READING THE AMERICAN PAST

EIGHTH EDITION

Selected Historical Documents
Volume 2: From 1865

MICHAEL P. JOHNSON
Johns Hopkins University

bedford/st.martin's
Macmillan Learning
Boston | New York

For Bedford/St. Martin's

Vice President, Editorial, Macmillan Learning Humanities: Edwin Hill
Senior Program Director for History: Michael Rosenberg
Senior Executive Program Manager for History: William J. Lombardo
History Marketing Manager: Melissa Rodriguez
Director of Content Development, Humanities: Jane Knetzger
Developmental Editor: Mollie Chandler
Senior Content Project Manager: Kendra LeFleur
Assistant Content Project Manager: Natalie Jones
Senior Workflow Project Supervisor: Susan Wein
Production Supervisor: Lawrence Guerra
Executive Media Project Manager: Michelle Camisa
Media Editor: Mary P. Starowicz
Editorial Services: Lumina Datamatics, Inc.
Composition: Lumina Datamatics, Inc.
Text Permissions Manager: Kalina Ingham
Text Permissions Editor: Michael McCarty
Photo Permissions Editor: Cecilia Varas
Photo Researcher: Naomi Kornhauser
Director of Design, Content Management: Diana Blume
Cover Design: William Boardman
Cover Image: Steve Dunwell/Getty Images
Printing and Binding: LSC Communications

Manufactured in the United States of America.

1 2 3 4 5 6   24 23 22 21 20 19

For information, write: Bedford/St. Martin's, 75 Arlington Street, Boston, MA 02116

ISBN 978-1-319-21201-8

Acknowledgments
Text acknowledgments and copyrights appear at the back of the book on page 298, which constitutes an extension of the copyright page. Art acknowledgments and copyrights appear on the same page as the art selections they cover.

Preface for Instructors

R *eading the American Past* is a collection of compelling documents that represent political, social, and cultural experiences critical to students' understanding of the scope and diversity of United States history. Created by people who shaped American history in ways both large and small, these primary sources reveal the views of the authors, the historical context in which they were written, and the major developments and controversies of their era. The documents give depth, breadth, and variety to textbook discussions of important developments in our nation's past. Organized chapter by chapter to parallel *The American Promise: A History of the United States* in all its versions (full-length, concise, and value), this wide-ranging set of documents offers teachers many pedagogical choices for discussion, analysis, writing assignments, and examinations. Above all, *Reading the American Past* seeks to ignite the sparks of historical imagination that every teacher hopes to see in students' eyes.

Reading a textbook discussion of Columbus's arrival in the New World, for example, gives students basic, up-to-date information that has been collected, sorted out, and synthesized over the past five hundred years. But reading the words Columbus wrote in his log shortly after he stepped ashore in the Western Hemisphere recaptures as no textbook can that moment of profound, mutual surprise when fifteenth-century Europeans and the people they called Indians first encountered one another. As every historian knows, primary sources bridge the gap from the present, when they are read, to the past, when they were written. They encourage students to venture across that span connecting present and past and to risk discovering a captivating and unexpected world.

FEATURES OF THIS BOOK

Three basic principles guided my selection of documents. First and fore-most, the sources highlight major events and significant perspectives of a given historical era. Second, I chose and edited documents to be accessible, interesting, and often surprising to students. Third, I sought sources that lend themselves to analysis in classroom discussion and writing assignments — documents that vividly portray controversies marking a particular historical moment and that offer multiple avenues of interpretation.

User-friendly editorial features help students read and interpret the sources. Introductory headnotes and follow-up questions accompany each document to aid students' reading and discussion. Unfamiliar words are defined when they are necessary to understand a document. Edito-rial intrusions have been kept brief, providing just enough information to allow students to explore the sources and make their own discoveries. By minimizing editorial interventions, I hope to encourage students to focus on the documents and to become astonished, perplexed, and invigorated by what they read.

Visual sources now in the eighth edition. Visual documents are included in the book for the first time, one in each chapter. Pictures can sometimes awaken students' curiosity more readily than written texts, but both images and texts require students to exercise their historical imagination, to read critically, and to ask questions about what the documents reveal and conceal.

This new edition incorporates the insights and suggestions of teach-ers who have used *Reading the American Past.* Guided by their classroom experiences, I have replaced one document per chapter in order to diver-sify the historical voices from each era and to give students and teachers fresh choices for investigating major developments. The visual documents include a wide range of images that challenge students to interrogate depictions of Native Americans and African Americans, of presidents and other politicians, of immigrants and pioneers, of common experiences of rural and urban Americans, and of moments of intense conflict.

Diverse perspectives and sources. The documents assembled here pro-vide students a generous cross-section of the diverse experiences that comprise the American past. The reflections of politicians and thieves, generals and privates, reformers and reprobates can be found here, along with those of the nation's countless ethnic and religious minorities. New text documents include a memorandum from American Jewish leaders to President Roosevelt, notifying him of the Holocaust (Document 25–2), President Carter's speech on energy conservation (Document 29–5), and President Bush's address on the Persian Gulf Crisis (Document 30–4). Barack Obama's 2009 speech in Cairo (Document 31–4) joins classic sources such as John Winthrop's *Arbella* sermon (Document 4–1), George Washington's Farewell Address (Document 9–5), and George Kennan's "Long Telegram" (Document 26–2), which disclose the perspectives of influential leaders. The no-less-significant views of common people are revealed by such documents as the memoir of an Englishwoman who became an indentured servant in eighteenth-century New York (Document 5–1), the letter from a slave to President Thomas Jefferson demanding that the president live up to his criticisms of slavery (Document 10–3), twentieth-century letters from American soldiers at war (Documents 22–3 and 25–4), and the interview of a Vietnamese immigrant (Document 30–3). Diaries and court cases convey the immediacy of history as lived experience. Reminiscences and oral histories illuminate the past with memories of participants. Speeches, manifestos, congressional testimony, and White House tape recordings spotlight the ends and means of political power. Essays, addresses, and passages from books offer the considered opinions of cultural leaders, whether captains of industry, novelists, or social critics.

Classroom flexibility. The selections in *Reading the American Past* allow instructors to choose documents that best serve their teaching needs. Teachers might, for example, ask students to read documents in preparation for lectures, then refer to the assigned selections as they explain, say, the encounter between Europeans and Native Americans, the tensions that led to the Civil War, or the origins and consequences of the Cold War. An instructor might devote a class to explicating a single source, such as Richard Frethorne's letter describing his life as an indentured servant at Jamestown, Virginia (Document 3–1), or Walter Wyckoff's observations about socialists and anarchists in 1890s Chicago (Document 19–4), or Mary Jenney Howe's parody of arguments made by opponents of women's suffrage (Document 21–4), or President Reagan's speech to American evangelicals (Document 30–1).

All the documents are ideally suited for provoking discussions during lecture sessions or in section meetings. Students can be asked to adopt and defend the viewpoint of a given source, to attack it from the perspective of a historical contemporary, to dissect its assumptions and evasions, or to compare and contrast it with other sources. Selections might also be used for quizzes, brief writing assignments, longer papers, or examinations. The documents open these and many other avenues for inspiring students to investigate the American past.

Tips for reading documents. A short introduction for students at the outset of each volume explains the significance of documents, both texts and images, for understanding history and outlines the basic questions that students should ask themselves in order to decipher any primary source. It encourages students to consider the historical context, author, date, audience, and language of the sources they are about to read.

Just the right amount of context. A brief paragraph begins each chapter, setting the documents in the larger historical context detailed in the corresponding chapter of the textbook. A headnote precedes every document, identifying its source, explaining when and by whom it was produced, and highlighting why it presents a revealing point of view. Rather than cluttering documents with numerous explanatory notes, I have assumed that students will—and they should—refer to a textbook for basic information about the people and events that appear in the sources, though notes are provided for more obscure words and people.

Thought-provoking questions. To guide students toward key passages and central ideas, "Questions for Reading and Discussion" follow each document. They are intended to help students identify fundamental points, analyze what a document means, and think about its larger historical significance. "Comparative Questions" at the end of each chapter ask students to ponder some of the similarities and differences among the chapter's documents, and to consider how the ideas, observations, and viewpoints expressed reveal the major historical developments of the time.

To see more clearly along the many angles of historical vision offered by the documents, students rely on the guidance, insight, and wisdom of their teachers. *Reading the American Past* gives instructors numerous opportunities to entice students to become active collaborators in the study of American history. Ideally, these documents will help persuade students that the American past is neither frozen in time nor entombed in books, but instead shapes their present and prefigures their future. Ideally, they will come to see that they do not simply read American history; they live it.

ACKNOWLEDGMENTS

For help with this edition of *Reading the American Past* I am indebted to many people, but to none more than the following historians who have shared their professional insights and classroom experiences to suggest ways to make the documents more useful and informative for students and teachers throughout the country: Ann Ackerman, Nashua Community College; Ian Aebel, Harris-Stowe State University; Joseph Bagley, Georgia State University Perimeter College; Ian Beamish, University of Louisiana-Lafayette; Timothy Buckner, Troy University; Kara Carroll, Central New Mexico Community College; Leilah Danielson, Northern Arizona University; Wayne Drews, Kennesaw State University, Marietta Campus; Donna Dunakey, Florida South Western State College; Robert Genter, Nassau Community College; Jessica Gerard, Ozarks Technical Community College; Diane Gill, North Lake College; Pat Herb, North Central State College; Peter Hoffer, University of Georgia; Andrew Hollinger, Tarrant County College; Robin Krawitz, Delaware State University; Alan Lehmann, Blinn College; Alexander Marriott,

Alvin Community College; Michael McCormick, Houston Community College; Stacy Reikowsky, New River Community and Technical College; Gary Ritter, Central Piedmont Community College; Carey Roberts, Liberty University; Scott Seagle, University of Tennessee at Chattanooga; Edward Simmons, Georgia Gwinnett College; John Smith, Texas A&M University-Commerce; David Toye, Northeast State Community College; James Tuten, Juniata College; Leah Vallely, Calhoun Community College; Stephanie Vincent, Kent State University; William Whisenhunt, College of DuPage.

I have also relied, as usual, on my coauthors of *The American Promise* — James L. Roark, François Furstenberg, Sarah Stage, and Sarah Igo — for advice and suggestions. Although I have benefited from the support of all of these colleagues, I am nonetheless solely responsible for the final selection of documents and edited passages in this volume.

Many others contributed their energy and creativity to this project. As always, the team at Bedford/St. Martin's, including Michael Rosenberg, Bill Lombardo, Leah Strauss, and Mollie Chandler, brought their benevolent and constructive stewardship to the project. Kendra LeFleur and Natalie Jones skillfully steered the book through the production process, while Kalina Ingham, Michael McCarty, and Cecilia Varas handled permissions.

Overall, this book represents the constructive efforts of teachers, students, colleagues, editors, and publishers, all enlisted in the common cause of helping students better understand our collective history. I am the grateful beneficiary of their generosity, intelligence, and insight.

Introduction for Students

H istorical documents allow us to peer into the past and learn what happened and what did not happen—crucial beginning points for understanding how and why the present came to be. They record bits of history and preserve the momentary ideas and experiences of individuals and groups. But how can you, a twenty-first-century student, read and truly comprehend a letter from a seventeenth-century indentured servant or a nineteenth-century woman on the frontier, full of irregular spelling and contemporary references? How can you determine the historical value and accuracy of documents recorded years or even centuries ago? How can you read documents to figure out what *really* happened in the past?

FLAWS OF MEMORY

It would be convenient if we did not need documents, if we could depend instead on our memory to tell us what happened. Unfortunately, memory is far from perfect, as we are reminded every time we misplace our keys. We not only forget things that did happen, but we also remember things that never occurred, such as erroneously thinking we put those keys right there on that shelf. Mark Twain once quipped, "When I was younger I could remember anything, whether it happened or not; but my faculties are decaying now, and soon I shall be so [old] I cannot remember any but the things that never happened."

Twain's witticism points to another important property of memory: It changes over time. Every good trial lawyer knows that memory is fragile, volatile, and subject to manipulation by our desires, intentions, and fears. Our memory is constantly reshaped to serve the needs of the present. Compounding the unreliability of memory are two stubborn realities: Most of the people who might remember something about what happened are dead, their memories erased forever; and no person, no single memory, ever knew all there is to know about what happened.

DOCUMENTS AS HISTORICAL SNAPSHOTS

These flaws of memory might cause us to shrug wearily and conclude that it is impossible to determine what happened. But documents make it possible to learn a great deal—although not every last thing—about what really happened. Because documents are created by humans, they are subject to all the frailties of memory, with one vital exception: Documents do not change. Unlike memory, documents freeze words at a moment in time. Ideas, perceptions, emotions, and assumptions expressed in a document allow us to learn now about what happened then. In effect, documents are a bridge from the present to the past. They allow us to cross over and to discover how we got from there to here.

Today you can stand where the audience stood in 1863 to listen to Abraham Lincoln's famous speech at the dedication of the cemetery for the Union soldiers killed at the battle of Gettysburg. Of course you can't hear Lincoln's voice, but you can read his words because the Gettysburg Address exists as a historical document; you can literally read this portion of the American past. The address transports the reader back to that crisp November day a century and a half ago, the outcome of the war very much in doubt, when the president and commander in chief of more than a million men in blue uniforms explained in a few words his view of the meaning of the war for the nation and the world. The address captured Lincoln's thoughts at that moment and preserved them, much like a historical snapshot. All documents have this property of stopping time, of indelibly recording somebody's views at a specific moment in the past.

The documents in *Reading the American Past* allow you to travel back in time without getting up from your chair. You can accompany a slave owner as he visits his former slaves for the first time after the Civil War and emancipation. You can listen to a young woman describe her life on the Great Plains frontier to her relatives back East. You can read the letters of soldiers during World War II who recount their part in the global maelstrom. You can witness the confession of the self-professed mastermind of the 9/11 terrorist attacks. These and the many other documents in this book bring the past alive in the words of the people who lived it.

DOCUMENTS CAPTURE DIVERSE VOICES AND EXPERIENCES

Documents record far more than the ideas of presidents. They disclose, for instance, Pueblo Indians' views of conquering Spaniards in the sixteenth century, Native American grievances against New Englanders who precipitated King Philip's War in the seventeenth century, a woman's passionate argument for equality of the sexes in the eighteenth century, the confessions of slave insurrectionists in the nineteenth century, the views of Vietnam War veterans in the twentieth century, and much, much more. These views and many others are recorded by the documents in this collection. They permit you to read the American past from the diversity of perspectives that contributed to the making of America: women and men, workers and bosses, newcomers and natives, slaves and masters, voters and politicians, conservatives and radicals, activists and reactionaries, westerners and easterners, northerners and southerners, farmers and urbanites, the famous and the forgotten. These people created historical documents when they stole a spare moment to write a letter or record thoughts in a diary, when they talked to a scribbling friend or stranger, when they appeared in court or made a will, and when they delivered a sermon, gave a speech, or penned a manifesto. Examples of all these kinds of documents are included in *Reading the American Past*. Together, they make it possible for you to learn a great deal about what really happened.

DOCUMENTS BRING YOU FACE-TO-FACE WITH THE PAST

From the almost limitless historical record, I chose documents that clearly and vividly express an important perspective about a major event or a widespread point of view during a certain historical era. I selected documents that are not only revealing but also often surprising, controversial, or troubling. My goal is to bring you face-to-face with the past through the eyes of the people who lived it.

Reading the American Past is designed to accompany *The American Promise: A History of the United States*. Each chapter in this volume parallels a chapter in *The American Promise*. The documents provide eyewitness accounts that broaden and deepen the textbook narrative. Chapter 16, for example, supplements the textbook discussion of Reconstruction with selections from five documents: a report on the attitudes of whites in the former Confederacy in the summer of 1865; advertisements of emancipated slaves seeking lost family members; a plantation owner's journal entry about his first visit with his former slaves after they became free following the Civil War; testimony of an African American Republican before the congressional committee investigating the Ku Klux Klan in 1871; and a political cartoon highlighting contemporary controversies about black suffrage and civil rights. Each selection is long enough to convey the central message of the author, but short enough to be read for the first time in ten minutes or so. In general, each chapter in this book contains four text documents of roughly similar length and one image that illustrates important experiences, conflicts, or ideas. Photos, drawings, paintings, cartoons, prints, and other images disclose information about an era that supplements and enriches the written documents. Reading and understanding these images require you to analyze not only what the images show on the surface but also what they suggest, omit, or obscure, just as you do with written documents.

READING AND UNDERSTANDING DOCUMENTS

To help you read and understand the documents, a brief paragraph at the beginning of each chapter sketches the larger historical context, which your textbook explains in more detail. A headnote precedes each document and identifies its source, explains who produced it and when, and suggests why it is revealing. Questions to aid your reading and discussion follow each selection, point you toward key passages and fundamental ideas, and ask you to consider both what a document says and what it means. More questions at the end of each chapter encourage you to compare and find connections among the different documents.

While reading the written documents and analyzing the images in this book, it's important to keep in mind the historical context; the author; date; audience; and the meanings of the words themselves. Here are some guidelines and questions to consider while reading any primary document, whether a written text or a picture.

ESTABLISH THE HISTORICAL CONTEXT

Getting the most out of these text and image documents requires reading with care and imagination. Historians are interested in what a document says and what it reveals about the historical reality that is only partly disclosed by the document itself. A document might be likened to a window that permits us to glimpse features of the past. A document challenges us to read and understand the words on the page as a way to look through the window and learn about the larger historical context.

Lincoln's Gettysburg Address, for example, hints that he believed many loyal Americans wondered whether the war was worth the effort, whether all those soldiers, as he said, "have died in vain." Lincoln's words do not explicitly say that many people thought the human tragedy of the war was too great, but that seems to be one of their meanings. His address attempted to answer such doubts by proclaiming the larger meaning of the war and the soldiers' deaths. His public statement of the noble ideals of the Union war effort hint at his private perception that many Americans had come to doubt whether the war had any meaning beyond the maiming or death of their loved ones.

To see such unstated historical reality in and through a document, readers must remain alert to exactly what the document says. The first step is to learn something about the era in which the document was written by reading *The American Promise* or another textbook of American history.

IDENTIFY AUTHOR, DATE, AND AUDIENCE

The next step in deciphering a document is to consider three important questions: Who wrote the document? When was it written? Who was the intended audience? These questions will help you understand the information in the brief headnote and answer the questions that accompany each document, as well as the concluding comparative questions that draw attention to similarities and differences among the documents in the chapter. While these editorial features will aid your investigation of the documents, you should always proceed by asking who wrote each document, when, and for what audience.

Author. Obviously, a document expresses the viewpoint of its author. Different people had different views about the same event. At Gettysburg, for example, the Confederacy suffered a painful defeat that weakened their ability to maintain their independence and to defend slavery. If Jefferson Davis, the president of the Confederacy, had delivered a Gettysburg Address, it would have been very different from Lincoln's. Documents also often convey their authors' opinions of the viewpoints of other people, including those who agree with them and those who don't. You should always ask, then: What does a document say about the viewpoint of the author? What does it say about the author's opinion about the views of other people? Does the document suggest the author's point of view was confined to a few others, shared by a substantial minority, or embraced by a great many people? What motivated the author to express his or her point of view in the first place? If the document has been translated or transcribed by another person, what relationship did that person have with the author, and can we trust that the document accurately represents the author's thoughts?

Date. A document conveys valuable information about the era when it was composed as well as about the author's point of view. Since a person's perspective often changes over time, it is critical to know exactly when a document was written in order to understand its meaning. When Lincoln delivered the Gettysburg Address, the outcome of the Civil War remained in doubt; seventeen months later, in April 1865, he was certain of northern victory. The address expresses the urgency and uncertainty of the wartime crisis of 1863 rather than the relief and confidence of 1865. As you read every document, you should ask: How does the document reflect the era when the author wrote it? What does it say about the events under way at the time? What does it suggest about how that particular time was perceived by the author and by other people? How did the times shape the author's thoughts and actions?

Audience. In addition to considering who wrote a document and when, you should think about the author's intended audience. A politician may say one thing in a campaign speech and something quite different in a private letter to a friend. An immigrant might send a rosy account of life in America to family members in the Old Country—an account at odds with the features of life in the New World he or she describes in a diary. The intended audience shapes the message an author seeks to send. The author's expectation of what the audience wants to hear contributes to what a document says, how it is said, and what is left unsaid. Lincoln knew that his audience at Gettysburg included many family members mourning the death of loved ones who "gave the last full measure of devotion" on the battlefield. He hoped his remarks would soothe the heartache of the survivors by ennobling the Union and those who died in its defense. To decipher any document, you should always ask: Who is the intended audience? How did the audience shape what the author says? Did consideration of the audience lead the author to emphasize some things and downplay or ignore others? How would the intended audience be likely to read the document? How would people who were not among the intended audience be likely to read it?

It is particularly important to consider the audience when reading interviews, since both the interviewer and interviewee can have different expectations of the same audience. If the interviewer's questions are provided, how do they guide and shape the responses of the interviewee? What is the interviewer's motivation for conducting the interview, and what is the interviewee's motivation for giving it?

DECIPHER THE LANGUAGE

The meanings of words, like the viewpoints of individuals, also reflect their historical moment. For the most part, the documents in this collection were written in English and the authors' original spelling has been preserved (unless stated otherwise), even if it fails to conform to common usage today. Numerous documents have been translated into English from Spanish, Portuguese, Latin, German, Swedish, or one of several Native American languages. But even documents originally written in English require you to translate the meaning of English words at the time the document was written into the meaning of English words today.

Readers must guard against imputing today's meanings to yesterday's words. When Lincoln said "this nation" in the Gettysburg Address, he referred to the United States in 1863, a vastly different nation from the one founded four score and seven years earlier and from the one that exists today, more than a century and a half later. The word is the same, but the meaning varies greatly.

Although the meaning of many words remains relatively constant, if you are on the lookout for key words whose meanings have changed, you will discover otherwise hidden insights into the documents. You can benefit simply from exercising your historical imagination about the changing meaning of words. To Lincoln, the phrase "all men are created equal" did not have the same meaning that it did for women's rights leaders at the time, or for slaves or slave owners.

You should always pay attention to the words used in a document and ask a final set of questions: How do the words in the document reflect the author, the time, and the intended audience? Would the same words have different meanings to other people at that time? Does the author's choice of words reveal covert assumptions and blind spots along with an overt message?

The Value of Documents

Historical documents not only provide readers with indelible markers of historical changes that have occurred, they also illuminate the role human beings played in making those changes. Documents instruct us about the achievements and limitations of the past as they inspire and caution us for the future. Documents also instill in us a strong sense of historical humility. Americans in the past were not less good or more evil, less right or more wrong, than we are today. Their ideas, their experiences, and their times were different from ours in many respects, but they made the nation we inhabit. Ideally, the documents in *Reading the American Past* will give you an appreciation of what it took, and will continue to take, to make American history happen.

Contents

Preface for Instructors   *iii*

Introduction for Students   *viii*

16. RECONSTRUCTION, 1863–1877   1

16–1 **Carl Schurz Reports on the Condition
of the Defeated South**   1
Report on the Condition of the South, 1865

16–2 **Former Slaves Seek to Reunite Their Families**   5
Advertisements from the Christian Recorder,
1865–1870

16–3 **Planter Louis Manigault Visits His Plantations
and Former Slaves**   11
*A Narrative of a Post–Civil War Visit to Gowrie
and East Hermitage Plantations*, March 22, 1867

16–4 **Klan Violence against Blacks**   15
Elias Hill, *Testimony before Congressional Committee
Investigating the Ku Klux Klan*, 1871

16–5 **The Ignorant Vote and the Election of 1876**   18
Thomas Nast, *"The Ignorant Vote,"* 1876

Comparative Questions   20

17. THE CONTESTED WEST, 1865–1900   21

17–1 **Transcontinental Railroad Completed, 1870**   21
"Through to the Pacific," ca. 1870

17–2 **Pun Chi Appeals to Congress in Behalf
of Chinese Immigrants in California**   22
A Remonstrance from the Chinese in California,
ca. 1870

17–3 **Mattie Oblinger Describes Life on a Nebraska Homestead**   26
Mattie V. Oblinger to George W. Thomas, Grizzie B. Thomas, and Wheeler Thomas Family, June 16, 1873

17–4 **Texas Rangers on the Mexican Border**   29
N. A. Jennings, A Texas Ranger, 1875

17–5 **In-mut-too-yah-lat-lat Describes White Encroachment**   33
Chief Joseph, Speech to a White Audience, 1879

COMPARATIVE QUESTIONS   36

18. **THE GILDED AGE, 1865–1900**   37

18–1 **William Graham Sumner on Social Obligations**   37
What Social Classes Owe to Each Other, 1883

18–2 **Henry Demarest Lloyd Attacks Monopolies**   40
Wealth against Commonwealth, 1894

18–3 **The Bosses of the Senate**   44
Joseph Keppler, "The Bosses of the Senate," 1889

18-4 **Andrew Carnegie Explains the Gospel of Wealth**   45
Wealth, 1889

18–5 **Henry George Explains Why Poverty Is a Crime**   48
An Analysis of the Crime of Poverty, 1885

COMPARATIVE QUESTIONS   52

19. **THE CITY AND ITS WORKERS, 1870–1900**   53

19–1 **A Textile Worker Explains the Labor Market**   53
Thomas O'Donnell, Testimony before a U.S. Senate Committee, 1885

19–2 **Domestic Servants on Household Work**   57
Interviews with Journalist Helen Campbell, 1880s

19–3 **Jacob Riis Photographs a Jewish Cobbler in New York City**   60
Jacob Riis, "Hebrew Making Ready for Sabbath Eve in his Coal Cellar," ca. 1890

19–4 **Walter Wyckoff Listens to Revolutionary Workers in Chicago**   61
Among the Revolutionaries, 1898

19–5 **George Washington Plunkitt Explains Politics**   65
William L. Riordon, *Plunkitt of Tammany Hall*, 1905

COMPARATIVE QUESTIONS   68

20. **DISSENT, DEPRESSION, AND WAR, 1890–1900**   69

20–1 **Mary Elizabeth Lease Reports on Women
in the Farmers' Alliance**   69
Women in the Farmers' Alliance, 1891

20–2 **Cherokee Strip Land Rush, 1893**   73
The Cherokee Strip Land Rush, 1893

20–3 **White Supremacy in Wilmington, North Carolina**   74
Gunner Jesse Blake, *Narrative of the Wilmington
"Rebellion" of 1898*

20–4 **Conflicting Views about Labor Unions**   79
N. F. Thompson, *Testimony before the Industrial
Commission on the Relations and Conditions
of Capital and Labor*, 1900
Samuel Gompers, *Letter to the* American
Federationist, 1894

20–5 **Emilio Aguinaldo Criticizes American
Imperialism in the Philippines**   84
Case against the United States, 1899

COMPARATIVE QUESTIONS   88

21. **PROGRESSIVE REFORM, 1890–1916**   89

21–1 **Jane Addams on Settlement Houses**   89
The Subjective Necessity for Social Settlements, 1892

21–2 **Pietro Learning to Write**   92
Jacob Riis, *Pietro Learning to Write*, 1892

21–3 **A Sociologist Studies Working-Class
Saloons in Chicago**   94
Royal Melendy, *Ethical Substitutes for
the Saloon*, 1900

21–4 **Marie Jenney Howe Parodies the Opposition
to Women's Suffrage**   98
An Anti-Suffrage Monologue, 1913

21–5 **Booker T. Washington on Racial Accommodation**   101
The Atlanta Exposition Address, 1895

21–6 W. E. B. Du Bois on Racial Equality   104
Booker T. Washington and Others, 1903

COMPARATIVE QUESTIONS   107

22. WORLD WAR I: THE PROGRESSIVE CRUSADE AT HOME AND ABROAD, 1914–1920   **108**

22–1 "The Human American Eagle," 1918   108
John D. Thomas and Arthur S. Mole, *"The Human American Eagle," Camp Gordon, Atlanta, Georgia,* 1918

22–2 Eugene V. Debs Attacks Capitalist Warmongers   109
Speech Delivered in Canton, Ohio, June 16, 1918

22–3 A Doughboy's Letter from the Front   113
Anonymous Soldier, *Letter to Elmer J. Sutters,* 1918

22–4 Attorney General A. Mitchell Palmer Defends America from Communists   116
The Case against the "Reds," 1920

22–5 An African American Responds to the Chicago Race Riot   120
Stanley B. Norvell, *Letter to Victor F. Lawson,* 1919

COMPARATIVE QUESTIONS   125

23. FROM NEW ERA TO GREAT DEPRESSION, 1920–1932   **126**

23–1 Demonstrating the Need for a Federal Highway System   126
Army Convoy Truck Stuck on the Road, 1919

23–2 Reinhold Niebuhr on Christianity in Detroit   127
Diary Entries, 1925–1928

23–3 The Ku Klux Klan Defends Americanism   131
Hiram W. Evans, *The Klan's Fight for Americanism,* 1926

23–4 Mothers Seek Freedom from Unwanted Pregnancies   135
Margaret Sanger, *Motherhood in Bondage,* 1928

23–5 Marcus Garvey Explains the Goals of the Universal Negro Improvement Association   138
The Negro's Greatest Enemy, 1923

COMPARATIVE QUESTIONS   142

24. THE NEW DEAL EXPERIMENT, 1932–1939   **143**

24–1 **Martha Gellhorn Reports on Conditions
in North Carolina in 1934**   143
Martha Gellhorn to Harry Hopkins, November 11, 1934

24–2 **Working People's Letters to New Dealers**   147
Letter to Frances Perkins, January 27, 1935
Letter to Frances Perkins, March 29, 1935
Letter to Franklin D. Roosevelt, November 23, 1936
Letter to Frances Perkins, July 27, 1937
Letter to Franklin D. Roosevelt, November 27, 1939

24–3 **Oklahoma Tenant Farmer Leads His Family
Down the Road, 1938**   152
Dorothea Lange, *"Family Walking on Highway,
five children,"* 1938

24–4 **Huey Long Proposes Redistribution of Wealth**   153
*Speech to Members of the Share Our Wealth
Society*, 1935

24–5 **Conservatives Criticize the New Deal**   156
Herbert Hoover, *Anti–New Deal Campaign
Speech*, 1936
Minnie Hardin, *Letter to Eleanor Roosevelt*,
December 14, 1937

COMPARATIVE QUESTIONS   160

25. THE UNITED STATES AND THE SECOND
WORLD WAR, 1939–1945   **161**

25–1 **A Japanese American War Hero Recalls
Pearl Harbor**   161
Grant Hirabayashi, *Oral History*, 1999

25–2 **American Jewish Leaders Notify FDR about
the Holocaust**   165
*Memorandum Submitted to the President of the
United States at the White House on Tuesday,
December 8, 1942*

25–3 **Rosies the Riveter Recall Working in War Industries**   169
Rosie the Riveter Memoirs, ca. 2004

25–4 **Soldiers Send Messages Home**   173
Sergeant Irving Strobing, *Radio Address from
Corregidor, Philippines*, May 5 or 6, 1942
John Conroy, *Letter*, December 24, 1942
Allen Spach, *Letter*, February 1943

James McMahon, *Letter*, March 10, 1944
David Mark Olds, *Letter*, July 12, 1945

25–5 **U.S. Generals Inspect Ohrdruf Concentration
Camp, 1945**   180
*U.S. Generals Inspect Ohrdruf Concentration Camp,
April 12, 1945*

COMPARATIVE QUESTIONS   181

26. THE NEW WORLD OF THE COLD WAR, 1945–1960   **183**

26–1 **General Marshall Summarizes the Lessons
of World War II**   183
For the Common Defense, 1945

26–2 **George F. Kennan Outlines Containment**   187
The Long Telegram, February 22, 1946

26–3 **Cold War Blueprint**   191
*NSC-68: U.S. Objectives and Programs for
National Security, 1950*

26–4 **Civilians Prepare for Nuclear Attack**   195
Miami Couple Honeymoons in Fallout Shelter, 1959

26–5 **A Veteran Recalls Combat in the Korean War**   196
Donald M. Griffith Interview, 2003

COMPARATIVE QUESTIONS   200

27. POSTWAR CULTURE AND POLITICS, 1945–1960   **201**

27–1 **Edith M. Stern Attacks the Domestic Bondage
of Women**   201
Women Are Household Slaves, 1949

27–2 **Vance Packard Analyzes the Age of Affluence**   206
The Status Seekers, 1959

27–3 **George E. McMillan Reports on Racial
Conditions in the South in 1960**   210
Sit-Downs: The South's New Time Bomb, 1960

27–4 **Youth Culture and the Draft**   214
Elvis Presley Joins the Army, 1958

27–5 **President Dwight D. Eisenhower Warns about
the Military-Industrial Complex**   215
Farewell Address, January 1961

COMPARATIVE QUESTIONS   218

28. RIGHTS, REBELLION, AND REACTION, 1960–1974   219

28–1 Martin Luther King Jr. Explains Nonviolent
Resistance   219
Letter from Birmingham City Jail, 1963

28–2 George C. Wallace Denounces the Civil
Rights Movement   224
The Civil Rights Movement: Fraud, Sham, and Hoax,
July 4, 1964

28–3 Equal Rights for Women   228
National Organization for Women, *Statement
of Purpose*, October 29, 1966

28–4 Black Power   232
*Chicago Student Non-Violent Coordinating
Committee Leaflet*, 1967

28–5 Students Protest the Vietnam War   236
*National Guard Soldiers Shoot Kent State
University Students*, 1970

COMPARATIVE QUESTIONS   238

29. CONFRONTING LIMITS, 1961–1979   239

29–1 A Secret Government Assessment
of the Vietnam War   239
Robert S. McNamara, *Actions Recommended
for Vietnam*, October 14, 1966

29–2 Military Discipline in an Unpopular War   244
Robert D. Heinl Jr., *The Collapse of the Armed Forces*,
June 7, 1971

29–3 The Evacuation of Saigon Exposes the Limits
of U.S. Military Power   248
Evacuation of Saigon, April 30, 1975

29–4 The Watergate Tapes: Nixon, Dean, and Haldeman
Discuss the Cancer within the Presidency   249
Transcript from Tape-Recorded Meeting, March 21, 1973

29–5 President Carter Declares Energy Conservation
the Moral Equivalent of War, 1977   256
*Address to the Nation on Proposed National Energy
Policy*, April 18, 1977

COMPARATIVE QUESTIONS   260

30. DIVISIONS AT HOME AND ABROAD IN A CONSERVATIVE ERA, 1980–2000   261

30–1 **President Ronald Reagan Defends American Morality**   261
Address to the National Association of American Evangelicals, 1983

30–2 **Norma McCorvey Explains How She Became "Roe" of *Roe v. Wade***   266
Affidavit, United States District Court, District of New Jersey, 2000

30–3 **A Vietnamese Immigrant on the West Coast**   270
Anonymous Man, *Oral History*, 1983

30–4 **President Bush Announces a New World Order, September 11, 1990**   273
Address Before a Joint Session of the Congress, September 11, 1990

30–5 **Police Brutality and Los Angeles Riots, 1992**   277
Pat Oliphant, *"Free at Last,"* 1992

COMPARATIVE QUESTIONS   278

31. AMERICA IN A NEW CENTURY, SINCE 2000   279

31–1 **National Security of the United States Requires Preemptive War**   279
The National Security Strategy of the United States, September 2002

31–2 **A Captured 9/11 Terrorist Confesses**   284
Khalid Sheikh Muhammad, *Confession*, 2007

31–3 **A Christian Leader Argues That Evangelical Christianity Has Been Hijacked**   288
Tony Campolo, *Interview*, 2004

31–4 **President Barack Obama Declares a New Beginning in U.S. Relations with the Muslim World**   291
On a New Beginning, June 4, 2009

31–5 **President Trump Addresses the Conservative Political Action Conference**   295
President Donald J. Trump Hugs the Flag, 2019

COMPARATIVE QUESTIONS   297

16 Reconstruction

1863–1877

During the turbulent years of Reconstruction, the character of freedom for former slaves was the subject of intense debate within the South and across the nation. Most southern whites sought the most limited form of freedom for African Americans. Most former slaves strove to exercise their liberty to the fullest, as they sought to reunite families and claim their independence from their former masters as much as possible. White vigilantes resorted to murder, lynching, and other acts of brutality to force blacks to limit their horizons. By the presidential election of 1876, most northern white Republicans concluded that once former slaves had the vote, the South—not the North or the federal government—should determine how best to define freedom and preserve order.

DOCUMENT 16–1

Carl Schurz Reports on the Condition of the Defeated South

In the summer of 1865, President Andrew Johnson sent Carl Schurz to investigate conditions in the defeated Confederacy. Born in Germany in 1829, Schurz immigrated to the United States in 1852 and became a leader in the Republican Party in Wisconsin. During the Civil War Schurz served as a general in the Union army, commanding troops at Gettysburg and other major battles. Schurz traveled throughout the South immediately after the war and spoke to hundreds of people to gauge the sentiment of leaders and ordinary people about their loyalty to the Union and their attitudes toward emancipation and the men and women recently emancipated from bondage. Schurz's report, excerpted here, discloses the views of southern whites toward the federal government and former slaves in the months following Confederate defeat. Those views shaped the course and consequences of federal efforts to reconstruct the former Confederacy.

From Carl Schurz, *Report on the Condition of the South*, 39th Cong., 1st Sess., Senate Ex. Doc. No. 2 (Washington, 1865).

Report on the Condition of the South, 1865

[A]ll organized attacks upon our military forces stationed in the south have ceased; but there are still localities where it is unsafe for a man wearing the federal uniform or known as an officer of the government to be abroad outside of the immediate reach of our garrisons. The shooting of single soldiers and government couriers was not unfrequently reported while I was in the south. . . . But no instance has come to my notice in which the people of a city or a rural district cordially fraternized with the army. Here and there the soldiers were welcomed as protectors against apprehended dangers; but general exhibitions of cordiality on the part of the population I have not heard of. . . . [U]pon the whole, the soldier of the Union is still looked upon as a stranger, an intruder—as the "Yankee," "the enemy." . . .

While the generosity and toleration shown by the [U.S.] government to the people lately in rebellion has not met with a corresponding generosity shown by those people to the government's friends, it has brought forth some results which, if properly developed, will become of value. It has facilitated the re-establishment of the forms of civil government, and led many of those who had been active in the rebellion to take part in the act of bringing back the States to their constitutional relations. . . . There is, at present, no danger of another insurrection against the authority of the United States on a large scale, and the people are willing to reconstruct their State governments, and to send their senators and representatives to Congress.

But as to the moral value of these results, we must not indulge in any delusions. There are two principal points to which I beg to call your attention. In the first place, the rapid return to power and influence of so many of those who but recently were engaged in a bitter war against the Union, has had one effect which was certainly not originally contemplated by the government. Treason does, under existing circumstances, not appear odious in the south. The people are not impressed with any sense of its criminality. And, secondly, there is, as yet, among the southern people an utter absence of national feeling. I made it a business, while in the South, to watch the symptoms of "returning loyalty" as they appeared not only in private conversation, but in the public press and in the speeches delivered and the resolutions passed at Union meetings. Hardly ever was there an expression of hearty attachment to the great republic, or an appeal to the impulses of patriotism; but whenever submission to the national authority was declared and advocated, it was almost uniformly placed upon two principal grounds: That, under present circumstances, the southern people could "do no better;" and then that submission was the only means by which they could rid themselves of the federal soldiers and obtain once more control of their own affairs. . . .

In speaking above of the improbability of an insurrectionary movement on a large scale, I did not mean to say that I considered resistance in detail to the execution of the laws of Congress and the measures of the government impossible. . . . [M]ost of the conversations I had with southerners upon this subject led me to apprehend that they . . . are rather inclined to ask money of the government as compensation for their emancipated slaves, for the rebuilding of the levees on the Mississippi, and various kinds of damage done by our armies for military purposes, than, as the current expression is, to "help paying the expenses of the whipping they have received." In fact, there are abundant indications in newspaper articles, public speeches, and electioneering documents of candidates, which render it eminently probable that on the claim of compensation for their emancipated slaves the southern States, as soon as readmitted to representation in Congress, will be almost a unit. In the Mississippi convention the idea was broached by Mr. Potter, in an elaborate speech, to have the late slave States relieved from taxation "for years to come," in consideration of "debt due them" for the emancipated slaves; and this plea I have frequently heard advocated in private conversations. . . .

In at least nineteen cases of twenty the reply I received to my inquiry about their views on the new [labor] system was uniformly this: "You cannot make the negro work, without physical compulsion." I heard this hundreds of times, heard it wherever I went, heard it in nearly the same words from so many different persons, that at last I came to the conclusion that this is the prevailing sentiment among the southern people. . . .

I found but few people who were willing to make due allowance for the adverse influence of exceptional circumstances. By a large majority of those I came in contact with, and they mostly belonged to the more intelligent class, every irregularity that occurred was directly charged against the system of free labor. If negroes walked away from the plantations, it was conclusive proof of the incorrigible instability of the negro, and the impracticability of free negro labor. If some individual negroes violated the terms of their contract, it proved unanswerably that no negro had, or ever would have, a just conception of the binding force of a contract, and that this system of free negro labor was bound to be a failure. If some negroes shirked, or did not perform their task with sufficient alacrity, it was produced as irrefutable evidence to show that physical compulsion was actually indispensable to make the negro work. If negroes, idlers or refugees crawling about the towns, applied to the authorities for subsistence, it was quoted as incontestably establishing the point that the negro was too improvident to take care of himself, and must necessarily be consigned to the care of a master. I heard a Georgia planter argue most seriously that one of his negroes had shown himself certainly unfit for freedom because he impudently refused to submit to a whipping. . . . It frequently struck me that persons who conversed about every other subject calmly and sensibly would lose their temper as soon as the negro question was touched. . . .

A belief, conviction, or prejudice, or whatever you may call it, so widely spread and apparently so deeply rooted as this, that the negro will not work without physical compulsion, is certainly calculated to have a very serious influence upon the conduct of the people entertaining it. It naturally produced a desire to preserve slavery in its original form as much and as long as possible . . . remember the admission made by one of the provisional governors, over two months after the close of the war, that the people of his State still indulged in a lingering hope slavery might yet be preserved—or to introduce into the new system that element of physical compulsion which would make the negro work. Efforts were, indeed, made to hold the negro in his old state of subjection, especially in such localities where our military forces had not yet penetrated, or where the country was not garrisoned in detail. Here and there planters succeeded for a limited period to keep their former slaves in ignorance, or at least doubt, about their new rights; but the main agency employed for that purpose was force and intimidation. In many instances negroes who walked away from the plantations, or were found upon the roads, were shot or otherwise severely punished, which was calculated to produce the impression among those remaining with their masters that an attempt to escape from slavery would result in certain destruction. A large proportion of the many acts of violence committed is undoubtedly attributable to this motive. . . .

The conviction, however, that slavery in the old form cannot be maintained has forced itself upon the minds of many of those who ardently desired its preservation. But while the necessity of a new system was recognized as far as the right of property in the individual negro is concerned, many attempts were made to introduce into that new system the element of physical compulsion, which . . . is so generally considered indispensable. This was done by simply adhering, as to the treatment of the laborers, as much as possible to the traditions of the old system, even where the relations between employers and laborers had been fixed by contract. The practice of corporal punishment was still continued to a great extent, although, perhaps, not in so regular a manner as it was practiced in times gone by. . . . The habit is so inveterate with a great many persons as to render, on the least provocation, the impulse to whip a negro almost irresistible. It will continue to be so until the southern people will have learned, so as never to forget it, that a black man has rights which a white man is bound to respect.

Here I will insert some remarks on the general treatment of the blacks as a class, from the whites as a class. It is not on the plantations and at the hands of the planters themselves that the negroes have to suffer the greatest hardships. Not only the former slaveholders, but the non-slaveholding whites, who, even previous to the war, seemed to be more ardent in their pro-slavery feelings than the planters themselves, are possessed by a singularly bitter and vindictive feeling against the colored race since the negro has ceased to be property. The pecuniary value which the individual negro formerly represented having disappeared, the maiming and killing of colored men seems to be looked upon by many as one of those venial offences which must be forgiven to the outraged feelings of a wronged and robbed people. Besides, the services rendered by the negro to the national cause during the war, which make him an object of special interest to the loyal people, make him an object of particular vindictiveness to those whose hearts were set upon the success of the rebellion. The number of murders and assaults perpetrated upon negroes is very great; we can form only an approximative estimate of what is going on in those parts of the south which are not closely garrisoned, and from which no regular reports are received, by what occurs under the very eyes of our military authorities. . . .

So far, the spirit of persecution has shown itself so strong as to make the protection of the freedman by the military arm of the government in many localities necessary—in almost all, desirable. It must not be forgotten that in a community a majority of whose members is peaceably disposed, but not willing or not able to enforce peace and order, a comparatively small number of bold and lawless men can determine the character of the whole. . . .

Aside from the assumption that the negro will not work without physical compulsion, there appears to be another popular notion prevalent in the south, which stands as no less serious an obstacle in the way of a successful solution of the problem. It is that the negro exists for the special object of raising cotton, rice and sugar for the whites, and that it is illegitimate for him to indulge, like other people, in the pursuit of his own happiness in his own way. Although it is admitted that he has ceased to be the property of a master, it is not admitted that he has a right to become his own master. As Colonel Thomas, assistant commissioner of the Freedmen's Bureau in Mississippi, in a letter addressed to me, very pungently expresses it: "The whites esteem the blacks their property by natural right, and, however much they may admit that the relations of masters and slaves have been destroyed by the war and by the President's emancipation proclamation, they still have an ingrained feeling that the blacks at large belong to the whites at large, and whenever opportunity serves, they treat the colored people just as their profit, caprice or passion may dictate."

QUESTIONS FOR READING AND DISCUSSION

1. What did Schurz see as "some results" that "will become of value" in reconstructing the South? What was his view of the "moral value of these results"?
2. What significance did Schurz give to white Southerners' demand for "compensation for emancipated slaves"? What did this demand suggest about the meaning of defeat and emancipation to slaveholders?
3. How did the racial views of white Southerners influence their responses to emancipation? Why did they almost universally insist that "You cannot make the negro work, without physical compulsion"?
4. Schurz reported that white Southerners had "a desire to preserve slavery in its original form as much and as long as possible." What evidence of that desire did Schurz report?
5. What evidence did Schurz find of the "ingrained feeling that the blacks at large belong to the whites at large"? To what degree was this feeling influential in shaping southern whites' responses to emancipation? To what extent was it influential in shaping federal policy toward Reconstruction?

DOCUMENT 16–2

Former Slaves Seek to Reunite Their Families

With freedom, former slaves tried to reunite families slavery had separated. Some freed people traveled far and wide searching for kinfolk. Others appealed for help from the Freedmen's Bureau or enlisted literate friends to write letters of inquiry. But hundreds of former slaves placed advertisements in newspapers, asking for help in locating lost family members. The advertisements below appeared in the Christian Recorder, *the weekly newspaper of the African Methodist Episcopal Church in Philadelphia. The ads provide a glimpse of the scars of slavery and the meanings of freedom for millions of former slaves.*

Advertisements from the Christian Recorder, 1865–1870

January 25, 1865

INFORMATION WANTED

Jacob Brown wishes to find his sister and friends, from whom he was sold about eight years ago. He belonged to George Fisher, of Hardy County, Va., near Morefield. His sister Louisa, who was sold with him into Louisiana, has been back home once. She left three children, named respectively Peter, Isaac, and Moses.

From *Christian Recorder*, 1865–1870.

She is in New Orleans, and is anxious to hear of them. Another sister remained, named Arena or "Arenir," whose husband was named Paul Peterson. His uncles were Richard and Jacob Cassam, owned by McCoy.

Any person knowing any thing of them will confer a great favor upon the undersigned, who is their young brother, and who escaped from imprisonment in the jail, at Winchester, Va., by writing such information as shall unite those separated by slavery.

Respectfully,
Jacob Brown,
Baton Rouge, Louisiana

July 29, 1865

INFORMATION WANTED

Information is wanted of Cayrel Robinson, who left Liberty, Clay County, Missouri, about four years ago, to join the Union army at Wyandotte, Kansas; and he has not been heard from since. Any information of his whereabouts will be thankfully received by his wife.

Mrs. Fannie Robinson
Care of P. C. Cooper
Box 1129
Davenport, Iowa

August 5, 1865

INFORMATION WANTED

Edith Chappel left Columbia, South Carolina, on February 20th, 1865, with the army of Gen. Sherman, from the residence of Mrs. Henry Lyons. Her aunt, Fannie Bostick, can be found with

Mr. A. L. Hart
827 Lombard St.
Philadelphia

November 18, 1865

NOTICE

Information wanted of my two brothers Nelson, and Wesley Smothers, and my six sisters, Mary Ann Russell, Harriet, Matilda, Elizabeth, Henrietta, and Cornelia Smothers.

They formerly belonged to Ruth Rigla, who resided two miles from the Old Harper's Ferry Road, Frederick County, Md.

In 1837, we were all sold to South Carolina. I have not seen them since. Any information will be thankfully received by

Rev. Cyrus Boey
Oswego, N.Y.

March 10, 1866

INFORMATION WANTED

By a mother concerning her children. Mrs. Elizabeth Williams, who now resides in Marysville, California, was formerly owned, together with her children viz.: Lydia, William, Allen, and Parker, by one John Petty, who lived about six miles from the town of Woodbury, Franklin County, Tennessee. At that time she was the wife of Sandy Rucker, and was familiarly known as Betsy, sometimes called Betsy Petty.

About twenty-five years ago, the mother was sold to Mr. Marshal Stroud, by whom some twelve or fourteen years later, she was, for the second time since purchased by him, taken to Arkansas. She has never seen the above named children since. Any information given concerning them, however, will be very gratefully received by one whose love for her children survives the bitterness and hardships of many long years spent in slavery.

Preachers in the neighborhood of Woodbury, Tennessee, are especially requested to make inquiry, and communicate any information they may deem valuable either by letter or through the columns of the "Recorder."

April 7, 1866

INFORMATION WANTED

Of the children of Hagar Outlaw, who went from Wake Forest. Three of them, (their names being Cherry, Viny, and Mills Outlaw,) were bought by Abram Hester. Noah Outlaw was taken to Alabama by Joseph Turner Hillsborough. John Outlaw was sold to George Vaughan. Eli Outlaw was sold by Joseph Outlaw. He acted as watchman for old David Outlaw. Thomas Rembry Outlaw was taken away by Wm. Outlaw. Julia Outlaw was sold in New Orleans by Dr. Outlaw. I live in Raleigh, and I hope they will think enough of their mother to come and look for her, as she is growing old, and needs help. She will be glad to see them again at [illegible word]. The place is healthy, and they can all do well here. As the hand of time steals over me now so rapidly, I wish to see my dear ones once more clasped to their mother's heart as in days of yore. Come to the capital of North Carolina, and you will find your mother there, eagerly awaiting her loved ones.

Hugh Outlaw, if you should find any or all of my children, you will do me an incalculable favor by immediately informing them that their mother still lives.

May 5, 1866

INFORMATION WANTED

Of the oldest daughter Jane's children. One son by the name of Andrew, another by the name of Ransom, and another by the name of George, who were taken from me and sold when they were very small.

Also two others, (twins) one called Martha Ann and the other had no name. The name of the father of these children is Washington. He belonged to a man in Franklinton, Ky., whose name was Joseph Kearney.

The mother of these children belonged to a man in Franklin Co., Ky., by the name of Seth Ward, her name is Charity Ward, wife of Washington Kearney, who was killed by a fall from a wagon. Any information concerning any of the above will be thankfully received by addressing

W. A. Bookram
Franklinton, North Carolina

June 9, 1866

INFORMATION WANTED

Charles Metts wishes to hear from his family. His wife's name is Jane, and his children are named Margaret, Drucilla, Elizabeth, and Chas. Henry. He has not seen them for ten years. The last he heard from them was when in the Rebel Army. They were at Columbia, S.C. He could not get a chance to go to see them. He came on to Philadelphia, and is now living here.

Baptist ministers at Columbia, S.C., will please make inquiry concerning the above family. All information will be thankfully received by addressing

Chas. Metts
Care of R. A. Black
"Christian Recorder" Office.
Philadelphia, Pa.

July 14, 1866

INFORMATION WANTED

Lewis Wade wishes to learn the whereabouts of his wife, Lucy, and three children, named respectively, Benjamin, Harriet and Charlotte. He left them in 1850, they then being in Rockbridge county, Virginia. He belonged to Wm. Thompson, while his wife and children belonged to James Watts. Any information respecting them will be thankfully received by the subscriber at Chatham, Canada West,—and Heaven will bless the hand that guides the wanderers home.

Chatham, Canada West

August 11, 1866

INFORMATION WANTED

Phoebe Ann Jackson, formerly Phoebe Nichols is desirous of informing her brother, Thomas G. Nichols, of Galveston, Texas, of her location in Richmond, Va.

Her proper name was Nichols. She was called Robertson, her eldest brother being known by that name.

In the family, beside father and mother, there were twelve brothers and three sisters. Nancy and Peter Robertson were sold to New Orleans; Brother Samuel went to Georgia. Mother could only learn that Francis and Thomas were on the same boat. Mother and father have since died, as also our stepfather, whose name was Africa Hanes.

Address
Phoebe Ann Jackson
1015 Marshall street, corner 11th
Richmond, Va.

September 22, 1866

INFORMATION WANTED

Information wanted of the whereabouts of my husband, Richard Jones, and my two sons, John and Thomas. We were separated in the woods, near a place called Alleywhite, in November, 1862. I was carried back to Suffolk by the Union troops. I have heard nothing of them since.

We were owned by Birven Jones, of Smithfield, Suffolk County, Virginia. I am the granddaughter of old Tom Peet Wilson. I am much in want at this time. Ministers will please read this notice in the churches.

Matilda Jones
Direct to Anthony Bowen
Agent, *Christian Recorder*
No. 85 E St., betw'n 9th and 10th (Island)
Washington, D.C.

November 17, 1866

INFORMATION WANTED

Information wanted of Silvey Lynch, wife of Sandy Lynch, who was carried away from Carolina county, Virginia, by her "master," Wm. Goodman, in 1862. Her maiden name is Silvey Wilkins. She took with her three children. The name of the eldest is Jane; the next eldest is Henrietta; and the youngest is a boy named Alexander.

When my wife was taken away, I was in the army, performing the duties of a servant. My wife was formerly claimed as the property of one Nicholas Wilkins. She is of the Baptist persuasion. Any information concerning her whereabouts will be thankfully received from any one who will please address a letter to

Sandy Lynch
Care of Rev. J. R. V. Thomas
Box 90
Portsmouth, Virginia

March 23, 1867

INFORMATION WANTED

Information wanted of John and Lavinia Teamer, or Teamoh, who were sold in 1853, from Richmond, Va., by one John Lindsay, formally of Fortress Monroe, Va. John was nine years old, and Lavinia eight, at the time of the sale. Their mother Sarah was sold by the same party to Rosinfield, of Richmond, Va. It was thought they were sold to Texas. Ministers of the Christian Church will please inquire, as any information of the parties, will be thankfully received by their father.

Geo. Teamoh
Portsmouth, Va.
P.O. Box 152

November 2, 1867

INFORMATION WANTED

Canton, Ind., Oct. 19, 1867

John Grantson and Albert Thurston Robinson, brothers, aged respectvely about 16 and 13 years, were sent from Missouri to Kentucky in the year 1863. Andrew Robinson, of Clay County, Missouri, was the owner of the boys' father, Coyed Robinson, whose wife, Frances was owned by Whiton Drew, of the same County and State, and after his death fell to his son, Dalphin Drew, who, in 1860, sold her to a man by the name of Pitcher, the former owner of her mother. This man formerly lived in Platt city, Platt county, Missouri. Albert, the youngest boy, was brought to Kentucky in August, 1863, by Dalphin Drew's wife, as nurse for her babe. John the elder boy, and his sister, Mary Eliza, with several others, were sent there a few months later to the care of Washington Gordon, Logan County, Kentucky. From thence they came back here a few months since, intending to get back to Missouri as soon as possible; but the parents may be elsewhere now. A kind, elderly colored man, by the name of Peter Garland, has voluntarily taken charge of them, and placed them in comfortable, but transient homes, but they wish very much to be united to their relatives.

Susan Trueblood

P.S. If any one should wish further information, they can write to me, and I will give it, if possible. My address is Canton, Washington, Co., Indiana.

May 8, 1869

INFORMATION WANTED

Of my son Charles Blackwell. He was sold from me in Lancaster county, Virginia, ten years ago, when quite young. He was sold from the estate of Mr. Joseph Beacham to Mr. Lewis Dix, and then taken to Mississippi. I am an old man and need the companionship of my son. Any assistance in securing information of his where-abouts will be thankfully received. Ministers in Mississippi and throughout the entire country will please read in their churches. Address information to my address,

Lewis Blackwell
Lancaster Court House, Virginia

April 2, 1870

INFORMATION WANTED

Information wanted of Sarah Williams, who I left at Halifax Court House, Va., about 25 years ago. She belonged to a man whose name was William Early, who kept a dry-goods store. Any information of her will be thankfully received by her sister, Martha Ann Good, who was taken away from Nathan Dexter, who kept a hotel at Halifax, at 12 o'clock at night, when quite small, and sold in Alabama, but who now lives at 225 Currant Alley, Philadelphia, Pa.

N.B. Ministers in the South, please read in your churches.

July 2, 1870

INFORMATION WANTED

Of my sisters, Jennette, Eliza, Caroline, America, and Elizabeth, and of my brother Harry. Also of our mother, whose name was Dinah Hickson. They were sold from Liberty, Mo., over 30 years ago, and the last time I heard of them they were on Red River. They belonged to Andy Hickson, and were sold to a man named Francis Benware. Any information of these parties will be gladly received by Moses Hickson,

Now Moses Sisseney
St. Joseph, Mo., Box 507

N.B. Pastors of churches will please read this.

December 10, 1870

INFORMATION WANTED

Of my mother Isabella, my sister Sallie, and of my grandmother, named Minna. I left them in Georgia about thirty years ago. They belonged to a man named Joe Marshall; my mother belonged to a man named Wm. Bell. They lived near Green Brier Meeting House. Any information address, Jas. Bell, Helena, Ark.

QUESTIONS FOR READING AND DISCUSSION

1. How did the people who placed these ads expect readers to recognize their lost family members?
2. What audiences did the people who placed these ads intend to reach? What was the significance of statements such as, "Ministers in Mississippi and throughout the entire country will please read in their churches"?
3. What do these ads suggest about slavery? What do these ads suggest about family relationships among slaves?
4. Do you think such ads actually helped to reunite families? Why or why not? What do these ads suggest about the meanings of freedom for former slaves?

DOCUMENT 16–3

Planter Louis Manigault Visits His Plantations and Former Slaves

For many years before the Civil War, Louis Manigault owned two large and very profitable rice plantations located on Argyle Island in the Savannah River, not far from the city of Savannah, Georgia. He abandoned the plantations when General Sherman's army approached in 1864. His numerous slaves remained on the plantations without white supervision through the end of the war, and more or less made them their own. After emancipation, most of the freed men and women stayed on Manigault's land, where they made contracts with a white man who rented the plantations from Manigault. In 1867 Manigault decided to return to his plantations for the first time since he left in 1864. In his plantation journal, excerpted here, he recorded what he discovered. His observations illustrate the mind-boggling changes the war and emancipation brought to plantations, as well as certain unexpected continuities. As you read Manigault's comments about his former slaves, try to imagine how the freedmen and women viewed their former master.

A Narrative of a Post–Civil War Visit to Gowrie and East Hermitage Plantations, March 22, 1867

I conversed with several Negroes from plantations in our vicinity, from them I received some River News and likewise sent word to some of our former Negroes that I was in Savannah and would visit them. . . .

Some six miles from Savannah we came in sight of the Charleston and Savannah Rail Road, which had not been touched since the advance of Sherman's Army but the twisted and ruined Rails remained as left by the Yankees. . . . The vestiges of former Encampments of large Bodies of Troops were still perceptible on either side of the road. . . . The cruel hand of War was now clearly to be seen; in fact most startling was the change on every side since my last visit here in Dec'r 1864. The large Rice Pounding Mill with its Wheel in the centre similar to the Gowrie Mill was burnt down. This was also the case with the fine wooden Barn close at hand. . . . With far deeper pain however did I contemplate the Ruins of Mr James Potter's handsome Residence. As a Country House it was superior to any on the River, and had been built by Mr Potter about the year of 1854 and with its furniture cost about Twenty Thousand Dollars. Many a time had I spent a pleasing hour at this hospitable Gentleman's House, surrounded by his family of charming Young Ladies not forgetting to mention "Miss Gilby" the English Governess. . . .

General Harrison [who rented Manigault's plantations] was soon pointed out to me. He was in his black-smith Shop overlooking the repair of some Plantation Utensil.

I advanced and introduced myself. He is a Man of commanding appearance, upwards of six feet in heighth, about fifty years of age, married; with five Children . . . and very fine looking, who had served in a [Confederate] Cavalry Regiment throughout the War. The General said he had not visited [Manigault's plantations on] Argyle Island for two or three days and would be happy to accompany me. His Canoe, with old Negro and paddle, was soon in readiness, and with our horse and buggy placed in charge of the Servant to be taken to the Stable we pushed off in the River. . . .

Proceeding now on foot along the Canal Bank . . . we took our nearest course towards Gowrie Settlement. When about half across the Island our progress was impeded by the freshet water knee deep over the check banks. The General pushed on, and Louis [Manigault's son] and I were soon soaked from knees down as we followed; the water becoming deeper still, it was determined he should endeavour to reach Gowrie Settlement and send us some Negro Man to take us on his back. After some delay I recognized our former Cooper "George" approaching, delighted to meet us and calling me "Maussa" as of yore. He [carried us on his back and] placed us in safety on dry land and we walked up to the Settlement. Reaching Gowrie Settlement I placed Louis in charge of (the above mentioned) George's Wife "Betty" a woman I had known for many years and who always bore a good character. She made a fire for him in her house, dried his shoes and stockings and as I learnt afterwards boiled several eggs for him to his great delight. . . .

From Louis Manigault, Manigault Plantation Journal (manuscript), pp. 56–71. Manigault Papers, Southern Historical Collection, University of North Carolina, Chapel Hill.

Not having visited the Plantation since the Advance of Sherman's Army in December 1864 my present visit was one of painful interest. [On my] . . . final visit to the plantation in Dec'r 1864 . . . although the sound of Musketry from the advancing Pickets grew more and more distinct from hour to hour, still up to the very last moment our Negroes behaved well and I left the entire Gang unloading the flat of rice, still pleased to see me, and singing as they bore the heavy loads on their heads from the flat to the Stacks in the Barn Yard. Standing near the ruins of my former dwelling I contemplated the spot. Where once stood this Country House could alone now be seen a few scattering brick, and the tall chimney to denote that spot. Here the most happy period of my boyish days, together with the early years of my married life had been spent. No remnant of my Kitchen, Fine Stable, both built just previous to the War, remained; not even a brick to mark the spot, as all of these had been stolen by the Negroes and sold in Savannah at $5 whilst the Market value was $18. . . .

Trees, Plants, Shrubs, Fences, not a vestige remained, not even the stumps of the trees being visible, all had been used as fire-wood by the Negroes. . . .

The Change in the appearance of Gowrie Settlement is, I may say, from a Village to a Wilderness. There remain in this Gowrie Settlement Four large double Negro Houses, all new, having been built by myself just previous to the War upon high brick foundations elevating them beyond the reach of . . . [flooding]. With the exception of these the Settlement is a barren waste and presents a most abandoned and forlorn appearance. About a half a dozen Negroes crawled out of their houses as we approached, dirty and sluggish in appearance and stupefied by sleep, not knowing whether under the new regime, it would be proper to meet me politely or not, but in every case I advanced and shook hands, calling each by name, which seemed to please them highly. I thought it best to appear but little concerned at the marked change in my situation and joked with them as was my former habit. Five or six were talking to me in this Settlement when one of them remarked "My God, Maussa! Wha mek You trow we side so long; Wha mek You no come back?" My answer amused them highly. Smiling, and turning to the tall chimney of my former happy Home, alone standing to indicate the spot where stood the House; I remarked "Lord! a Massy! You tink I can lib in de Chimney?" which they for the first time appeared to consider true. . . .

Proceeding in front of General Harrison and followed by some of his "Foremen" (none other than our former Negroes "Driver John" [who, before emancipation, supervised the labor of other slaves], "George" Cooper [who built rice barrels], "Big Hector," and "Charles" the Trunk Minder [who supervised sluices for flooding and draining rice fields]) I imagined myself for the moment a Planter once more as if followed by Overseer and Driver. The weather was most beautiful, not a cloud on the Horizon, and so clear and pure the atmosphere that the Presbyterian Church Steeple in Savannah loomed up as if one half its distance. I wished my horse with me to ride over the entire Tract as of yore. But these were only passing momentary thoughts, and soon dispelled by the sad reality of affairs. . . .

Passing through the Settlement and about leaving we were met by Twelve of our former Negroes. They all seemed pleased to see me, calling me "Maussa" the Men still showing respect by taking off their caps. It was singular that after an absence of two and a half years from the Plantation I should now return to visit the place just after the Death of one of three Original Negroes purchased with Gowrie, January 1833. A Woman Known by the Name of "Currie Binah" . . . died yesterday and was buried this morning. Two of the Original Negroes now remain, both as cunning as Negroes can be. These are "Charles the Trunk Minder"; and "Capt'n Hector" for Thirty Years our chief Boat Hand, always spoiled both by my Father and Myself, greatly indulged, and one of the first to give trouble upon the out-break of the War. Amongst the twelve Negroes who advanced to meet me at East Hermitage was, strange to say, the greatest Villain on the Plantation, the most notoriously bad character and worst Negro of the place. Tall, black, lousy, in rags, and uncombed, kinky, knotty-hair approached "Jack Savage." This Negro was bought in 1839. . . . He was an exceedingly lazy Man, although quite smart and our best plantation Carpenter. He was always giving trouble and ever appeared dissatisfied. He was the only Negro ever in our possession who I considered capable of Murdering me, or burning my dwelling at night, or capable of committing any act. The Trunks [sluice gates for flooding and draining rice fields] built by Jack Savage . . . were perfect, and his large Flood-Gates were all that one could desire and specimens of good work. This Man we sold in 1863, he causing trouble on the place, and I had not seen him since 1862. As we met I gave him my hand and made a few friendly remarks. I always gave him many presents such as bacon, and tobacco and rice. Even now I felt sad in contemplating his condition, as in fact was the case with all of them. . . . That former mutual and pleasing feeling of Master towards Slave and vice versa is now as a dream of the past. Our "Northern Brethren" inform us that we Southerners "knew nothing of the Negro Character." This I have always considered perfectly true, but they further state that They (the Yankees) have always known the true Character of the Negro which I consider entirely false in the extreme. So deceitful is the Negro that as far as my own experience extends I could never in a single instance decipher his character. Here at present the last one I should have dreamt of, advances to greet me; whilst sitting idly upon the Negro-House steps dirty and sluggish, I behold young Women to whom I had most frequently presented Ear-Rings, Shoes, Calicos, [and] Kerchief . . . formerly pleased to meet me, but now not even lifting the head as I passed. In former days also fear in a great measure guided the action of the Negro and we Planters could never get at the truth. I am of opinion that very many Negroes are most unhappy in their changed condition, but this however they do not care to admit. . . .

At last I put the simple question to [General Harrison], "out of curiosity, could you give me an idea of [how] you make a 'Contract' with the Negroes, and how do you work the Plantation from your experience as a Planter, since the 'Termination of the War?' " His reply was as follows; and his Plan as far as I can judge, appears to me quite good. "Contract" The portion of the Plantation rented to General Harrison contains 390 Acres. This is divided into 5 Divisions, each Division containing 78 Acres. An intelligent Negro, and one experienced in Rice Culture is chosen. The new appellation of "Foreman" is given him, and he takes full charge of One Division (of in this case 78 Acres). The "Foreman" is to cultivate and in every respect superintend his Division, until his [rice] Crop is threshed, and ready for Market. For this purpose He selects or procures his own Hands, which in this instance requires about 10 for each "Foreman." A "Contract" is signed in Savannah between Gen'l Harrison and his "Foreman" . . . and for this purpose they two appear at the Government [Freedmen's] Bureau where the transaction is effected in proper form established by Law. Little or no intercourse is thus held between Gen'l Harrison and the Mass of the Negroes, and provided the Work is performed it is immaterial what Hands are employed whether the same or others. . . .

All [about the visit] had passed off in a most satisfactory manner, with the exception that upon reaching Savannah I found that the Gen'l's Servant (who had taken charge of horse and buggy up at the place) had stolen nearly every thing I had in the buggy, but I have never thought it worth my while to mention it to the General, as I have no doubt he has from his contact with Negroes annoyance enough.

QUESTIONS FOR READING AND DISCUSSION

1. What evidence did Manigault discover of the "cruel hand of War"?
2. What was responsible for what Manigault called the "change in appearance" of his Gowrie plantation "from a Village to a Wilderness"?
3. How did Manigault's former slaves behave toward him on his visit? How did he account for their behavior? How would you explain their behavior?
4. Why did Manigault believe that, "So deceitful is the Negro that as far as my own experience extends I could never in a single instance decipher his character"? How might his former slaves have described Manigault?
5. Manigault confirmed for himself "the sad reality of affairs" on his visit to his plantations. How, specifically, might his former slaves have described the reality of affairs on his plantations in 1867?

DOCUMENT 16–4

Klan Violence against Blacks

White vigilantes often terrorized African Americans after emancipation. The campaign of terror intensified with congressional Reconstruction and the mobilization of black voters in the Republican Party. The violence attracted the attention of Congress, which held committee hearings throughout the South in 1871 to investigate the Ku Klux Klan. The following testimony of Elias Hill — a black preacher and teacher who lived in York County, South Carolina — illustrates the tactics and purposes of white vigilantes.

Elias Hill

Testimony before Congressional Committee Investigating the Ku Klux Klan, 1871

[The committee included a brief description of Hill.] Elias Hill is a remarkable character. He is crippled in both legs and arms, which are shriveled by rheumatism; he cannot walk, cannot help himself, has to be fed and cared for personally by others; was in early life a slave, whose freedom was purchased, his father buying his mother and getting Elias along with her, as a burden of which his master was glad to be rid. Stricken at seven years old with disease, he never was afterward able to walk, and he presents the appearance of a dwarf with the limbs of a child, the body of a man, and a finely developed intellectual head. He learned his

From U.S. Congress, *Report of the Joint Select Committee to Inquire into the Condition of Affairs in the Late Insurrectionary States* (Washington, DC, 1872), 1:44–46.

letters and to read by calling the school children into the cabin as they passed, and also learned to write. He became a Baptist preacher, and after the war engaged in teaching colored children, and conducted the business correspondence of many of his colored neighbors. He is a man of blameless character, of unusual intelligence, speaks good English, and we put the story of his wrongs in his own language:

On the night of the 5th of last May, after I had heard a great deal of what they had done in that neighborhood, they came. It was between 12 and 1 o'clock at night when I was awakened and heard the dogs barking, and something walking, very much like horses. As I had often laid awake listening for such persons, for they had been all through the neighborhood, and disturbed all men and many women, I supposed that it was them. They came in a very rapid manner, and I could hardly tell whether it was the sound of horses or men. At last they came to my brother's door, which is in the same yard, and broke open the door and attacked his wife, and I heard her screaming and mourning. I could not understand what they said, for they were talking in an outlandish and unnatural tone, which I had heard they generally used at a negro's house. I heard them knocking around in her house. I was lying in my little cabin in the yard. At last I heard them have her in the yard. She was crying and the Ku-Klux were whipping her to make her tell where I lived. I heard her say, "Yon is his house." She has told me since that they first asked who had taken me out of her house. They said, "Where's Elias?" She said, "He doesn't stay here; yon is his house." They were then in the yard, and I had heard them strike her five or six licks when I heard her say this. Some one then hit my door. It flew open. One ran in the house, and stopping about the middle of the house, which is a small cabin, he turned around, as it seemed to me as I lay there awake, and said, "Who's here?" Then I knew they would take me, and I answered, "I am here." He shouted for joy, as it seemed, "Here he is! Here he is! We have found him!" and he threw the bedclothes off of me and caught me by one arm, while another man took me by the other and they carried me into the yard between the houses, my brother's and mine, and put me on the ground beside a boy. The first thing they asked me was, "Who did that burning? Who burned our houses?" — gin-houses, dwelling houses and such. Some had been burned in the neighborhood. I told them it was not me; I could not burn houses; it was unreasonable to ask me. Then they hit me with their fists, and said I did it, I ordered it. They went on asking me didn't I tell the black men to ravish all the white women. No, I answered them. They struck me again with their fists on my breast, and then they went on, "When did you hold a night-meeting of the Union League,[1] and who were the officers? Who was the president?" I told them I had been the president, but that there had been no Union League meeting held at that place where they were formerly held since away in the fall. This was the 5th of May. They said that Jim Raney, that was hung, had been at my house since the time I had said the League was last held, and that he had made a speech. I told them that he had not, because I did not know the man. I said, "Upon honor." They said I had no honor, and hit me again. They went on asking me hadn't I been writing to Mr. A. S. Wallace, in Congress, to get letters from him. I told them I had. They asked what I had been writing about? I told them, "Only tidings." They said, with an oath, "I know the tidings were d —— d

---

[1] **Union League**: Republican organization that helped mobilize African American voters.

good, and you were writing something about the Ku-Klux, and haven't you been preaching and praying about the Ku-Klux?" One asked, "Haven't you been preaching political sermons?" Generally, one asked me all the questions, but the rest were squatting over me — some six men I counted as I lay there, Said one, "Didn't you preach against the Ku-Klux," and wasn't that what Mr. Wallace was writing to me about? "Not at all," I said. "Let me see the letter," said he; "what was it about?" I said it was on the times. They wanted the letter. I told them if they would take me back into the house, and lay me in the bed, which was close adjoining my books and papers, I would try and get it. They said I would never go back to that bed, for they were going to kill me. "Never expect to go back; tell us where the letters are." I told them they were on the shelf somewhere, and I hoped they would not kill me. Two of them went into the house. . . . They staid in there a good while hunting about and then came out and asked me for a lamp. I told them there was a lamp somewhere. They said "Where?" I was so confused I said I could not tell exactly. They caught my leg — you see what it is — and pulled me over the yard, and then left me there, knowing I could not walk nor crawl, and all six went into the house. I was chilled with the cold lying in the yard at that time of night, for it was near 1 o'clock, and they had talked and beat me and so on until half an hour had passed since they first approached. After they had staid in the house for a considerable time, they came back to where I lay and asked if I wasn't afraid at all. They pointed pistols at me all around my head once or twice, as if they were going to shoot me, telling me they were going to kill me; wasn't I ready to die, and willing to die? Didn't I preach? That they came to kill me — all the time pointing pistols at me. This second time they came out of the house, after plundering the house, searching for letters, they came at me with these pistols, and asked if I was ready to die. I told them that I was not exactly ready; that I would rather live; that I hoped they would not kill me that time. They said they would; I had better prepare. One caught me by the leg and hurt me, for my leg for forty years has been drawn each year, more and more year by year, and I made moan when it hurt so. One said "G —— d d —— n it, hush!" He had a horsewhip, and he told me to pull up my shirt, and he hit me. He told me at every lick, "Hold up your shirt." I made a moan every time he cut with the horsewhip. I reckon he struck me eight cuts right on the hip bone; it was almost the only place he could hit my body, my legs are so short — all my limbs drawn up and withered away with pain. I saw one of them standing over me or by me motion to them to quit. They all had disguises on. I then thought they would not kill me. One of them then took a strap, and buckled it around my neck and said, "Let's take him to the river and drown him." . . . After pulling the strap around my neck, he took it off and gave me a lick on my hip where he had struck me with the horsewhip. One of them said, "Now, you see, I've burned up the d —— d letter of Wallace's and all," and he brought out a little book and says, "What's this for?" I told him I did not know; to let me see with a light and I could read it. They brought a lamp and I read it. It was a book in which I had keep an account of the school. I had been licensed to keep a school. I read them some of the names. He said that would do, and asked if I had been paid for those scholars I had put down. I said no. He said I would now have to die. I was somewhat afraid, but one said not to kill me. They said "Look here! Will you put a card in the paper next week like June Moore and Sol Hill?" They had been prevailed on to put a card in the paper to renounce all republicanism and never vote. I said, "If I had the money to pay the expense, I could." They said I could borrow, and gave me another lick. They asked me, "Will you quit preaching?" I told them I did not know. I said that to save my life. They said I must stop that republican paper that was coming to Clay Hill. It has been only a few weeks since it stopped. The republican weekly paper was then coming to me from Charleston. It came to my name. They said I must stop it, quit preaching, and put a card in the newspaper renouncing republicanism, and they would not kill me; but if I did not they would come back the next week and kill me. With that one of them went into the house where my brother and my sister-in-law lived, and brought her to pick me up. As she stooped down to pick me up one of them struck her, and as she was carrying me into the house another struck her with a strap. She carried me into the house and laid me on the bed. Then they gathered around and told me to pray for them. I tried to pray. They said, "Don't you pray against Ku-Klux, but pray that God may forgive Ku-Klux. Don't pray against us. Pray that God may bless and save us." I was so chilled with cold lying out of doors so long and in such pain I could not speak to pray, but I tried to, and they said that would do very well, and all went out of the house.

QUESTIONS FOR READING AND DISCUSSION

1. What did the Klan want from Hill? Why didn't they kill him?
2. Why was the Klan concerned about Hill's preaching, teaching, and newspaper reading?
3. Why did the Klan use such brutal violence against Hill and his relatives? According to Hill, how had others been treated by the Klan? Does it appear that the Klan randomly chose people to terrorize? Why or why not?
4. What significance, if any, should be attributed to the Klan's demand that Hill "pray that God may forgive Ku-Klux"? For what did they seek forgiveness? Why?

DOCUMENT 16–5

The Ignorant Vote and the Election of 1876

The Republican and Democratic parties mobilized sectional, racial, and ethnic coalitions in the presidential election of 1876. Republicans hoped to pick up electoral votes from southern states—where most whites hated northerners and Republicans—by depending on the votes of recently enfranchised former slaves. Southern Democrats in turn hoped to pick up electoral votes from northern states—where many whites hated white southerners who killed their relatives during the Civil War—by mobilizing the votes of Irish immigrants and others who bitterly opposed anti-Catholic Republicans. The Democratic candidate Samuel J. Tilden won the popular vote, which seemed to signal the failure of the unwieldy Republican coalition of white northern farmers and businessmen with black former slaves. A Tilden victory would end Republican control of the government and reverse postwar reconstruction policies. But the election deadlocked since Tilden lacked one electoral vote for a majority. An electoral commission eventually handed the presidency to the Republican candidate, Rutherford B. Hayes, in what became known as the Compromise of 1877. Popular cartoonist Thomas Nast drew this cartoon after the 1876 election, when it appeared that Tilden had won, but before the electoral deadlock was settled in favor of Hayes. Nast, who supported Republican policies of black suffrage and civil rights, attributed the 1876 popular vote to what he termed, "The Ignorant Vote."

Thomas Nast
"The Ignorant Vote," 1876

Library of Congress/Corbis/VCG via Getty Images

QUESTIONS FOR READING AND DISCUSSION

1. How did Nast portray common racial and ethnic stereotypes in the cartoon?

2. Though neither blacks nor Irish immigrants were majorities in the South or North, why did Nast still choose to portray them as balancing each other?

3. How did Nast try to convey the idea that these voters were ignorant? Does the cartoon suggest what motivated these voters? How might a cartoon that portrayed intelligent voters differ?

4. Did Nast's cartoon blame one party more than another for what he considered the electoral influence of the ignorant vote?

5. In what ways does Nast's cartoon depict widespread doubts about democracy in the United States going into the election of 1876?

6. How does Nast's cartoon portray Republicans' retreat from Reconstruction policies of black suffrage and civil rights?

COMPARATIVE QUESTIONS

1. How do the views of southern whites as reported by Carl Schurz differ from those expressed by Louis Manigault? To what extent do they contrast with the meanings of freedom documented in the advertisements from the *Christian Recorder*?

2. To what extent did the Klan's campaign of terror against black Republicans like Hill confirm or contradict Schurz's report on race relations in the South?

3. How did the activities of Hill and other Republicans compare with those of the freedmen and women on Manigault's plantations? How did they compare with the voters' activities as depicted in the cartoon about the 1876 election?

4. In what ways did Schurz's conclusions about the South differ from those presented in the other documents in this chapter? What explains the differences? How does race factor into these differences?

5. Documents in this chapter provide evidence that Reconstruction profoundly challenged fundamental assumptions among Northerners and Southerners, whites and blacks. Judging from these documents, what assumptions were challenged, and how, if at all, did those assumptions change during Reconstruction?

17 The Contested West

1865–1900

After the Civil War, hundreds of thousands of migrants settled the prairies, the mountainous West, and the Pacific coast, most of them moving westward, some of them on recently built railroads. Migration was not all westward. Some Mexicans moved north and some Chinese moved east. Native Americans displaced from their tribal lands onto reservations sought to resist cultural extermination. The uprooting that accompanied this restless movement strengthened some ties while weakening or breaking others. The struggles of Chinese immigrants, homesteaders, Texas ranchers, Mexicans in the Texas borderlands, and Native Americans to come to terms with the consequences of migration and settlement are disclosed in the following documents.

DOCUMENT 17–1

Transcontinental Railroad Completed, 1870

In May 1869, tracks of the Central Pacific Railroad that headed east and the Union Pacific Railroad that headed west met north of Salt Lake City, Utah, causing jubilation about the conquest of the West's vast distances by this transportation technology. Now a trip from the East Coast to the Pacific that previously was dangerous and time-consuming could ideally be completed in the comparative comfort of a railroad car in about two weeks, assuming one could afford the ticket. To celebrate the completion of the transcontinental railroad, in 1870 the printmakers Currier and Ives published "Through to the Pacific." The print highlights the last miles of a transcontinental journey from east to west, the direction most passengers traveled. The print does not depict a specific geographical location. Instead, it assembles a generalized portrait of the human and environmental context of the new rail connection to the Pacific coast.

"Through to the Pacific," ca. 1870

Library of Congress, 3a04026

QUESTIONS FOR READING AND DISCUSSION

1. How does the train contrast with the environment it is passing through?
2. What sources of energy are depicted in the print and how is the energy harnessed for practical uses?
3. What forms of commerce are portrayed in the print? How does the rail connection to the Pacific affect commerce?
4. How, if at all, is the railroad connection between the Eastern and Pacific coasts likely to change the lives of people who live in the village? Would passengers on the train be likely to find life in the village familiar or alien?
5. How does this portrait of the far West in 1870 compare with common American ideas that the West was uncivilized and lawless?
6. Who is the audience for this print? How does the print try to appeal to the audience?

DOCUMENT 17–2

Pun Chi Appeals to Congress in Behalf of Chinese Immigrants in California

The strong anti-Chinese sentiment in California led a group of Chinese merchants in San Francisco to petition Congress for a redress of grievances. Pun Chi, one of the merchants, drafted a statement in Chinese that was subsequently translated by William Speer, a Presbyterian missionary who worked in Chinatown. Pun Chi outlined the many ways life in California had betrayed the hopes of Chinese immigrants and violated basic principles of common humanity. His petition disclosed the views of many Chinese immigrants about how and why they were persecuted.

A Remonstrance from the Chinese in California, ca. 1870

We are natives of the empire of China, each following some employment or profession—literary men, farmers, mechanics or merchants. When your honorable government threw open the territory of California, the people of other lands were welcomed here to search for gold and to engage in trade. The ship-masters of your respected nation came over to our country, lauded the equality of your laws, extolled the beauty of your manners and customs, and made it known that your officers and people were extremely cordial toward the Chinese. Knowing well the harmony which had existed between our respective governments, we trusted in your sincerity. Not deterred by the long voyage, we came here presuming that our arrival would be hailed with cordiality and favor. But, alas! what times are these!—when former kind relations are forgotten, when we Chinese are viewed like thieves and enemies, when in the administration of justice our testimony is not received, when in the legal collection of the licenses we are injured and plundered, and villains of other nations are encouraged to rob and do violence to us! Our numberless wrongs it is most painful even to recite. At the present time, if we desire to quit the country, we are not possessed of the pecuniary means; if allowed to remain, we dread future troubles. But yet, on the other hand, it is our presumption that the conduct of the officers of justice here has been influenced by temporary prejudices and that your honorable government will surely not uphold their acts. We are sustained by the confidence that the benevolence of your eminent body, contemplating the people of the whole world as one family, will most assuredly not permit the Chinese population without guilt to endure injuries to so cruel a degree. . . .

1. THE UNRIGHTEOUSNESS OF HUMILIATING AND HATING THE CHINESE AS A PEOPLE.

We have heard that your honorable nation reverences Heaven. But if they comprehend the reverence that is due to the heavenly powers, of necessity they cannot humiliate and hate the Chinese. Why do we aver this? At the very beginning of time, Heaven produced a most holy man, whose name was Pwan-ku. He was the progenitor of the people of China. All succeeding races have branched off from them. . . . Hence we see that Heaven most loves our Chinese people, and multiplies its gifts to them beyond any other race. . . .

After some centuries, Heaven again produced a sage preeminent and alone in his excellence, whose name was Confucius, whom it made the great teacher of China. He combined what was greatest and best in all that preceded him, and became the teacher and exemplar of all ages. As to things on high, he showed men the fear of Heaven; as to things on earth, he taught them virtue. The sages of whom we have spoken had the wisdom to discern that all men on earth are one family. Now what is meant in styling all men on earth one family? It is, that the people of China, or of countries foreign to it, are all embraced, as it were, in one great circle of kindred, with its parents and children, its elder and younger

---

From William Speer, *The Oldest and the Newest Empire: China and the United States* (Cincinnati: National Publishing Co., 1870), 588–601.

branches, its bonds of unity; the pervading principle, love; no one member debased, none treated with dislike. Again, after several centuries, Heaven brought forth one Jesus, and ordained him to be a teacher to foreign lands. Now Jesus also taught mankind the fear of Heaven. He showed that the chief end is to pray for eternal life. He comprehended the reverence due to Heaven, and the obligations of virtue. He was in accord with the holy men of China. He looked on all beneath the sky as one great family. He did not permit distinctions of men into classes to be loved or despised. But now, if the religion of Jesus really teaches the fear of Heaven, how does it come that the people of your honorable country on the contrary trample upon and hate the race which Heaven most loves, that is, the Chinese? Should this not be called rebellion against Heaven? . . .

The wise men of China plant at the very foundation of government the idea of virtue, not that of physical power, just as do those professing the religion of Jesus Christ. Virtue is that which commands the intuitive submission of the human will. Great vessels of war and powerful artillery may destroy cities and devastate a country. That is physical power. But moral power is essentially different from mechanical power. The noblest illustration of moral power is the teacher at the head of his school—as much so as the locomotive and the telegraph are of mechanical skill. It is the spirit of man that deserves respect, not his form. If the spirit be noble and good, although the man be poor and humble, his features homely and his apparel mean, we honor him and love him. If the spirit be not so, though the man have wealth and position, though his countenance be beautiful and his clothing rich, we regard him with contempt and dislike. But we do affirm that the reason why the people of your honorable country dislike the Chinese is this, and no other—they look at the plain appearance and the patched clothes of their poor, and they do not think how many spirits there are among them whom they could respect and love. . . .

Now why is it that, when our people come to your country, instead of being welcomed with unusual respect and kindness, on the contrary they are treated with unusual contempt and evil? Hence many lose their lives at the hands of lawless wretches. Yet though there be Chinese witnesses of the crime, their testimony is rejected. The result is our utter abandonment to be murdered and that of our business to be ruined. How hard for the spirit to sustain such trials! It . . . is to be considered that we Chinese are universally a law-abiding people and that our conduct is very different from the lawlessness and violence of some other foreigners. Were it not that each so little understands the other's tongue, and mutual kind sentiments are not communicated, would not more cordial intercourse probably exist? . . .

4. THE PERPETUAL VEXATIONS OF THE CHINESE.
The class that engage in digging gold are, as a whole, poor people. We go on board the ships. There we find ourselves unaccustomed to winds and waves and to the extremes of heat and cold. We eat little; we grieve much. Our appearance is plain and our clothing poor. At once, when we leave the vessel, boatmen extort heavy fares; all kinds of conveyances require from us more than the usual charges; as we go on our way we are pushed and kicked and struck by the drunken and the brutal; but as we cannot speak your language, we bear our injuries and pass on. Even when within doors, rude boys throw sand and bad men stones after us. Passers by, instead of preventing these provocations, add to them by their laughter. We go up to the mines; there the collectors of the licenses make unlawful exactions and robbers strip, plunder, wound and even murder some of us. Thus we are plunged

into endless uncommiserated wrongs. But the first root of them all is that very degradation and contempt of the Chinese as a race of which we have spoken, which begins with your honorable nation, but which they communicate to people from other countries, who carry it to greater lengths. . . .

5. FATAL INJURIES UNPUNISHED.

Your Supreme Court has decided that the Chinese shall not bring action or give testimony against white men. Of how [many] great wrongs is this the consummation! To the death of how many of us has it led! In cases that are brought before your officers of justice, inasmuch as we are unable to obtain your people as witnesses, even the murderer is immediately set free! Sanctioned by this, robbers of foreign nations commit the greatest excesses. It is a small thing with them to drive us away and seize our property. They proceed to do violence and kill us; they go on in a career of bloodshed without limit, since they find there are none to bear testimony against them. . . . Because here and there a Chinese or two has proved a perjurer, shall it prejudice our entire nation? Shall this degrade us beneath the negro and the Indian? . . .

6. THE PERSECUTION OF THE CHINESE MINERS.

If a Chinese earns a dollar and a half in gold per day, his first desire is to go to an American and buy a mining claim. But should this yield a considerable result, the seller, it is possible, compels him to relinquish it. Perhaps robbers come and strip him of the gold. He dare not resist, since he cannot speak the language, and has not the power to withstand them. On the other hand, those who have no means to buy a claim seek some ground which other miners have dug over and left, and thus obtain a few dimes. From the proceeds of a hard day's toil, after they pay for food and clothes very little remains. It is hard for them to be prepared to meet the collector when he comes for the license money. . . . If these refuse to pay them, the collectors seize their purses and take their last grain of gold. Should the Chinese dispute with them, they assault them with pistols and other weapons, and some of the miners may lose their lives, and there is no redress. Hence, when it is reported that the collectors are coming, those who have no gold are forced to fly in terror; those who could pay are thus frightened and follow; then they are pursued and beaten, perhaps killed. Occurrences like these are common. . . .

When we were first favored with the invitations of your ship-captains to emigrate to California, and heard the laudations which they published of the perfect and admirable character of your institutions, and were told of your exceeding respect and love toward the Chinese, we could hardly have calculated that we would now be the objects of your excessive hatred — that your courts would refuse us the right of testimony; your legislature load us with increasing taxes and devise means how to wholly expel us; . . . that foreign villains, witnessing your degrading treatment of us, would assume the right to harass, plunder and rob us, possibly kill us; that injuries of every kind would be inflicted on us, and unceasing wrongs be perpetrated; that if we would desire to go, we would be unable to do so, and if we desired to remain, we could not. . . . If . . . you grant us as formerly to mine and trade here, then it is our request that you will give instructions to your courts that they shall again receive Chinese testimony; that they shall cease their incessant discussions about expelling the Chinese; that they shall quit their frequent agitations as to raising the license fees; that they shall allow the Chinese peace in the pursuit of their proper employments; and that they shall effectually repress the acts of violence common among the mountains, so that robbers shall not upon one pretext or another injure and plunder us. Thus shall your distinguished favor revive us like a continual dew.

QUESTIONS FOR READING AND DISCUSSION

1. What did Pun Chi consider "the perpetual vexations of the Chinese"? Why did he believe these vexations occurred?

2. Why did Pun Chi consider the treatment of the Chinese in California to be a "rebellion against Heaven"? According to Pun Chi, how did Christianity and Confucianism compare? Why did people in California persecute the Chinese, according to Pun Chi?

3. To what extent was "the first root" of all the wrongs Pun Chi pointed out the "degradation and contempt of the Chinese as a race"? Why did he ask if this treatment would "degrade us beneath the negro and the Indian"?

4. How realistic were the legal and political reforms Pun Chi suggested?

DOCUMENT 17–3

Mattie Oblinger Describes Life on a Nebraska Homestead

Uriah Oblinger moved to Fillmore County, Nebraska, in the fall of 1872 to claim a homestead and establish a farm on the prairie. A poor man, Uriah had served with an Indiana regiment for three years during the Civil War. After he married Mattie Thomas in 1869, the young couple rented a farm in Indiana. Along with Mattie's brothers Giles and Sam, Uriah decided to try his luck on a homestead in Nebraska. Mattie joined him there in May 1873. Shortly after she arrived, Mattie wrote the following letter to her relatives back in Indiana. Her letter vividly describes experiences shared by many other prairie homesteaders in the 1870s. Since Mattie did not use periods at the end of her sentences, it helps to read her letter aloud.

Mattie V. Oblinger to George W. Thomas, Grizzie B. Thomas, and Wheeler Thomas Family, June 16, 1873

Fillmore County Neb
June 16th 1873
Dear Brother & Sister & all of Uncle Wheelers

Thinking you would like to hear from us and hear how we are prospering I thought I must write you a letter and to fulfill the promise I made when I last saw you

The reason I have not written sooner I have not had the time I have wrote a letter almost every sunday to send home and that has occupied most all my

From Mattie V. Oblinger to George W. Thomas, Grizzie B. Thomas, and Wheeler Thomas Family, June 16, 1873, Uriah Oblinger Family Letters (manuscript), Library of Congress.

leisure time Sunday is rather a poor day for us to get a chance to write too for we have went to Church and sunday school every sunday I have been here two sundays we went about 9 miles the rest of the time we went to Giles [Mattie's brother, homesteading nearby] the next preaching will be at Giles which is in two weeks The man that preaches is quite old and is a baptist minister but when he preaches he makes no distinction in denominations We have a good sunday school in progress now I suppose there must be about fifty enrolled We have not the means yet to carry on sunday school . . . as they do in older settlments but we have our bibles and hymn books and we all gather together and read a lesson and then ask questions and sing and offer prayers and I think we do about as much good as any sunday school I know it is not quite so interesting as if we had money to buy papers and books I think we have Just as enterpriseing people here as any where There was methodist [the denomination of Mattie's family in Indiana] preaching yesterday about four miles from here Mr Elliotts and us had intended to go but it threatened rain and it was so late when our sunday school and society meeting was out that we did not go I think there will be a methodist preaching place established in the neighborhood before long as there was a methodist preacher around a few days ago hunting up the scattered members in the country He said the conference had sent him here so you see we are not entirely out of civilizatian I know if you was here you would not think so I have just as good neighbors as I ever had any where and they are very sociable I was never in a neighborhood where all was as near on equality as they are here Those that have been here have a little the most they all have cows and that is quite a help here I get milk & butter from Mrs Furgison who lives 1/4 of a mile from us get the milk for nothing and pay twelve cents a pound for butter she makes good butter Most all of the people here live in Sod houses and dug outs I like the sod house the best they are the most convenient I expect you think we live miserable because we are in a sod house but I tell you in solid earnest I never enjoyed my self better but George [Mattie's brother in Indiana] I expect you are ready to say It is because it is somthing new No this not the case it is because we are . . . on our own and the thoughts of moving next spring does not bother me and every lick we strike is for our selves and not half for some one else I tell you this is quite a consolation to us who have been renters so long there are no renters here every one is on his own and doing the best he can and not much a head yet for about all that are here was renters and it took about all they had to get here Some come here and put up temporary frame houses thought they could not live in a sod house This fall they are going to build sod houses so they can live . . . comfortable this winter a temporary frame house here is a poor thing a house that is not plastered the wind and dust goes right through and they are very cold A sod house can be built so they are real nice and comfortable build nice walls and then plaster and lay a floor above and below and then they are nice Uriah is going to build one after that style this fall The one we are in at present is 14 by 16 and a dirt floor Uriah intends takeing it for a stable this winter I will be a nice comfortable stable A little ways from the door is a small pond that has watter the year round we use out of it for all purposes but drinking and cooking We have the drinking water cary about 1/4 of a mile and the best of water We have two neighbors only 1/4 of a mile from us

I must stop and get supper

Supper is over and dishes washed I wish I had a cow or two to milk I would feel quite proud then think will get one after harvest Uriah is going up near Crete [a Nebraska town nearby] to harvest The wheat and Oats looks well here but there is not so much sown as in older settlements each man calculates to do his own harvesting in this neighborhood this year there is several men going from this settlement in to older ones to get harvesting Mrs Elliot and I are talking of staying together while our men go harvesting Almost every man here does his own work yet for they are not able to hire I think it will be quite different in a few years Uriah has 23 acres of sod corn planted it looks real well I tell you it is encourageing to have out a lot of corn and all your own We have a nice lot of Squashes and Cucumbers & Mellons & Beans comeing on There was a striped bug worked some on our squashes but did not bother our other vines We have our Potatoes and cabbage up at Giles as they do not so well on sod I set a hundred & thirty cabbages last week they are every one growing We have the nicest patch of early rose potatoes in the neighborhood will not be long until we will have new potatoes We have fared pretty well in the potato line as Uriah bought ten bushel when I come to Crete he bought for seed and to use we will have plenty until new potatoes come If nothing happens we will have a nice lot this fall I have nice Tomato plants comeing on I want to set more Tomatoes and Cabbage this week I get Garden vegetables in Giles garden I could not make garden here as we had no sod subdued and I have such good neighbors they said they would divide their garden vegetables I planted a lot of beet seed in Mrs Alkires garden they look real nice Uriah is breaking sod to day he will soon have 40 acres turned over then it will be ready to go into right next Spring It looks like it was fun to turn the sod over here there are no roots or stpumps to be jerkinking the plows out It has been very warm for a few days and it makes old buck pant considerable he is almost fat enough for beef old bright is not so fat so he gets along the best

We have had an immense lot of rain here this season but I guess this has been the general complaint every where I think we had the hardest storm saturday night or evening that has been since I come the wind blew very hard I do not know how long it lasted for I went to sleep and the wind was blowing yet We can not notice the wind so much in a sod house as in a frame Giles . , . came home with us yesterday I heard them & Uriah laughing about going out to see if the fences was blown down I looks very strange to me to see Crops growing here and no fence around them They have a herd law here and the stock a man has for use about home he must Lariett them out his other cattle he puts them in herds in the neighbor hood gets them herded for 25 cts per month The prarie looks beautiful now as the grass is so nice and green and the most pretty flowers I can not tell how many different kinds I have noticed I have seen three Antelopes one Jack Rabbit and one swift and lots of prarie squirrels I thought when I left the timber I would not see any more birds but there are lots of them here some that are entirely different to any I ever saw in Ind[iana] There is more Rattle snakes here than there are garter snakes in Ind[iana] Uriah has killed two on our place there are not so plent[y] right in our neighborhood as they are three miles east of here near a prarie dog town some men over there have killed as high 18 & 20 John how is this for high hardly any one gets bit with them they are mostly black rattle snakes Sam [Mattie's brother] has sold out to Mr . . . McClain he [Sam] had not improved as much as the law requested he should and he was afraid some one would jump his claim and then he would be out he sold very cheap only got fifty dollars I ask him if he was going back with out secureing a peice of land he said no I['ll bet I dont go back home with out owning some of this nice prarie he said he was bound to have land here He is going to buy RR land and then he will not have to stay by it I think he will go to Ind[iana] this fall I have not heard him say for certain This is a lonely place for a single man for there are not many young ladies here for them to go with but there are lots comeing on a little too young. . . . Geo do you and Grizzie [think] of comeing west yet if you do I wish you would come here I am quite sure you would like the country for it is as pretty and good as it can be of course it has some draw backs as all other places do Ella [Mattie's young daughter] is fat and hearty she said I should tell you to come over and bring Earny [a cousin] she often speaks of him I got her a little kitten last evening she is trying to comb it We are all well hope this will find you all well and Aunt Eliza getting better I washed to day Now Geo I send this in your name but I want you to besure and give it Uncle Wheels too as postage is scarce I thoughgt this would do all I want you all to besure and write soon We send our love and best wishes from U[riah] W O[blinger] & M[attie] V Oblinger

Direct to Sutton Clay County Neb Excuse letter paper

Questions for Reading and Discussion

1. What did Mattie Oblinger mean by telling her family, "we are not entirely out of civilizatian"? What features of her new life did Mattie consider "civilized"?
2. What led Mattie to conclude that "I was never in a neighborhood where all was as near on equality as they are here"? What did her observation say about her former home in Indiana as well as her new home in Nebraska?
3. What was the significance of Mattie's report that "every lick we strike is for our selves and not half for some one else"?
4. How did neighbors and family members cooperate, according to Mattie? Did Mattie recommend homesteading for all her family members? Why or why not?

Document 17–4

Texas Rangers on the Mexican Border

Texas Rangers patrolled south Texas against cattle rustlers and vigilantes. Organized as state law enforcement officials in 1874, the Rangers had existed unofficially since the 1830s and had fought in the campaigns for Texas independence and in the Civil War. The Rangers often repressed lawlessness among both whites and Mexicans along the Texas–Mexico border, as described in the following selection from a memoir by Ranger N. A. Jennings. The document recounts forms of rough-and-ready law enforcement common in Texas and other parts of the West, especially in encounters between white Americans and people of color, whether or not they were American citizens.

N. A. Jennings

A Texas Ranger, 1875

We went by easy stages across the country to Corpus Christi, the pretty little old town on the Gulf of Mexico. We were ordered there because Mexican raiders had come across the Rio Grande and spread terror throughout that part of Texas.

From N. A. Jennings, *A Texas Ranger* (New York: Scribners, 1899), 129–43.

We arrived at Corpus Christi on the morning of April 22, 1875, and found the country in the wildest state of excitement. We were told how large bands of raiders were coming from every direction to lay waste the countryside and burn the town. The most extravagant rumors found ready credence from the terrorized people. The civil authorities seemed helpless. Large parties of mounted and well-armed men, residents of Nueces County, were riding over the country, committing the most brutal outrages, murdering peaceable Mexican farmers and stockmen who had lived all their lives in Texas. These murderers called themselves vigilance committees and pretended that they were acting in the cause of law and order. . . .

It seemed that the excitement had been first caused by a raid made by Mexicans (from Mexico) in the neighborhood of Corpus Christi. These raiders had stolen cattle and horses, burned ranch houses, murdered men and ravished women, and then escaped back to Mexico. The excitement which followed was seized upon by a number of white men living in Nueces County as a fitting time to settle up old scores with the Mexican residents of that and some of the adjoining counties. Many of these Mexicans, it must be admitted, had been making a livelihood by stealing and skinning cattle, and the sheriffs and constables had failed to make any efforts to detect and punish them.

On the evening of April 24th a report was brought in that a party of raiders from Mexico had been seen at La Para about sixty miles from Corpus Christi. [Captain Leander H.] McNelly at once started with the troop to that place and arrived the following day. There we learned that the party reported to be Mexican raiders was really a posse of citizens from Cameron County, under a deputy sheriff, and that they "had come out to protect the people of La Para from further outrages from the citizens of Nueces County," meaning certain lawless bands organized in Nueces County.

McNelly ordered the deputy sheriff to take his posse back and disband it. After some demurring on the part of the posse, this was done. We went into camp and McNelly sent scouting parties out in every direction to disband the various vigilance committees and "regulators" which were roaming through the country.

On April 26th two companies of white men, commanded by T. Hynes Clark and M. S. Culver, cattlemen, came to our camp and said they wanted to cooperate with the Rangers.

"We need no one to cooperate with us," said the Captain. "I have heard that some of you men are the very ones accused of a number of outrages committed on Mexican citizens of this State, and you must disband at once and not reassemble, except at the call and under the command of an officer of the State. If you don't do as I say, you will have us to fight."

The Texans didn't like this high-handed way of talking and were disposed at first to dispute McNelly's authority, but the Captain showed them very quickly that he meant business and they disbanded. . . .

On May 20th we moved down the Rio Grande. We found the frontier in a state of great excitement. Reports of a dozen different raiding parties would be brought in daily and the scouting parties had no rest. I was in the saddle almost continually. At night we would either camp where we happened to be, or continue riding, in the attempt to head off some party of raiders of whom we had heard. Many of the reports of raiders brought to us were groundless, but the greater number were true. Through fear of the robbers, the law-abiding citizens withheld information which would have insured the capture of the marauders.

The people said that large droves of cattle and horses were stolen and driven across the Rio Grande into Mexico almost nightly. This, we found, had been going on for years. The United States military authorities had never made a determined effort to put a stop to the wholesale stealing, although the raiders at times would pass close to the frontier posts.

McNelly continued to keep out scouting parties of Rangers, and this course had the effect of lessening the number of raids, but not of wholly putting an end to them.

While we were encamped . . . a Mexican brought the information to Captain McNelly that a party of raiders was crossing into Texas, below Brownsville. . . . McNelly at once ordered us to saddle up, and within fifteen minutes we were trotting after him and a Mexican guide over the prairie. . . .

It was three days . . . before we managed to head off the raiders. They had fourteen men and we had eighteen, including Captain McNelly. We found them with the cattle on a little bit of wooded rising ground surrounded by a swamp. . . . They were drawn up in line and were evidently expecting us. When they saw us, they drew off behind the rising ground and fired at a range of about one hundred and fifty yards with carbines.

"Boys," said Captain McNelly, "the only way we can get at those thieves is to cross through the mud of the swamp and ride them down. I don't think they can shoot well enough to hit any of us, but we'll have to risk that. Don't fire at them until you're sure of killing every time."

Following the Captain, we started across the swamp for the little hill, the Mexican marauders continually firing at us. When we got near the hill, the Captain put spurs to his horse and we followed him with a yell as we flew through the mud and up the hill. The Mexicans answered our yell with one of defiance and a volley. At first, we thought they had not done any execution, but we soon saw they had aimed only too well, for three of our horses went crashing to the ground, one after the other, throwing their riders over their heads. . . .

Then came a single shot from the Mexicans, and one of the Rangers . . . popularly known in the troop as "Sonny," threw his arms above his head, reeled in his saddle for a moment and fell headlong to the ground. We all saw him fall and the sight roused a fury in our hearts that boded ill for the men in front of us.

The Mexicans fired at us again, but this time did no harm. The next instant we were upon them, shooting and yelling like demons. They stood their ground for a moment only; then turned and fled. As they went they leaned forward on their horses' necks and fired back at us, but they were demoralized by the fury of our onslaught and could hit nothing.

Crack! bang! bang! went our revolvers, and at nearly every shot one of the raiders went tumbling from his saddle. We had ridden hard to get to that place and our horses were played out, but we never thought of giving up the chase on that account. The remembrance of poor young Smith's face, as he threw up his hands and reeled from his horse, was too fresh in our minds for us to think of anything but revenge.

Some of our enemies were well mounted, but even these we gradually overhauled. We flew over the prairie at a killing pace, intent only on avenging our comrade's death. When we finally did halt, our horses were ready to drop from exhaustion; but the work had been done—every man of the raiders but one was dead. . . .

The Mexican guerrilla chief, Cortina[1] . . . was a Mexican general, and at the head of all the cattle raiding. He had a contract to deliver in Cuba six hundred head of Texas cattle every week. About three thousand robbers were under him, and he was virtually the ruler of the Mexican border. . . .

We recovered 265 stolen cattle after the fight. We procured a wagon and took the body of young Smith to Brownsville. The next day the bodies of the thirteen dead Mexicans were brought to Brownsville and laid out in the plaza. Nearly the entire population of Matamoras, the Mexican town immediately across the Rio Grande from Brownsville, came over to see their dead countrymen. The Mexicans were very angry, and we heard many threats that Cortina would come across with his men and kill us all. McNelly sent back word to Cortina that he would wait for him and his men. Cortina's bandits outnumbered the Rangers and the United States forces . . . about ten to one at that time. . . .

We gave Smith a fine military funeral. The Mexican raiders were all buried in one trench. The Mexican inhabitants of the town stood in their doorways and scowled at us whenever we passed, but they were afraid to express their hatred openly. They contented themselves with predicting that Cortina would come over and kill us. . . .

At the time of which I write, Matamoras was full of Mexican soldiers, and Cortina had put the place under martial rule. No person was allowed on the streets after sunset, except by special permit; that is, no Mexican was allowed on the streets. For some reason best known to Cortina, Americans were not included in the rule, and the Mexican sentries had orders to pass Americans. The Rangers were not slow to take advantage of this state of affairs, and we paid frequent visits to Matamoras after nightfall. We went there for two reasons: to have fun, and to carry out a set policy of terrorizing the Mexicans at every opportunity. Captain McNelly assumed that the more we were feared, the easier would be our work of subduing the Mexican raiders; so it was tacitly understood that we were to gain a reputation as fire-eating, quarrelsome dare-devils as quickly as possible, and to let no opportunity go unimproved to assert ourselves and override the "Greasers." Perhaps everyone has more or less of the bully inherent in his make-up, for certain it is that we enjoyed this work hugely.

"Each Ranger was a little standing army in himself," was the way [one ranger] . . . put it to me, speaking, long afterward, of those experiences. The Mexicans were afraid of us, collectively and individually, and added to the fear was a bitter hatred. . . .

The news of our big fight with the raiders reached everyone's ears, and none was so bold as to attempt to resist our outrages upon the peace and dignity of the community, for such they undoubtedly were. But we accomplished our purpose. In a few weeks we were feared as men were never before feared on that border, and, had we given the opportunity, we should undoubtedly have been exterminated by the Mexicans, but there was "method in our madness," and we never gave them the chance to get the better of us.

Questions for Reading and Discussion

1. Why were white men in Nueces County committing "brutal outrages" and what did the Rangers do about it, according to N. A. Jennings? Who were "regulators" and what did they seek?

---

[1]**Cortina**: Refers to Juan Nepomuceno Cortinas, a famous Mexican leader on the Texas–Mexico border.

2. There "was 'method in our madness,'" Jennings declared. What did he mean? What goals did the Rangers hope to achieve with their methods? Were the methods lawful? Just? Justified?

3. Who were "Greasers," according to Jennings? How did they differ from other people? What attitudes did Mexicans have toward the Rangers and why, according to Jennings?

4. What conclusions does Jennings's memoir suggest about violence, racism, law, and justice along the Texas–Mexico border? Do you think Jennings's account describes typical or atypical behavior and attitudes?

DOCUMENT 17–5

In-mut-too-yah-lat-lat Describes White Encroachment

The steady encroachment of white settlers on Native American lands intensified after 1870. Soldiers who had fought in the Civil War now tried to confine tribes onto reservations. In 1877, the chief of the Chute-pa-lu, or Nez Percé, resisted the U.S. government's demands that his tribe relinquish their land. In-mut-too-yah-lat-lat, or Chief Joseph as he was called by the whites, fought against overwhelming odds, was defeated, and was moved with his tribe to Fort Leavenworth, then to Baxter Springs, Kansas, and finally to Indian Territory. In 1879, In-mut-too-yah-lat-lat explained to a white audience why he fought. His explanation, excerpted here, described experiences shared by countless other Native Americans.

Chief Joseph
Speech to a White Audience, 1879

My friends, I have been asked to show you my heart. I am glad to have a chance to do so. I want the white people to understand my people. Some of you think an Indian is like a wild animal. This is a great mistake. I will tell you all about our people, and then you can judge whether an Indian is a man or not. I believe much trouble and blood would be saved if we opened our hearts more. I will tell you in my way how the Indian sees things. . . .

My name is In-mut-too-yah-lat-lat (Thunder Traveling over the Mountains). I am chief of the Wal-lam-wat-kin band of Chute-pa-lu, or Nez Percés (nose-pierced Indians). I was born in eastern Oregon, thirty-eight winters ago. My father was chief before me. When a young man, he was called Joseph by Mr. Spaulding, a missionary. He died a few years ago. There was no stain on his hands of the blood of a white man. He left a good name on the earth. He advised me well for my people.

Our fathers gave us many laws, which they had learned from their fathers. These laws were good. They told us to treat all men as they treated us; that we

---

From "An Indian's Views of Indian Affairs," *North American Review* 128 (April 1879), 412–33.

should never be the first to break a bargain; that it was a disgrace to tell a lie; that we should speak only the truth; that it was a shame for one man to take from another his wife, or his property without paying for it. We were taught to believe that the Great Spirit sees and hears everything, and that he never forgets; that hereafter he will give every man a spirit-home according to his deserts: if he has been a good man, he will have a good home; if he has been a bad man, he will have a bad home. This I believe, and all my people believe the same.

We did not know there were other people besides the Indian until about one hundred winters ago, when some men with white faces came to our country. They brought many things with them to trade for furs and skins. They brought tobacco, which was new to us. They brought guns with flint stones on them, which frightened our women and children. Our people could not talk with these white-faced men, but they used signs which all people understand. These men were Frenchmen, and they called our people "Nez Percés," because they wore rings in their noses for ornaments. Although very few of our people wear them now, we are still called by the same name. . . . The first white men of your people who came to our country were named Lewis and Clark. They also brought many things that our people had never seen. They talked straight, and our people gave them a great feast, as a proof that their hearts were friendly. These men were very kind. They made presents to our chiefs and our people made presents to them. We had a great many horses, of which we gave them what they needed, and they gave us guns and tobacco in return. All the Nez Percés made friends with Lewis and Clark, and agreed to let them pass through their country, and never to make war on white men. This promise the Nez Percés have never broken. No white man can accuse them of bad faith, and speak with a straight tongue. It has always been the pride of the Nez Percés that they were the friends of the white men. When my father was a young man there came to our country a white man [Mr. Spaulding] who talked spirit law. He won the affections of our people because he spoke good things to them. At first he did not say anything about white men wanting to settle on our lands. Nothing was said about that until about twenty winters ago, when a number of white people came into our country and built houses and made farms. At first our people made no complaint. They thought there was room enough for all to live in peace, and they were learning many things from the white men that seemed to be good. But we soon found that the white men were growing rich very fast, and were greedy to possess everything the Indian had. My father was the first to see through the schemes of the white men, and he warned his tribe to be careful about trading with them. He had suspicion of men who seemed so anxious to make money. I was a boy then, but I remember well my father's caution. He had sharper eyes than the rest of our people.

Next there came a white officer [Governor Stevens], who invited all the Nez Percés to a treaty council. After the council was opened he made known his heart. He said there were a great many white people in the country, and many more would come; that he wanted the land marked out so that the Indians and white men could be separated. If they were to live in peace it was necessary, he said, that the Indians should have a country set apart for them, and in that country they must stay. My father, who represented his band, refused to have anything to do with the council, because he wished to be a free man. He claimed that no man owned any part of the earth, and a man could not sell what he did not own.

Mr. Spaulding took hold of my father's arm and said, "Come and sign the treaty." My father pushed him away, and said: "Why do you ask me to sign away my country? It is your business to talk to us about spirit matters, and not to talk to us about parting with our land." Governor Stevens urged my father to sign his treaty, but he refused. "I will not sign your paper," he said; "you go where you please, so do I; you are not a child, I am no child; I can think for myself. No man can think for me. I have no other home than this. I will not give it up to any man. My people would have no home. Take away your paper. I will not touch it with my hand."

My father left the council. Some of the chiefs of the other bands of the Nez Percés signed the treaty, and then Governor Stevens gave them presents of blankets. My father cautioned his people to take no presents, for "after a while," he said, "they will claim that you have accepted pay for your country." Since that time four bands of the Nez Percés have received annuities from the United States. My father was invited to many councils, and they tried hard to make him sign the treaty, but he was firm as the rock, and would not sign away his home. His refusal caused a difference among the Nez Percés.

Eight years later [1863] was the next treaty council. A chief called Lawyer, because he was a great talker, took the lead in this council, and sold nearly all the Nez Percés country. . . . In this treaty Lawyer acted without authority from our band. He had no right to sell the Wallowa . . . country. That had always belonged to my father's own people, and the other bands had never disputed our right to it. . . .

In order to have all people understand how much land we owned, my father planted poles around it and said: "Inside is the home of my people—the white man may take the land outside. Inside this boundary all our people were born. It circles around the graves of our fathers, and we will never give up these graves to any man."

The United States claimed they had bought all the Nez Percés country outside of Lapwai Reservation, from Lawyer and other chiefs, but we continued to live in this land in peace until eight years ago, when white men began to come inside the bounds my father had set. We warned them against this great wrong, but they would not leave our land, and some bad blood was raised. The white men represented that we were going upon the war-path. They reported many things that were false.

The United States Government again asked for a treaty council. . . . It was then that I took my father's place as chief. In this council I made my first speech to white men. I said to the agent who held the council:

"I did not want to come to this council, but I came hoping that we could save blood. The white man has no right to come here and take our country. We have never accepted any presents from the Government. Neither Lawyer nor any other chief had authority to sell this land. It has always belonged to my people. It came unclouded to them from our fathers, and we will defend this land as long as a drop of Indian blood warms the hearts of our men."

The agent said he had orders, from the Great White Chief at Washington, for us to go upon the Lapwai Reservation, and that if we obeyed he would help us in many ways. "You must move to the agency," he said. I answered him: "I will not. I do not need your help; we have plenty and we are contented and happy if the white man will let us alone. The reservation is too small for so many people with all their stock. You can keep your presents; we can go to your towns and pay for all we need; we have plenty of horses and cattle to sell, and we won't have any help from you; we are free now; we can go where we please. Our fathers were born here. Here they lived, here they died, here are their graves. We will never leave them." The agent went away, and we had peace for a little while. . . .

Year after year we have been threatened, but no war was made upon my people until General Howard came to our country two years ago [1877] and told us that he was the white war-chief of all that country. He said: "I have a great many soldiers at my back. . . . The country belongs to the Government, and I intend to make you go upon the reservation." . . .

I said to General Howard: ". . . I do not believe that the Great Spirit Chief gave one kind of men the right to tell another kind of men what they must do."

QUESTIONS FOR READING AND DISCUSSION

1. In what ways did Chute-pa-lu laws differ from white laws? Did the two groups share some beliefs about laws? What was the significance of "spirit law," and how did it differ from other laws, if at all?

2. How did whites gain control of some Chute-pa-lu land? To what extent did conflicting concepts of land ownership divide the Chute-pa-lu from whites and from one another?

3. In-mut-too-yah-lat-lat told General Howard, "I do not believe that the Great Spirit Chief gave one kind of men the right to tell another kind of men what they must do." What gave General Howard "the right" to insist that the Chute-pa-lu "go upon the reservation," regardless of their wishes? To what extent was the conflict between the Chute-pa-lu and the federal government rooted in disagreements about what "kind of men" Americans were and could be?

COMPARATIVE QUESTIONS

1. How did Mattie Oblinger's experiences compare with those of In-mut-too-yah-lat-lat, Pun Chi, the Texas Rangers, and the Mexican raiders with whom the Rangers fought? To what extent did they have different concepts of property, ownership, law, and social order?

2. What similarities and differences characterized the migrant experiences of the Chinese in San Francisco, the Oblingers in Nebraska, and Native Americans?

3. How did Oblinger's experiences compare to the depiction of western society and environment in the print "Through to the Pacific"?

4. Do the documents in this chapter suggest that Americans in the West had conflicting ideas about civilization and race? Why or why not?

5. Based on the documents in this chapter, how did migrants' assumptions about their familiar worlds influence their adjustments to their new lives in the West? To what extent did their experiences in the West cause them to change their old assumptions?

The Gilded Age
1865–1900

The growth of huge corporations during the Gilded Age concentrated great power in the hands of wealthy industrialists and financiers. Their power to hire and fire employees, to make or break the fortunes of many, and to shape the economic fate of the nation raised the question of how the principles of democracy should apply to corporations. Should the government attempt to regulate the relations between labor and capital? Should lawmakers set rates for public services such as railroads or telegraphs? What should be done about the growing disparity between rich and poor? Did wealthy capitalists have special social obligations? Captains of industry and their supporters answered these questions by declaring that things were as they should be. Critics pointed out that the actual relations between government and industry, employers and workers, and the rich and the poor were very different from the laissez-faire claims of business leaders.

DOCUMENT 18–1

William Graham Sumner on Social Obligations

Many Americans wondered what to do about those who suffered more than they benefited from the phenomenal economic development of the Gilded Age. Should one give spare change to a beggar? Should one donate money to a home for unwed mothers? Should the government somehow help those who needed it? William Graham Sumner, a Yale professor whose ideas attracted a large national audience, answered these questions in his 1883 book, What Social Classes Owe to Each Other, *excerpted here.*

What Social Classes Owe to Each Other, 1883

There is no possible definition of "a poor man." A pauper is a person who cannot earn his living; whose producing powers have fallen positively below his necessary consumption; who cannot, therefore, pay his way. A human society

From William Graham Sumner, *What Social Classes Owe to Each Other* (New York: Harper & Brothers, 1883), 84–90.

needs the active co-operation and productive energy of every person in it. A man who is present as a consumer, yet who does not contribute either by land, labor, or capital to the work of society, is a burden. On no sound political theory ought such a person to share in the political power of the State. He drops out of the ranks of workers and producers. Society must support him. It accepts the burden, but he must be cancelled from the ranks of the rulers likewise. So much for the pauper. About him no more need be said. But he is not the "poor man." . . .

Neither is there any possible definition of "the weak." Some are weak in one way, and some in another; and those who are weak in one sense are strong in another. In general, however, it may be said that those whom humanitarians and philanthropists call the weak are the ones through whom the productive and conservative forces of society are wasted. They constantly neutralize and destroy the finest efforts of the wise and industrious, and are a dead-weight on the society in all its struggles to realize any better things. . . .

Under the names of the poor and the weak, the negligent, shiftless, inefficient, silly, and imprudent are fastened upon the industrious and prudent as a responsibility and a duty. On the one side, the terms are extended to cover the idle, intemperate, and vicious, who, by the combination, gain credit which they do not deserve, and which they could not get if they stood alone. On the other hand, the terms are extended to include wage-receivers of the humblest rank, who are degraded by the combination. . . .

The humanitarians, philanthropists, and reformers, looking at the facts of life as they present themselves, find enough which is sad and unpromising in the condition of many members of society. They see wealth and poverty side by side. They note great inequality of social position and social chances. They eagerly set about the attempt to account for what they see, and to devise schemes for remedying what they do not like. In their eagerness to recommend the less fortunate classes to pity and consideration they forget all about the rights of other classes; they gloss over all the faults of the classes in question, and they exaggerate their misfortunes and their virtues. They invent new theories of property, distorting rights and perpetrating injustice, as any one is sure to do who sets about the re-adjustment of social relations with the interests of one group distinctly before his mind, and the interests of all other groups thrown into the background. When I have read certain of these discussions I have thought that it must be quite disreputable to be respectable, quite dishonest to own property, quite unjust to go one's own way and earn one's own living, and that the only really admirable person was the good-for-nothing. The man who by his own effort raises himself above poverty appears, in these discussions, to be of no account. The man who has done nothing to raise himself above poverty finds that the social doctors flock about him, bringing the capital which they have collected from the other class, and promising him the aid of the State to give him what the other had to work for. In all these schemes and projects the organized intervention of society through the State is either planned or hoped for, and the State is thus made to become the protector and guardian of certain classes. The agents who are to direct the State action are, of course, the reformers and philanthropists. . . . [O]n the theories of the social philosophers to whom I have referred, we should get a new maxim of judicious living: Poverty is the best policy. If you get wealth, you will have to support other people; if you do not get wealth, it will be the duty of other people to support you.

No doubt one chief reason for the unclear and contradictory theories of class relations lies in the fact that our society, largely controlled in all its organization by one set of doctrines, still contains survivals of old social theories which are totally inconsistent with the former. In the Middle Ages men were united by custom and prescription into associations, ranks, guilds, and communities of various kinds. These ties endured as long as life lasted. Consequently society was dependent, throughout all its details, on status, and the tie, or bond, was sentimental. In our modern state, and in the United States more than anywhere else, the social structure is based on contract, and status is of the least importance. Contract, however, is rational—even rationalistic. It is also realistic, cold, and matter-of-fact. A contract relation is based on a sufficient reason, not on custom or prescription. It is not permanent. It endures only so long as the reason for it endures. In a state based on contract sentiment is out of place in any public or common affairs. It is relegated to the sphere of private and personal relations. . . .

A society based on contract is a society of free and independent men, who form ties without favor or obligation, and cooperate without cringing or intrigue. A society based on contract, therefore, gives the utmost room and chance for individual development, and for all the self-reliance and dignity of a free man. That a society of free men, co-operating under contract, is by far the strongest society which has ever yet existed; that no such society has ever yet developed the full measure of strength of which it is capable; and that the only social improvements which are now conceivable lie in the direction of more complete realization of a society of free men united by contract, are points which cannot be controverted. It follows, however, that one man, in a free state, cannot claim help from, and cannot be charged to give help to, another. . . .

Every honest citizen of a free state owes it to himself, to the community, and especially to those who are at once weak and wronged, to go to their assistance and to help redress their wrongs. Whenever a law or social arrangement acts so as to injure any one, and that one the humblest, then there is a duty on those who are stronger, or who know better, to demand and fight for redress and correction. . . .

We each owe it to the other to guarantee rights. Rights do not pertain to results, but only to chances. They pertain to the conditions of the struggle for existence, not to any of the results of it; to the pursuit of happiness, not to the possession of happiness. It cannot be said that each one has a right to have some property, because if one man had such a right some other man or men would be under a corresponding obligation to provide him with some property. Each has a right to acquire and possess property if he can. . . . If we take rights to pertain to results, and then say that rights must be equal, we come to say that men have a right to be equally happy, and so on in all the details. Rights should be equal, because they pertain to chances, and all ought to have equal chances so far as chances are provided or limited by the action of society. This, however, will not produce equal results, but it is right just because it will produce unequal results—that is, results which shall be proportioned to the merits of individuals. We each owe it to the other to guarantee mutually the chance to earn, to possess, to learn, to marry, etc., etc., against any interference which would prevent the exercise of those rights by a person who wishes to prosecute and enjoy them in peace for the pursuit of happiness. If we generalize this, it means that All-of-us ought to guarantee rights to each of us. . . .

The only help which is generally expedient, even within the limits of the private and personal relations of two persons to each other, is that which consists in helping a man to help himself. This always consists in opening the chances. . . .

Now, the aid which helps a man to help himself is not in the least akin to the aid which is given in charity. If alms are given, or if we "make work" for a man, or "give him employment," or "protect" him, we simply take a product from one and give it to another. If we help a man to help himself, by opening the chances around him, we put him in a position to add to the wealth of the community by putting new powers in operation to produce. . . .

The men who have not done their duty in this world never can be equal to those who have done their duty more or less well. If words like wise and foolish, thrifty and extravagant, prudent and negligent, have any meaning in language, then it must make some difference how people behave in this world, and the difference will appear in the position they acquire in the body of society, and in relation to the chances of life. They may, then, be classified in reference to these facts. Such classes always will exist; no other social distinctions can endure. If, then, we look to the origin and definition of these classes, we shall find it impossible to deduce any obligations which one of them bears to the other. The class distinctions simply result from the different degrees of success with which men have availed themselves of the chances which were presented to them. Instead of endeavoring to redistribute the acquisitions which have been made between the existing classes, our aim should be to increase, multiply, and extend the chances. Such is the work of civilization. Every old error or abuse which is removed opens new chances of development to all the new energy of society. Every improvement in education, science, art, or government expands the chances of man on earth. Such expansion is no guarantee of equality. On the contrary, if there be liberty, some will profit by the chances eagerly and some will neglect them altogether. Therefore, the greater the chances, the more unequal will be the fortune of these two sets of men. So it ought to be, in all justice and right reason.

QUESTIONS FOR READING AND DISCUSSION

1. According to Sumner, what did one class owe to another? What defined classes?
2. What, according to Sumner, were the advantages of a "social structure . . . based on contract"? What was the relationship between contracts and freedom?
3. "Rights do not pertain to results, but only to chances," Sumner declared. Why was that distinction important to him? Why did increasing chances create greater inequality? Was great inequality therefore a sign of the health and strength of American society? Why or why not?
4. In Sumner's view, what was the proper role for government and politics in a society based on "justice and right reason"? In what ways might "agents who are to direct the State action" have disagreed with him?

DOCUMENT 18–2

Henry Demarest Lloyd Attacks Monopolies

Muckraking journalists attacked the pompous rhetoric of free markets and self-made men. They argued that the realities of the Gilded Age had more to do with monopolies and greed than with hard work and virtuous perseverance. Henry Demarest Lloyd,

a Chicago muckraker, assailed monopolies in his book Wealth against Commonwealth, *excerpted here. Lloyd contrasted the rhetoric of competition with the reality of
monopolies and lambasted the wealthy for the evil social consequences of their gains.
Lloyd articulated a widespread view among working people that, for them, the age was
not gilded.*

Wealth against Commonwealth, 1894

Nature is rich; but everywhere man, the heir of nature, is poor. Never in this
happy country or elsewhere—except in the Land of Miracle, where "they did all
eat and were filled"—has there been enough of anything for the people. Never
since time began have all the sons and daughters of men been all warm, and all
filled, and all shod and roofed. Never yet have all the virgins, wise or foolish,
been able to fill their lamps with oil.

The world, enriched by thousands of generations of toilers and thinkers, has
reached a fertility which can give every human being a plenty undreamed of even
in the Utopias. But between this plenty ripening on the boughs of our civilization
and the people hungering for it step the "cornerers," the syndicates, trusts, combinations, with the cry of "over-production"—too much of everything. Holding
back the riches of earth, sea, and sky from their fellows who famish and freeze
in the dark, they declare to them that there is too much light and warmth and
food. They assert the right, for their private profit, to regulate the consumption
by the people of the necessaries of life, and to control production, not by the
needs of humanity, but by the desires of a few for dividends. The coal syndicate
thinks there is too much coal. There is too much iron, too much lumber, too much
flour—for this or that syndicate.

The majority have never been able to buy enough of anything; but this
minority have too much of everything to sell.

Liberty produces wealth, and wealth destroys liberty. . . . Our bignesses—
cities, factories, monopolies, fortunes, which are our empires, are the obesities
of an age gluttonous beyond its powers of digestion. Mankind are crowding
upon each other in the centres, and struggling to keep each other out of the
feast set by the new sciences and the new fellowships. Our size has got beyond
both our science and our conscience. The vision of the railroad stockholder is
not far-sighted enough to see into the office of the General Manager; the people
cannot reach across even a ward of a city to rule their rulers; Captains of Industry "do not know" whether the men in the ranks are dying from lack of food
and shelter; we cannot clean our cities nor our politics; the locomotive has more
man-power than all the ballot-boxes, and millwheels wear out the hearts of
workers unable to keep up beating time to their whirl. If mankind had gone on
pursuing the ideals of the fighter, the time would necessarily have come when
there would have been only a few, then only one, and then none left. This is
what we are witnessing in the world of livelihoods. . . . This era is but a passing
phase in the evolution of industrial Caesars, and these Caesars will be of a new
type—corporate Caesars. . . .

From Henry Demarest Lloyd, *Wealth against Commonwealth* (New York: Harper,
1894).

In an incredible number of the necessaries and luxuries of life, from meat to tombstones, some inner circle of the "fittest" has sought, and very often obtained, the sweet power which Judge Barrett [of the New York Supreme Court] found the sugar trust had: It "can close every refinery at will, close some and open others, limit the purchases of raw material (thus jeopardizing, and in a considerable degree controlling, its production), artificially limit the production of refined sugar, enhance the price to enrich themselves and their associates at the public expense, and depress the price when necessary to crush out and impoverish a foolhardy rival."

Laws against these combinations have been passed by Congress and by many of the States. There have been prosecutions under them by the State and Federal governments. The laws and the lawsuits have alike been futile. . . .

Nothing has been accomplished by all these appeals to the legislatures and the courts, except to prove that the evil lies deeper than any public sentiment or public intelligence yet existent, and is stronger than any public power yet at call.

What we call Monopoly is Business at the end of its journey. The concentration of wealth, the wiping out of the middle classes, are other names for it. To get it is, in the world of affairs, the chief end of man. . . .

If our civilization is destroyed . . . , it will not be by . . . barbarians from below. Our barbarians come from above. Our great money-makers have sprung in one generation into seats of power kings do not know. The forces and the wealth are new, and have been the opportunity of new men. Without restraints of culture, experience, the pride, or even the inherited caution of class or rank, these men, intoxicated, think they are the wave instead of the float, and that they have created the business which has created them. To them science is but a never-ending repertoire of investments stored up by nature for the syndicates, government but a fountain of franchises, the nations but customers in squads, and a million the unit of a new arithmetic of wealth written for them. They claim a power without control, exercised through forms which make it secret, anonymous, and perpetual. The possibilities of its gratification have been widening before them without interruption since they began, and even at a thousand millions they will feel no satiation and will see no place to stop. They are gluttons of luxury and power, rough, unsocialized, believing that mankind must be kept terrorized. Powers of pity die out of them, because they work through agents and die in their agents, because what they do is not for themselves. . . .

By their windfall of new power they have been forced into the position of public enemies. Its new forms make them seem not to be within the jurisdiction of the social restraints which many ages of suffering have taught us to bind about the old powers of man over man. A fury of rule or ruin has always in the history of human affairs been a characteristic of the "strong men" whose fate it is to be in at the death of an expiring principle. The leaders who, two hundred years ago, would have been crazy with conquest, to-day are crazy with competition. To a dying era some man is always born to enfranchise it by revealing it to itself. Men repay such benefactors by turning to rend them. Most unhappy is the fate of him whose destiny it is to lead mankind too far in its own path. Such is the function of these men, such will be their lot, as that of those for whom they are building up these wizard wealths. . . .

Business motived by the self-interest of the individual runs into monopoly at every point it touches the social life—land monopoly, transportation monopoly, trade monopoly, political monopoly in all its forms, from contraction of the currency to corruption in office. The society in which in half a lifetime a man without a penny can become a hundred times a millionaire is as over-ripe, industrially, as was, politically, the Rome in which the most popular bully could lift himself from the ranks of the legion on to the throne of the Caesars. Our rising issue is with business. Monopoly is business at the end of its journey. It has got there. The irrepressible conflict is now as distinctly with business as the issue so lately met was with slavery. Slavery went first only because it was the cruder form of business.

Against the principles, and the men embodying them and pushing them to extremes—by which the powers of government, given by all for all, are used as franchises for personal aggrandizement; by which, in the same line, the common toil of all and the common gifts of nature, lands, forces, mines, sites, are turned from service to selfishness, and are made by one and the same stroke to give gluts to a few and impoverishment to the many—we must plan our campaign. The yacht of the millionaire incorporates a million days' labor which might have been given to abolishing the slums, and every day it runs the labor of hundreds of men is withdrawn from the production of helpful things for humanity, and each of us is equally guilty who directs to his own pleasure the labor he should turn to the wants of others. Our fanatic of wealth reverses the rule that serving mankind is the end and wealth an incident, and has made wealth the end and the service an accident, until he can finally justify crime itself if it is a means to the end—wealth—which has come to be the supreme good; and we follow him.

It is an adjudicated fact of the business and social life of America that to receive the profits of crime and cherish the agents who commit it does not disqualify for fellowship in the most "solid" circles—financial, commercial, religious, or social. It illustrates . . . the "morbid" character of modern business that the history of its most brilliant episodes must be studied in the vestibules of the penitentiary. The riches of the combinations are the winnings of a policy which, we have seen, has certain constant features. Property to the extent of uncounted millions has been changed from the possession of the many who owned it to the few who hold it:

1. Without the knowledge of the real owners.
2. Without their consent.
3. With no compensation to them for the value taken.
4. By falsehood, often under oath.
5. In violation of the law.

Our civilization is builded on competition, and competition evolves itself crime—to so acute an infatuation has the lunacy of self-interest carried our dominant opinion. We are hurried far beyond the point of not listening to the new conscience which, pioneering in moral exploration, declares that conduct we think right because called "trade" is really lying, stealing, murder. . . . Two social energies have been in conflict, and the energy of reform has so far proved the weaker. We have chartered the self-interest of the individual as the rightful sovereign of conduct; we have taught that the scramble for profit is the best method of administering the riches of earth and the exchange of services. Only those can attack this system who attack its central principle, that strength gives the strong in the market the right to destroy his neighbor. Only as we have denied that right to the strong elsewhere have we made ourselves as civilized as we are. And we cannot make a change as long as our songs, customs, catchwords, and public opinions tell all to do the same thing if they can. Society, in each person of its multitudes, must recognize that the same principles of the interest of all being the rule of all, of the strong serving the weak, of the first being the last—"I am among you as one that serves"—which have given us the home where the weakest is the one surest of his rights and of the fullest service of the strongest, and have given us the republic in which all join their labor that the poorest may be fed, the weakest defended, and all educated and prospered, must be applied where men associate in common toil as wherever they associate. Not until then can the forces be reversed which generate those obnoxious persons—our fittest.

Our system, so fair in its theory and so fertile in its happiness and prosperity in its first century, is now, following the fate of systems, becoming artificial, technical, corrupt; and, as always happens in human institutions, after noon, power is stealing from the many to the few. Believing wealth to be good, the people believed the wealthy to be good. But, again in history, power has intoxicated and hardened its possessors, and Pharaohs are bred in counting-rooms as they were in palaces. Their furniture must be banished to the world-garret, where lie the out-worn trappings of the guilds and slavery and other old lumber of human institutions.

QUESTIONS FOR READING AND DISCUSSION

1. Why, according to Lloyd, was "nature . . . rich" and "man . . . poor"? What were the social consequences of "bignesses"? How did competition contribute to monopolies?
2. According to Lloyd, who were the "barbarians . . . from above," and why were they barbarians? What did Lloyd object to about "corporate Caesars"?
3. Why did laws and courts fail to control monopolies? How did monopolies compare to slavery?
4. Why was wealth against commonwealth? How, according to Lloyd, might those interested in commonwealth strike back against wealth?

DOCUMENT 18–3

The Bosses of the Senate

The concentrated economic power of trusts controlled many basic industries during the Gilded Age. This economic power translated into potent political influence that called democracy into question. Did the government represent the people or the trusts? The following 1889 cartoon by Joseph Keppler answered the question in no uncertain terms. The sign on the wall of the United States Senate (top center) reads, "This is a Senate of the Monopolists, By the Monopolists, and For the Monopolists!" Keppler's cartoon suggested that democratic institutions as they currently existed were unwilling and unable to govern the trusts.

Joseph Keppler
"The Bosses of the Senate," 1889

Library of Congress, 3b52004

Questions for Reading and Discussion

1. What evidence in the cartoon shows who "the Bosses of the Senate" were?
2. According to the cartoon, what values motivate the trusts? What do they want from the Senate?
3. How do senators go about deciding what to do? Why? Do they listen to the people in their states?
4. How might one of the trusts—the Standard Oil Trust, for example—criticize this portrayal of the Senate?
5. According to the cartoon, how is the national interest defined and defended in the Senate?
6. What audience is this cartoon attempting to persuade? What is the cartoon arguing against?

Document 18–4

Andrew Carnegie Explains the Gospel of Wealth

Gilded Age critics argued that the concentration of wealth in the bank accounts of the rich robbed workers of just compensation and gave the few too much power. Andrew Carnegie, one of the nation's leading industrialists and among the richest Americans of the era, defended the concentration of wealth. In an article published in 1889—the source of the following selection—Carnegie declared that the wealthy knew best how to use their riches for the public welfare.

Wealth, 1889

The problem of our age is the proper administration of wealth, that the ties of brotherhood may still bind together the rich and poor in harmonious relationship. The conditions of human life have not only been changed, but revolutionized, within the past few hundred years. In former days there was little difference between the dwelling, dress, food, and environment of the chief and those of his retainers. The Indians are today where civilized man then was. . . . The contrast between the palace of the millionaire and the cottage of the laborer with us to-day measures the change which has come with civilization. This change, however, is not to be deplored, but welcomed as highly beneficial. It is well, nay, essential, for the progress of the race that the houses of some should be homes for all that is highest and best in literature and the arts,—and for all the refinements of civilization, rather than that none should be so. Much better this great irregularity than universal squalor. . . . The "good old times" were not good old times. Neither master nor servant was as well situated then as to-day. A relapse to old conditions would be disastrous to both—not the least so to him who serves—and would sweep away civilization with it. But whether the change be for good or ill, it is upon us, beyond our power to alter, and, therefore, to be accepted and made the best of. It is a waste of time to criticize the inevitable.

It is easy to see how the change has come. . . . In the manufacture of products we have the whole story. . . . Formerly, articles were manufactured at the domestic hearth, or in small shops which formed part of the household. The master and his apprentices worked side by side, the latter living with the master, and therefore subject to the same conditions. When these apprentices rose to be masters, there was little or no change in their mode of life, and they, in turn, educated succeeding apprentices in the same routine. There was, substantially, social equality, and even political equality, for those engaged in industrial pursuits had then little or no voice in the State.

The inevitable result of such a mode of manufacture was crude articles at high prices. To-day the world obtains commodities of excellent quality at prices which even the preceding generation would have deemed incredible. . . . The poor enjoy what the rich could not before afford. What were the luxuries have become the necessaries of life. The laborer has now more comforts than the farmer had a few generations ago. The farmer has more luxuries than the landlord had, and is more richly clad and better housed. The landlord has books and pictures rarer and appointments more artistic than the king could then obtain.

The price we pay for this salutary change is, no doubt, great. We assemble thousands of operatives in the factory, and in the mine, of whom the employer can know little or nothing, and to whom he is little better than a myth. All intercourse between them is at an end. Rigid castes are formed, and, as usual, mutual ignorance breeds mutual distrust. Each caste is without sympathy with the other, and ready to credit anything disparaging in regard to it. Under the law of competition, the employer of thousands is forced into the strictest economies, among which the rates paid to labor figure prominently, and often there is friction between the employer and the employed, between capital and labor, between rich and poor. Human society loses homogeneity.

From Andrew Carnegie, "Wealth," *North American Review* (1889).

The price which society pays for the law of competition, like the price it pays for cheap comforts and luxuries, is also great; but the advantages of this law are also greater still than its cost—for it is to this law that we owe our wonderful material development, which brings improved conditions in its train. But, whether the law be benign or not, we must say of it, as we say of the change in the conditions of men to which we have referred: It is here; we cannot evade it; no substitutes for it have been found; and while the law may be sometimes hard for the individual, it is best for the race, because it insures the survival of the fittest in every department. We accept and welcome, therefore, as conditions to which we must accommodate ourselves, great inequality of environments; the concentration of business, industrial and commercial, in the hands of a few; and the law of competition between these, as being not only beneficial, but essential to the future progress of the race. . . .

What is the proper mode of administering wealth after the laws upon which civilization is founded have thrown it into the hands of the few? And it is of this great question that I believe I offer the true solution. It will be understood that fortunes are here spoken of, not moderate sums saved by many years of effort, the returns from which are required for the comfortable maintenance and education of families. This is not wealth, but only competence, which it should be the aim of all to acquire, and which it is for the best interests of society should be acquired. . . .

There remains . . . only one mode of using great fortunes; . . . in this we have the true antidote for the temporary unequal distribution of wealth, the reconciliation of the rich and the poor—a reign of harmony. . . . It is founded upon the present most intense Individualism, and the race is prepared to put it in practice by degrees whenever it pleases. Under its sway we shall have an ideal State, in which the surplus wealth of the few will become, in the best sense, the property of the many, because administered for the common good; and this wealth, passing through the hands of the few, can be made a much more potent force for the elevation of our race than if distributed in small sums to the people themselves. Even the poorest can be made to see this, and to agree that great sums gathered by some of their fellow-citizens and spent for public purposes, from which the masses reap the principal benefit, are more valuable to them than if scattered among themselves in trifling amounts through the course of many years. . . .

Poor and restricted are our opportunities in this life, narrow our horizon, our best work most imperfect; but rich men should be thankful for one inestimable boon. They have it in their power during their lives to busy themselves in organizing benefactions from which the masses of their fellows will derive lasting advantage, and thus dignify their own lives. The highest life is probably to be reached, not by such imitation of the life of Christ as Count Tolstoi[1] gives us, but, while animated by Christ's spirit, by recognizing the changed conditions of this age, and adopting modes of expressing this spirit suitable to the changed conditions under which we live, still laboring for the good of our fellows, which was the essence of his life and teaching, but laboring in a different manner.

This, then, is held to be the duty of the man of wealth: To set an example of modest, unostentatious living, shunning display or extravagance; to provide

---

[1]**Count Tolstoi**: Russian novelist and philosopher Leo Tolstoy (1828–1910), whose later works focused on separating what he saw as the true teachings of Jesus from Christian doctrine.

moderately for the legitimate wants of those dependent upon him; and, after doing so, to consider all surplus revenues which come to him simply as trust funds, which he is called upon to administer, and strictly bound as a matter of duty to administer in the manner which, in his judgment, is best calculated to produce the most beneficial results for the community—the man of wealth thus becoming the mere trustee and agent for his poorer brethren, bringing to their service his superior wisdom, experience, and ability to administer, doing for them better than they would or could do for themselves. . . .

[O]ne of the serious obstacles to the improvement of our race is indiscriminate charity. It were better for mankind that the millions of the rich were thrown into the sea than so spent as to encourage the slothful, the drunken, the unworthy. Of every thousand dollars spent in so-called charity to-day, it is probable that nine hundred and fifty dollars is unwisely spent—so spent, indeed, as to produce the very evils which it hopes to mitigate or cure. . . .

[T]he best means of benefiting the community is to place within its reach the ladders upon which the aspiring can rise—free libraries, parks, and means of recreation, by which men are helped in body and mind; works of art, certain to give pleasure and improve the public taste; and public institutions of various kinds, which will improve the general condition of the people; in this manner returning their surplus wealth to the mass of their fellows in the forms best calculated to do them lasting good.

Thus is the problem of rich and poor to be solved. The laws of accumulation will be left free, the laws of distribution free. Individualism will continue, but the millionaire will be but a trustee for the poor, intrusted for a season with a great part of the increased wealth of the community, but administering it for the community far better than it could or would have done for itself. . . .

Such, in my opinion, is the true gospel concerning wealth, obedience to which is destined some day to solve the problem of the rich and the poor, and to bring "Peace on earth, among men good will."

QUESTIONS FOR READING AND DISCUSSION

1. According to Carnegie, what were the revolutionary changes that made it possible for "the poor [to] enjoy what the rich could not before afford"?
2. What did Carnegie believe were the relative advantages and disadvantages of competition, the concentration of wealth, and the "law of competition"?
3. Why should the goal of the truly wealthy be to bring about "the reconciliation of the rich and the poor"? How should they accomplish that goal, according to Carnegie?
4. To what extent would "the millionaire" be a better "trustee for the poor" than government agencies, reform societies, or the poor themselves?

DOCUMENT 18–5

Henry George Explains Why Poverty Is a Crime

A California journalist and reformer, Henry George was a fierce critic of the economic inequality of the Gilded Age. His book Progress and Poverty, *published in 1879, became a nationwide best seller. In a speech delivered in Burlington, Iowa, excerpted here, George summarized the basic theme of his book—that poverty was neither inevitable nor natural, but instead resulted from the concentration of wealth in land. George's speech addresses a widespread perception that the economic inequalities so evident during the Gilded Age were somehow wrong.*

An Analysis of the Crime of Poverty, 1885

I should like to show you . . . that poverty is a crime. I do not mean that it is a crime to be poor. Murder is a crime; but it is not a crime to be murdered; and a man who is in poverty, I look upon, not as a criminal in himself, so much as the victim of a crime for which others, as well perhaps as himself, are responsible. . . . The curse born of poverty is not confined to the poor alone; it runs through all classes, even to the very rich. They, too, suffer; they must suffer; for there cannot be suffering in a community from which any class can totally escape. The vice, the crime, the ignorance, the meanness born of poverty, poison, so to speak, the very air which rich and poor alike must breathe. . . .

But while a man who chooses to be poor cannot be charged with crime, it is certainly a crime to force poverty on others. And it seems to me clear that the great majority of those who suffer from poverty are poor not from their own particular faults, but because of conditions imposed by society at large. Therefore I hold that poverty is a crime—not an individual crime, but a social crime, a crime for which we all, poor as well as rich, are responsible. . . .

If poverty is appointed by the [divine] power which is above us all, then it is no crime; but if poverty is unnecessary, then it is a crime for which society is responsible and for which society must suffer. I hold . . . that poverty is utterly unnecessary. It is not by the decree of the Almighty, but it is because of our own injustice, our own selfishness, our own ignorance, that this scourge, worse than any pestilence, ravages our civilisation, bringing want and suffering and degradation, destroying souls as well as bodies. . . . And yet the peculiar characteristic of this modern poverty of ours is that it is deepest where wealth most abounds.

Why, to-day, while over the civilised world there is so much distress, so much want, what is the cry that goes up? What is the current explanation of the hard times? Over-production! There are so many clothes that men must go ragged, so much coal that in the bitter winters people have to shiver, such over-filled granaries that people actually die by starvation! Want due to over-production! Was a greater absurdity ever uttered? How can there be over-production till all have enough? It is not over-production; it is unjust distribution. . . .

The dangerous man is not the man who tries to excite discontent; the dangerous man is the man who says that all is as it ought to be. Such a state of things cannot continue; such tendencies as we see at work here cannot go on without bringing at last an overwhelming crash.

I say that all this poverty and the ignorance that flows from it is unnecessary; I say that there is no natural reason why we should not all be rich, in the sense, not of having more than each other, but in the sense of all having enough

From Henry George, *The Crime of Poverty: An Address Delivered in the Opera House, Burlington, Iowa, April 1, 1885, under the auspices of Burlington Assembly, No. 3135. Knights of Labor* (Cincinnati: The Joseph Fels Fund of America, 1885).

to completely satisfy all physical wants; of all having enough to get such an easy living that we could develop the better part of humanity. There is no reason why wealth should not be so abundant, that no one should think of such a thing as little children at work, or a woman compelled to a toil that nature never intended her to perform; wealth so abundant that there would be no cause for that harassing fear that sometimes paralyses even those who are not considered *the poor*, the fear that every man of us has probably felt, that if sickness should smite him, or if he should be taken away, those whom he loves better than his life would become charges upon charity. . . . I believe that in a really Christian community, in a society that honoured not with the lips but with the act, the doctrines of Jesus, no one would have occasion to worry about physical needs any more than do the lilies of the field. There is enough and to spare. . . .

There is a cause for this poverty; and, if you trace it down, you will find its root in a primary injustice. Look over the world to-day — poverty everywhere. The cause must be a common one. You cannot attribute it to the tariff, or to the form of government, or to this thing or to that in which nations differ; because, as deep poverty is common to them all, the cause that produces it must be a common cause. What is that common cause? There is one sufficient cause that is common to all nations; and that is the appropriation as the property of some of that natural element on which and from which all must live. . . .

Now, think of it — is not land monopolisation a sufficient reason for poverty? What is man? In the first place, he is an animal, a land animal who cannot live without land. All that man produces comes from land; all productive labour, in the final analysis, consists in working up land; or materials drawn from land, into such forms as fit them for the satisfaction of human wants and desires. Why, man's very body is drawn from the land. Children of the soil, we come from the land, and to the land we must return. . . . Therefore he who holds the land on which and from which another man must live, is that man's master; and the man is his slave. The man who holds the land on which I must live can command me to life or to death just as absolutely as though I were his chattel. Talk about abolishing slavery — we have not abolished slavery; we have only abolished one rude form of it, chattel slavery. There is a deeper and a more insidious form, a more cursed form yet before us to abolish, in this industrial slavery that makes a man a virtual slave, while taunting him and mocking him with the name of freedom. Poverty! want! they will sting as much as the lash. Slavery! God knows there are horrors enough in slavery; but there are deeper horrors in our civilised society today. . . .

This land question is the bottom question. Man is a land animal. Suppose you want to build a house; can you build it without a place to put it? What is it built of? Stone, or mortar, or wood, or iron — they all come from the earth. Think of any article of wealth you choose, any of those things which men struggle for, where do they come from? From the land. It is the bottom question. The land question is simply the labour question; and when some men own that element from which all wealth must be drawn, and upon which all must live, then they have the power of living without work, and, therefore, those who do work get less of the products of work.

Did you ever think of the utter absurdity and strangeness of the fact that, all over the civilised world, the working classes are the poor classes? . . .

Nature gives to labour, and to labour alone; there must be human work before any article of wealth can be produced; and in the natural state of things the man who toiled honestly and well would be the rich man, and he who did not work would be poor. We have so reversed the order of nature that we are accustomed to think of the workingman as a poor man.

And if you trace it out I believe you will see that the primary cause of this is that we compel those who work to pay others for permission to do so. You may buy a coat, a horse, a house; there you are paying the seller for labour exerted, for something that he has produced, or that he has got from the man who did produce it; but when you pay a man for land, what are you paying him for? You are paying for something that no man has produced; you pay him for something that was here before man was, or for a value that was created, not by him individually, but by the community of which you are a part. What is the reason that the land here, where we stand tonight, is worth more than it was twenty-five years ago? What is the reason that land in the centre of New York, that once could be bought by the mile for a jug of whiskey, is now worth so much that, though you were to cover it with gold, you would not have its value? Is it not because of the increase of population? Take away that population, and where would the value of the land be? Look at it in any way you please. . . .

[O]ur treatment of land lies at the bottom of all social questions. . . . [D]o what you please, reform as you may, you never can get rid of wide-spread poverty so long as the element on which and from which all men must live is made the private property of some men. It is utterly impossible. Reform government—get taxes down to the minimum—build railroads; institute co-operative stores; divide profits, if you choose, between employers and employed—and what will be the result? The result will be that the land will increase in value—that will be the result—that and nothing else. Experience shows this. Do not all improvements simply increase the value of land—the price that some must pay others for the privilege of living? . . .

I cannot go over all the points I would like to try, but I wish to call your attention to the utter absurdity of private property in land! Why, consider it, the idea of a man's selling the earth—the earth, our common mother. A man selling that which no man produced—a man passing title from one generation to another. Why, it is the most absurd thing in the world. Why, did you ever think of it? What right has a dead man to land? For whom was this earth created? It was created for the living, certainly, not for the dead. Well, now we treat it as though it was created for the dead. Where do our land titles come from? They come from men who for the most part are past and gone. Here in this new country you get a little nearer the original source; but go to the Eastern States and go back over the Atlantic. There you may clearly see the power that comes from land ownership. As I say, the man that owns the land is the master of those who must live on it. . . . That which a man produces, that is his against all the world, to give or to keep, to lend, to sell or to bequeath; but how can he get such a right to land when it was here before he came? Individual claims to land rest only on appropriation. . . .

[T]he way of getting rid of land monopoly . . . is not . . . to divide up the land. All that is necessary is to divide up the income that comes from the land. In that way we can secure absolute equality; nor could the adoption of this principle involve any rude shock or violent change. It can be brought about gradually and easily by abolishing taxes that now rest upon capital, labour and improvements, and raising all our public revenues by the taxation of land values; and the longer you think of it the clearer you will see that in every possible way will it be a benefit.

QUESTIONS FOR READING AND DISCUSSION

1. In what ways, according to George, was poverty a "social crime"? Why was it a "crime" rather than simply the inevitable result of the differing talents and energies of individuals?

2. Why did George believe it an "absurdity" that overproduction caused poverty? What caused overproduction? What caused poverty? What did George mean by saying that "there is no natural reason why we should not all be rich"?

3. Why did George believe that "he who holds the land on which and from which another man must live, is that man's master; and the man is his slave"?

4. Why did George believe that "private property in land" was an "utter absurdity"? How did private property in land create poverty, according to George? Do you think George considered private land ownership a crime?

5. Why did George believe a single tax on land, unlike other reforms, would reduce or eliminate poverty?

COMPARATIVE QUESTIONS

1. How did Andrew Carnegie's views of the obligations of wealthy people compare with those of Henry George and William Graham Sumner?

2. How did Henry Demarest Lloyd's critique of monopolies compare with that in "The Bosses of the Senate" cartoon?

3. Carnegie, George, and Lloyd offered sharply contrasting characterizations of rich people and the social consequences of their wealth. What accounted for their differences? How would George and Lloyd have replied to Carnegie and vice versa?

4. What can you detect about Sumner and Carnegie's views of democracy? How did views of democracy differ in the documents by George and Lloyd and "The Bosses of the Senate"? To what extent did these documents argue that democracy and freedom were compatible? What did they think was the proper source of political power?

5. Each of the documents in this chapter focuses on the striking inequalities among Americans in the Gilded Age. To what extent did these authors perceive inequality as a problem, and what did they propose to do about it? Did they believe in the ideal of equality? If so, to what degree?

19 The City and Its Workers

1870–1900

The economic achievements of the Gilded Age did not appear to be miraculous to working people. Factory workers knew that profits often meant low wages, long hours, and frequent unemployment. Domestic servants knew how much work it took to supply their employers with the comforts of home. Immigrants streamed into America where they hoped to find jobs, security, and a new life for themselves and their children. Union members hoped that strikes might win them a share of gains in productivity. Radicals argued that only revolutionary change could remedy injustice and inequality. As the following documents illustrate, the Gilded Age looked different when viewed from the shop floor rather than the corner office.

DOCUMENT 19–1

A Textile Worker Explains the Labor Market

Wageworkers had jobs as long as they could be hired. Employers laid off workers during business slumps or replaced those whose jobs could be done more cheaply by a machine or a worker with a lower wage. In 1883, Thomas O'Donnell, who had worked as a mule spinner (operating a machine that spun cotton fibers into yarn) for eleven years in textile mills in Fall River, Massachusetts, testified before the U.S. Senate Committee on Relations between Labor and Capital. O'Donnell explained to Senator Henry W. Blair of New Hampshire what it was like to be a working man in the 1880s.

Thomas O'Donnell

Testimony before a U.S. Senate Committee, 1885

Senator Blair: Are you a married man?

Thomas O'Donnell: Yes, sir; I am a married man; have a wife and two children. I am not very well educated. I went to work when I was young, and have

---

From U.S. Congress, Senate, *Report of the Senate Committee on Relations between Labor and Capital* (Washington, DC: Government Printing Office, 1885).

been working ever since in the cotton business; went to work when I was about eight or nine years old. I was going to state how I live. My children get along very well in summer time, on account of not having to buy fuel or shoes or one thing and another. I earn $1.50 a day and can't afford to pay a very big house rent. I pay $1.50 a week for rent, which comes to about $6.00 a month.

Blair: That is, you pay this where you are at Fall River?

O'Donnell: Yes, Sir.

Blair: Do you have work right along?

O'Donnell: No, sir; since that strike we had down in Fall River about three years ago I have not worked much more than half the time, and that has brought my circumstances down very much.

Blair: Why have you not worked more than half the time since then?

O'Donnell: Well, at Fall River if a man has not got a boy to act as "back-boy" it is very hard for him to get along. In a great many cases they discharge men in that work and put in men who have boys.

Blair: Men who have boys of their own?

O'Donnell: Men who have boys of their own capable enough to work in a mill, to earn $.30 or $.40 a day.

Blair: Is the object of that to enable the boy to earn something for himself?

O'Donnell: Well, no; the object is this: They are doing away with a great deal of mule-spinning there and putting in ring-spinning,[1] and for that reason it takes a good deal of small help to run this ring work, and it throws the men out of work. . . . For that reason they get all the small help they can to run these ring-frames. There are so many men in the city to work, and whoever has a boy can have work, and whoever has no boy stands no chance. Probably he may have a few months of work in the summer time, but will be discharged in the fall. That is what leaves me in poor circumstances. Our children, of course, are very often sickly from one cause or another, on account of not having sufficient clothes, or shoes, or food, or something. And also my woman; she never did work in a mill; she was a housekeeper, and for that reason she can't help me do anything at present, as many women do help their husbands down there, by working, like themselves. . . .

Blair: How much [work] have you had within a year?

O'Donnell: Since Thanksgiving I happened to get work in the Crescent Mill, and worked there exactly thirteen weeks. I got just $1.50 a day, with the exception of a few days that I lost because in following up mule-spinning you are obliged to lose a day once in a while; you can't follow it up regularly.

Blair: Thirteen weeks would be seventy-eight days, and, at $1.50 a day, that would make $117, less whatever time you lost?

O'Donnell: Yes. I worked thirteen weeks there and ten days in another place, and then there was a dollar I got this week, Wednesday.

Blair: Taking a full year back can you tell how much you have had?

O'Donnell: That would be about fifteen weeks' work. . . .

Blair: That would be somewhere about $133, if you had not lost any time?

O'Donnell: Yes, sir.

Blair: That is all you have had?

O'Donnell: Yes, sir.

---

[1]**ring-spinning**: A method of spinning that expedited the process and allowed mills to hire children and pay lower wages.

Blair: To support yourself and wife and two children?

O'Donnell: Yes, sir.

Blair: Have you had any help from outside?

O'Donnell: No, sir.

Blair: Do you mean that yourself and wife and two children have had nothing but that for all this time?

O'Donnell: That is all. I got a couple dollars' worth of coal last winter, and the wood I picked up myself. I goes around with a shovel and picks up clams and wood.

Blair: What do you do with the clams?

O'Donnell: We eat them. I don't get them to sell, but just to eat, for the family. That is the way my brother lives, too, mostly. He lives close by us.

Blair: How many live in that way down there?

O'Donnell: I could not count them, they are so numerous. I suppose there are one thousand down there.

Blair: A thousand that live on $150 a year?

O'Donnell: They live on less.

Blair: Less than that?

O'Donnell: Yes; they live on less than I do.

Blair: How long has that been so?

O'Donnell: Mostly so since I have been married.

Blair: How long is that?

O'Donnell: Six years this month.

Blair: Why do you not go West on a farm?

O'Donnell: How could I go, walk it?

Blair: Well, I want to know why you do not go out West on a $2,000 farm, or take up a homestead and break it and work it up, and then have it for yourself and family?

O'Donnell: I can't see how I could get out West. I have got nothing to go with.

Blair: It would not cost you over $1,500.

O'Donnell: Well, I never saw over a $20 bill, and that is when I have been getting a month's pay at once. If someone would give me $1,500 I will go. . . .

Blair: Are you a good workman?

O'Donnell: Yes, sir.

Blair: Were you ever turned off because of misconduct or incapacity or unfitness for work?

O'Donnell: No, sir.

Blair: Or because you did bad work?

O'Donnell: No, sir.

Blair: Or because you made trouble among the help?

O'Donnell: No, sir. . . .

Blair: How old are you?

O'Donnell: About thirty.

Blair: Is your health good?

O'Donnell: Yes, sir.

Blair: What would you work for if you could get work right along; if you could be sure to have it for five years, staying right where you are?

O'Donnell: Well, if I was where my family could be with me, and I could have work every day I would take $1.50, and be glad to. . . .

Blair: You spoke of fuel — what do you have for fuel?

O'Donnell: Wood and coal.

Blair: Where does the wood come from?

O'Donnell: I pick it up around the shore—any old pieces I see around that are not good for anything. There are many more that do the same thing.

Blair: Do you get meat to live on much?

O'Donnell: Very seldom.

Blair: What kinds of meat do you get for your family?

O'Donnell: Well, once in a while we get a piece of pork and some clams and make a clam chowder. That makes a very good meal. We sometimes get a piece of corn beef or something like that. . . .

Blair: What have you eaten?

O'Donnell: Well, bread mostly, when we could get it; we sometimes couldn't make out to get that, and have had to go without a meal.

Blair: Has there been any day in the year that you have had to go without anything to eat?

O'Donnell: Yes, sir, several days.

Blair: More than one day at a time?

O'Donnell: No. . . .

Blair: What have the children got on in the way of clothing?

O'Donnell: They have got along very nicely all summer, but now they are beginning to feel quite sickly. One has one shoe on, a very poor one, and a slipper, that was picked up somewhere. The other has two odd shoes on, with the heel out. He has got cold and is sickly now.

Blair: Have they any stockings?

O'Donnell: He had got stockings, but his feet comes through them, for there is a hole in the bottom of the shoe.

Blair: What have they got on the rest of their person?

O'Donnell: Well, they have a little calico shirt—what should be a shirt; it is sewed up in some shape—and one little petticoat, and a kind of little dress.

Blair: How many dresses has your wife got?

O'Donnell: She has got one since she was married, and she hasn't worn that more than half a dozen times; she has worn it just going to church and coming back. She is very good in going to church, but when she comes back she takes it off, and it is pretty near as good now as when she bought it.

Blair: She keeps that dress to go to church in?

O'Donnell: Yes, sir.

Blair: How many dresses aside from that has she?

O'Donnell: Well, she got one here three months ago.

Blair: What did it cost?

O'Donnell: It cost $1.00 to make it and I guess about a dollar for the stuff, as near as I can tell . . . she has an undershirt that she got given to her, and she has an old wrapper, which is about a mile too big for her; somebody gave it to her. . . . That is all that I know that she has. . . .

Blair: Do you see any way out of your troubles—what are you going to do for a living—or do you expect to have to stay right there?

O'Donnell: Yes. I can't run around with my family.

Blair: You have nowhere to go to, and no way of getting there if there was any place to go to?

O'Donnell: No, sir; I have no means nor anything, so I am obliged to remain there and try to pick up something as I can.

Blair: Do the children go to school?

O'Donnell: No, sir; they are not old enough; the oldest child is only three and a half; the youngest one is one and a half years old.

Blair: Is there anything else you wanted to say?

O'Donnell: Nothing further, except that I would like some remedy to be got to help us poor people down there in some way. Excepting the government decides to do something with us we have a poor show. We are all, or mostly all, in good health; that is, as far as the men who are at work go.

Blair: You do not know anything but mule-spinning, I suppose?

O'Donnell: That is what I have been doing, but I sometimes do something with pick and shovel. I have worked for a man at that, because I am so put on. I am looking for work in a mill. The way they do there is this: There are about twelve or thirteen men that go into a mill every morning, and they have to stand their chance, looking for work. The man who has a boy with him he stands the best chance, and then, if it is my turn or a neighbor's turn who has no boy, if another man comes in who has a boy he is taken right in, and we are left out. I said to the boss once it was my turn to go in, and now you have taken on that man; what am I to do; I have got two little boys at home, one of them three years and a half and the other one year and a half old, and how am I to find something for them to eat; I can't get my turn when I come here. He said he could not do anything for me. I says, "Have I got to starve; ain't I to have any work?" They are forcing these young boys into the mills that should not be in mills at all; forcing them in because they are throwing the mules out and putting on ring-frames. They are doing everything of that kind that they possibly can to crush down the poor people—the poor operatives there.

QUESTIONS FOR READING AND DISCUSSION

1. What wages did O'Donnell earn? Why didn't he work more? How did he account for his poverty? To what extent did O'Donnell possess freedom to negotiate for better wages and working conditions?

2. O'Donnell requested "some remedy to . . . help us poor people." What remedies did he appear to favor? What remedies might have improved his prospects of employment?

3. Why did he believe the employers were doing "everything . . . that they possibly can to crush down the poor people"? How might employers have responded?

4. How representative do you think O'Donnell and his family were of working-class Americans in the late nineteenth century?

DOCUMENT 19–2

Domestic Servants on Household Work

Millions of women worked in factories and shops during the Gilded Age. Millions more worked as domestic servants for people who could afford to pay somebody else to do household chores. Many women preferred to become factory laborers or shop clerks rather than domestic servants. In the 1880s, journalist Helen Campbell interviewed a number of former servants to try to find out why. A selection of Campbell's interviews follows.

Interviews with Journalist Helen Campbell, 1880s

First on the list stands Margaret M——, an American, twenty-three years old, and for five years in a paper-box factory. Seven others nodded their assent, or added a word here and there as she gave her view, two of them Irish-Americans who had had some years in the public schools.

"It's freedom that we want when the day's work is done. I know, some nice girls, Bridget's cousins, that make more money and dress better and everything for being in service. They're waitresses, and have Thursday afternoon out and part of every other Sunday. But they're never sure of one minute that's their own when they're in the house. Our day is ten hours long, but when it's done it's done, and we can do what we like with the evenings. That's what I've heard from every nice girl that ever tried service. You're never sure that your soul's your own except when you are out of the house, and I couldn't stand that a day. Women care just as much for freedom as men do. Of course they don't get so much, but I know I'd fight for mine."

"Women are always harder on women than men are," said a fur sewer, an intelligent American about thirty. "I got tired of always sitting, and took a place as chambermaid. The work was all right and the wages good, but I'll tell you what I couldn't stand. The cook and the waitress were just common, uneducated Irish, and I had to room with one and stand the personal habits of both, and the way they did at table took all my appetite. I couldn't eat, and began to run down; and at last I gave notice, and told the truth when I was asked why. The lady just looked at me astonished: 'If you take a servant's place, you can't expect to be one of the family,' she said. 'I never asked it,' I said; 'all I ask is a chance at common decency.' 'It will be difficult to find an easier place than this,' she said, and I knew it; but ease one way was hardness another, and she couldn't see that I had any right to complain. That's one trouble in the way. It's the mixing up of things, and mistresses don't think how they would feel in the same place."

Third came an Irish-American whose mother had been cook for years in one family, but who had, after a few months of service, gone into a jute-mill, followed gradually by five sisters.

"I hate the very words 'service' and 'servant,'" she said. "We came to this country to better ourselves, and it's not bettering to have anybody ordering you round."

"But you are ordered in the mill."

"That's different. A man knows what he wants, and doesn't go beyond it; but a woman never knows what she wants, and sort of bosses you everlastingly. If there was such a thing as fixed hours it might be different, but I tell every girl I know, 'Whatever you do, don't go into service. You'll always be prisoners and always looked down on.' You can do things at home for them as belongs to you that somehow it seems different to do for strangers. Anyway, I hate it, and there's plenty like me."

"What I minded," said a gentle, quiet girl, who worked at a stationer's, and who had tried household service for a year,—"what I minded was the awful lonesomeness. I went for general housework, because I knew all about it, and there were only three in the family. I never minded being alone evenings in my own room, for I'm always reading or something, and I don't go out hardly at all, but then I always

From Helen Campbell, *Prisoners of Poverty: Women Wage Workers, Their Trades and Their Lives* (Boston: Little, Brown and Company, 1900), pp. 224–231.

know I can, and that there is somebody to talk to if I like. But there, except to give orders, they had nothing to do with me. It got to feel sort of crushing at last. I cried myself sick, and at last I gave it up, though I don't mind the work at all. . . ."

"Oh, nobody need to tell me about poor servants," said an energetic woman of forty, Irish-American, and for years in a shirt factory. "Don't I know the way the hussies'll do, comin' out of a bog maybe, an' not knowing the names even, let alone the use, of half the things in the kitchen, and asking their twelve and fourteen dollars a month? Don't I know it well, an' the shame it is to 'em! but I know plenty o' decent, hard-workin' girls too, that give good satisfaction, an' this is what they say. They say the main trouble is, the mistresses don't know, no more than babies, what a day's work really is. A smart girl keeps on her feet all the time to prove she isn't lazy, for if the mistress finds her sitting down, she thinks there can't be much to do and that she doesn't earn her wages. Then if a girl tries to save herself or is deliberate, they call her slow. They want girls on tap from six in the morning till ten and eleven at night. 'Tisn't fair. And then, if there's a let-up in the work, maybe they give you the baby to see to. I like a nice baby, but I don't like having one turned over to me when I'm fit to drop scrabbling to get through and sit down a bit. . . . Women make hard mistresses, and I say again, I'd rather be under a man, that knows what he wants. That's the way with most."

"I don't see why people are surprised that we don't rush into places," said a shop-girl. "Our world may be a very narrow world, and I know it is; but for all that, it's the only one we've got, and right or wrong, we're out of it if we go into service. A teacher or cashier or anybody in a store, no matter if they have got common-sense, doesn't want to associate with servants. Somehow you get a sort of smooch. Young men think and say, for I have heard lots of them, 'Oh, she can't amount to much if she hasn't brains enough to make a living outside of a kitchen!' You're just down once [and] for all if you go into one."

"I don't agree with you at all," said a young teacher who had come with her. "The people that hire you go into kitchens and are not disgraced. What I felt was, for you see I tried it, that they oughtn't to make me go into livery. I was worn out with teaching, and so I concluded to try being a nurse for a while. I found two hard things: one, that I was never free for an hour from the children, for I took meals and all with them, and any mother knows what a rest it is to go quite away from them, even for an hour; and the other was that she wanted me to wear the nurse's cap and apron. She was real good and kind; but when I said, 'Would you like your sister, Miss Louise, to put on cap and apron when she goes out with them?' she got very red, and straightened up. 'It's a very different matter,' she said; 'you must not forget that in accepting a servant's place you accept a servant's limitations.' That finished me. I loved the children, but I said, 'If you have no other thought of what I am to the children than that, I had better go.' I went, and she put a common, uneducated Irish girl in my place. . . ."

"I've tried it," said one who had been a dressmaker and found her health going from long sitting. "My trouble was, no conscience as to hours; and I believe you'll find that is, at the bottom, one of the chief objections. My first employer was a smart, energetic woman, who had done her own work when she was first married and knew what it meant, or you'd think she might have known. But she had no more thought for me than if I had been a machine. She'd sit in her sitting room on the second floor and ring for me twenty times a day to do little things, and she wanted me up till eleven to answer the bell, for she had a great deal of company. I had a good room and everything nice, and she gave me a great many things, but I'd have spared them all if only I could have had a little time to myself.

I was all worn out, and at last I had to go. There was another reason. I had no place but the kitchen to see my friends. I was thirty years old and as well born and well educated as she, and it didn't seem right. The mistresses think it's all the girls' fault, but I've seen enough to know that women haven't found out what justice means, and that a girl knows it, many a time, better than her employer. Anyway, you couldn't make me try it again."

"My trouble was," said another, who had been in a cotton-mill and gone into the home of one of the mill-owners as chambermaid, "I hadn't any place that I could be alone a minute. We were poor at home, and four of us worked in the mill, but I had a little room all my own, even if it didn't hold much. In that splendid big house the servants' room was over the kitchen, hot and close in summer, and cold in winter, and four beds in it. We five had to live there together, with only two bureaus and a bit of a closet, and one washstand for all. There was no chance to keep clean or your things in nice order, or anything by yourself, and I gave up. Then I went into a little family and tried general housework, and the mistress taught me a great deal, and was good and kind, only there the kitchen was a dark little place and my room like it, and I hadn't an hour in anything that was pleasant and warm. A mistress might see, you'd think, when a girl was quiet and fond of her home, and treat her different from the kind that destroy everything; but I suppose the truth is, they're worn out with that kind and don't make any difference. It's hard to give up your whole life to somebody else's orders, and always feel as if you was looked at over a wall like; but so it is, and you won't get girls to try it, till somehow or other things are different."

QUESTIONS FOR READING AND DISCUSSION

1. What did these women object to about their experiences as domestic servants? Why did some consider factory work preferable to domestic service?

2. Why did these former servants think that "women are always harder on women [servants] than men are"? Why did a servant woman often "know what justice means . . . better than her employer"?

3. Several of these women testified about their desire for freedom. What kind of freedom did they seek, and how did they hope to attain it?

4. Given the many dissatisfactions of household service, why did these women become servants? In what ways did their experiences conflict with their expectations and those of their employers?

DOCUMENT 19–3

Jacob Riis Photographs a Jewish Cobbler in New York City

Jacob Riis worked as a journalist and photographer in New York slums crowded with immigrants. An immigrant himself, Riis was born in Denmark and migrated to New York in 1870 at the age of twenty-one. In his most famous book, How the Other Half Lives, *published in 1890, Riis called attention to the wretched living conditions endured by poor New Yorkers. Riis took the following photo on one of his visits to what he called "Jewtown" in New York City. Riis titled this picture, "Hebrew Making Ready for Sabbath Eve in his Coal Cellar." The photo captures major features of the lives of millions of other immigrants in Gilded Age cities.*

Jacob Riis

"Hebrew Making Ready for Sabbath Eve in his Coal Cellar," ca. 1890

Jacob A. Riis/Getty Images

QUESTIONS FOR READING AND DISCUSSION

1. What evidence in the photo shows the man is Jewish?
2. What does the title "Making Ready for Sabbath" indicate about the importance of his faith? What is the importance of the bread and the tablecloth?
3. What does the sign (on the left) advertising his skill as a cobbler suggest about where he worked and who employed him?
4. What evidence suggests the man lived in the coal cellar? How did the coal cellar influence him?
5. How does the photo suggest this man's values and aspirations?

DOCUMENT 19–4

Walter Wyckoff Listens to Revolutionary Workers in Chicago

In 1891 Walter Wyckoff, a young man from Connecticut who had recently graduated from Princeton University, set off to walk across America and earn his living as a laborer. After two years on the road, Wyckoff, who went on to teach at Princeton, published a book about his experiences among workingmen. In the excerpt below, Wyckoff described his encounters with socialist and anarchist workers at meetings in Chicago. Wyckoff emphasized the ideological differences among radical workers as well as their shared bitterness about inequality and the hypocrisy and complacency of supporters of the status quo.

Among the Revolutionaries, 1898

By this time I had attended several of the Socialists' meetings, and had come to know personally a number of the members of the order. . . . [One] I had learned to know was a near approach to my original preconception of a revolutionary. He was a Communistic Anarchist. . . . It puzzled me not a little; for . . . Socialism and Anarchy, as two schools of social doctrine, are at the very poles of hostile opposition to each other.

I soon learned that Socialist and Anarchist are not interchangeable terms, to be used with light indifference in describing the general advocate of revolution against established order. Indeed, to my great surprise, I found that a policy of active, aggressive revolution among these men had almost no adherents. Certainly none among the Socialists, for they repudiated the bare suggestion of violence as being wholly inadequate and absurd, and pinned their faith instead to what they called the "natural processes of evolution." These [processes], to their belief, would . . . work out the appointed ends with men, but their operation could be stimulated by education, they said, and helped on by organized effort toward the achievement of manifest destiny in the highly centralized and perfected order which is to result from the common ownership and administration by all the people of all land and capital used in production and distribution, for the common good of all.

And even among the Anarchists the upholders of a policy of bloody revolt against social order were rare. Most of those whom I came to know were distinctly of a metaphysical turn of mind. . . . Their views, reduced to simplest terms [were] . . . that "the cure for the evils of freedom is more freedom." The removal of all artificial restraint in the form of man-made laws would result eventually, to their thinking, in a society as natural and as wholesome as is all physical order, which is the exact resultant of the free play of natural law.

It was the Socialist's conception of a highly centralized administration which drove the Anarchist into a frenzy of vehement antagonism. And it was the Anarchist's *laissez faire* ideal which roused the latent fighting-spirit of the Socialist. The Anarchist would maintain with stout conviction that centralized administration is already the core of the malady of the world, and that our need is for freedom in the absence of artificial limitations wherein natural forces can work their rightful ends. And the Socialist would retort, with rising anger, that it is from anarchy—the absence of wisely regulated system—that the world even now suffers most, and that the hope of men lies in the orderly management of their own affairs in the interests of all, and in the light of the revelations of science. They [the Socialist and Anarchist] were heartily at one in their dislike for what they were

From Walter A. Wyckoff, *The Workers: An Experiment in Reality* (New York: Charles Scribner's Sons, 1898), 210–36.

fond of calling the present *"bourgeois* society," and for the existing rights of private property, which they regarded as its chiefest bulwark, but they parted company at once . . . on the grounds of their dislike, and of their purposes and hopes for a regenerated state of things.

Such Anarchists were of the "Individualistic" type. Not all of those I met were so philosophical, however. The Communistic one . . . notably was not. Very much the reverse. He was for open revolution to the death, and he made no secret of it. He had little patience for the slow pace of evolution believed in by the Socialists, but he had less . . . for the *laissez faire* conception of his brother Anarchists. At all events, I found him most commonly in the meetings of the [Socialists], where his revolutionary views were frowned down, but his invectives against society were tolerated in a spirit of free speech, and as being warranted by the evils of the existing state.

He was a German, of tall, muscular frame, erect, square-shouldered, well-poised, as a result of long service, most bitterly against his will, in the Prussian Army, and he hated kings and potentates and all government authority, with a burning hatred. . . . He was a mechanic by trade, and a good one. . . .

My acquaintance among the Socialists had not gone far before I began to observe that I was meeting men who, whatever their mental vagaries, were craftsmen of no mean order. They were machinists and skilled workmen mostly, and some were workers in sweat-shops. All of them had known the full stress of the struggle for bread, but they were decidedly not the inefficient of their class, having fought their way to positions of some advantage in the general fight. . . .

[At a Socialist meeting to debate whether the Chicago World's Fair should be open on Sunday] Christianity was assailed [by the main speaker] as the giant superstition of historic civilization, still, daring, to the shame of high intelligence, to hold its fetich [superstitious] head aloft in the light of modern science. Its ministers were attacked as sycophantic parasites, whose only motive, in urging the closing of the Fair on Sunday, was the fear of the spread among working people of that enlightenment which will achieve the overthrow of capitalistic society and with it the tottering structure of the Church. . . . The Romish [Catholic] Church, he said, keeps many of them in bondage yet, but the Protestant organizations have all but lost their hold upon them; and the widening gulf between the two great classes in society has left these churches in the nakedness of their true character, as mere centres of the social life of the very rich and of the upper *bourgeoisie*, and as a prop to the social order from which these idle classes so richly profit, at the merciless cost of the wage-earners. . . .

The applause which greeted [the speech] was genuine and prolonged. . . . [M]en began ardently to speak to this new theme: Modern Christianity a vast hypocrisy—a cloak made use of by vested interest to conceal from the common people the real nature of the grounds on which it stands. . . .

At one moment an American workman was speaking, a Socialist of the general school of Social Democracy. . . . The Christian Church served as well as any institution of the capitalistic order, he said, to measure the growing cleavage between the classes in society. But, to his mind, . . . [the main speaker] had emphasized unnecessarily the existence of the *bourgeoisie*; for economically considered, there is no longer a middle-class. . . . There remain simply the capitalists and the proletarians. The old middle-class, which had made its living by individual enterprise, was fast being forced (by the play of natural laws, which showed themselves in the increasing centralization of capital) out of the possibility of successful competition with aggregated wealth, and down, for the most part, to the level of those who can bring to their native qualities of physical strength, or manual skill or mental ability—proletarians, all of them, whether manual or intellectual, and coming surely, in the slow development of evolution, to a conscious knowledge of their community of interest as against the vested "right" of monopoly in the material interests of production. But athwart this path of progress rose the hardened structure of the Christian Church, bringing to bear against it all her temporal power and the full force of her accumulated superstitions. . . .

[W]ith the fervor of his hate, [this speaker] cried out against the ministers of Christ, who preach to the wronged and downtrodden poor the duty of patience with their "divinely appointed lot," and who try to soothe them to blind submission with promises of an endless future of ecstatic blessedness, when the rich of this world shall burn in the unquenchable fires of hell.

"Oh! The fiendishness of these men," he shouted, "who hide from ignorant minds the truth, which they themselves know full well, that for no mortal man is there any heaven or hell which he does not realize in the span of his earthly history, and if he misses here the happiness to which he was rightly born, he misses it forever! And the miserable paltriness of their motive in working this cruel wrong—merely that they may exempt themselves from toil and live in comfort upon the labor of others, instead of being, where most of them belong, out in the open fields hoeing corn!" . . .

The Communistic Anarchist [rose to speak in imperfect English]. . . . "God a decaying myth, and the Bible a silly legend, and Jesus a good man seeing some human truth, but gone mad in the credulous ignorance of his age, and dead these two thousand years, and Christianity a hoary superstition, made use of in its last days by *bourgeois* civilization to stave off a little longer its own fateful day of reckoning! . . ."

[At the conclusion of the meeting, the leader of the meeting said] he had been brought up under the influence of the Protestant religion, [but] he found himself in very little sympathy with modern Christianity. . . . [H]e felt justified in judging in the light of every-day facts that Christianity was a failure. . . .

"Let us take an illustration," he went on. "A very urgent problem in our city [Chicago] just now is that of 'the unemployed.' . . . [W]ithin the city limits to-day, there are at least thirty thousand men out of work. There may be fifty thousand. . . .

"And how does the Christian Church among us hold itself in relation to this problem? Its members profess themselves the disciples of 'the meek and lowly Jesus,' whom they call 'divine.' He said of Himself that 'He had not where to lay his Head,' and He was the first Socialist in His teaching of universal brotherhood.

"His followers build gorgeous temples to His worship in our city, and out of fear, apparently, that some of the shelterless waifs [of the unemployed], whom He taught them to know as brothers and who are in the very plight their Master was, should lay their weary heads upon the cushioned seats, they keep the churches tight locked through the six days of the week, and then open them on one day for the exclusive purpose of praising that Master's name! Nor is this condition truer of Chicago than it is of any other large industrial centre in this country, or even in all of Christendom." . . .

[After the meeting] I found myself beside a young German mechanic . . . [who] was a Socialist and was employed in a large factory. . . . He was a Socialist of serene temperament, with boundless faith in the silent processes of development. . . .

"There could be no propaganda in behalf of Socialism," he said to me, "one hundredth part so effective as the unchecked activity of men who imagine themselves the bulwarks of social order and the bitterest foes of Socialism. We have no quarrel with the increasing centralization of capital. The opposition to 'trusts' and the like comes mainly from the *bourgeoisie*, who feel themselves being forced out of independent business. We Socialists are already of the proletariat, and we see clearly that all trusts and syndicates are the inevitable forerunner of still greater centralization. The men who are employing their rare abilities in eliminating the useless wastes of competitive production, by unifying its administration and control, and so reducing greatly the cost of the finished article, and who are perfecting the machinery of transportation and distribution by like unity of administration, are doing far more in a year to bring about a co-operative organization of society than we could do by preaching the theory of collectivism, in a hundred years.

"The collectivist order of society may be distant, but, at least, we have this comfort—that the day of the old individualist, anarchical order is past. We can never return to it. The centralization of capital has proved the inadequacy of all that, in the present stage of progress. We have no choice but to go on to further centralization, and the logical outcome must be eventually, not the monopoly of everything by a few, but the common ownership of all land and capital by all the people."

QUESTIONS FOR READING AND DISCUSSION

1. According to Wyckoff, how did socialists differ from anarchists? Where did they find common ground?

2. Why did the socialists at the meeting Wyckoff attended assail Christianity as a "giant superstition," ministers as "sycophantic parasites," and churches as "a prop to the social order"?

3. Why, according to one socialist, were "men who imagine themselves the bulwarks of social order and the bitterest foes of Socialism" in reality working to bring about changes that would lead to socialism?

4. Who did the socialists and anarchists identify as the leading agents of economic and social change? Why did they act as they did? How should they behave? What goals should they seek?

5. To what extent did the socialists and anarchists Wyckoff heard rely on evolution to lead to the "collectivist order of society"? How did they believe evolution differed from revolution? Why?

DOCUMENT 19–5

George Washington Plunkitt Explains Politics

Political machines ruled big cities, and none was more successful—or notorious—than New York's Tammany Hall. George Washington Plunkitt, a loyal Tammany boss, liked to hold court at the county courthouse shoeshine stand, explaining how things really worked to anyone willing to listen. In 1897, freelance journalist William L. Riordon began recording Plunkitt's remarks and followed him for a day to see what he did. Riordon's account appeared in the New York Evening Post *and was later published in the volume* Plunkitt of Tammany Hall *in 1905. Plunkitt's statements are excerpted here, followed by Riordon's diary of one day in the life of a big-city boss.*

William L. Riordon
Plunkitt of Tammany Hall, 1905

Everybody is talkin' these days about Tammany men growin' rich on graft, but nobody thinks of drawin' the distinction between honest graft and dishonest graft. There's all the difference in the world between the two. Yes, many of our men have grown rich in politics. I have myself. I've made a big fortune out of the game, and I'm gettin' richer every day, but I've not gone in for dishonest graft—blackmailin' gamblers, saloon-keepers, disorderly people, etc.—and neither has any of the men who have made big fortunes in politics.

There's an honest graft, and I'm an example of how it works. I might sum up the whole thing by sayin': "I seen my opportunities and I took 'em."

Just let me explain by examples. My party's in power in the city, and it's goin' to undertake a lot of public improvements. Well, I'm tipped off, say, that they're going to lay out a new park at a certain place.

I see my opportunity and I take it. I go to that place and I buy up all the land I can in the neighborhood. Then the board of this or that makes its plan public, and there is a rush to get my land, which nobody cared particular for before.

Ain't it perfectly honest to charge a good price and make a profit on my investment and foresight? Of course, it is. Well, that's honest graft. . . .

It's just like lookin' ahead in Wall Street or in the coffee or cotton market. It's honest graft, and I'm lookin' for it every day in the year. I will tell you frankly that I've got a good lot of it, too. . . .

I seen my opportunity and I took it. I haven't confined myself to land; anything that pays is in my line. . . .

I've told you how I got rich by honest graft. Now, let me tell you that most politicians who are accused of robbin' the city get rich the same way.

They didn't steal a dollar from the city treasury. They just seen their opportunities and took them. That is why, when a reform administration comes in and spends a half million dollars in tryin' to find the public robberies they talked about in the campaign, they don't find them.

The books are always all right. The money in the city treasury is all right. Everything is all right. All they can show is that the Tammany heads of departments looked after their friends, within the law, and gave them what opportunities they could to make honest graft. Now, let me tell you that's never going to hurt Tammany with the people. Every good man looks after his friends, and any man who doesn't isn't likely to be popular. If I have a good thing to hand out in private life, I give it to a friend. Why shouldn't I do the same in public life? . . .

There's the biggest kind of a difference between political looters and politicians who make a fortune out of politics by keepin' their eyes wide open. The looter goes in for himself alone without considerin' his organization or his city. The politician looks after his own interests, the organization's interests, and the city's interests all at the same time. See the distinction? . . .

The Irish was born to rule, and they're the honestest people in the world. Show me the Irishman who would steal a roof off an almshouse! He don't exist. Of course, if an Irishman had the political pull and the roof was much worn, he might get the city authorities to put on a new one and get the contract for it himself, and buy the old roof at a bargain—but that's honest graft. . . .

From William L. Riordon, *Plunkitt of Tammany Hall* (New York: McClure, Phillips & Co., 1905).

One reason why the Irishman is more honest in politics than many Sons of the Revolution is that he is grateful to the country and the city that gave him protection and prosperity when he was driven by oppression from the Emerald Isle. . . . His one thought is to serve the city which gave him a home. He has this thought even before he lands in New York, for his friends here often have a good place in one of the city departments picked out for him while he is still in the old country. Is it any wonder that he has a tender spot in his heart for old New York when he is on its salary list the mornin' after he lands? . . .

[H]ave you ever thought what would become of the country if the bosses were put out of business, and their places were taken by a lot of cart-tail orators and college graduates? It would mean chaos. . . .

This is a record of a day's work by Plunkitt:

2 A.M.   Aroused from sleep by the ringing of his door bell; went to the door and found a bartender, who asked him to go to the police station and bail out a saloon-keeper who had been arrested for violating the excise law. Furnished bail and returned to bed at three o'clock.

6 A.M.   Awakened by fire engines passing his house. Hastened to the scene of the fire, according to the custom of the Tammany district leaders, to give assistance to the fire sufferers, if needed. Met several of his election district captains who are always under orders to look out for fires, which are considered great vote-getters. Found several tenants who had been burned out, took them to a hotel, supplied them with clothes, fed them, and arranged temporary quarters for them until they could rent and furnish new apartments.

8:30 A.M.   Went to the police court to look after his constituents. Found six "drunks." Secured the discharge of four by a timely word with the judge, and paid the fines of two.

9 A.M.   Appeared in the Municipal District Court. Directed one of his district captains to act as counsel for a widow against whom dispossess proceedings had been instituted and obtained an extension of time. Paid the rent of a poor family about to be dispossessed and gave them a dollar for food.

11 A.M.   At home again. Found four men waiting for him. One had been discharged by the Metropolitan Railway Company for neglect of duty, and wanted the district leader to fix things. Another wanted a job on the road. The third sought a place on the Subway and the fourth, a plumber, was looking for work with the Consolidated Gas Company. The district leader spent nearly three hours fixing things for the four men, and succeeded in each case.

3 P.M.   Attended the funeral of an Italian as far as the ferry. Hurried back to make his appearance at the funeral of a Hebrew constituent. Went conspicuously to the front both in the Catholic church and the synagogue, and later attended the Hebrew confirmation ceremonies in the synagogue.

7 P.M.   Went to district headquarters and presided over a meeting of election district captains. Each captain submitted a list of all the voters in his district, reported on their attitude toward Tammany, suggested who might be won over and how they could be won, told who were in need, and who were in trouble of any kind and the best way to reach them. District leader took notes and gave orders.

8 P.M.   Went to a church fair. Took chances on everything, bought ice-cream for the young girls and the children. Kissed the little ones, flattered their mothers and took their fathers out for something down at the corner.

9 P.M.   At the club-house again. Spent $10 on tickets for a church excursion and promised a subscription for a new church-bell. Bought tickets for a base-ball game to be played by two nines from his district. Listened to the complaints of a dozen pushcart peddlers who said they were persecuted by the police and assured them he would go to Police Headquarters in the morning and see about it.

10:30 P.M.   Attended a Hebrew wedding reception and dance. Had previously sent a handsome wedding present to the bride.

12 P.M.   [*sic*] In bed.

That is the actual record of one day in the life of Plunkitt.

QUESTIONS FOR READING AND DISCUSSION

1. According to Plunkitt, what was "honest graft"? How did it differ from dishonest graft or from ordinary business deals?
2. What did reformers object to about Tammany and honest graft? What did Tammany's supporters object to about reformers? How did political bosses differ from bosses at places of employment?
3. How did Tammany win the loyalty of voters? In what ways did it matter to Tammany that many New Yorkers were immigrants?
4. Why did Plunkitt think chaos would result "if the bosses were put out of business, and their places were taken by a lot of cart-tail orators and college graduates"?
5. To Plunkitt, what was politics? Did Riordon seem to have a different view of politics?

COMPARATIVE QUESTIONS

1. What portrait of factory and political bosses emerges from the descriptions in these documents? How did bosses differ from working people? Why? To what extent did working people cooperate with bosses? Why?
2. How did Thomas O'Donnell's experiences with factory work compare with the experiences of women domestic servants and the Jewish cobbler?
3. To what extent were Plunkitt's notions of politics shared by the socialists and anarchists Wyckoff heard in Chicago? How were working people affected by politics as practiced by Plunkitt?
4. How did the people described in these documents define economic justice and injustice? In their views, what might lead to greater justice? Politics? Unions? Bosses? Religion?
5. These documents focus on the deep class divisions in American society in the late nineteenth century. Judging from these documents, what had created these divisions, and what might be done to bridge them? To what extent did working people share the ideals and aspirations of employers? To what extent did working people agree among themselves?

20 Dissent, Depression, and War

1890–1900

Profound moral conflict generated intense strife during the 1890s. Many Americans believed that the basic principles of order in the economy, in society, and in politics were immoral and unjust. Numerous others believed the opposite. Supporters of the Farmers' Alliance and the Populists voiced some of the moral doubts, while their opponents reaffirmed their faith in the conventional virtues. This conflict was more than a debate, as African Americans, labor activists, and Filipino nationalists knew. The following documents disclose the contours of the moral conflict of the 1890s and some of its many consequences.

DOCUMENT 20-1

Mary Elizabeth Lease Reports on Women in the Farmers' Alliance

Hard times in agriculture pushed farmers in the Midwest and South to organize a wide variety of local reform movements. Selling their crops in distant markets for prices that often seemed to be rigged against them, shipping their produce on railroads that manipulated rates to their disadvantage, borrowing money for land and supplies at what seemed extravagant interest rates—these and other common experiences bred a sense of helplessness that many farmers came to believe could only be overcome by cooperation and organizations such as the Farmers' Alliance, the Populists, and the Knights of Labor. Mary Elizabeth Lease, a Kansas schoolteacher who had lived for years on a hardscrabble farm, became a popular and charismatic speaker who encouraged farmers—and especially farm women—to come together in the Farmers' Alliance. As the following excerpt from Lease's speech to the National Council of Women illustrates, Lease believed farm women could help change America for the better.

Women in the Farmers' Alliance, 1891

It must be evident to every intelligent man and woman to-day that there is something radically wrong in the affairs of the Nation. It must be evident to every thinking man and woman that we have reached a crisis in the affairs of this Nation which is of more importance, more fraught with mighty consequence for the weal or woe for the American people, than was even that crisis that engaged the attention of the people of this Nation in the dark and bleeding years of civil war. We are confronted to-day by a crisis in which every instinct of common duty, of justice, and of patriotism demands prompt and decisive action.

Twelve years ago . . . [a United States senator] said, "There is no use in any longer trying to disguise the truth. We are on the verge of an impending revolution. Old issues are dead, and the people are arraying themselves on one side or the other of a portentous conflict. On one side is capital, strongly intrenched and privileged, grown arrogant by repeated triumphs and repeated success; on the other side is labor demanding employment, labor starving and sullen in cities, resolutely determined to endure no further [the status quo] under which the rich are growing richer and the poor are growing poorer, a system that gives a [capitalist such as Jay] Gould or a Vanderbilt possession of wealth beyond even the dreams of avarice and condemns the poor to a poverty from which there is no refuge but starvation and the grave." . . .

What means it that [another United States senator] . . . stood in the Senate a few days ago and bade this Nation beware of further ignoring the will of the people, and prophesied dark, disastrous days to come if the will of the people be longer defied? What means it that that grand old Governor of Iowa stood before the Republican Club of New York and prophesied that a storm would break over this country that would bring ruin, devastation, and bloodshed? What means it that John J. Ingalls [Republican Senator from Kansas], whom the women of Kansas had the pleasure of defeating (applause), — what means it that in his death-bed speech a few days ago he bade the House, the Senate, and the Executive beware of further ignoring and defying the will of the people, and told us most emphatically and plainly that there were two great dangers that menaced the safety, ay, threatened the very existence of this Republic to-day — a corrupt ballot and the tyranny of combined, incorporated, conscienceless capital? . . .

Senator [William Morris] Stewart [of Nevada] tells us in a recent speech . . . that every act of legislation since the close of the [Civil] war has been in pursuance of the policy of the combined bondholders to enslave the American people and contract the currency of this Nation, and [former president James A.] Garfield and [former Senator John Alexander] Logan [of Illinois] unite in telling us that whoever controls the money of the Nation controls the commerce, the industrial interest of the Nation.

From Mary E. Lease, "Women in the Farmers' Alliance," *Transactions of the National Council of Women of the United States, Assembled in Washington, D.C., February 22 to 25, 1891*, ed. Rachel Foster Avery (Philadelphia: J. B. Lippincott, 1891), 157–59, 214–16.

My friends, the lash of the slave-driver's whip is no longer heard in this country, but the lash of necessity is driving thousands to unrequited toil. Conscienceless capital is robbing manhood of its prime, mothers of their motherhood, and sorrowful children of sunshine and joy. Look around you. What do you behold to-day? A land which less than four hundred years ago we received fresh from the hands of God, a continent of unparalleled fertility, magnificent in golden promise for all humanity, a land where we have all diversity of soil and clime, a land where the bounteous hand of Nature has given a wonderful heritage to each and every one of her children; and yet, in this land of plenty and unlimited resources, the cry of humanity is going up from every corner of this Nation. The plaint of motherhood, the moans of starving children! Capital buys and sells to-day the very heart-beats of humanity. . . .

[T]o-day the American toiler in his bitterness and wrath asks us, Which is the worst, the black slavery that has gone or the white slavery that has come? Has the American laborer nothing to show for twenty years of toil? Oh yes: he can point to the rivers bridged, to the transcontinental railway connecting ocean with ocean, to wonderful churches and cathedrals; he can point to the most wonderful system of agriculture that ever brought joy to a hungry world; he can jostle his rags against the silken garments his toil has secured; he can walk shelterless and sad by the side of the home he has helped to build; he can wipe the sweat from his weary face and reflect that the twenty thousand of American millionaires who own one billion five hundred million dollars, gathered from the toils and tears of sixty-four millions of American people, have it in their power to name their Governors and our legislators and representatives and Congressmen—and they *do* name them, and they *have* named them for the last quarter of a century, and they have it in their power to fix the price of labor and to fix the price for every ton of coal.

For one hundred years the speculators, the land-robbers, the pirates and gamblers of this Nation have knocked unceasingly at the door of Congress, and Congress has in every case acceded to their demands. They have gotten money out of the public treasury amounting to tens of millions of dollars. They were permitted to tap the veins of trade and commerce and withdraw from the body politic the circulating medium which is the life-blood of the Nation, and our law-makers term these [acts] constitutional, and when for the first time in one hundred years farmers come timidly knocking at the doors of Congress asking for relief, a howl went up. . . .

We are living in a grand and wonderful time; we are living in a day when old ideas, old traditions, and old customs have broken loose from their moorings . . . ; we are living in a time when the gray old world begins to dimly comprehend that there is no difference between the brain of an intelligent woman and the brain of an intelligent man; . . . we are living in a day and age when the women of industrial societies and the [Farmers'] Alliance women have become a mighty factor in the politics of this nation; when the mighty dynamite of thought is stirring the hearts of men of this world from centre to circumference, and this thought is crystallizing into action.

Organization is becoming the key-note among the farmers of this nation. The farmers, slow to think and slow to act, are to-day thinking for themselves; they have been compelled to think. They have been awakened by the load of oppressive taxation, unjust tariffs, and they find themselves standing to-day on the very brink of their own despair. In all the years which have flown, the farmers, in their unswerving loyalty and patriotism to [political] party, have been too mentally lazy to do their own thinking. They have been allowing the unprincipled demagogues of both the old political parties to do their thinking for them, and they have voted poverty and degradation not only upon themselves but upon their wives and their children.

But to-day these farmers, thank God! are thinking, and also their mothers, wives, and daughters, "their sisters, their cousins, and their aunts." We find, as a result of this mighty thought in the hearts of the people, a movement of the great common people of this nation, and that is the protest of the patient burden-bearers of the world against political superstition, a movement which is an echo of the life of Jesus of Nazareth, a movement that means revolution,—not a revolution such as deluged the streets of Paris with blood in 1793 [during the French Revolution], but the revolution of brain and ballots that shall shake this continent and move humanity everywhere. The voice which is coming up to-day from the mystic cords of the American heart is the same voice which Lincoln heard blending with the guns of Fort Sumter. It is breaking into a clarion cry which will be heard round the world, and thrones will fall and crowns will crumble, and the divine right of kings and capital will fade away like the mists of the morning when the angel of liberty shall kindle the fires of justice in the hearts of men.

An injury to one is the concern of all. Founded upon the eternal principles of truth and right, with special privileges to none, the farmers' movement could not well exclude the patient burden-bearers of the home. And so we find them opening wide the doors of this new and mighty movement, the Farmer's Alliance, admitting women into the ranks of the organization, actually recognizing the fact that they are human beings, and treating them as such, with full privileges of membership and promotion. And the women who have borne the heat and the burden of the day were not slow to accept the newly-offered privileges, undeterred by the fact that the new organization was political, though non-partisan, and they gladly accepted the privileges extended them, until we find to-day upwards of half a million women in the Farmers' Alliance, who have taken up the study of social and political problems, and are studying and investigating the great issues of the day, fully cognizant of the fact that in the political arena alone can these great problems be satisfactorily settled.

You will wonder, perhaps, why the women of the West are interested so much in this great uprising of the common people. . . . I will tell you, friends: if you will refer to your old school-maps, you will find that that portion of our country now the valuable, teeming, fruitful West, was twenty-five or thirty years ago marked there as the "Great American Desert, the treeless plain." About that time, the women of the East turned their faces towards the boundless, billowy prairies of the West. They accompanied their husbands, sons, and brothers; they came with the roses of health on their cheeks; they left home and friends, school and church, and all which makes life dear to you and me, and turned their faces towards the untried West, willing to brave the dangers of pioneer life upon the lonely prairies with all its privations; their children were born there, and there upon the prairies our little babes lie buried. After all our years of sorrow, loneliness, and privation, we are being robbed of our farms, of our homes, at the rate of five hundred a week, and turned out homeless paupers, outcasts and wanderers, robbed of the best years of our life and our toil. Do you wonder that women are joining the Farmers' Alliance and the Knights of Labor? Let no one . . . for one moment suppose that this Alliance movement is but a passing episode of a brief political career. We have come to stay, for we are advocating principles of truth, right, and justice. Our demands are founded on the Sermon on the Mount, and that other command, that ye love one another. We seek to put into practical operation the teachings of Christ, who was sent to bring about a better day. Then there shall be no more coal kings nor silver kings, but a better day when there shall be no more millionaires, no more paupers, and no more waifs in our streets.

QUESTIONS FOR READING AND DISCUSSION

1. What, according to Lease, was "radically wrong in the affairs of the Nation"? Who did she believe shared her views about "a crisis"?

2. What did Lease mean by declaring, "Capital buys and sells to-day the very heart-beats of humanity"?

3. Why did Lease say that farmers had "been too mentally lazy to do their own thinking"? In her opinion, who had been thinking for them? What ideas would ignite "the mighty dynamite of thought" that Lease believed would bring about change?

4. How had women contributed to the Farmers' Alliance, according to Lease? How did the Alliance aid women?

5. What reason did Lease give to explain why women in the West were "interested so much in this great uprising of the common people"?

DOCUMENT 20–2

Cherokee Strip Land Rush, 1893

In September 1893 about 150,000 people gathered on the boundaries of the so-called Cherokee Strip (or Outlet) in what is now north-central Oklahoma for the largest land rush in U.S. history. The Cherokee had been granted the Strip's seven million acres when they were removed to Indian Territory back in 1835. Since then, railroads, ranchers, and farmers coveted the land and continually tried to claim portions of it. The U.S. Army tried to remove these illegal settlers, called "boomers." With hard times in agriculture, the severe 1893 depression throughout the nation, and a drought-plagued summer, camps of poor, hungry people formed on boundaries of the Strip and demanded to settle it. The army and federal marshals tried to keep so-called "sooners" from illegally crossing into the Strip before it was officially open. The federal government finally opened the Strip to homestead claims at noon on September 16, 1893, in a great, chaotic land rush, a portion of which is shown in the following photo. Would-be homesteaders streaked into the Strip in every way possible and tried to stake a claim that would eventually become ownership. In the end, about three-fourths of the people who staked claims did not manage to get deeds of ownership.

The Cherokee Strip Land Rush, 1893

First train leaving the Line north of O-lembo for Perry South, 1893.

National Archives photo no. 49-AR-7

QUESTIONS FOR READING AND DISCUSSION

1. Judging from the photo, what preparations had these people made for the land rush?
2. How do the expectations of the people in wagons differ from those of the passengers on the train?
3. With such hard times in agriculture, why did so many people rush to claim land in the Cherokee Strip?
4. How did the Cherokee Strip land rush exhibit attitudes and values common among Americans in the 1890s?
5. Was the land rush a democratic method of land distribution? What might the Cherokee say?

DOCUMENT 20–3

White Supremacy in Wilmington, North Carolina

Black southerners affiliated with the Republican Party often cooperated with Populists to defeat Democrats. Such a fusion of Republicans and Populists carried North Carolina in 1894 and 1896, resulting in the election and appointment of a number of black office-holders, including the mayor and aldermen of Wilmington. In 1898, Democrats struck back with a campaign of terror and intimidation, which culminated two days after their victory at the polls by what Gunner Jesse Blake called a "rebellion" that established white supremacy by killing at least twenty blacks. Blake, a Confederate veteran who participated in the "rebellion," recalled the event for a sympathetic white writer in the 1930s. Blake's narrative, excerpted here, illustrates the explosive racism that confronted southern blacks every day and ultimately undermined the Populist revolt in the South.

Gunner Jesse Blake
Narrative of the Wilmington "Rebellion" of 1898

"So, I am going to give you the inside story of this insurrection," he proceeded, "wherein the white people of Wilmington overthrew the constituted municipal authority overnight and substituted a reform rule, doing all this legally and with some needless bloodshed, to be sure, but at the same time they eliminated the Negroes from the political life of the city and the state. This Rebellion was the very beginning of Negro disfranchisement in the South and an important step in the establishment of 'White Supremacy' in the Southland. . . .

"The Rebellion was an organized resistance," Mr. Blake said, "on the part of the white citizens of this community to the established government, which had long irked them because it was dominated by 'Carpet Baggers' and Negroes, and also because the better element here wished to establish 'White Supremacy' in the city, the state and throughout the South, and thereby remove the then stupid and ignorant Negroes from their numerically dominating position in the government. . . .

"The older generation of Southern born men were at their wits' end. They had passed through the rigors of the North-South war and through the tyrannies of Reconstruction when Confiscation . . . of properties without due process of law, was the rule rather than the exception. They had seen 'Forty Acres and a Mule' buy many a Negro's vote.

"Black rapists were attacking Southern girls and women, those pure and lovely creatures who graced the homes in Dixie Land, and the brutes were committing this dastardly crime with more frequency while the majority of them were escaping punishment through the influence of the powers that be.

"These old Southern gentlemen had calculated that time and time only would remove the terrors of Reconstruction, a condition that was imposed upon the conquered Southerners by the victorious Northerners, but they were not willing to sit supinely by and see their girls and women assaulted by beastly brutes.

"The better element among the Northerners in the North could not want them and their little friends to grow up amid such conditions. . . .

"A group of nine citizens met at the home of Mr. Hugh MacRae and there decided that the attitude and actions of the Negroes made it necessary for them to take some steps towards protecting their families and homes in their immediate neighborhood, Seventh and Market Streets. . . .

"This group of citizens, . . . referred to as the 'Secret Nine,' divided the city into sections, placing a responsible citizen as captain in charge of each area. . . .

"The better element planned to gain relief from Negro impudence and domination, from grafting and from immoral conditions; the 'Secret Nine' and the white leaders marked time, hoping something would happen to arouse the citizenry to concerted action.

"But the 'watch-and-wait policy' of the 'Secret Nine' did not obtain for long, as during the latter part of October [1898] there appeared in the columns of [t]he *Wilmington* (Negro) *Daily Record* an editorial, written by the Negro editor, Alex Manly, which aroused a state-wide revulsion to the city and state administrations then in the hands of the Republicans and Fusionists [Populists]. The editorial

From Harry Hayden, *The Wilmington Rebellion* (Wilmington, NC, 1936), 231–36.

attempted to justify the Negro rape fiends at the expense of the virtue of Southern womanhood."

Mr. Blake . . . read the following . . . editorial from [t]he *Wilmington Record*:

Poor whites are careless in the matter of protecting their women, especially on the farm. They are careless of their conduct towards them, and our experience among the poor white people in the county teaches us that women of that race are not more particular in the matter of clandestine meetings with colored men, than are the white man and colored women. Meetings of this kind go on for some time until the woman's infatuation, or the man's boldness, bring attention to them, and the man is lynched for rape. Every Negro lynched is called a "big, burly, black brute," when in fact, many of those who have been thus dealt with had white men for their fathers, and were not only not "black" and "burly," but were sufficiently attractive for white girls of culture and refinement to fall in love with them, as is very well known to all.

"That editorial," Mr. Blake declared . . . , "is the straw that broke Mister Nigger's political back in the Southland." . . .

"Excitement reigned supreme on election day and the day following," Mr. Blake said, adding that "the tension between the races was at the breaking point, as two Pinkerton detectives, Negroes, had reported to their white employers that the Negro women, servants in the homes of white citizens, had agreed to set fire to the dwellings of their employers, and the Negro men had openly threatened to 'burn the town down' if the 'White Supremacy' issue was carried in the political contest. The very atmosphere was surcharged with tinder, and only a spark, a misstep by individuals of either race, was needed to set the whites and the blacks at each other's throats.

"When Mr. Hugh MacRae was sitting on his porch on Market Street on the afternoon of the election, he saw a band of 'Red Shirts,'[1] fifty in number, with blood in their eyes; mounted upon fiery and well caparisoned[2] steeds and led by Mike Dowling, an Irishman, who had organized this band of vigilantes. The hot headed 'Red Shirts' paused in front of Mr. MacRae's home and the level headed Scotsman walked toward the group to learn what was amiss.

"Dowling told Mr. MacRae that they were headed for 'The Record' building to lynch Editor Manly and burn the structure. Mr. MacRae pleaded with Dowling and his 'Red Shirts' to desist in their plans. Messrs. MacRae, Dowling and other leaders of the 'Red Shirts' repaired across the street to Sasser's Drug store and there he, Mr. MacRae, showed them a 'Declaration of White Independence' that he had drawn up for presentation at a mass meeting of white citizens the next day.

"The 'Red Shirts' were finally persuaded by Mr. MacRae to abandon their plans for the lynching, but only after Mr. MacRae had called up the newspapers on the telephone and dictated a call for a mass meeting of the citizens for the next morning. . . .

"A thousand or more white citizens, representative of all walks of life . . . attended the mass meeting in the New Hanover county court house the next morning, November 10, at 11 o'clock.

"Colonel Alfred Moore Waddell, a mild mannered Southern gentleman, noted for his extremely conservative tendencies, was called upon to preside over

---

[1] **Red Shirts**: Paramilitary white supremacist Democrats.
[2] **caparisoned**: Dressed in an ornamented covering.

the gathering. In addressing this meeting, Colonel Waddell said: . . . 'We will not live under these intolerable conditions. No society can stand it. We intend to change it, if we have to choke the current of Cape Fear River with (Negro) carcasses!' "

"*That* declaration," Mr. Blake said, "brought forth tremendous applause from the large gathering of white men at the mass meeting. . . .

"Colonel Waddell . . . announced that he heartily approved the set of resolutions which had been prepared by Mr. Hugh MacRae and which included the latter's 'Declaration of White Independence.'

"These resolutions were unanimously approved by the meeting, followed by a wonderful demonstration, the assemblage rising to its feet and cheering: 'Right! Right! Right!' and there were cries of 'Fumigate' the city with 'The Record' and 'Lynch Manly.' "

Blake then read the resolutions from the scrap book, as follows:

> Believing that the Constitution of the United States contemplated a government to be carried on by an enlightened people; believing that its framers did not anticipate the enfranchisement of an ignorant population of African origin, and believing that those men of the state of North Carolina, who joined in framing the union, did not contemplate for their descendants subjection to an inferior race.

> We, the undersigned citizens of the city of Wilmington and county of New Hanover, do hereby declare that we will no longer be ruled and will never again be ruled, by men of African origin.

> This condition we have in part endured because we felt that the consequences of the war of secession were such as to deprive us of the fair consideration of many of our countrymen. . . .

"Armed with a Winchester rifle, Colonel Waddell ordered the citizens to form in front of the Armory for an orderly procession out to 'The Record' plant. . . .

"As this band of silent yet determined men marched up Market Street it passed the beautiful colonial columned mansion, the Bellamy home. From the balcony of this mansion, a Chief Justice of the United States Supreme Court, Salmon P. Chase, delivered an address shortly after Lincoln's tragic assassination, advocating Negro suffrage and thereby sowing the seeds that were now blossoming forth into a white rebellion.

"The printing press of 'The Record' was wrecked by the maddened white men, who also destroyed other equipment, and the type that had been used in producing the editorial that had reflected upon the virtue and character of Southern womanhood was scattered to the four winds by these men, who stood four-square for the virtue of their women and for the supremacy of the white race over the African.

"Some lamps that had been hanging from the ceiling of the plant were torn down and thrown upon the floor, which then became saturated with kerosene oil; and then a member of the band struck a match, with the result that the two-story frame building was soon in flames.

"The leaders and most of the citizens had designed only to destroy the press," Mr. Blake averred, adding . . . "all of which proves that a mob, no matter how well disciplined, is no stronger than its weakest link.

"The crowd of armed men, which had destroyed the plant and building of the nefarious *Wilmington* (Negro) *Daily Record*, dispersed, repairing peacefully to their respective homes," Mr. Blake said. . . .

"But in about an hour the tension between the two races broke with the shooting of William H. (Bill) Mayo, a white citizen, who was wounded by the first shot that was fired in the Wilmington Rebellion as he was standing on the sidewalk near his home. . . . Mayo's assailant, Dan Wright, was captured by members of the Wilmington Light Infantry and the Naval Reserves after he had been riddled by 13 bullets. Wright died next day in a hospital.

"Then the 'Red Shirts' began to ride and the Negroes began to run. . . . The Africans, or at least those Negroes who had foolishly believed in the remote possibility of social equality with the former masters of their parents, began to slink before the Caucasians. They, the Negroes, appeared to turn primal, slinking away like tigers at bay, snarling as they retreated before the bristling bayonets, barking guns and flaming 'Red Shirts.'

"Six Negroes were shot down near the corner of Fourth and Brunswick Streets, the Negro casualties for the day—November 11, 1898—totaling nine. One of these, who had fired at the whites from a Negro dance hall, 'Manhattan,' over in 'Brooklyn,' was shot 15 or 20 times. . . .

"One 'Red Shirt' said he had seen six Negroes shot down near the Cape Fear Lumber Company's plant and that their bodies were buried in a ditch. . . . Another 'Red Shirt' described the killing of nine Negroes by a lone white man, who killed them one at a time with his Winchester rifle as they filed out of a shanty door in 'Brooklyn' and after they had fired on him. . . . Another told of how a Negro had been killed and his body thrown in Cape Fear River after he had approached two white men on the wharf. . . .

"Other military units came to Wilmington to assist the white citizens in establishing 'White Supremacy' here. . . . Military organizations from as far South as New Orleans telegraphed offering to come here if their services were needed in the contest.

"When the Rebellion was in full blast 'The Committee of Twenty-five' appointed . . . a committee to call upon Mayor Silas P. Wright and the Board of Aldermen and demand that these officials resign. The mayor had expressed a willingness to quit, but not during the crisis. He changed his mind, however, when he saw white citizens walking the streets with revolvers in their hands. The Negroes, too, had suddenly turned submissive, they were carrying their hats in their hands. . . .

"African continued to cringe before Caucasian as the troops paraded the streets, as the guns barked and the bayonets flared, for a new municipal administration of the 'White Supremacy' persuasion had been established in a day! The old order of Negro domination over the white citizenry had ended."

QUESTIONS FOR READING AND DISCUSSION

1. According to Blake, why did the "better element" want "to establish 'White Supremacy' in the city, the state and throughout the South"? How did Blake's description of the behavior of African Americans serve his own political agenda?

2. Why did an editorial in the local newspaper precipitate violence, according to Blake? Who was offended by the editorial? Why?

3. Who was responsible for the violence? Why did it occur?

4. To what extent did the Declaration of White Independence express the views of all whites? How did the declaration undermine partisan loyalties of white voters?

DOCUMENT 20–4

Conflicting Views about Labor Unions

Many employers vehemently opposed labor unions while many working people just as vehemently defended them and—more important—joined them. Bitter, often violent conflict between capital and labor over wages, working conditions, jobs, strikes, and boycotts fueled the debate. A forceful argument against labor unions was made in 1900 by N. F. Thompson, a representative of the Southern Industrial Convention and the Chamber of Commerce of Huntsville, Alabama, in testimony before the Industrial Commission on the Relations and Conditions of Capital and Labor. Samuel Gompers, who served as president of the American Federation of Labor almost continuously from 1886 to 1924, defended labor unions in a letter published in 1894—six years before Thompson's testimony—in the union journal American Federationist. *Gompers's letter responded to a judge who had issued an injunction against the leaders of the strike and boycott against the Pullman Company in 1894 and who subsequently called for federal troops to suppress the strike. The arguments made by Thompson and Gompers reveal clashing views of the period's industrial order, its strengths and weaknesses, achievements and failures, virtues and vices. The debate about labor unions also highlighted fundamental disagreements about the roles of capitalists, working people, and governments on the path toward progress.*

N. F. Thompson

Testimony before the Industrial Commission on the Relations and Conditions of Capital and Labor, 1900

Labor organizations are to-day the greatest menace to this Government that exists inside or outside the pale of our national domain. Their influence for disruption and disorganization of society is far more dangerous to the perpetuation of our Government in its purity and power than would be the hostile array on our borders of the army of the entire world combined. I make this statement from years of close study and a field of the widest opportunities for observation, embracing the principal industrial centers both of the North and the South. I make this statement entirely from a sense of patriotic duty and without prejudice against any class of citizens of our common country.

If I could make this statement any stronger or clearer, I would gladly do so, for it is not until an evil or a danger is made strongly apparent that adequate measures of relief are likely to be applied. That such a menace is real and not imaginary the most casual investigation of existing tendencies among the laboring classes will make the facts discernible. On every hand, and for the slightest provocation, all classes of organized labor stand ready to inaugurate a strike with all its attendant evils, or to place a boycott for the purpose of destroying the business of some one against whom their enmity has been evoked.

In addition to this, stronger ties of consolidation are being urged all over the country among labor unions with the view of being able to inaugurate a

From *Report of the Industrial Commission on the Relations and Conditions of Capital and Labor*, vol. 7 (Washington, DC: U.S. Government Printing Office, 1901), 755–57; *American Federationist* 1 (September 1894), 150–52.

sympathetic strike that will embrace all classes of labor, simply to redress the grievances or right the wrong of one class, however remotely located or however unjust may be the demands of that class. To recognize such a power as this in any organization, or to permit such a theory to be advanced without a protest or counteracting influence, is so dangerous and subversive of government that it may justly be likened to the planting of deadly virus in the heart of organized society, death being its certain and speedy concomitant.

Organizations teaching such theories should be held as treasonable in their character and their leaders worse than traitors to their country. It is time for the plainest utterances on this subject, for the danger is imminent, and in view of the incidents that have occurred recently in strikes it can be considered little less than criminal in those who control public sentiment that such scenes are possible anywhere in this country.

This language may seem needlessly harsh and severe, but in some classes of diseases it is the sharpest knife that effects the speediest remedy, and so, in this case, if the public are to be awakened to their real danger the plainest speech becomes necessary.

No one questions the right of labor to organize for any legitimate purpose, but when labor organizations degenerate into agencies of evil, inculcating theories dangerous to society and claiming rights and powers destructive to government, there should be no hesitancy in any quarter to check these evil tendencies even if the organizations themselves have to be placed under the ban of law.

That these organizations are thus degenerating is seen in the following facts:

1. Many labor leaders are open and avowed socialists and are using labor organizations as the propaganda of socialistic doctrines.
2. These organizations are weakening the ties of citizenship among thousands of our people in that they have no other standard of community obligations than what these organizations inculcate.
3. They are creating widespread disregard for the rights of others equally as entitled to the protection of organized society as their own, as evidenced in every strike that occurs and the increasing arbitrariness of labor demands on their employers.
4. They are destroying respect for law and authority among the working classes, as many have no higher conception of these than such as are embodied in the commands and demands of labor organizations and labor leaders.
5. They are educating the laboring classes against the employing classes, thus creating antagonisms between those whose mutuality of interests should be fostered and encouraged by every friend of good government; for the success of government hangs on no less a basis than the harmony and happiness of the people, embracing alike employers and the employed.
6. They are demanding of Federal, State, and municipal authorities class legislation and class discrimination utterly at variance with the fundamental principles of our Government, in that they are demanding of these various authorities the employment of only union labor, thus seeking to bring the power of organized society to crush out all nonunion workers.
7. They are destroying the right of individual contract between employees and employers and forcing upon employers men at arbitrary wages, which is unjust alike to other labor more skilled, and to capital, which is thus obliged to pay for more than it receives in equivalent.

8. They demand the discharge of men who risk life to protect employers' interests during strikes to reinstate those who were formerly employed, but who have been instrumental, directly or indirectly, in the destruction of life and property, thereby placing a premium upon disloyalty and crime.

9. They are bringing public reproach upon the judicial tribunals of our Country by public abuse of these tribunals and often open defiance of their judgments and decrees, thus seeking to break down the only safeguards of a free people. . . .

A further law should be enacted that would make it justifiable homicide for any killing that occurred in defense of any lawful occupation, the theory of our government being that anyone has a right to earn an honest living in this country, and any endeavor to deprive one of that right should be placed in the same legal status with deprivation of life and property.

Samuel Gompers
Letter to the American Federationist, 1894

You say that . . . you believe in labor organizations within such lawful and reasonable limits as will make them a service to the laboring man, and not a menace to the lawful institutions of the country. . . .

You would certainly have no objection . . . to workingmen organizing, and in their meetings discuss perhaps "the origin of man," benignly smiling upon each other, and declaring that all existing things are right, going to their wretched homes to find some freedom in sleep from gnawing hunger. You would have them extol the virtues of monopolists and wreckers of the people's welfare. You would not have them consider seriously the fact that more than two million of their fellows are unemployed, and though willing and able, cannot find the opportunity to work, in order that they may sustain themselves, their wives and their children. You would not have them consider seriously the fact that Pullman who has grown so rich from the toil of his workingmen, that he can riot in luxury, while he heartlessly turns these very workmen out of their tenements into the streets and leave to the tender mercies of corporate greed. Nor would you have them ponder upon the hundreds of other Pullmans of different names.

You know, or ought to know, that the introduction of machinery is turning into idleness thousands, faster than new industries are founded, and yet, machinery certainly should not be either destroyed or hampered in its full development. The laborer is a man, he is made warm by the same sun and made cold—yes, colder—by the same winter as you are. He has a heart and brain, and feels and knows the human and paternal instinct for those depending upon him as keenly as do you.

What shall the workers do? Sit idly by and see the vast resources of nature and the human mind be utilized and monopolized for the benefit of the comparative few? No. The laborers must learn to think and act, and soon, too, that only by the power of organization, and common concert of action, can either their manhood be maintained, their rights to life (work to sustain it) be recognized, and liberty and rights secured.

Since you say that you favor labor organizations within certain limits, will you kindly give to thousands of your anxious fellow citizens what you believe the workers could and should do in their organizations to solve this great problem? Not what they should not do. . . .

I am not one of those who regards the entire past as a failure. I recognize the progress made and the improved conditions of which nearly the entire civilized world are the beneficiaries. I ask you to explain . . . how is it that thousands of able-bodied, willing, earnest men and women are suffering the pangs of hunger? We may boast of our wealth and civilization, but to the hungry man and woman and child our progress is a hollow mockery, our civilization a sham, and our "national wealth" a chimera [an illusion].

You recognize that the industrial forces set in motion by steam and electricity have materially changed the structure of our civilization. You also admit that a system has grown up where the accumulations of the individual have passed from his control into that of representative combinations and trusts, and that the tendency in this direction is on the increase. How, then, can you consistently criticize the workingmen for recognizing that as individuals they can have no influence in deciding what the wages, hours of toil and conditions of employment shall be?

You evidently have observed the growth of corporate wealth and influence. You recognize that wealth, in order to become more highly productive, is concentrated into fewer hands, and controlled by representatives and directors, and yet you sing the old siren song that the working man should depend entirely upon his own "individual effort."

The school of *laissez faire*, of which you seem to be a pronounced advocate, has produced great men in advocating the theory of each for himself, and his Satanic Majesty taking the hindermost, but the most pronounced advocates of your school of thought in economics have, when practically put to the test, been compelled to admit that combination and organization of the toiling masses are essential both to prevent the deterioration and to secure an improvement in the condition of the wage earners.

If, as you say, the success of commercial society depends upon the full play of competition, why do not you and your confreres turn your attention and direct the shafts of your attacks against the trusts and corporations, business wreckers and manipulators in the food products — the necessities of the people. Why garland your thoughts in beautiful phrase when speaking of these modern vampires, and steep your pen in gall when writing of the laborers' efforts to secure some of the advantages accruing from the concentrated thought and genius of the ages? . . .

One becomes enraptured in reading the beauty of your description of modern progress. Could you have had in mind the miners of Spring Valley or Pennsylvania, or the clothing workers of the sweat shops of New York or Chicago when you grandiloquently dilate, "Who is not rich to-day when compared with his ancestors of a century ago? The steamboat and the railroad bring to his breakfast table the coffees of Java and Brazil, the fruit from Florida and California, and the steaks from the plains. The loom arrays him in garments and the factories furnish him with a dwelling that the richest contemporaries of his grandfather would have envied. With health and industry he is a prince."

Probably you have not read within the past year of babies dying of starvation at their mothers' breasts. More than likely the thousands of men lying upon the bare stones night after night in the City Hall of Chicago last winter escaped your notice. You may not have heard of the cry for bread that was sounded through this land of plenty by thousands of honest men and women. But should these and many other painful incidents have passed you by unnoticed, I am fearful that you may learn of them with keener thoughts with the coming sleets and blasts of winter.

You say that "labor cannot afford to attack capital." Let me remind you that labor has no quarrel with capital, as such. It is merely the possessors of capital who refuse to accord to labor the recognition, the right, the justice which is the laborers' due, with whom we contend. . . .

Inquire from the thousands of women and children whose husbands or fathers were suffocated or crushed in the mines through the rapacious greed of stockholders clamoring for more dividends. Investigate the sweating dens of the large cities. Go to the mills, factories, through the country. Visit the modern tenement houses or hovels in which thousands of workers are compelled to eke out an existence. . . . Ascertain from employers whether the laborer is not regarded the same as a machine, thrown out as soon as all the work possible has been squeezed out of him.

Are you aware that all the legislation ever secured for the ventilation or safety of mines, factory or work-shop is the result of the efforts of organized labor? Do you know that the trade unions were the shield for the seven-year-old children . . . until they become somewhat older? And that the reformatory laws now on the statute books, protecting or defending . . . both sexes, young and old, from the fond care of the conquerors, were wrested from Congresses, legislatures and parliaments despite the Pullmans. . . .

By what right, sir, do you assume that the labor organizations do not conduct their affairs within lawful limits, or that they are a menace to the lawful institutions of the country? Is it because some thoughtless or overzealous member at a time of great excitement and smarting under a wrong may violate . . . a law or commit an improper act? Would you apply the same rule to the churches, the other moral agencies and organizations that you do to the organizations of labor? If you did, the greatest moral force of life to-day, the trade unions, would certainly stand out the clearest, brightest and purest. Because a certain class (for which you and a number of your colleagues on the bench seem to be the special pleaders) have a monopoly in their lines of trade, I submit that this is no good reason for their claim to have a monopoly on true patriotism or respect for the lawful institutions of the country.

Year by year man's liberties are trampled under foot at the bidding of corporations and trusts, rights are invaded and law perverted. In all ages wherever a tyrant has shown himself he has always found some willing judge to clothe that tyranny in the robes of legality, and modern capitalism has proven no exception to the rule.

You may not know that the labor movement as represented by the trades unions, stands for right, for justice, for liberty. You may not imagine that the issuance of an injunction depriving men of a legal as well as a natural right to protect themselves, their wives and little ones, must fail of its purpose. Repression or oppression never yet succeeded in crushing the truth or redressing a wrong.

In conclusion let me assure you that labor will organize and more compactly than ever and upon practical lines, and despite relentless antagonism, achieve for humanity a nobler manhood, a more beautiful womanhood and a happier childhood.

QUESTIONS FOR READING AND DISCUSSION

1. Why were labor unions "the greatest menace to this Government," according to Thompson? How did Gompers's arguments respond to such claims? How did Thompson and Gompers differ in their views of strikes?

2. In what ways did labor unions violate the rights of others, according to Thompson? What workers' rights and liberties did Thompson recognize?

3. How did Gompers and Thompson differ in their beliefs about the benefits and liabilities of competition? Why was government important to each of them?

4. How did Gompers respond to accusations that labor unions were treasonous? Did Gompers oppose capitalism and industrialization?

5. How did Thompson and Gompers view the future? How did they differ in their assumptions about a just society?

DOCUMENT 20–5

Emilio Aguinaldo Criticizes American Imperialism in the Philippines

Emilio Aguinaldo commanded Filipino forces that allied with the United States to erad-icate Spanish control of the Philippines in 1898, and he became the first president of the newly independent nation. But when the United States refused to recognize Philippine independence, Aguinaldo led his troops in a guerrilla war against American military intervention. More than 120,000 U.S. soldiers battled the guerrillas with ruthless tac-tics that included killing prisoners, burning civilian villages, and creating concentration camps. In 1899, Aguinaldo published a scathing critique, excerpted below, of America's imperialist effort to deny Philippine independence. Aguinaldo demanded that the United States recognize the humanity of Filipinos and live up to the heritage of the American Revolution.

Case against the United States, 1899

We Filipinos have all along believed that if the American nation at large knew exactly, as we do, what is daily happening in the Philippine Islands, they would rise en masse, and demand that this barbaric war should stop. There are other methods of securing sovereignty—the true and lasting sovereignty that has its foundation in the hearts of the people. . . . And, did America recognize this fact, she would cease to be the laughing stock of other civilized nations, as she became when she abandoned her traditions and set up a double standard of government—government by consent in America, government by force in the Philippine Islands. . . .

Politically speaking, we [in the Philippines] know that we are simply regarded as the means to an end. For the time being, we are crushed under the wheels of the modern political Juggernaut, but its wheels are not broad enough to crush us all. Perfidious Albion[1] is the prime mover in this dastardly business—she at one side of the lever, America at the other, and the fulcrum is the Philippines. England has set her heart on the Anglo-American alliance. . . . What she cannot obtain by

---

From A Filipino [Emilio Aguinaldo], "Aguinaldo's Case against the United States," *North American Review* 169 (September 1899), 425–32.

[1]**Albion**: Great Britain.

force, she intends to secure by stratagem. Unknown to the great majority of the American people, she has taken the American government into her confidence, and shown it "the glorious possibilities of the East." The temptation has proved too strong. . . . If America should win, all is well; England has her ally safely installed in the East, ready at her beck and call to oppose, hand in hand with her, the other powers in the dismemberment of the Orient. If America loses, she will be all the more solicitous to join in the Anglo-American alliance. The other powers stand by and see this political combination effected . . . and are deaf to the wail of the widows and the orphans, and to the cry of an oppressed race struggling to be free. . . .

You have been deceived all along the line. You have been greatly deceived in the personality of my countrymen. You went to the Philippines under the impression that their inhabitants were ignorant savages, whom Spain had kept in subjection at the bayonet's point. . . . We have been represented by your popular press as if we were Africans or Mohawk Indians. We smile, and deplore the want of ethnological knowledge on the part of our literary friends. We are none of these. We are simply Filipinos. You know us now in part: you will know us better, I hope, by and by. . . .

I will not deny that there are savages in the Philippine Islands, if you designate by that name those who lead a nomad life, who do not pay tribute or acknowledge sovereignty to any one save their chief. For, let it be remembered, Spain held these islands for three hundred years, but never conquered more than one-quarter of them, and that only superficially and chiefly by means of priest-craft. The Spaniards never professed to derive their just powers from the consent of those whom they attempted to govern. What they took by force, they lost by force at our hands; and you deceived yourselves when you bought a revolution for twenty million dollars, and entangled yourselves in international politics. . . . You imagined you had bought the Philippines and the Filipinos for this mess of pottage. Your imperialism led you, blind-fold, to purchase "sovereignty" from a third party who had no title to give you—a confidence trick, certainly, very transparent; a bad bargain, and one we have had sufficient perspicuity and education to see through.

In the struggle for liberty which we have ever waged, the education of the masses has been slow; but we are not, on that account, an uneducated people. . . . It is the fittest and the best of our race who have survived the vile oppression of the Spanish Government, on the one hand, and of their priests on the other; and, had it not been for their tyrannous "sovereignty" and their execrable colonial methods, we would have been, ere this time, a power in the East, as our neighbors, the Japanese, have become by their industry and their modern educational methods.

You repeat constantly the dictum that we cannot govern ourselves. . . . With equal reason, you might have said the same thing some fifty or sixty years ago of Japan; and, little over a hundred years ago, it was extremely questionable, when you, also, were rebels against the English Government, if you could govern yourselves. You obtained the opportunity, thanks to political combinations and generous assistance at the critical moment. You passed with credit through the trying period when you had to make a beginning of governing yourselves, and you eventually succeeded in establishing a government on a republican basis, which, theoretically, is as good a system of government as needs be, as it fulfils the just ideals and aspirations of the human race.

Now, the moral of all this obviously is: Give us the chance; treat us exactly as you demanded to be treated at the hands of England, when you rebelled against her autocratic methods. . . .

Now, here is an unique spectacle—the Filipinos fighting for liberty, the American people fighting them to give them liberty. The two peoples are fighting on parallel lines for the same object. We know that parallel lines never meet. Let us look back to discover the point at which the lines separated and the causes of the separation, so that we may estimate the possibility of one or the other or both being turned inwards so that they shall meet again.

You declared war with Spain for the sake of Humanity. You announced to the world that your programme was to set Cuba free, in conformity with your constitutional principles. One of your ablest officials gave it as his opinion that the Filipinos were far more competent to govern themselves than the Cuban people were. . . .

You entered into an alliance with our chiefs at Hong Kong and at Singapore, and you promised us your aid and protection in our attempt to form a government on the principles and after the model of the government of the United States. Thereupon you sent a powerful fleet to Manila and demolished the old Spanish hulks, striking terror into the hearts of the Spanish garrison in Manila. In combination with our forces, you compelled Spain to surrender, and you proclaimed that you held the city, port and bay of Manila until such time as you should determine what you meant by the word "control," as applied to the rest of the islands. By some mysterious process, heretofore unknown to civilized nations, you resolved "control" into "sovereignty," on the pretense that what is paid for is "possession," no matter what the quality of the title may be.

Let us go into details. You went to Manila under a distinct understanding with us, fully recognized by Admiral [George] Dewey, that your object and ours was a common one. We were your accepted allies; we assisted you at all points. We besieged Manila, and we prevented the Spaniards from leaving the fortified town. We captured all the provinces of Luzon. We received arms from you. Our chiefs were in constant touch with your naval authorities. Your consuls vied with each other in their efforts to arrange matters according to the promise made to us by your officials. We hailed you as the long-prayed-for Messiah.

Joy abounded in every heart, and all went well . . . until . . . the Government at Washington . . . commenc[ed] by ignoring all promises that had been made and end[ed] by ignoring the Philippine people, their personality and rights, and treating them as a common enemy.

Never has a greater mistake been made in the entire history of the nations. Here you had a people who placed themselves at your feet, who welcomed you as their savior, who wished you to govern them and protect them. In combination with the genius of our countrymen and their local knowledge, you would have transformed the Philippine Islands from a land of despotism, of vicious governmental methods and priestcraft, into an enlightened republic, with America as its guide—a happy and contented people—and that in the short space of a few months, without the sacrifice of a single American life. The means were there, and it only required the magic of a master-hand to guide them, as your ships were guided into Manila Bay. . . .

You have been deceived from the beginning, and deception is the order of the day. You continue to deceive yourselves by the thought that once the military power is established in the Philippines, the rest is a matter for politicians.

Verily you are falling into the pit you have dug for yourselves. Your officials and generals have broken their promises with our countrymen over and over again. Your atrocious cruelties are equalled only by those of Spain.

You take into your confidence the odious reptiles of Spanish priestcraft. . . . In the face of the world you emblazon humanity and Liberty upon your standard, while you cast your political constitution to the winds and attempt to trample down and exterminate a brave people whose only crime is that they are fighting for their liberty. You ask my countrymen to believe in you, to trust you, and you assure them that, if they do so, all will be well. . . .

You will never conquer the Philippine Islands by force alone. How many soldiers in excess of the regular army do you mean to leave in every town, in every province? How many will the climate claim as its victims, apart from those who may fall in actual warfare? What do the American people, who have thousands of acres yet untilled, want with the Philippines? Have you figured up the cost?

The conclusion of the whole matter is this: You were duped at the beginning. You took a wrong step, and you had not sufficient moral courage to retrace it. You must begin by conquering the hearts of the Philippine people. Be absolutely just, and you can lead them with a silken cord where chains of steel will not drag them. . . . But this question of sovereignty — why, such a transparent farce has never before been flouted before an intelligent people and the world in general. Can you wonder our people mistrust . . . ? They do not even regard you as being serious — a nation which professes to derive its just power of government from the consent of the governed.

"Lay down your arms," you say. Did you lay down your arms when you, too, were rebels, and the English under good King George demanded your submission? How in the name of all that is serious do you demand that we shall do what you, being rebels, refused to do?

Therefore, we Filipinos say: . . . try . . . methods of fair dealing, make our countrymen believe that you are sincere, and be sincere and just in your dealings with them. Suspend the order for these rabble volunteers, the scum of your country, whom you propose to send across the sea to die of the effect of the climate, and you will find you can do more in a month than you will do by force in twenty years. Your scheme of military occupation has been a miserable failure. You have gained practically nothing. . . . Our forces are manufacturing thousands of cartridges and other improved means to continue the struggle, and it will continue until you are convinced of your error.

Our friend, Admiral Dewey . . . caught the genius of the Philippine people, and if he had been left alone many valuable lives would have been spared and many millions of treasure saved. Be convinced, the Philippines are for the Filipinos. We are a virile race. We have never assimilated with our former oppressors, and we are not likely to assimilate with you.

QUESTIONS FOR READING AND DISCUSSION

1. What did Aguinaldo mean by asserting that the United States had "set up a double standard of government"? What did he see as America's goal in the Philippines?

2. How did American perceptions of Filipinos as "ignorant savages" influence U.S. policy? How did those perceptions influence American "imperialism," according to Aguinaldo?

3. How did American policy in the Philippines compare to Spanish rule, according to Aguinaldo? What did he mean by the "unique spectacle" of "Filipinos fighting for liberty, [and] the American people fighting them to give them liberty"? Why did the United States ally with Aguinaldo, then turn against him?

4. Why did Americans ask Filipinos to "Lay down your arms"? What was the significance of "sovereignty"?

5. Aguinaldo portrayed American war against Filipinos as a violation of the nation's heritage. To what extent do you think that argument was valid? What evidence do you find most persuasive?

COMPARATIVE QUESTIONS

1. To what extent did Mary Lease's concepts of justice, freedom, and equality agree with those of people in the Cherokee Strip land rush? Of Samuel Gompers and Emilio Aguinaldo?

2. How did N. F. Thompson's concepts of justice, freedom, and democracy compare with the ideals of American policy in the Philippines?

3. In what ways did the experiences of Filipinos compare with those of black Republicans in Wilmington and the Cherokee in the Oklahoma land rush? Does the comparison suggest a significant relationship between American racial oppression and imperialism?

4. Judging from the documents in this chapter, what ideals and values united Americans in the 1890s under the deep fissures of class, race, and region?

21 Progressive Reform

1890–1916

Progressives sought to reunite Americans, to overcome the many bitter divisions that separated rich and poor, employers and employees, native citizens and immigrants, adherents of one faith and those of all others. The settlement house movement reflected the desire to bridge divisions by bringing the ideas and energies of middle-class Americans to poor immigrant neighborhoods. Many Americans did not share progressives' aspiration to find some middle ground between conflicting groups. Working people, suffragists, and black Americans feared that the middle ground would be nothing more than the continuation of a status quo they found unacceptable. The following documents illustrate the attitudes and experiences that drew some people toward progressive reforms and caused others to seek change by insisting on the recognition of fundamental differences among Americans.

DOCUMENT 21–1

Jane Addams on Settlement Houses

Progressives engaged in many reform activities besides electoral politics. Settlement houses were among the most important centers of progressive reform. Jane Addams, founder of Chicago's Hull House, explained her motives in a paper she presented in 1892 to a group of women considering settlement work. In "The Subjective Necessity for Social Settlements," Addams revealed attitudes and perceptions that motivated many other progressive reformers.

The Subjective Necessity for Social Settlements, 1892

This paper is an attempt to analyze the motives which underlie a movement based, not only upon conviction, but upon genuine emotion, wherever educated young people are seeking an outlet for that sentiment of universal brotherhood,

---

From Jane Addams, *Twenty Years at Hull House* (New York: Macmillan, 1910).

which the best spirit of our times is forcing from an emotion into a motive. These young people accomplish little toward the solution of this social problem, and bear the brunt of being cultivated into unnourished, oversensitive lives. They have been shut off from the common labor by which they live which is a great source of moral and physical health. They feel a fatal want of harmony between their theory and their lives, a lack of coordination between thought and action. I think it is hard for us to realize how seriously many of them are taking to the notion of human brotherhood, how eagerly they long to give tangible expression to the democratic ideal. These young men and women, longing to socialize their democracy, are animated by certain hopes which may be thus loosely formulated; that if in a democratic country nothing can be permanently achieved save through the masses of the people, it will be impossible to establish a higher political life than the people themselves crave; that it is difficult to see how the notion of a higher civic life can be fostered save through common intercourse; that the blessings which we associate with a life of refinement and cultivation can be made universal and must be made universal if they are to be permanent; that the good we secure for ourselves is precarious and uncertain, is floating in mid-air, until it is secured for all of us and incorporated into our common life. It is easier to state these hopes than to formulate the line of motives, which I believe to constitute the trend of the subjective pressure toward the Settlement. . . .

You may remember the forlorn feeling which occasionally seizes you when you arrive early in the morning a stranger in a great city: the stream of laboring people goes past you as you gaze through the plate-glass window of your hotel; you see hard workingmen lifting great burdens; you hear the driving and jostling of huge carts and your heart sinks with a sudden sense of futility. The door opens behind you and you turn to the man who brings you in your breakfast with a quick sense of human fellowship. You find yourself praying that you may never lose your hold on it all. . . . You turn helplessly to the waiter and feel that it would be almost grotesque to claim from him the sympathy you crave because civilization has placed you apart, but you resent your position with a sudden sense of snobbery. . . .

I have seen young girls suffer and grow sensibly lowered in vitality in the first years after they leave school. In our attempt . . . to give a girl pleasure and freedom from care we succeed, for the most part, in making her pitifully miserable. She finds "life" so different from what she expected it to be. She is besotted with innocent little ambitions, and does not understand this apparent waste of herself, this elaborate preparation, if no work is provided for her. There is a heritage of noble obligation which young people accept and long to perpetuate. The desire for action, the wish to right wrong and alleviate suffering haunts them daily. Society smiles at it indulgently instead of making it of value to itself. . . .

[F]rom babyhood the altruistic tendencies of these daughters are persistently cultivated. They are taught to be self-forgetting and self-sacrificing, to consider the good of the whole before the good of the ego. But when all this information and culture show results, when the daughter comes back from college and begins to recognize her social claim to the "submerged tenth," and to evince a disposition to fulfill it, the family claim is strenuously asserted; she is told that she is unjustified, ill-advised in her efforts. . . .

We have in America a fast-growing number of cultivated young people who have no recognized outlet for their active faculties. They hear constantly of the great social maladjustment, but no way is provided for them to change it, and their uselessness hangs about them heavily. . . . These young people have had advantages of college, of European travel, and of economic study, but they are sustaining this shock of inaction. They have pet phrases, and they tell you that the things that make us all alike are stronger than the things that make us different. They say that all men are united by needs and sympathies far more permanent and radical than anything that temporarily divides them and sets them in opposition to each other. . . .

This young life, so sincere in its emotion and good phrase and yet so undirected, seems to me as pitiful as the other great mass of destitute lives. One is supplementary to the other, and some method of communication can surely be devised. . . . Our young people feel nervously the need of putting theory into action, and respond quickly to the Settlement form of activity.

Other motives which I believe make toward the Settlement are the result of a certain renaissance going forward in Christianity. The impulse to share the lives of the poor, the desire to make social service, irrespective of propaganda, express the spirit of Christ, is as old as Christianity itself. . . .

I believe that there is a distinct turning among many young men and women toward this simple acceptance of Christ's message. They resent the assumption that Christianity is a set of ideas which belong to the religious consciousness, whatever that may be. They insist that it cannot be proclaimed and instituted apart from the social life of the community and that it must seek a simple and natural expression in the social organism itself. The Settlement movement is only one manifestation of that wider humanitarian movement which throughout Christendom . . . is endeavoring to embody itself, not in a sect, but in society itself.

I believe that this turning, this renaissance of the early Christian humanitarianism, is going on in America, in Chicago, if you please, without leaders who write or philosophize, without much speaking, but with a bent to express in social service and in terms of action the spirit of Christ. Certain it is that spiritual force is found in the Settlement movement, and it is also true that this force must be evoked and must be called into play before the success of any Settlement is assured. There must be the overmastering belief that all that is noblest in life is common to men as men, in order to accentuate the likenesses and ignore the differences which are found among the people whom the Settlement constantly brings into juxtaposition. . . .

In a thousand voices singing the Hallelujah Chorus in Handel's Messiah, it is possible to distinguish the leading voices, but the differences of training and cultivation between them and the voices of the chorus, are lost in the unity of purpose and in the fact that they are all human voices lifted by a high motive. This is a weak illustration of what a Settlement attempts to do. It aims, in a measure, to develop whatever of social life its neighborhood may afford, to focus and give form to that life, to bring to bear upon it the results of cultivation and training; but it receives in exchange for the music of isolated voices the volume and strength of the chorus. It is quite impossible for me to say in what proportion or degree the subjective necessity which led to the opening of Hull-House combined the three trends: first, the desire to interpret democracy in social terms; secondly, the impulse beating at the very source of our lives, urging us to aid in the race progress; and, thirdly, the Christian movement toward humanitarianism. . . .

The Settlement, then, is an experimental effort to aid in the solution of the social and industrial problems which are engendered by the modern conditions of life in a great city. It insists that these problems are not confined to any one portion of a city. It is an attempt to relieve, at the same time, the overaccumulation at one end of society and the destitution at the other; but it assumes that this overaccumulation and destitution is most sorely felt in the things that pertain to social and educational privileges. From its very nature it can stand for no political or social propaganda. . . . The one thing to be dreaded in the Settlement is that it lose its flexibility, its power of quick adaptation, its readiness to change its methods as its environment may demand. It must be open to conviction and must have a deep and abiding sense of tolerance. It must be hospitable and ready for experiment. It should demand from its residents a scientific patience in the accumulation of facts and the steady holding of their sympathies as one of the best instruments for that accumulation. It must be grounded in a philosophy whose foundation is on the solidarity of the human race, a philosophy which will not waver when the race happens to be represented by a drunken woman or an idiot boy. Its residents must be emptied of all conceit of opinion and all self-assertion, and ready to arouse and interpret the public opinion of their neighborhood. They must be content to live quietly side by side with their neighbors, until they grow into a sense of relationship and mutual interests. Their neighbors are held apart by differences of race and language which the residents can more easily overcome. They are bound to see the needs of their neighborhood as a whole, to furnish data for legislation, and to use their influence to secure it. In short, residents are pledged to devote themselves to the duties of good citizenship and to the arousing of the social energies which too largely lie dormant in every neighborhood given over to industrialism. . . .

I may be forgiven the reminder that the best speculative philosophy sets forth the solidarity of the human race; that the highest moralists have taught that without the advance and improvement of the whole, no man can hope for any lasting improvement in his own moral or material individual condition; and that the subjective necessity for Social Settlements is therefore identical with that necessity, which urges us on toward social and individual salvation.

QUESTIONS FOR READING AND DISCUSSION

1. According to Addams, what was subjective about the necessity for social settlements? What did she see as major problems in her society?

2. In what ways did Addams believe settlements would make "universal" those "blessings which we associate with a life of refinement and cultivation"? What differences did she notice among people? What did she identify as the unity underlying those differences?

3. To what extent did Addams think social settlements would serve the interests of educated middle-class women, as well as immigrants? How might immigrants have described their own and Addams's interests in settlement houses?

4. To what degree did settlement houses exemplify progressive approaches to the solution of social and industrial problems?

DOCUMENT 21–2

Pietro Learning to Write

Progressives firmly believed education made social progress possible. By learning English, for example, immigrants could hope to better themselves and their families and take full advantage of opportunities in America. Jacob Riis took this photo of Pietro, *a thirteen-year-old Italian boy in New York City who was trying to learn to write English. Pietro's father (at the table) told Riis, "Pietro he good boy; make Englis', Englis'." Pietro's father immigrated from Italy with his wife and five children. He worked as a laborer, earning $9 a week at best. He paid that much each month to rent the room pictured here and a small alcove for sleeping. A year earlier Pietro had learned the alphabet and stopped attending school in order to work shining shoes at a saloon. Crossing the street to his new job he was run over by a street car, crippling him and landing him in the hospital for months. Since the accident left him unable to shine shoes, he was trying to learn to write English in order to find a job he could do. Riis wrote that Pietro and his father were "dead set on becoming American citizens, and tremendously impressed with the privileges of citizenship."*

Jacob Riis
Pietro Learning to Write, 1892

The Museum of the City of New York/Art Resource, NY

Questions for Reading and Discussion

1. What evidence in the photo depicts Pietro's injury? How did his injury influence his desire to learn to write English?

2. How does the photo suggest Pietro struggled to write English?

3. Does Pietro's father encourage him to learn to write English, according to the photo? If so, how?

4. Why would it be important to Pietro's family that he learn to write English?

5. How does the photo reflect the aspirations of many other immigrants?

DOCUMENT 21–3

A Sociologist Studies
Working-Class Saloons in Chicago

Progressive temperance reformers believed that saloons seduced customers into lives of drunkenness, crime, and debauchery. Many progressives also believed social problems such as saloons should be studied scientifically. Sociologist Royal Melendy investigated saloons in a working-class neighborhood of Chicago as part of an "Ethical Subcommittee" set up to study "the liquor problem," as he put it. Venturing out from a progressive social settlement house in an industrial district of the city, Melendy discovered that saloons met major needs of working people. His study, excerpted below, revealed the gap between the realities of working-class life and the assumptions and preconceptions of many progressives.

Royal Melendy
Ethical Substitutes for the Saloon, 1900

In considering the subject "Ethical Substitutes for the Saloon," . . . [w]e must try to ascertain the secret of its hold upon our civilization. . . .

The popular conception of the saloon as a "place where men and women revel in drunkenness and shame," or "where the sotted beasts gather nightly at the bar," is due to exaggerated pictures, drawn by temperance lecturers and evangelists, intended to excite the imagination with a view to arousing public sentiment. I am not charging them with intended falsehood, but with placing in combination things which never so exist in real life; with blending into one picture hideous incidents taken here and there from the lives of those whom the saloon has wrecked; with portraying vividly the dark side of saloon life and calling this picture "the saloon." . . .

The term "saloon" is too general to admit of concise definition. It is an institution grown up among the people, not only in answer to their demand for its wares, but to their demand for certain necessities and conveniences, which it supplies, either alone or better than any other agency. It is a part of the neighborhood, which must change with the neighborhood; it fulfills in it the social functions which unfortunately have been left to it to exercise. With keen insight into human nature and into the wants of the people, it anticipates all other agencies in supplying them, and thus claims its right to existence. In some sections of the city it has the appearance of accomplishing more for the laboring classes from business interests than we from philanthropic motives. . . .

Hedged in on every side by law, opposed by every contrivance the mind of man could invent, the saloon persists in existing and flourishing. . . . The saloon in Chicago is restricted by every kind of law, yet it sells liquor to minors, keeps open door all night and Sundays, from January 1 to January 1. . . .

When the poor, underpaid, and unskilled laborer returns from his day's work, go with him, if you will, into the room or rooms he calls "home." Eat with

From Royal Melendy, "The Saloon in Chicago," *The American Journal of Sociology* 6 (November 1900), 289–306.

him there, in the midst of those squalid surroundings and to the music of crying children, a scanty, poorly cooked meal served by an unkempt wife. Ask yourself if this is just the place where he would want to spend his evenings, night after night. . . . Is there no escape from the inevitable despair that must come to him whose long hours of heavy physical labor preclude any mental enjoyment, if his few leisure hours are to be spent in the wretched surroundings of a home, or, worse yet, of the ordinary cheap lodging-house, either of which must constantly remind him of his poverty? Are there not places in the neighborhood where the surroundings will be more congenial; where his mental, yes, his moral, nature will have a better chance for development? Are there not some in the neighborhood who have recognized and sought to satisfy the social cravings of these men, which the home at best does not wholly satisfy?

Yes, business interests have occupied this field. With a shrewd foresight, partially due to the fierce competition between the great brewing companies, they have seen and met these needs. The following table, made by a careful investigation of each of the 163 saloons of the seventeenth ward—a fairly representative ward of the working people—shows some of the attractions offered by these saloons:

Number of saloons				163
Number offering free lunches				111
"	"		business lunches	24
"	supplied with tables			147
"	"	"	papers	139
"	"	"	music	8
"	"	"	billiard tables	44
"	"	"	stalls	56
"	"	"	dance halls	6
"	allowing gambling			3

In the statement, now current among those who have studied the saloon "at first hand," that it is the workingman's club, lies the secret of its hold upon the vast working and voting populace of Chicago. That same instinct in man which leads those of the more resourceful classes to form such clubs as the Union League Club . . . which leads the college man into the fraternity, leads the laboring men into the clubs furnished them by the saloonkeeper, not from philanthropic motives, but because of shrewd business foresight. The term "club" applies; for, though unorganized, each saloon has about the same constituency night after night. Its character is determined by the character of the men who, having something in common, make the saloon their rendezvous. Their common ground may be their nationality, as the name "Italian Headquarters" implies; or it may be their occupation, as indicated by the names "Mechanics' Exchange," "Milkman's Exchange," etc.; or, if their political affiliations are their common ground, there are the "Democratic Headquarters of the Eighteenth Ward," etc. . . . As you step in, you find a few men standing at the bar, a few drinking, and farther back men are seated about the tables, reading, playing cards, eating, and discussing, over a glass of beer, subjects varying from the political and sociological problems of the day to the sporting news and the lighter chat of the immediate neighborhood. Untrammeled by rules and restrictions, it surpasses in spirit the organized club. That general atmosphere of freedom, that spirit of democracy, which men crave, is here realized; that men seek it and that the saloon tries to cultivate it is blazoned forth in such titles as "The Freedom," "The Social," "The Club," etc. Here men "shake out their hearts together." . . .

In many of these discussions, to which I have listened and in which I have joined, there has been revealed a deeper insight into the real cause of present evils than is often manifested from lecture platforms, but their remedies are wide of the mark, each bringing forward a theory which is the panacea for all social ills. The names of Karl Marx and leaders of political and social thought are often heard here. This is the workingman's school. He is both scholar and teacher. The problems of national welfare are solved here. Many as patriotic men as our country produces learn here their lessons in patriotism and brotherhood. Here the masses receive their lessons in civil government, learning less of our ideals, but more of the practical workings than the public schools teach. It is the most cosmopolitan institution in the most cosmopolitan of cities. One saloon advertises its cosmopolitanism by this title, "Everybody's Exchange." Men of all nationalities meet and mingle, and by the interchange of views and opinions their own are modified. Nothing short of travel could exert so broadening an influence upon these men. It does much to assimilate the heterogeneous crowds that are constantly pouring into our city from foreign shores. But here, too, they learn their lessons in corruption and vice. It is their school for good and evil. . . .

The saloon is, in short, the clearing-house for the common intelligence—the social and intellectual center of the neighborhood. . . .

For the large floating population of these districts, and for the thousands of men whose only home is in the street or the cheap lodging-house, where they are herded together like cattle, the saloon is practically the basis of food supply. [Our study shows that] 68 per cent. furnish free lunches, and 15 per cent. business lunches. On the free-lunch counters are dishes containing bread, several kinds of meats, vegetables, cheeses, etc., to which the men freely help themselves. Red-hots [frankfurters], clams, and egg sandwiches are dispensed with equal freedom to those who drink and to those who do not. . . .

That the saloons are able to put out such an abundance, and of such variety and quality, is due to the competition of the large brewing companies. These companies own a very large number of the saloons in Chicago. Thus the cost of not only the beer, but the meat, bread, and vegetables, bought in vast quantities, is greatly reduced. Only a portion of those who drink patronize the lunch counter. . . . I believe it is true that all the charity organizations in Chicago combined are feeding fewer people than the saloons. No questions are asked about the "deserving poor;" no "work test" is applied; and again and again relief is given in the shape of money, "loaned expecting no return."

Another function of the Charity Organization Society the saloon has taken unto itself and exercises more or less perfectly: the laboring man out of employment knows that in some saloon he is likely to find, not only temporary relief, but assistance in finding work. That these saloons pose as labor bureaus is evidenced by the names placed above their doors. The significance of these names is this: Men of the same trade, having common interests, make the saloon that represents their interests their rendezvous. To the "Stonecutters' Exchange," for example, men seeking stonecutters often apply. But information concerning positions is dependent more upon that gathered by the men themselves and made common property. Many a man has been "put on his feet" by just this kind of help, nor does he feel that he is accepting charity, but that he is as likely to give as to receive.

He is asked neither his age nor his pedigree. His past history is not desired as long as he is in need now. . . . Grateful is he to the saloon that was his "friend in need;" bitter toward those who, without offering anything better, propose to take from him the only institution that has befriended him.

Scattered throughout the city, within easy reach of any neighborhood, are saloons offering a form of entertainment to the people not unlike the cheap vaudeville. Passing back of the screen, we enter a large room filled with tables and chairs; at the end of the room is a stage. While men and women sit around these tables, drinking beer and smoking, the painted, bawdy girls entertain them with the latest popular songs and the skirt dance. The regular vaudeville bill, including the comic man, acrobatic feats, cake-walks, etc., is presented. The character of the entertainment is but a reflection of the character of the neighborhood. In some communities no obscene word is uttered, and but little that is suggestive of evil is presented. It affords an opportunity for the hard-worked men and women to escape from their stuffy homes and thoughts of poverty into a clean, well-lighted room, where with their families they can enjoy an evening of pleasure. . . . Patriotic songs are never missing, and I have heard them join heartily in the chorus. Cheer after cheer greets the names of our heroes, as they appear in the songs of the girls. The sense of the masses on the Cuban war policy could easily be determined by their applause and hisses at the saloon vaudevilles. . . . Then too prostitutes often come here and mingle with the crowd. . . .

While it is true that a vast army of the laboring men and boys of Chicago find the saloon the best place in their neighborhood for the development of their social, intellectual, and physical natures, they find there also things which appeal to their lower natures. . . .

Where is the respectable young woman, who is but one member of a large family, all living, or rather existing, in a single room which serves as kitchen, dining-room, parlor, and bedroom for the entire family, to receive her young men friends? Is it strange that she takes advantage of these [saloons]? Here her father goes; her mother and brothers are often there. They come here on cold nights to save fuel and light. Here, when a little tot, she used to come for the pitcher of beer; here, barefooted and dirty, she would run to hear the music of the German band; if she were pretty and could sing, many a bright ribbon did she buy with the money earned here. No, they are not all directly evil places, but the temptation is tremendous. How can a child, brought up in such a locality, forced to receive from the saloon even the common necessities and conveniences of life, grow up into noble and beautiful womanhood?

QUESTIONS FOR READING AND DISCUSSION

1. By studying "Ethical Substitutes for the Saloon," what did Melendy discover about who patronized saloons and why? To what degree did Melendy discover that saloons were ethical substitutes for other institutions?

2. How did saloons function as "the social and intellectual center of the neighborhood"? How did patrons of saloons learn "more of the practical workings" of government "than the public schools teach"? What political influence did saloons have?

3. Why did Melendy liken saloons to "the Charity Organization Society"? What motivated the "charity" of saloons? What part did "business interests" play in saloons?

4. Why did Melendy consider saloons "the most cosmopolitan institution in the most cosmopolitan of cities"? Who frequented saloons and why? Were saloons more dangerous to young women than to young men? Why or why not?

5. How did Melendy account for the conventional view of saloons as dens of iniquity, drunkenness, and vice? How might a progressive temperance reformer respond to Melendy's report?

DOCUMENT 21–4

Marie Jenney Howe Parodies the Opposition to Women's Suffrage

Women's rights activists had struggled for decades to obtain the right to vote along with full and equal civil rights as citizens. While suffragists had won victories in most western states and some local communities by 1910, they continued to confront stubborn opposition from legislatures, most men, and many women. Marie Jenney Howe, a member of the recently formed National Woman Suffrage Association and a progressive activist, dramatized the contradictions and assumptions of suffrage opponents in her Anti-Suffrage Monologue, *excerpted below. Howe ridiculed anti-suffrage arguments in this parody of the views of her adversaries. As you read, keep in mind that Howe—a strong advocate of women's suffrage—was imitating (or parodying) ideas and convictions she believed were widely shared by opponents of suffrage.*

An Anti-Suffrage Monologue, 1913

Woman suffrage is the reform against nature. Look at these [pro-suffrage] ladies sitting on the platform. Observe their physical inability, their mental disability, their spiritual instability and general debility! Could they walk up to the ballot box, mark a ballot, and drop it in? Obviously not. Let us grant for the sake of argument that they could mark a ballot. But could they drop it in? Ah, no. All nature is against it. The laws of man cry out against it. The voice of God cries out against it—and so do I.

Enfranchisement is what makes man man. Disfranchisement is what makes woman woman. If women were enfranchised every man would be just like every woman and every woman would be just like every man. There would be no difference between them. And don't you think this would rob life of just a little of its poetry and romance?

Man must remain man. Woman must remain woman. If man goes over and tries to be like woman, if woman goes over and tries to be like man, it will become so very confusing and so difficult to explain to our children. . . .

I know you begin to see how strongly I *feel* on this subject, but I have some reasons as well. These reasons are based on logic. Of course, I am not logical. I am a creature of impulse, instinct, and intuition—and I glory in it. But I know that these reasons are based on logic because I have culled them from the men whom it is my privilege to know.

From Marie Jenney Howe, *An Anti-Suffrage Monologue* (New York: National American Woman Suffrage Association, 1913).

My first argument against suffrage is that the women would not use it if they had it. You couldn't drive them to the polls. My second argument is, if the women were enfranchised they would neglect their homes, desert their families, and spend all their time at the polls. You may tell me that the polls are only open once a year. But I know women. They are creatures of habit. If you let them go to the polls once a year, they will hang round the polls all the rest of the time.

I have arranged these arguments in couplets. They go together in such a way that if you don't like one you can take the other. This is my second anti-suffrage couplet. If the women were enfranchised they would vote exactly as their husbands do and only double the existing vote. Do you like that argument? If not, take this one. If the women were enfranchised they would vote against their own husbands, thus creating dissension, family quarrels, and divorce.

My third anti-suffrage couplet is—women are angels. Many men call me an angel and I have a strong instinct which tells me it is true; that is why I am an anti, because "I want to be an angel and with the angels stand." And if you don't like that argument take this one. Women are depraved. They would introduce into politics a vicious element which would ruin our national life.

Fourth anti-suffrage couplet: women cannot understand politics. Therefore there would be no use in giving women political power, because they would not know what to do with it. On the other hand, if the women were enfranchised, they would mount rapidly into power, take all the offices from all the men, and soon we would have women governors of all our states and dozens of women acting as President of the United States.

Fifth anti-suffrage couplet: women cannot band together. They are incapable of organization. No two women can even be friends. Women are cats. On the other hand, if women were enfranchised, we would have all the women banded together on one side and all the men banded together on the other side, and there would follow a sex war which might end in bloody revolution.

Just one more of my little couplets: the ballot is greatly over-estimated. It has never done anything for anybody. Lots of men tell me this. And the corresponding argument is—the ballot is what makes man man. It is what gives him all his dignity and all of his superiority to women. Therefore if we allow women to share this privilege, how could a woman look up to her own husband? Why, there would be nothing to look up to.

I have talked to many woman suffragists and I find them very unreasonable. I say to them: "Here I am, convince me." I ask for proof. Then they proceed to tell me of Australia and Colorado and other places where women have passed excellent laws to improve the condition of working women and children. But I say, "What of it?" These are facts. I don't care about facts. I ask for proof.

Then they quote the eight million women of the United States who are now supporting themselves, and the twenty-five thousand married women in the City of New York who are self-supporting. But I say again, what of it? These are statistics. I don't believe in statistics. Facts and statistics are things which no truly womanly woman would ever use.

I wish to prove anti-suffrage in a womanly way—that is, by personal example. This is my method of persuasion. Once I saw a woman driving a horse, and the horse ran away with her. Isn't that just like a woman? Once I read in the newspapers about a woman whose house caught on fire, and she threw the children out of the window and carried the pillows downstairs. Does that show political acumen, or does it not? Besides, look at the hats that women wear!

And have you ever known a successful woman governor of a state? Or have you ever known a really truly successful woman president of the United States? Well, if they could they would, wouldn't they? Then, if they haven't, doesn't that show they couldn't? As for the militant suffragettes, they are all hyenas in petticoats. Now do you want to be a hyena and wear petticoats?

Now, I think I have proved anti-suffrage; and I have done it in a womanly way — that is, without stooping to the use of a single fact or argument or a single statistic.

I am the prophet of a new idea. No one has ever thought of it or heard of it before. I well remember when this great idea first came to me. It waked me in the middle of the night with a shock that gave me a headache. This is it: woman's place is in the home. Is it not beautiful as it is new, new as it is true? Take this idea away with you. You will find it very helpful in your daily lives. You may not grasp it just at first, but you will gradually grow into understanding of it.

I know the suffragists reply that all our activities have been taken out of the home. The baking, the washing, the weaving, the spinning are all long since taken out of the home. But I say, all the more reason that something should stay in the home. Let it be woman. Besides, think of the great modern invention, the telephone. That has been put into the home. Let woman stay at home and answer the telephone.

We antis have so much imagination! Sometimes it seems to us that we can hear the little babies in the slums crying to us. We can see the children in factories and mines reaching out their little hands to us, and the working women in the sweated industries, the underpaid, underfed women, reaching out their arms to us — all, all crying as with one voice, "Save us, save us, from Woman Suffrage." Well may they make this appeal to us, for who knows what woman suffrage might not do for such as these. It might even alter the conditions under which they live.

We antis do not believe that any conditions should be altered. We want everything to remain just as it is. All is for the best. Whatever is, is right. If misery is in the world, God has put it there; let it remain. If this misery presses harder on some women than others, it is because they need discipline. Now, I have always been comfortable and well cared for. But then I never needed discipline. Of course I am only a weak, ignorant woman. But there is one thing I do understand from the ground up, and that is the divine intention toward woman. I *know* that the divine intention toward woman is, let her remain at home. . . .

Let me speak one word to my sister women who are here to-day. Women, we don't need to vote in order to get our own way. Don't misunderstand me. Of course I want you to get your own way. That's what we're here for. But do it indirectly. If you want a thing, tease. If that doesn't work, nag. If that doesn't do, cry — crying always brings them around. Get what you want. Pound pillows. Make a scene. Make home a hell on earth, but do it in a womanly way. That is so much more dignified and refined than walking up to a ballot box and dropping in a piece of paper. Can't you see that?

Let us consider for a moment the effect of woman's enfranchisement on man. I think some one ought to consider the men. What makes husbands faithful and loving? The ballot, and the monopoly of that privilege. If women vote, what will become of men? They will all slink off drunk and disorderly. We antis understand men. If women were enfranchised, men would revert to their natural instincts such as regicide, matricide, patricide and race-suicide. . . .

It comes down to this. Some one must wash the dishes. Now, would you expect man, man made in the image of God, to roll up his sleeves and wash the dishes? Why, it would be blasphemy. I know that I am but a rib [woman] and so I wash the dishes. Or I hire another rib to do it for me, which amounts to the same thing.

Let us consider the argument from the standpoint of religion. The Bible says, "Let the women keep silent in the churches." Paul says, "Let them keep their hats on for fear of the angels." My minister says, "Wives, obey your husbands." And my husband says that woman suffrage would rob the rose of its fragrance and the peach of its bloom. I think that is so sweet. . . .

I don't want to be misunderstood in my reference to woman's inability to vote. Of course she could get herself to the polls and lift a piece of paper. I don't doubt that. What I refer to is the pressure on the brain, the effect of this mental strain on woman's delicate nervous organization and on her highly wrought sensitive nature. Have you ever pictured to yourself Election Day with women voting? Can you imagine how women, having undergone this terrible ordeal, with their delicate systems all upset, will come out of the voting booths and be led away by policemen, and put into ambulances, while they are fainting and weeping, half laughing, half crying, and having fits upon the public highway? Don't you think that if a woman is going to have a fit, it is far better for her to have it in the privacy of her own home?

And how shall I picture to you the terrors of the day after election? Divorce and death will rage unchecked, crime and contagious disease will stalk unbridled through the land. Oh, friends, on this subject I feel—I feel, so strongly that I can—not think!

QUESTIONS FOR READING AND DISCUSSION

1. According to Howe, why did anti-suffragists believe "all nature is against" women's suffrage? Why were suffragists "hyenas in petticoats"?

2. Why did Howe arrange anti-suffrage arguments in "couplets"? What points do her couplets make?

3. What arguments, illuminated in Howe's parody, "prove anti-suffrage in a womanly way"? Why should women be "saved" from women's suffrage?

4. Why did anti-suffragists believe, according to Howe, that "Whatever is, is right"?

5. By ridiculing the contradictions and assumptions of anti-suffrage arguments, what pro-suffrage arguments did Howe suggest?

DOCUMENT 21–5

Booker T. Washington on Racial Accommodation

Most progressives showed little interest in changing race relations. Many in fact actively supported white supremacy. Beset by the dilemmas of sharecropping, Jim Crow laws, disfranchisement, poverty, illiteracy, and the constant threat of violence, black southerners had few champions among progressives. Booker T. Washington, perhaps the era's most celebrated black leader, spelled out a plan of racial accommodation as a path toward progress. In an address to white business leaders gathered at the Cotton States and International Exposition in Atlanta in 1895, Washington outlined ideas that remained at the center of debate among black Americans for decades.

The Atlanta Exposition Address, 1895

Mr. President and Gentlemen of the Board of Directors and Citizens,

One-third of the population of the South is of the Negro race. No enterprise seeking the material, civil, or moral welfare of this section can disregard this element of our population and reach the highest success. I but convey to you . . . the sentiment of the masses of my race when I say that in no way have the value and manhood of the American Negro been more fittingly and generously recognized than by the managers of this magnificent Exposition at every stage of its progress. It is a recognition that will do more to cement the friendship of the two races than any occurrence since the dawn of our freedom.

Not only this, but the opportunity here afforded will awaken among us a new era of industrial progress. Ignorant and inexperienced, it is not strange that in the first years of our new life we began at the top instead of at the bottom; that a seat in Congress or the state legislature was more sought than real estate or industrial skill; that the political convention or stump speaking had more attractions than starting a dairy farm or truck garden.

A ship lost at sea for many days suddenly sighted a friendly vessel. From the mast of the unfortunate vessel was seen a signal, "Water, water; we die of thirst!" The answer from the friendly vessel at once came back, "Cast down your bucket where you are." . . . The captain of the distressed vessel, at last heeding the injunction, cast down his bucket, and it came up full of fresh, sparkling water from the mouth of the Amazon River. To those of my race who depend on bettering their condition in a foreign land or who underestimate the importance of cultivating friendly relations with the Southern white man, who is their next-door neighbor, I would say: "Cast down your bucket where you are" — cast it down in making friends in every manly way of the people of all races by whom we are surrounded.

Cast it down in agriculture, mechanics, in commerce, in domestic service, and in the professions. And in this connection it is well to bear in mind that whatever other sins the South may be called to bear, when it comes to business, pure and simple, it is in the South that the Negro is given a man's chance in the commercial world, and in nothing is this Exposition more eloquent than in emphasizing this chance. Our greatest danger is that in the great leap from slavery to freedom we may overlook the fact that the masses of us are to live by the productions of our hands, and fail to keep in mind that we shall prosper in proportion as we learn to dignify and glorify common labour and put brains and skill into the common occupations of life; shall prosper in proportion as we learn to draw the line between the superficial and the substantial, the ornamental gewgaws [knick-knacks] of life and the useful. No race can prosper till it learns that there is as much dignity in tilling a field as in writing a poem. It is at the bottom of life we must begin, and not at the top. Nor should we permit our grievances to overshadow our opportunities.

To those of the white race who look to the incoming of those of foreign birth and strange tongue and habits for the prosperity of the South, were I permitted I would repeat what I say to my own race, "Cast down your bucket where you are." Cast it down among the eight millions of Negroes whose habits you know, whose

---

From Booker T. Washington, *Up from Slavery* (New York: A. L. Burt Company, 1901).

fidelity and love you have tested in days when to have proved treacherous meant the ruins of your firesides. Cast down your bucket among these people who have, without strikes and labour wars, tilled your fields, cleared your forests, builded your railroads and cities, and brought forth treasures from the bowels of the earth, and helped make possible this magnificent representation of the progress of the South. Casting down your bucket among my people, helping and encouraging them as you are doing on these grounds, and to education of head, hand, and heart, you will find that they will buy your surplus land, make blossom the waste places in your fields, and run your factories. While doing this, you can be sure in the future, as in the past, that you and your families will be surrounded by the most patient, faithful, law-abiding, and unresentful people that the world has seen. As we have proved our loyalty to you in the past, in nursing your children, watching by the sick-bed of your mothers and fathers, and often following them with tear-dimmed eyes to their graves, so in the future, in our humble way, we shall stand by you with a devotion that no foreigner can approach, ready to lay down our lives, if need be, in defence of yours, interlacing our industrial, commercial, civil, and religious life with yours in a way that shall make the interests of both races one. In all things that are purely social we can be as separate as the fingers, yet one as the hand in all things essential to mutual progress. . . .

Nearly sixteen millions of hands will aid you in pulling the load upward, or they will pull against you the load downward. We shall constitute one-third and more of the ignorance and crime of the South, or one-third its intelligence and progress; we shall contribute one-third to the business and industrial prosperity of the South, or we shall prove a veritable body of death, stagnating, depressing, retarding every effort to advance the body politic. . . .

The wisest among my race understand that the agitation of questions of social equality is the extremest folly, and that progress in the enjoyment of all the privileges that will come to us must be the result of severe and constant struggle rather than of artificial forcing. No race that has anything to contribute to the markets of the world is long in any degree ostracized. It is important and right that all privileges of the law be ours, but it is vastly more important that we be prepared for the exercises of these privileges. The opportunity to earn a dollar in a factory just now is worth infinitely more than the opportunity to spend a dollar in an operahouse.

QUESTIONS FOR READING AND DISCUSSION

1. What did Washington mean by "Cast down your bucket where you are"?
2. Washington expressed a distinctive vision of racial equality and progress in his famous statement, "In all things that are purely social we can be as separate as the fingers, yet one as the hand in all things essential to mutual progress." What were the implications of his vision for blacks who sought equality and progress? What significance did Washington attach to the words *separate* and *mutual*?
3. In what ways did Washington's argument appeal to his white audience? Would his speech have been different if he had been addressing a black audience? If so, how and why?
4. To what extent did Washington's speech exemplify the dilemmas of African Americans in the Progressive Era?

DOCUMENT 21–6

W. E. B. Du Bois on Racial Equality

Many educated African Americans, especially in the North, objected to Booker T. Washington's policy of racial accommodation. In 1903, W. E. B. Du Bois attacked Washington's ideas and proposed alternatives that made sense to many black Americans, then and since. One of the organizers of the Niagara Movement and of the National Association for the Advancement of Colored People, Du Bois had earned a doctorate in history from Harvard and was a professor at Atlanta University when he published his criticisms of Washington, excerpted from his work The Souls of Black Folk.

Booker T. Washington and Others, 1903

Easily the most striking thing in the history of the American Negro since 1876 is the ascendancy of Mr. Booker T. Washington. It began at the time when war memories and ideals were rapidly passing; a day of astonishing commercial development was dawning; a sense of doubt and hesitation overtook the freedmen's sons, — then it was that his leading began. Mr. Washington came, with a simple definite programme, at the psychological moment when the nation was a little ashamed of having bestowed so much sentiment on Negroes, and was concentrating its energies on Dollars. His programme of industrial education, conciliation of the South, and submission and silence as to civil and political rights, was not wholly original. . . . But Mr. Washington first indissolubly linked these things; he put enthusiasm, unlimited energy, and perfect faith into this programme, and changed it from a by-path into a veritable Way of Life. . . .

It startled the nation to hear a Negro advocating such a programme after many decades of bitter complaint; it startled and won the applause of the South, it interested and won the admiration of the North; and after a confused murmur of protest, it silenced if it did not convert the Negroes themselves.

To gain the sympathy and cooperation of the various elements comprising the white South was Mr. Washington's first task; and [it] . . . seemed, for a black man, well-nigh impossible. And yet ten years later it was done in the words spoken at Atlanta: "In all things purely social we can be as separate as five fingers, and yet one as the hand in all things essential to mutual progress." This "Atlanta Compromise" is by all odds the most notable thing in Mr. Washington's career. The South interpreted it in different ways: the radicals received it as a complete surrender of the demand for civil and political equality; the conservatives, as a generously conceived working basis for mutual understanding. . . .

So Mr. Washington's cult has gained unquestioning followers, his work has wonderfully prospered, his friends are legion, and his enemies are confounded. To-day he stands as the one recognized spokesman of his ten million fellows, and one of the most notable figures in a nation of seventy million. . . .

But Booker T. Washington arose as essentially the leader not of one race but of two, — a compromiser between the South, the North, and the Negro. Naturally

---

From W. E. B. Du Bois, *The Souls of Black Folk* (Chicago: A. C. McClurg & Company, 1903).

the Negroes resented, at first bitterly, signs of compromise which surrendered their civil and political rights, even though this was to be exchanged for larger chances of economic development. The rich and dominating North, however, was not only weary of the race problem, but was investing largely in Southern enterprises, and welcomed any method of peaceful cooperation. Thus, by national opinion, the Negroes began to recognize Mr. Washington's leadership; and the voice of criticism was hushed.

Mr. Washington represents in Negro thought the old attitude of adjustment and submission; but adjustment at such a peculiar time as to make his programme unique. This is an age of unusual economic development, and Mr. Washington's programme naturally takes an economic cast, becoming a gospel of Work and Money to such an extent as apparently almost completely to overshadow the higher aims of life. Moreover, this is an age when the more advanced races are coming in closer contact with the less developed races, and the race-feeling is therefore intensified; and Mr. Washington's programme practically accepts the alleged inferiority of the Negro races. Again, in our own land, the reaction from the sentiment of war time has given impetus to race-prejudice against Negroes, and Mr. Washington withdraws many of the high demands of Negroes as men and American citizens. . . .

In answer to this, it has been claimed that the Negro can survive only through submission. Mr. Washington distinctly asks that black people give up, at least for the present, three things,

> First, political power,
> Second, insistence on civil rights,
> Third, higher education of Negro youth, —

and concentrate all their energies on industrial education, the accumulation of wealth, and the conciliation of the South. This policy has been courageously and insistently advocated for over fifteen years, and has been triumphant for perhaps ten years. As a result of this tender of the palm-branch, what has been the return? In these years there have occurred:

1. The disfranchisement of the Negro.
2. The legal creation of a distinct status of civil inferiority for the Negro.
3. The steady withdrawal of aid from institutions for the higher training of the Negro.

These movements are not, to be sure, direct results of Mr. Washington's teachings; but his propaganda has, without a shadow of doubt, helped their speedier accomplishment. The question then comes: Is it possible, and probable, that nine millions of men can make effective progress in economic lines if they are deprived of political rights, made a servile caste, and allowed only the most meagre chance for developing their exceptional men? If history and reason give any distinct answer to these questions, it is an emphatic *No.* And Mr. Washington thus faces the triple paradox of his career:

1. He is striving nobly to make Negro artisans, business men and property-owners; but it is utterly impossible, under modern competitive methods, for workingmen and property-owners to defend their rights and exist without the right of suffrage.

2. He insists on thrift and self-respect, but at the same time counsels a silent submission to civic inferiority such as is bound to sap the manhood of any race in the long run.

3. He advocates common-school and industrial training, and depreciates institutions of higher learning. . . .

This triple paradox in Mr. Washington's position is the object of criticism by two classes of colored Americans. One class is spiritually descended from Toussaint the Savior, through Gabriel, Vesey, and Turner,[1] and they represent the attitude of revolt and revenge; they hate the white South blindly and distrust the white race generally, and so far as they agree on definite action, think that the Negro's only hope lies in emigration beyond the borders of the United States. And yet, by the irony of fate, nothing has more effectively made this programme seem hopeless than the recent course of the United States toward weaker and darker peoples in the West Indies, Hawaii, and the Philippines, — for where in the world may we go and be safe from lying and brute force?

The other class of Negroes who cannot agree with Mr. Washington has hitherto said little aloud. . . . Such men feel in conscience bound to ask of this nation three things:

1. The right to vote.
2. Civic equality.
3. The education of youth according to ability.

They acknowledge Mr. Washington's invaluable service in counselling patience and courtesy in such demands; they do not ask that ignorant black men vote when ignorant whites are debarred, or that any reasonable restrictions in the suffrage should not be applied; they know that the low social level of the mass of the race is responsible for much discrimination against it, but they also know, and the nation knows, that relentless color prejudice is more often a cause than a result of the Negro's degradation; they seek the abatement of this relic of barbarism, and not its systematic encouragement and pampering by all agencies of social power. . . . They advocate, with Mr. Washington, a broad system of Negro common schools supplemented by thorough industrial training; but they are surprised that a man of Mr. Washington's insight cannot see that no educational system ever has rested or can rest on any other basis than that of the well equipped college and university, and they insist that there is a demand for a few such institutions throughout the South to train the best of the Negro youth as teachers, professional men, and leaders. . . .

They do not expect that the free right to vote, to enjoy civic rights, and to be educated, will come in a moment; they do not expect to see the bias and prejudices of years disappear at the blast of a trumpet; but they are absolutely certain that the way for a people to gain their reasonable rights is not by voluntarily throwing them away and insisting that they do not want them; that the way for a people to gain respect is not by continually belittling and ridiculing themselves; that, on the contrary, Negroes must insist continually, in season and out of

---

[1]**Toussaint the Savior . . . Gabriel, Vesey, and Turner:** Toussaint L'Ouverture was a former slave who led the Haitian Revolution in 1798. African Americans Gabriel Prosser, Denmark Vesey, and Nat Turner were executed for attempts to lead slave rebellions in the United States in 1800, 1822, and 1831, respectively.

season, that voting is necessary to modern manhood, that color discrimination is barbarism, and that black boys need education as well as white boys. . . .

[T]he distinct impression left by Mr. Washington's propaganda is, first, that the South is justified in its present attitude toward the Negro because of the Negro's degradation; secondly, that the prime cause of the Negro's failure to rise more quickly is his wrong education in the past; and, thirdly, that his future rise depends primarily on his own efforts. Each of these propositions is a dangerous half-truth. The supplementary truths must never be lost sight of: first, slavery and race-prejudice are potent if not sufficient causes of the Negro's position; second, industrial and common-school training were necessarily slow in planting because they had to await the black teachers trained by higher institutions . . . ; and, third, while it is a great truth to say that the Negro must strive and strive mightily to help himself, it is equally true that unless his striving be not simply seconded, but rather aroused and encouraged, by the initiative of the richer and wiser environing group, he cannot hope for great success.

In his failure to realize and impress this last point, Mr. Washington is especially to be criticised. His doctrine has tended to make the whites, North and South, shift the burden of the Negro problem to the Negro's shoulders and stand aside as critical and rather pessimistic spectators; when in fact the burden belongs to the nation, and the hands of none of us are clean if we bend not our energies to righting these great wrongs.

QUESTIONS FOR READING AND DISCUSSION

1. According to Du Bois, what were the shortcomings of the "Atlanta Compromise"? What was compromised, and why? What consequences did the compromise have for black Americans?

2. In what ways did Washington's "gospel of Work and Money" involve a "triple paradox"?

3. What alternatives did Du Bois propose to Washington's plan? How did the political implications of Du Bois's proposals differ from those of Washington?

4. Who did Du Bois consider his audience? To what extent did Du Bois and Washington differ in their assessments of their white and black audiences?

COMPARATIVE QUESTIONS

1. How did the views of Marie Jenney Howe about the possibility of harmony between classes compare with those of Jane Addams?

2. How did Addams's views of the necessity of settlement houses compare with Pietro's desire to learn to write English and to Royal Melendy's description of working-class saloons?

3. To what extent did Booker T. Washington's ideas about progress for black Americans differ from Howe's characterization of anti-suffrage arguments? In what ways did W. E. B. Du Bois's beliefs about the necessity of equality and political conflict compare with Howe's depiction of anti-suffragist arguments?

4. The documents in this chapter provide evidence of both the aspirations and limitations of progressivism. Judging from these documents, to what extent did the limitations of progressive reforms arise from the character of progressive aspirations? In what ways, if at all, did the commonly held aspirations of progressives differ from those of working people, suffragists, and African Americans?

22 | World War I: The Progressive Crusade at Home and Abroad

1914–1920

With the declaration of war against Germany in 1917, the United States unmistakably asserted its status as a major power in world affairs. European nations had admired American economic might for decades and watched the politics of the nation's constitutional democracy with interest for more than a century. Now, by entering the war and claiming a decisive voice in the peace, the United States took its place as one of the powerful industrial nations that would shape global history. The following documents illustrate the mobilization of Americans for the war effort, the bitter criticism of the war by American socialists, the experience of combat, the postwar suppression of political radicals, and outbreaks of violence against African Americans.

DOCUMENT 22–1

"The Human American Eagle," 1918

Before Americans entered the war, the U.S. Army had fewer than 130,000 soldiers. The declaration of war required the army to recruit, train, and support millions of American civilians. By the end of the war, more than four million men and over 30,000 women had served in uniform, while millions of others worked in war industries or volunteered to sell Liberty Bonds or support the war effort in other ways. This massive mobilization of civilians into soldiers took place at hastily constructed training camps scattered across the nation. The following photo, made in 1918 at a training camp near Atlanta, Georgia, shows 12,500 soldiers and nurses assembled into the shape of a giant "American Eagle." Camp Gordon trained the Eighty-second Division, also known as the All American Division since it included soldiers from all 48 states and many immigrants from Italy, Poland, Greece, and elsewhere. The division ultimately fought with distinction in the Meuse-Argonne offensive during the last months of the war.

John D. Thomas and Arthur S. Mole

"The Human American Eagle,"
Camp Gordon, Atlanta, Georgia, 1918

Library of Congress, 2b11329

QUESTIONS FOR READING AND DISCUSSION

1. How does "The Human American Eagle" display the results of military training and discipline? Did organizing the Eagle detract from military training?
2. How does the Eagle reflect the "All American" reputation of the Eighty-second Division?
3. What features of civilian life needed to be altered in the barracks and training fields of the camp to turn these people into soldiers and military nurses?
4. To what extent does the photo portray the ideals of President Woodrow Wilson?

DOCUMENT 22–2

Eugene V. Debs Attacks Capitalist Warmongers

The Socialist Party opposed American entry into World War I, calling it "a crime against the people of the United States." In June 1918, Eugene V. Debs, the party's perennial presidential candidate, spoke in Canton, Ohio, to a group of working people. In his speech, excerpted here, Debs explained that socialists opposed the war not because they were pro-German but because they were anticapitalist. This speech precipitated Debs's arrest for violating the Espionage Act; he was convicted and sentenced to ten years in prison. In 1920, he campaigned for president from his prison cell.

Speech Delivered in Canton, Ohio, June 16, 1918

Why should a Socialist be discouraged on the eve of the greatest triumph in all the history of the Socialist movement? It is true that these are anxious, trying days for us all—testing days for the women and men who are upholding the banner of labor in the struggle of the working class of all the world against the exploiters of all the world. . . .

Are we opposed to Prussian militarism? Why, we have been fighting it since the day the Socialist movement was born; and we are going to continue to fight it, day and night, until it is wiped from the face of the earth. Between us there is no truce—no compromise. . . . Multiplied thousands of Socialists have languished in the jails of Germany because of their heroic warfare upon the despotic ruling class of that country. . . .

I hate, I loathe, I despise Junkers[1] and junkerdom. I have no earthly use for the Junkers of Germany, and not one particle more use for the Junkers in the United States.

They tell us that we live in a great free republic; that our institutions are democratic; that we are a free and self-governing people. This is too much, even for a joke. But it is not a subject for levity; it is an exceedingly serious matter.

To whom do the Wall Street Junkers in our country marry their daughters? After they have wrung their countless millions from your sweat, your agony and your life's blood, in a time of war as in a time of peace, they invest these untold millions in the purchase of titles of broken-down aristocrats, such as princes, dukes, counts, and other parasites and no-accounts. Would they be satisfied to wed their daughters to honest workingmen? To real democrats? Oh, no! . . .

These are the gentry who are today wrapped up in the American flag, who shout their claim from the housetops that they are the only patriots, and who have their magnifying glasses in hand, scanning the country for evidence of disloyalty, eager to apply the brand of treason to the men who dare to even whisper their opposition to junker rule in the United States. No wonder Sam Johnson declared that "patriotism is the last refuge of the scoundrel." He must have had this Wall Street gentry in mind, or at least their prototypes, for in every age it has been the tyrant, the oppressor, and the exploiter who has wrapped himself in the cloak of patriotism, or religion, or both to deceive and overawe the people. . . .

Socialism is a growing idea, an expanding philosophy. It is spreading over the entire face of the earth. It is as vain to resist it as it would be to arrest the sunrise on the morrow. It is coming, coming, coming all along the line. . . . It is the mightiest movement in the history of mankind. . . . It has enabled me . . . to feel life truly worth while; . . . to be class-conscious, and to realize that, regardless

---

From Jean Y. Tussey, ed., Eugene V. Debs, "Speech at Canton, Ohio," June 16, 1918, in *Eugene V. Debs Speaks* (New York: Pathfinder Press, 1970).

[1]**Junkers**: Members of the Prussian aristocracy, an especially militaristic and politically reactionary class in German society at that time.

of nationality, race, creed, color, or sex, every man, every woman who toils, who renders useful service, every member of the working class without an exception, is my comrade, my brother and sister—and that to serve them and their cause is the highest duty of my life. . . .

[O]ur hearts are with the Bolsheviki of Russia. Those heroic men and women, those unconquerable comrades have by their incomparable valor and sacrifice added fresh lustre to the fame of the international movement. . . . The very first act of the triumphant Russian revolution was to proclaim a state of peace with all mankind, coupled with a fervent moral appeal, not to kings, not to emperors, rulers or diplomats, but to the people of all nations. . . .

Wars throughout history have been waged for conquest and plunder. . . . The feudal barons of the Middle Ages, the economic predecessors of the capitalists of our day, declared all wars. And their miserable serfs fought all the battles. The poor, ignorant serfs had been taught to revere their masters; to believe that when their masters declared war upon one another, it was their patriotic duty to fall upon one another and to cut one another's throats for the profit and glory of the lords and barons who held them in contempt. And that is war in a nutshell. The master class has always declared the wars; the subject class has always fought the battles. The master class has had all to gain and nothing to lose, while the subject class has had nothing to gain and all to lose—especially their lives. . . .

And here let me emphasize the fact—and it cannot be repeated, too often— that the working class who fight all the battles, the working class who make the supreme sacrifices, the working class, who freely shed their blood and furnish the corpses, have never yet had a voice in either declaring war or making peace. It is the ruling class that invariably does both. They alone declare war and they alone make peace. . . .

What a compliment it is to the Socialist movement to be persecuted for the sake of the truth! The truth alone will make the people free. And for this reason the truth must not be permitted to reach the people. The truth has always been danger- ous to the rule of the rogue, the exploiter, the robber. So the truth must be ruthlessly suppressed. That is why they are trying to destroy the Socialist movement. . . .

We do not attack individuals. We do not seek to avenge ourselves upon those opposed to our faith. . . . There is no room in our hearts for hate, except for the sys- tem, the social system in which it is possible for one man to amass a stupendous fortune doing nothing, while millions of others suffer and struggle and agonize and die for the bare necessities of existence. . . .

To turn your back on the corrupt Republican party and the corrupt Democratic party—the gold-dust lackeys of the ruling class counts for some- thing. It counts for still more after you have stepped out of those popular and corrupt capitalist parties to join a minority party that has an ideal, that stands for a principle, and fights for a cause. This will be the most important change you have ever made. . . .

Give me a hundred capitalists and let me ask them a dozen simple questions about the history of their own country and I will prove to you that they are as ignorant and unlettered as any you may find in the so-called lower class. They know little of history; they are strangers to science; they are ignorant of sociology and blind to art but they know how to exploit, how to gouge, how to rob, and do it with legal sanction. They always proceed legally for the reason that the class which has the power to rob upon a large scale has also the power to control the government and legalize their robbery. . . .

They are continually talking about your patriotic duty. It is not their but your patriotic duty that they are concerned about. There is a decided difference. Their patriotic duty never takes them to the firing line or chucks them into the trenches.

And now among other things they are urging you to "cultivate" war gardens, while at the same time a government war report just issued shows that practically 52 percent of the arable, tillable soil is held out of use by the landlords, speculators, and profiteers. They themselves do not cultivate the soil. They could not if they would. Nor do they allow others to cultivate it. They keep it idle to enrich themselves, to pocket the millions of dollars of unearned increment. Who is it that makes this land valuable while it is fenced in and kept out of use? It is the people. Who pockets this tremendous accumulation of value? The landlords. And these landlords who toil not and spin not are supreme among American "patriots." . . .

This lord who practically owns the earth tells you that we are fighting this war to make the world safe for democracy—he, who shuts out all humanity from his private domain; he, who profiteers at the expense of the people who have been slain and mutilated by multiplied thousands, under pretense of being the great American patriot. It is he, this identical patriot who is in fact the arch-enemy of the people; it is he that you need to wipe from power. It is he who is a far greater menace to your liberty and your well-being than the Prussian junkers on the other side of the Atlantic Ocean. . . .

[W]ar comes in spite of the people. When Wall Street says war the press says war and the pulpit promptly follows with its Amen. In every age the pulpit has been on the side of the rulers and not on the side of the people. . . .

Political action and industrial action must supplement and sustain each other. You will never vote the Socialist republic into existence. You will have to lay its foundations in industrial organization. The industrial union is the forerunner of industrial democracy. In the shop where the workers are associated is where industrial democracy has its beginning. Organize according to your industries! . . .

Then unite in the Socialist party. Vote as you strike and strike as you vote. . . .

When we unite and act together on the industrial field and when we vote together on election day we shall develop the supreme power of the one class that can and will bring permanent peace to the world. . . . We shall conquer the public power. We shall then transfer the title deeds of the railroads, the telegraph lines, the mines, mills, and great industries to the people in their collective capacity; we shall take possession of all these social utilities in the name of the people. We shall then have industrial democracy. We shall be a free nation whose government is of and by and for the people.

And now for all of us to do our duty! The clarion call is ringing in our ears and we cannot falter without being convicted of treason to ourselves and to our great cause.

Do not worry over the charge of treason to your masters, but be concerned about the treason that involves yourselves. Be true to yourself and you cannot be a traitor to any good cause on earth.

QUESTIONS FOR READING AND DISCUSSION

1. According to Debs, why were "these . . . anxious, trying days"? What was the significance of his slogan "Vote as you strike and strike as you vote"?

2. Why did Debs object to Wilson's pledge that the war would make the world safe for democracy? Did Debs and Wilson agree about the democratic possibilities of developments in Russia?

3. According to Debs, how should working-class people respond to the patriotic appeals of leaders? How should they avoid treason? In what way could peace be achieved?

4. Do you think Debs should have opposed the war, even though U.S. troops were fighting in it? Why or why not?

DOCUMENT 22–3

A Doughboy's Letter from the Front

More than a million American soldiers, "doughboys" in contemporary slang, fought fierce German resistance in decisive battles in the Argonne forest of northern France during the fall of 1918. One anonymous soldier described his experiences to a friend back home in the following letter. The letter expresses the risks, fears, horrors, and exhilaration that many soldiers experienced in combat.

Anonymous Soldier
Letter to Elmer J. Sutters, 1918

Cote D'Or France

Dear Old Bunkie,

Now don't go into epileptic fits or something like that when you read this letter, that is because I sent one to you as I know I haven't written you a letter for some time. Too busy with Uncle Sam's affairs just now and am working to beat hell.

I guess you would like to know of a few of my experiences over here while the scrimmage was on so I'll give you a few little yarns.

We were in the line up at Thiacourt (St. Michel Sector) at first and although we did no actual fighting as we were in reserve at first and then in support, we got a lot of strafing from Jerry[1] in the nature of Artillery fire and Air raids.

But in the Argonne Forest was where we got in it in earnest and even if I do say it myself, the good old Lightning (78th) Division will go down in history as second to none for the work they did there.

It was here, old man, that I got my first Hun[2] with the bayonet. That was on the day prior to taking Grandpre and we had just broke through the enemy first line defenses when this happened.

We were pressing through a thicket when this big plug-ugly Hun suddenly loomed up in front of me and made a one-armed stab at me with his bayonet. You can make a hell of a long reach this way, but it's a rather awkward thrust as the bayonet makes the rifle heavy at the muzzle when you've got hold of your rifle at the small of the stock like this guy had. A homelier guy I never saw before in all my life and he'd make two in size compared to Dad and you know what a big man my old Dad is.

Anonymous soldier to Elmer J. Sutters, 1918 (pp. 162–67), from *War Letters: Extraordinary Correspondence from American Wars* (New York: Washington Square Press, 2001), edited by Andrew Carroll. Reprinted by permission of Andrew Carroll.

[1]**Jerry**: Slang term for a German soldier.
[2]**Hun**: Slang term for a German soldier.

Well you can imagine that this bud did not catch me unawares.

I was ready for him. I thought I was going to have a pretty stiff one-sided fight on my hands, with the odds in his favor, but he was a cinch. Before I even realized it myself I parried off his blow and had him through the throat. It was my first hand to hand fight.

It was all over in a second, that is it for Jerry. He never even made a shriek. He went down like a log.

It was hand to hand all the way through that section of the woods as it was considered a vulnerable point, but we finally cleared them out and opened up the way for an attack on Grandpre itself. . . .

We took it, but at heavy cost. I lost a buddie in that last charge. If short five or ten yard dashes can be called a charge and I certainly didn't have much love for the Boches[3] after he went west. We can't mention any names of boys who were killed in our letters so I'll have to postpone it until I get home but he came from New Hampshire and a whiter fellow never lived. He was an only child too, old chap and his parents certainly have my sympathy.

Although I don't know his people I wrote a letter to them trying to make it as soft as I could. Well, he gave his all to the cause and you can't expect a fellow to do more. If a fellow goes down, it's up to the next one to carry on and make them pay dearly for every life taken. You know what I mean.

I know that the first thing you would ask me when you see me again for the first if I was afraid. Now I am not going to stick my chest out and exclaim "Like hell I was" or anything of the sort. I sure was afraid, and you and any other chap would be too, but what I was afraid of most was that I would be yellow.

If a fellow gets a yellow streak and backs down the other boys won't have anything to do with him and that was what I was afraid of the most, of getting a yellow streak.

But I didn't. I was as plucky as any other doughboy and carried on all the way through and although I didn't get as much as a scratch I had many a close call. Enough of them to make a fellow's hair turn white. I crouched for three hours one night up to my waist in water in a shell hole waiting for our barrage to lift.

The water was like ice and there [were] four or five dead Huns floating around in it too. Not very pleasant, eh?

While sneaking about the ruins of Grandpre "Mopping Up" we came across a Prussian Chap in a ruined building with a rifle. He was a sniper, alive and the reason he was still there was because he could not get out although the opening was big enough for him to crawl through. During the bombardment the roof of the building had fell through in such a way as to pin him there by the feet and although he was practically uninjured he could not get himself free. I'll explain better when I see you, as I can tell it better than I can write it. He begged us to help him and although we had been cautioned against treatury [treachery] one of the fellows who was with me put down his rifle and started to crawl through to free him. The moment he got his head and shoulders through the hole which had been smashed by a shell, by the way, this Hun hauls off and lets him have a charge right square in the face.

Poor Dan never knew what happened. His face was unrecognizable. We didn't do a thing but riddle that hole, we were that furious, and we didn't stop shooting until our magazines were empty.

---

[3]**Boches:** Slang term for German soldiers.

That Hun was the dirtiest skunk that every lived. . . . Dan was some husky boy and boasted of being a foot-ball player somewhere out in Tennessee where he came from. . . .

Up near Brickemay we ran into another pretty stiff proposition. We had to fight through the woods that seemed to be full of machine gun nests. We had just cleared out one of them with hand grenades and while we were sneaking up a rather steep hill, thickly wooded, we saw these Huns suddenly appear and run about a dozen paces and disappear down into a clearly camouflaged dug-out.

The Yanks were pressing the Huns hard, they were some of the Famous Prussian Guard too, and after these three birds had gone down into their hole we sneaked right up. There were three of us together, all Buck Privates. I took a hand grenade out of my bag, pulled out the retaining pin and heaved it down into the dug-out. . . . There was a helluva an explosion in about six seconds. I threw two more down to join the first and keep it company. Well after the big noise had stopped down there we crept down to investigate.

There was only one room down there, a big concrete affair and only one entrance, the one we came down, and that room was a mess. There were fifteen dead Huns down there and the walls, floor and ceiling were splashed with red, so you can see what damage a hand grenade can do. I don't know whether my grenades killed them all, we didn't have time to ascertain, as we had to hurry right out again, but I know I got the three we saw beating it down there.

I was also with a detachment of men who took a dozen prisoners out of a dug-out and the worst of the whole thing was that they were only mere kids.

Just think of it old man. Mere kids, that is the most of them and they all expected to be killed immediately.

They were all scared stiff. We bagged the lot and sent them to the man under guard.

Well I was there to the finish old man and we had just mashed Fritz's[4] last resistance up near Sedan when we were relieved by a French Division who captured Sedan next day. . . .

Fritz pulled off a peach of an air raid. . . . It was about 7:30 pm and quiet, yes very dark outside when the thing started and he came back again and again at regular intervals of ten minutes and bombed the hell out of everything in sight, but what he really wanted to get . . . was our Supply and Ammunition Depots. . . . Now there is only one sane thing to do and I did it. Nothing heroic about it old man, just common sense and it wasn't the first time I did it either, even though my heart was trying to pound a hole through my ribs at the time. I went outside and walked out on the railroad and lay down flat in a shallow trench I had stumbled upon . . . along the tracks and I stayed there all night too. It was an organized raid, or rather a general raid and I saw the flashes from the exploding bomb all around me all night. . . . [O]ne bomb struck right near a small wooden shack where the Engineers use to store tools and blew that thing to hallaballoo.

That shed stood only about 100 or 150 yards from where I was laying . . . and a big piece of that shed came down ker-smak only six feet from where I was.

The next instant another landed right on the railroad and exploded with terrific force. . . .

This one burst about 500 yards away from me, but those things can kill at 1,000 yards and the concussion lifted me up out of this trench between the rails,

---

[4]**Fritz:** Slang term for a German soldier.

about a foot or so in the air and I came down again ker-flump. It wasn't a pleasant sensation, but nothing hit me and that was better than anything. . . .

Well I guess this will be all for just now so with best regard and good wishes to you, Elmer, Mother Sutters, Pop, Mutt, and all the kyoodles. I close.

Your Old Friend and Comrade in Mischief
Dickwitch

P.S. Say you old slab of a lop-sided tin-eared Jackass, what's wrong with you anyhow. Got writer's cramp or what? Pick up a pen for the Love of Pete and write to your old buddie in France. Dick

QUESTIONS FOR READING AND DISCUSSION

1. What was this soldier most afraid of? Why? What did his fear suggest about motivation for combat? What did he seem to mean by the term "the cause"?

2. Did this "doughboy" take pride in killing "Huns"? Did he express regrets or doubts about killing? Why or why not?

3. To what extent did his combat experiences seem different from his prewar life? Did his prewar experiences and expectations seem to influence his life as a soldier?

DOCUMENT 22–4

Attorney General A. Mitchell Palmer Defends America from Communists

The Bolshevik Revolution in Russia terrified many Americans. They feared communism would spread in the United States with the help of political radicals and immigrants. To suppress this "Red menace," U.S. Attorney General A. Mitchell Palmer organized a series of raids to round up and deport immigrants suspected to be Communists. Civil liberties defenders denounced Palmer's raids as violations of the U.S. Constitution. Palmer defended the anti-Red crackdown in an essay, excerpted below, that described his perception of the Red menace and what had to be done to defeat it.

The Case against the "Reds," 1920

[Forum *editor's note: The plans for fomenting a nation-wide revolution in this country, prepared by [Leon] Trotzky in Moscow, are in the files of the Attorney-General's office. It is upon these proofs that the Attorney-General has decided upon a vigorous system of arrest and deportation of radical aliens, which he says he will pursue till the United States is purged of Bolshevism. . . .]*

In this brief review of the work which the Department of Justice has undertaken, to tear out the radical seeds that have entangled American ideas in their poisonous theories, I desire not merely to explain what the real menace of communism is, but also to tell how we have been compelled to clean up the country

---

From A. Mitchell Palmer, "The Case against the 'Reds,' " *Forum* 63 (February 1920), 173–85.

almost unaided by any virile legislation. Though I have not been embarrassed by political opposition, I have been materially delayed because the present sweeping processes of arrests and deportation of seditious aliens should have been vigorously pushed by Congress last spring. . . .

The anxiety of that period in our responsibility when Congress, ignoring the seriousness of these vast organizations that were plotting to overthrow the Government, failed to act, has passed. The time came when it was obviously hopeless to expect the hearty co-operation of Congress, in the only way to stamp out these seditious societies in their open defiance of law by various forms of propaganda.

Like a prairie-fire, the blaze of revolution was sweeping over every American institution of law and order a year ago. It was eating its way into the homes of the American workman, its sharp tongues of revolutionary heat were licking the altars of the churches, leaping into the belfry of the school bell, crawling into the sacred corners of American homes, seeking to replace marriage vows with libertine laws, burning up the foundations of society.

Robbery, not war, is the ideal of communism. This has been demonstrated in Russia, Germany, and in America. As a foe, the anarchist is fearless of his own life, for his creed is a fanaticism that admits no respect of any other creed. Obviously it is the creed of any criminal mind, which reasons always from motives impossible to clean thought. Crime is the degenerate factor in society.

Upon these two basic certainties, first that the "Reds" were criminal aliens, and secondly that the American Government must prevent crime, it was decided that there could be no nice distinctions drawn between the theoretical ideals of the radicals and their actual violations of our national laws. An assassin may have brilliant intellectuality, he may be able to excuse his murder or robbery with fine oratory, but any theory which excuses crime is not wanted in America. This is no place for the criminal to flourish, nor will he do so, so long as the rights of common citizenship can be exerted to prevent him.

OUR GOVERNMENT IN JEOPARDY

It has always been plain to me that when American citizens unite upon any national issue, they are generally right, but it is sometimes difficult to make the issue clear to them. If the Department of Justice could succeed in attracting the attention of our optimistic citizens to the issue of internal revolution in this country, we felt sure there would be no revolution. The Government was in jeopardy. My private information of what was being done by the organization known as the Communist Party of America, with headquarters in Chicago, of what was being done by the Communist Internationale under their manifesto planned at Moscow last March by Trotzky, Lenin and others addressed "To the Proletariats of All Countries," of what strides the Communist Labor Party was making, removed all doubt. In this conclusion we did not ignore the definite standards of personal liberty, of free speech, which is the very temperament and heart of the people. The evidence was examined with the utmost care, with a personal leaning toward freedom of thought and word on all questions.

The whole mass of evidence, accumulated from all parts of the country, was scrupulously scanned, not merely for the written or spoken differences of viewpoint as to the Government of the United States, but, in spite of these things, to see if the hostile declarations might not be sincere in their announced motive to improve our social order. There was no hope of such a thing.

By stealing, murder and lies, Bolshevism has looted Russia not only of its material strength, but of its moral force. A small clique of outcasts from the East Side of New York has attempted this, with what success we all know. Because a disreputable alien — Leon Bronstein, the man who now calls himself Trotzky — can inaugurate a reign of terror from his throne room in the Kremlin; because this lowest of all types known to New York can sleep in the Czar's bed, while hundreds of thousands in Russia are without food or shelter, should Americans be swayed by such doctrines?

Such a question, it would seem, should receive but one answer from America.

My information showed that communism in this country was an organization of thousands of aliens, who were direct allies of Trotzky. Aliens of the same misshapen caste of mind and indecencies of character, and it showed that they were making the same glittering promises of lawlessness, of criminal autocracy to Americans, that they had made to the Russian peasants. How the Department of Justice discovered upwards of 60,000 of these organized agitators of the Trotzky doctrine in the United States is the confidential information upon which the Government is now sweeping the nation clean of such alien filth. . . .

There were other activities of the Reds . . . for which there was no legislation. These were:

"... The preaching of anarchy and sedition is not a crime under the general criminal statutes of the United States.

"... Advising the defiance of law is not a crime under the general criminal laws whether the same be done by printing and circulating literature or by the spoken word.

"... Nor is the advising and openly advocating the unlawful obstruction of industry and the unlawful and violent destruction of property a crime under the United States general statutes." . . .

One of the chief incentives for the present activity of the Department of Justice against the "Reds" has been the hope that American citizens will, themselves, become voluntary agents for us, in a vast organization for mutual defense against the sinister agitation of men and women aliens, who appear to be either in the pay or under the criminal spell of Trotzky and Lenin. . . .

WILL DEPORTATIONS CHECK BOLSHEVISM?

Behind, and underneath, my own determination to drive from our midst the agents of Bolshevism with increasing vigor and with greater speed, until there are no more of them left among us, so long as I have the responsible duty of that task, I have discovered the hysterical methods of these revolutionary humans with increasing amazement and suspicion. In the confused information that sometimes reaches the people, they are compelled to ask questions which involve the reasons for my acts against the "Reds." I have been asked, for instance, to what extent deportation will check radicalism in this country. Why not ask what will become of the United States Government if these alien radicals are permitted to carry out the principles of the Communist Party as embodied in its so-called laws, aims and regulations?

There wouldn't be any such thing left. In place of the United States Government we should have the horror and terrorism of bolsheviki tyranny such as is destroying Russia now. Every scrap of radical literature demands the overthrow of our existing government. All of it demands obedience to the instincts of criminal minds, that is, to the lower appetites, material and moral. The whole purpose of communism appears to be a mass formation of the criminals of the world to overthrow the decencies of private life, to usurp property that they have not earned, to disrupt the present order of life regardless of health, sex or religious rights. By a literature that promises the wildest dreams of such low aspirations, that can occur to only the criminal minds, communism distorts our social law.

The chief appeal communism makes is to "The Worker." If they can lure the wage-earner to join their own gang of thieves, if they can show him that he will be rich if he steals, so far have they succeeded in betraying him to their own criminal course.

Read this manifesto issued in Chicago:

THE COMMUNIST PARTY MANIFESTO

"The world is on the verge of a new era. Europe is in revolt. The masses of Asia are stirring uneasily. Capitalism is in collapse. The workers of the world are seeing a new light and securing new courage. Out of the night of war is coming a new day.

"The spectre of communism haunts the world of capitalism. Communism [is] the hope of the workers to end misery and oppression.

"The workers of Russia smashed the front of international Capitalism and Imperialism. They broke the chains of the terrible war; and in the midst of agony, starvation and the attacks of the Capitalists of the world, they are creating a new social order.

"The class war rages fiercely in all nations. Everywhere the workers are in a desperate struggle against their capitalist masters. The call to action has come. The workers must answer the call!

"The Communist Party of America is the party of the working class. The Communist Party proposes to end Capitalism and organize a workers' industrial republic. The workers must control industry and dispose of the product of industry. . . . The Communist Party insists that the problems of the American worker are identical with the problems of the workers of the world." . . .

Their manifesto further embraces the various organizations in this country of men and women obsessed with discontent, having disorganized relations to American society. These include the I.W.W.'s,[1] the most radical socialists, the misguided anarchists, the agitators who oppose the limitations of unionism, the moral perverts and the hysterical neurasthenic[2] women who abound in communism. . . .

It has been inferred by the "Reds" that the United States Government, by arresting and deporting them, is returning to the autocracy of Czardom, adopting the system that created the severity of Siberian banishment. My reply to such charges is, that in our determination to maintain our government we are treating our alien enemies with extreme consideration. To deny them the privilege of remaining in a country which they have openly deplored as an unenlightened

---

[1]**I.W.W.**: Industrial Workers of the World.

[2]**neurasthenic**: Weakened by a nervous disorder.

community, unfit for those who prefer the privileges of Bolshevism, should be no hardship. It strikes me as an odd form of reasoning that these Russian Bolsheviks who extol the Bolshevik rule, should be so unwilling to return to Russia. The nationality of most of the alien "Reds" is Russian and German. There is almost no other nationality represented among them.

It has been impossible in so short a space to review the entire menace of the internal revolution in this country as I know it, but this may serve to arouse the American citizen to its reality, its danger, and the great need of united effort to stamp it out, under our feet, if needs be. It is being done. The Department of Justice will pursue the attack of these "Reds" upon the Government of the United States with vigilance, and no alien, advocating the overthrow of existing law and order in this country, shall escape arrest and prompt deportation.

It is my belief that while they have stirred discontent in our midst, while they have caused irritating strikes, and while they have infected our social ideas with the disease of their own minds and their unclean morals, we can get rid of them! [A]nd not until we have done so shall we have removed the menace of Bolshevism for good.

QUESTIONS FOR READING AND DISCUSSION

1. What did Palmer consider "the real menace of communism"? What did he propose to do "to clean up the country"?
2. Why did he believe Congress ignored "the seriousness of these vast organizations that were plotting to overthrow the Government"? What evidence did Palmer believe showed that " 'Reds' were criminal aliens"?
3. In what ways did the "blaze of revolution" sweep "over every American institution of law and order"? What evidence did Palmer cite of this "prairie-fire"? What legal basis did Palmer claim for his actions?
4. To what extent did Palmer believe that Communists were successful in recruiting American members? To what extent did "men and women obsessed with discontent" advance the cause of communism, according to Palmer?
5. Do you think Palmer successfully defended his policy? Why or why not? What did Palmer say about democracy and the Constitution? Do you think his view that the "Government was in jeopardy" was accurate? Why or why not?

DOCUMENT 22–5

An African American Responds to the Chicago Race Riot

Race riots exploded in almost two dozen American cities during the summer of 1919. White mobs attacked African Americans, indiscriminately beating, shooting, and lynching them. Shortly after the bloody riot in Chicago, the governor of Illinois appointed a biracial commission to study the causes of the melee. Stanley B. Norvell, an African American Chicagoan, wrote the following letter to Victor F. Lawson, editor of the Chicago Daily News, *who had just been appointed as one of the white members of the commission to study the riot. Norvell described whites' ignorance of blacks and pointed out that a "new Negro" had been created by the experiences of World War I and the continuing injustices of white racism.*

Stanley B. Norvell
Letter to Victor F. Lawson, 1919

My dear Mr. Lawson:

. . . I take it that the object of this commission is to obtain by investigation . . . the cause or causes of the friction between the two races that started the molecules of race hatred into such violent motion as to cause the heterogeneous mixture to boil over in the recent race riots.

Few white men know the cause, for the simple reason that few white men know the Negro as an entity. On the other hand, I daresay that almost any Negro that you meet on the street could tell you the cause, if he would, for it is doubtful — aye, very doubtful — if he would tell you, because Negroes have become highly suspicious of white men, even such white men as they deem their friends ordinarily. The Negro has always been and is now largely a menial dependent upon the white man's generosity and charity for his livelihood, and for this reason he has become an expert cajoler of the white man and a veritable artist at appearing to be that which he is not. To resort to the vernacular, "conning" the white man has become his profession, his stock in trade. Take for example the Negro in Chicago — and Chicago is fairly representative — sixty per cent of the male Negro population is engaged in menial and servile occupations such as hotel waiters, dining car waiters, sleeping car porters, barbershop porters, billiard room attendants, etc., where "tips" form the greater part of their remuneration. Thirty per cent are laborers and artisans, skilled and unskilled, governmental and municipal employees; while the remaining ten per cent are business and professional men.

Unfortunately it is always by the larger class — the menial, servitor and flunky class — that the race is judged. Even at that, we would not object to being judged by this class of our race, if those who did the judging had a thorough knowledge of the individuals who make up this class. Unfortunately they have not this knowledge nor can they get it except through the instrumentality of just such a commission as that to which you gentlemen have been assigned. The white man of America knows just about as much about the mental and moral calibre, the home life and social activities of this class of colored citizens as he does about the same things concerning the inhabitants of the thus far unexplored planet of Mars. . . . [W]ere you to ask any white man concerning these dusky servitors he . . . will discuss him in a general superficial sort of way and if you press him further you will be surprised to know that in spite of his years of acquaintance with the subject he knows absolutely nothing about intellect, ability, ambitions, the home life and environment of one with whom he has come into daily contact for years. He is just a "nigger" and he takes him for granted, as a matter of course. . . .

I can walk down the "Boul Mich"[1] and be surveyed by the most critical of Sherlock Holmeses and I will wager that none of them can accurately deduce what I am or what I represent. They cannot tell whether I am well off or hard up; whether I am educated or illiterate; whether I am a northerner or a southerner; whether I am a native born Negro or a foreigner; whether I live among beautiful

[1]**Boul Mich**: Michigan Avenue in Chicago.

surroundings or in the squalor of the "black belt." I defy the shrewdest of your pseudo detectives to know whether I am a reputable citizen or whether I am a newly arrived crook. They cannot tell by looking at me what my income is. . . . The point is that I am only an ordinary, average Negro and that the white man is constantly making the mistake of discounting us and rating us too cheaply. He should wake up to the fact that brain is not peculiar to any race or nationality but is merely a matter of development. . . .

The further causes of the apparent increased friction between the two races, in my opinion is due to the gradual, and inevitable evolution—metamorphosis, if you please—of the Negro. The Negro has also progressed in knowledge by his study of the white man, while the white man blinded by either his prejudice or by his indifference has failed to study the Negro judiciously, and as a consequence, he knows no more about him than he did fifty years ago and still continues to judge him and to formulate opinions about him by his erstwhile standards. Today we have with us a new Negro. A brand new Negro, if you please. What opportunities have you better class white people for getting into and observing the homes of the better class of colored people[?] Yet the duties of the colored man in his menial capacities gives him an insight of your home life. As a suggestion, if I may be permitted to make one, I suggest that the white members of this commission make it their business to try to obtain an opportunity through some of the colored members of the commission to visit the homes of some of our better class people. You will find that "Uncle Tom" that charming old figure of literature contemporary with the war of the rebellion is quite dead now and that his prototypes are almost as extinct as is the great auk, the dodo bird, old Dobbin and the chaise[2]. . . . This was all brought about by education. . . . When a young colored boy of Chicago goes through the eight grades of grammar school and wins the cherished . . . diploma; then through a four year high school course and wins a university scholarship; and then goes to college and wins a degree . . . and is highly popular and well received among his fellow classmates, it is a very difficult thing for him to get it into his head that he is inferior to anybody that has no more knowledge, ability nor money than himself. Regardless of what the eminent sociologists may say, and the fiery and usually groundless claims of the southern negrophile [negrophobe] to the contrary notwithstanding, there is no amount of logic, nor philosophy, nor ethnology, nor anthropology, nor sociology that can convince him to his own satisfaction that he is not the possessor of all the lesser and major attributes that go to make up a good citizen by all of the standards which our republican conventions hold near and dear.

Take the late war for example, and consider the effect that it has had upon the Negro, by and large. I believe that the mental attitude of the Negro that went to war is comparable in a certain degree to the mental attitude of most of the Negroes throughout the country; so far as the awakenings are concerned. The Negro of this country has gone through the same evolution that the white man has, in his own way; and in a large percentage of the total, that way is not far removed from the way the white man's mind thought out the matter or is thinking it out, especially the soldier mind. The Negro of our country . . . the Negro of the mass I mean, is comparable in his awakening and in his manner of thought after that awakening, to these white boys who went to war. The white soldiers—being young—had

---

[2]**old Dobbin and the chaise**: Horse and carriage.

but little thought of anything but their immediate concerns, and the Negro, until lately, had but little thought of anything but his immediate concerns—being segregated. How I loathe that word.

. Since the war the Negro has been jolted into thinking by circumstances. . . . [Negroes] have learned that there were treaties and boundaries and Leagues of Nations and mandatories, and Balkan states, and a dismembered Poland, a ravished Belgium, a stricken France, a soviet Russia and a republic in Ireland and so on, and they have . . . for the first time in their lives taken a peep of their own volition and purely because they wanted to know, into the workings of governmental things of those other countries, and have tried to reason out the possible real cause of all of this bloodshed and woe and misery along such international, allied and foreign government and other vague lines.

Now then, this has logically . . . brought us round to a sort of realization of how our government was made and is conducted. I venture to claim that any average Negro of some education, if closely questioned, and the questions were put to him in simple understandable form, will tell you that he finally has come to know that he counts as a part of his government, that he is a unit in it. It took a world war to get that idea into general Negro acceptance, but it is there now. Centuries of the dictum, which heretofore not many of us disputed, that, "This was a white man's country and that we were destined to always be hewers of wood and carriers of water," was set aside by circumstances and conditions and reactions and reflexes and direct contacts of this war. Negroes were pulled out of their ordinary pursuits all over the country and called upon to do things that they had to do because there was nobody at hand to do them, and those circumstances induced an awakening that must inevitably continue for all time.

The five hundred thousand Negroes who were sent overseas to serve their country were brought into contacts that widened both their perceptions and their perspectives, broadened them, gave them new angles on life, on government, and on what both mean. They are now new men and world men, if you please. . . .

What the Negro wants and what the Negro will not be satisfied with until he gets is that treatment and that recognition that accords him not one jot or tittle less than that which any other citizen of the United States is satisfied with. He has become tired of equal rights. He wants the same rights. He is tired of equal accommodations. He wants [the] same accommodations. He is tired of equal opportunity. He wants the same opportunity. He must and will have industrial, commercial, civil and political equality. America has already given him these inalienable rights, but she has not always seen to it that he has received them. America must see that the Negro is not deprived of any right that she has given him otherwise the gift is bare, and in view of her recent international exploits she will stand in grave danger of losing her national integrity in the eyes of Europe and she will be forced to admit to her European adversaries that her constitution is but a scrap of paper.

Social equality — that ancient skeleton in the closet of the southern negrophile, whose bones are always brought out and rattled ominously whenever the Negro question is discussed—is in no way a factor in the solution of the problem, but is a condition that will quite naturally exist when the problem is eventually solved—just a little prior to the millennium. Leastwise considering the unsettled condition of the world at large, the white man of this country has a great deal more to be sensibly alarmed about than the coming of social equality. Looking into the future I can see more ominous clouds on the horizon of this country's destiny than the coming of social equality.

When the Negro ponders the situation — and now he is beginning to seriously do that — it is with a feeling of poignant resentment that he sees his alleged inferiority constantly and blatantly advertised at every hand, by the press, the pulpit, the stage and by the glaring and hideous sign-boards of segregation. Try to imagine, if you can, the feelings of a Negro army officer, who clothed in the full panoply of his profession and wearing the decorations for valor of three governments, is forced to the indignity of a jim-crow car and who is refused a seat in a theatre and a bed in a hotel. Think of the feelings of a colored officer, who after having been graduated from West Point and having worked up step by step to the rank of colonel to be retired on account of blood pressure — and other pressure — in order that he might not automatically succeed to the rank of general officer. Try to imagine the smouldering hatred within the breast of an overseas veteran who is set upon and mercilessly beaten by a gang of young hoodlums simply because he is colored. Think of the feelings in the hearts of boys and girls of my race who are clean, intelligent and industrious who apply for positions only to meet with the polite reply that, "We don't hire niggers." Think how it must feel to pass at the top of the list and get notice of appointment to some nice civil service position that is paid for out of the taxes of the commonwealth, and upon reporting to assume the duties thereof, to be told that there has been a mistake made in the appointment.

When you think of these things, and consider them seriously it is easy to see the underlying, contributory causes of the friction that led up to the recent racial troubles. It is a well known fact that civilization is but a veneer which lightly covers the surface of mankind; that if slightly scratched, with the right kind of tool, a man will turn into a bloodthirsty savage in the twinkling of an eye. The overt act that is alleged to have started the recent conflagration, would not have in itself been sufficient to have ignited and exploded such vials of wrath had not the structure of society been long soaked in the inflammable gasolene of smouldering resentment.

As soon as the white man is willing to inform himself about the true status of the Negro as he finds him today, and is willing to take off the goggles of race prejudice and to study the Negro with the naked eye of fairness, and to treat him with justice and equity, he will come to the conclusion that the Negro has "arrived" and then voila, you have the solution to the problem.

We ask not charity but justice. We no longer want perquisites but wages, salary and commissions. Much has been said . . . [about] the white man's burden. We admit to having been a burden, just as an infant that cannot walk is at one time a burden. But in the natural order of things the infant soon ceases to be a burden and eventually grows up to be a crutch for the arm that once carried him. We feel that now we are able to take our first, feeble diffident steps, and we implore the white man to set his burden down and let us try to walk. Put us in your counting rooms, your factories and in your banks. The young people who went to school with us and who learned the three R's from the same blackboard as ourselves will surely not object to working with us after we have graduated. If they do, it will only be because they are not yet accustomed to the new conditions. That is nothing. People soon become accustomed to new things and things that seem at first preposterous soon become commonplace. We have surely proven by years of unrequited toil and by constant and unfaltering loyalty and fealty that we are worthy of the justice that we ask. For God's sake give it to us!

Stanley B. Norvell

QUESTIONS FOR READING AND DISCUSSION

1. According to Norvell, what were the causes of the Chicago race riot?
2. Why did few white men "know the Negro"? How did whites judge "the race"? Why could whites not "accurately deduce what I am or what I represent," according to Norvell?
3. What did Norvell mean by saying, "Today we have with us a new Negro"? How did education influence attitudes among blacks and whites? How did World War I contribute to new attitudes among African Americans?
4. How did "the goggles of race prejudice" shape the experiences of blacks and whites? What assumptions did Norvell make about the motivations of whites and blacks and how they might be changed?

COMPARATIVE QUESTIONS

1. How did the message portrayed in "The Human American Eagle" compare to Eugene V. Debs's antiwar views? What accounted for the differences? How might Debs have responded to the men and women in the Eagle and how might they have responded to him?
2. How does the doughboy's letter reinforce or dispute the stances taken by Debs and the soldiers and nurses in the Eagle?
3. To what extent were A. Mitchell Palmer's raids against the Red menace an outgrowth of President Wilson's wartime policies? Based on the documents in this chapter, how might Debs have responded to Palmer?
4. To what extent did Debs's advocacy of socialism address the issues raised by Stanley B. Norvell? Did Norvell endorse Debs's stance toward the war and other matters?
5. The wartime appeal to patriotism intensified domestic concerns about who was authentically American. Considering the documents in this chapter, what ideas existed about who genuine Americans were, how they could be recognized, and what their duties and responsibilities were?

From New Era to Great Depression

1920–1932

During the 1920s complacency became an article of faith among many comfortable Americans. Prosperous Americans celebrated business as the embodiment of the highest American ideals. President Calvin Coolidge and members of the Republican Party championed the unity of American values and business practices. Things were as they should be, business was good, America was strong, and God was in his heaven. Republican presidents and their supporters embraced the logic of contentment that appealed to many voters. Beneath the gaze of the satisfied, however, other Americans felt disoriented and dissatisfied by the economic, religious, political, social, racial, and ethnic status quo. For them complacency was a problem, rather than a happy consequence of all problems having been solved.

DOCUMENT 23–1

Demonstrating the Need for a Federal Highway System

In 1921 Congress passed the Federal Highway Act that authorized the expenditure of $75 million a year for the construction of roads that would connect American cities in a network stretching across the continent. The U.S. Army organized a convoy from Washington, D.C. to San Francisco in the summer of 1919 that demonstrated the miserable condition of many of the nation's roads. The convoy of 81 vehicles — mostly trucks — and almost 300 soldiers (including Major Dwight D. Eisenhower, who became president in 1952) averaged about 5 miles an hour on the journey of 62 days, a trip that could be driven in a little over 40 hours today. Between Illinois and California the roads were especially bad, as illustrated here by the photo of one of the convoy's trucks. Trucks broke down frequently and got stuck even more often. As the convoy crossed the Great Salt Lake Desert, Eisenhower jotted in his log book, "Practically every vehicle was mired and rescue work required almost superhuman effort of entire personnel from 2 p.m. until after midnight." That day the convoy covered 15 miles in slightly less than 8 hours. Although the truck drivers claimed to be experienced, Eisenhower noted that they had *"a longer association with teams of horses than with internal combustion engines."* And no wonder. At the time of the convoy, the nation had about 200,000 trucks, 3.5 million cars, and 21 million horses.

Army Convoy Truck Stuck on the Road, 1919

Eisenhower Presidential Library, K. C. Downing Collection

QUESTIONS FOR READING AND DISCUSSION

1. What does the photo suggest about the feasibility of trucks transporting heavy freight from city to city? Would travel by car be easier, according to the photo? What about travel by horse and buggy?
2. What commercial and national defense issues does the photo raise?
3. What social, economic, and political considerations might explain why the roads were so bad?
4. In practical terms, how might the roads be improved? Which constituencies would favor improving roads like this one and which would be likely to oppose?
5. How does the photo depict the troubled partnership between men and machines and between agriculture and industry in the 1920s?

DOCUMENT 23–2

Reinhold Niebuhr on Christianity in Detroit

What meaning did Christianity have in an industrial society? Many Americans answered that question by affirming that Christianity and industrial capitalism were perfectly compatible. Businessmen went to church, and ministers preached the gospel of business. Reinhold Niebuhr, a young minister in Detroit, criticized the comfortable equation of Christianity with industrialization in a diary he kept between 1915 and 1928. In his diary, excerpted here, Niebuhr noted the frequent conflict between Christian ideals and the industrial realities he encountered in Detroit.

Diary Entries, 1925–1928

1925   We went through one of the big automobile factories today. So artificial is life that these factories are like a strange world to me though I have lived close to them for many years. The foundry interested me particularly. The heat was terrific. The men seemed weary. Here manual labor is a drudgery and toil is slavery. The men cannot possibly find any satisfaction in their work. They simply work to make a living. Their sweat and their dull pain are part of the price paid for the fine cars we all run. And most of us run the cars without knowing what price is being paid for them. . . .

We are all responsible. We all want the things which the factory produces and none of us is sensitive enough to care how much in human values the efficiency of the modern factory costs. Beside the brutal facts of modern industrial life, how futile are all our homiletical spoutings [sermons]! The church is undoubtedly cultivating graces and preserving spiritual amenities in the more protected areas of society. But it isn't changing the essential facts of modern industrial civilization by a hair's breadth. It isn't even thinking about them.

The morality of the church is anachronistic. Will it ever develop a moral insight and courage sufficient to cope with the real problems of modern society? . . . We ministers maintain our pride and self-respect and our sense of importance only through a vast and inclusive ignorance. If we knew the world in which we live a little better we would perish in shame or be overcome by a sense of futility. . . .

1926   Several ministers have been commended for "courage" because they permitted labor leaders to speak in their churches who represented pretty much their own convictions and said pretty much what they had been saying for years.

It does seem pretty bad to have the churches lined up so solidly against labor and for the open shop policy[1] of the town. The ministers are hardly to blame, except if they are to be condemned for not bringing out the meaning of Christianity for industrial relations more clearly in their ministry previous to the moment of crisis. As it was, few of the churches were sufficiently liberal to be able to risk an heretical voice in their pulpits. The idea that these A. F. of L. leaders are dangerous heretics is itself a rather illuminating clue to the mind of Detroit. I attended several sessions of the [labor] convention and the men impressed me as having about the same amount of daring and imagination as a group of village bankers. . . .

There are few cities in which wealth, suddenly acquired and proud of the mechanical efficiency which produced it, is so little mellowed by social intelligence. Detroit produces automobiles and is not yet willing to admit that the poor automata who are geared in on the production lines have any human problems.

From Reinhold Niebuhr, *Leaves from the Notebook of a Tamed Cynic* (Chicago: Willet, Clark & Colby, 1929).

[1]**open shop policy**: Anti-union law that permitted employers to hire workers who did not belong to a union, thereby preventing the union from representing all the workers of a given employer.

Yet we differ only in degree from the rest of the country. The churches of America are on the whole thoroughly committed to the interests and prejudices of the middle classes. I think it is a bit of unwarranted optimism to expect them to make any serious contribution to the reorganization of society. . . .

If religion is to contribute anything to the solution of the industrial problem, a more heroic type of religion than flourishes in the average church must be set to the task. . . .

That resolution we passed in our pastors' meeting, calling upon the police to be more rigorous in the enforcement of law, is a nice admission of defeat upon the part of the church. Every one of our cities has a crime problem, not so much because the police are not vigilant as because great masses of men in an urban community are undisciplined and chaotic souls, emancipated from the traditions which guided their fathers and incapable of forming new and equally potent cultural and moral restraints. . . .

Perhaps the real reason that we live such chaotic lives in urban communities is because a city is not a society at all, and moral standards are formed only in societies and through the sense of mutual obligation which neighbors feel for one another. A big city is not a society held together by human bonds. It is a mass of individuals, held together by a productive process. Its people are spiritually isolated even though they are mechanically dependent upon one another. In such a situation it is difficult to create and preserve the moral and cultural traditions which each individual needs to save his life from anarchy.

All of us do not live in moral chaos. But in so far as we escape it, it is due to our loyalty to religious, moral and cultural traditions which have come out of other ages and other circumstances. That is why churches, Protestant, Catholic and Jewish, however irrelevant their ethical idealism may be to the main facts of an industrial civilization, are nevertheless indispensable. . . .

There is something very pathetic about the efforts of almost every one of our large cities to restore by police coercion what has been lost by the decay of moral and cultural traditions. But of course we do have to save ourselves from anarchy, even if it must be done by force. Only I think the church would do well to leave the police problem alone. If violence must be used temporarily, let the state do so without undue encouragement from the church. . . .

1927   Our city race commission has finally made its report after months of investigation and further months of deliberation on our findings. It has been a rare experience to meet with these white and colored leaders and talk over our race problems. The situation which the colored people of the city face is really a desperate one, and no one who does not spend real time in gathering the facts can have any idea of the misery and pain which exists among these people, recently migrated from the south and unadjusted to our industrial civilization. Hampered both by their own inadequacies and the hostility of a white world they have a desperate fight to keep body and soul together, to say nothing of developing those amenities which raise life above the brute level.

I wish that some of our romanticists and sentimentalists could sit through a series of meetings where the real social problems of a city are discussed. They would be cured of their optimism. A city which is built around a productive process and which gives only casual thought and incidental attention to its human problems is really a kind of hell. Thousands in this town are really living in torment while the rest of us eat, drink and make merry. What a civilization! . . .

Mother and I visited at the home of ――― today where the husband is sick and was out of employment before he became sick. The folks have few connections in the city. They belong to no church. What a miserable existence it is to be friendless in a large city. And to be dependent upon a heartless industry. The man is about 55 or 57 I should judge, and he is going to have a desperate time securing employment after he gets well. These modern factories are not meant for old men. They want young men and they use them up pretty quickly. Your modern worker, with no skill but what is in the machine, is a sorry individual. After he loses the stamina of youth, he has nothing to sell. . . .

According to the ethics of our modern industrialism men over fifty, without special training, are so much junk. It is a pleasure to see how such an ethic is qualified as soon as the industrial unit is smaller and the owner has a personal interest in his men. . . . But unfortunately the units are getting larger and larger and more inhuman. . . .

The new Ford car is out. The town is full of talk about it. Newspaper reports reveal that it is the topic of the day in all world centers. Crowds storm every exhibit to get the first glimpse of this new creation. Mr. [Henry] Ford has given out an interview saying that the car has cost him about a hundred million dollars and that after finishing it he still has about a quarter of a billion dollars in the bank.

I have been doing a little arithmetic and have come to the conclusion that the car cost Ford workers at least fifty million in lost wages during the past year. No one knows how many hundreds lost their homes in the period of unemployment, and how many children were taken out of school to help fill the depleted family exchequer, and how many more children lived on short rations during this period. Mr. Ford refuses to concede that he made a mistake in bringing the car out so late. He has a way of impressing the public even with his mistakes. We are now asked to believe that the whole idea of waiting a year after the old car stopped selling before bringing out a new one was a great advertising scheme which reveals the perspicacity of this industrial genius. But no one asks about the toll in human lives.

What a civilization this is! Naïve gentlemen with a genius for mechanics suddenly become the arbiters over the lives and fortunes of hundreds of thousands. Their moral pretentions are credulously accepted at full value. No one bothers to ask whether an industry which can maintain a cash reserve of a quarter of a billion ought not make some provision for its unemployed. It is enough that the new car is a good one. . . . The cry of the hungry is drowned in the song, "Henry has made a lady out of Lizzy."[2] . . .

1928   It is almost impossible to be sane and Christian at the same time, and on the whole I have been more sane than Christian. . . . The church can really be a community of love and can give one new confidence in the efficacy of the principles of brotherhood outside of the family relation. The questions and qualms of conscience arise when one measures the church in its relationships to society, particularly to the facts of modern industry. It is at this point where it seems to me that we had better admit failure than to claim any victory. . . .

Modern industry, particularly American industry, is not Christian. The economic forces which move it are hardly qualified at a single point by really

---

[2]**Lizzy**: "Tin Lizzie" was a nickname for Ford's Model T.

ethical considerations. If, while it is in the flush of its early triumphs, it may seem impossible to bring it under the restraint of moral law, it may strengthen faith to know that life without law destroys itself. If the church can do nothing else, it can bear witness to the truth until such a day as bitter experience will force a recalcitrant civilization to a humility which it does not now possess.

QUESTIONS FOR READING AND DISCUSSION

1. Why did Niebuhr believe that the "morality of the church is anachronistic"? What did he consider to be the proper role of Christianity in industrial society? In what ways was "modern industry, particularly American industry . . . not Christian"?

2. What were the consequences of "the churches of America" being "thoroughly committed to the interests and prejudices of the middle classes"?

3. Niebuhr argued that "a city is not a society at all." Why not? Why were the police important?

4. How did Henry Ford's new car exemplify the moral basis of business?

DOCUMENT 23–3

The Ku Klux Klan Defends Americanism

During the 1920s, the Ku Klux Klan attracted hundreds of thousands throughout the nation with its defense of "true" Americans from threats allegedly posed by immigrants, blacks, Catholics, Jews, and dissenters. In the following excerpt from an essay published in the North American Review, *the imperial wizard of the Klan, Hiram W. Evans, outlined who the KKK represented and why. Evans explained the Klan's racial definition of Americanism, a definition that seemed sensible to many native-born white Americans who never joined the KKK. Evans's essay disclosed the widespread sense that the familiar contours of American life were under assault and must, somehow, be defended.*

Hiram W. Evans
The Klan's Fight for Americanism, 1926

The Klan, therefore, has now come to speak for the great mass of Americans of the old pioneer stock. We believe that it does fairly and faithfully represent them, and our proof lies in their support. To understand the Klan, then, it is necessary to understand the character and present mind of the mass of old-stock Americans. The mass, it must be remembered, as distinguished from the intellectually mongrelized "Liberals."

These are, in the first place, a blend of various peoples of the so-called Nordic race, the race which, with all its faults, has given the world almost the whole of modern civilization. The Klan does not try to represent any people but these.

From Hiram W. Evans, "The Klan's Fight for Americanism," *North American Review* 223 (March–April–May 1926). Reprinted by permission of North American Review.

There is no need to recount the virtues of the American pioneers; but it is too often forgotten that in the pioneer period a selective process of intense rigor went on. From the first only hardy, adventurous and strong men and women dared the pioneer dangers; from among these all but the best died swiftly, so that the new Nordic blend which became the American race was bred up to a point probably the highest in history. This remarkable race character, along with the new-won continent and the new-created nation, made the inheritance of the old-stock Americans the richest ever given to a generation of men.

In spite of it, however, these Nordic Americans for the last generation have found themselves increasingly uncomfortable, and finally deeply distressed. There appeared first confusion in thought and opinion, a groping and hesitancy about national affairs and private life alike, in sharp contrast to the clear, straightforward purposes of our earlier years. There was futility in religion, too, which was in many ways even more distressing. Presently we began to find that we were dealing with strange ideas; policies that always sounded well, but somehow always made us still more uncomfortable.

Finally came the moral breakdown that has been going on for two decades. One by one all our traditional moral standards went by the boards, or were so disregarded that they ceased to be binding. The sacredness of our Sabbath, of our homes, of chastity, and finally even of our right to teach our own children in our own schools fundamental facts and truths were torn away from us. Those who maintained the old standards did so only in the face of constant ridicule.

Along with this went economic distress. The assurance for the future of our children dwindled. We found our great cities and the control of much of our industry and commerce taken over by strangers, who stacked the cards of success and prosperity against us. Shortly they came to dominate our government. The *bloc* system by which this was done is now familiar to all. Every kind of inhabitant except the Americans gathered in groups which operated as units in politics, under orders of corrupt, self-seeking and un-American leaders, who both by purchase and threat enforced their demands on politicians. Thus it came about that the interests of Americans were always the last to be considered by either national or city governments, and that the native Americans were constantly discriminated against, in business, in legislation and in administrative government.

So the Nordic American today is a stranger in large parts of the land his fathers gave him. Moreover, he is a most unwelcome stranger, one much spit upon, and one to whom even the right to have his own opinions and to work for his own interests is now denied with jeers and revilings. "We must Americanize the Americans," a distinguished immigrant said recently. Can anything more clearly show the state to which the real American has fallen in this country which was once his own?

Our falling birth rate, the result of all this, is proof of our distress. We no longer feel that we can be fair to children we bring into the world, unless we can make sure from the start that they shall have capital or education or both, so that they need never compete with those who now fill the lower rungs of the ladder of success. We dare no longer risk letting our youth "make its own way" in the conditions under which we live. So even our unborn children are being crowded out of their birthright.

All this has been true for years, but it was the World War that gave us our first hint of the real cause of our troubles, and began to crystallize our ideas. The war revealed that millions whom we had allowed to share our heritage and prosperity, and whom we had assumed had become part of us, were in fact not wholly so. They had other loyalties: each was willing — anxious! — to sacrifice the interests of the country that had given him shelter to the interests of the one he was supposed to have cast off; each in fact did use the freedom and political power we had given him against ourselves whenever he could see any profit for his older loyalty.

This, of course, was chiefly in international affairs, and the excitement caused by the discovery of disloyalty subsided rapidly after the war ended. But it was not forgotten by the Nordic Americans. They had been awakened and alarmed; they began to suspect that the hyphenism[1] which had been shown was only a part of what existed; their quiet was not that of renewed sleep, but of strong men waiting very watchfully. And presently they began to form decisions about all those aliens who were Americans for profit only.

They decided that even the crossing of salt-water did not dim a single spot on a leopard; that an alien usually remains an alien no matter what is done to him, what veneer of education he gets, what oaths he takes, nor what public attitudes he adopts. They decided that the melting pot was a ghastly failure, and remembered that the very name was coined by a member of one of the races — the Jews — which most determinedly refuses to melt. They decided that in every way, as well as in politics, the alien in the vast majority of cases is unalterably fixed in his instincts, character, thought and interests by centuries of racial selection and development, that he thinks first for his own people, works only with and for them, cares entirely for their interests, considers himself always one of them, and never an American. They decided that in character, instincts, thought, and purposes — in his whole soul — an alien remains fixedly alien to America and all it means.

They saw, too, that the alien was tearing down the American standard of living, especially in the lower walks. It became clear that while the American can out-work the alien, the alien can so far under-live the American as to force him out of all competitive labor. So they came to realize that the Nordic can easily survive and rule and increase if he holds for himself the advantages won by strength and daring of his ancestors in times of stress and peril, but that if he surrenders those advantages to the peoples who could not share the stress, he will soon be driven below the level at which he can exist by their low standards, low living and fast breeding. And they saw that the low standard aliens of Eastern and Southern Europe were doing just that thing to us.

They learned, though more slowly, that alien ideas are just as dangerous to us as the aliens themselves, no matter how plausible such ideas may sound. With most of the plain people this conclusion is based simply on the fact that the alien ideas do not work well for them. Others went deeper and came to understand that the differences in racial background, in breeding, instinct, character and emotional point of view are more important than logic. So ideas which may be perfectly healthy for an alien may also be poisonous for Americans.

Finally they learned the great secret of the propagandists; that success in corrupting public opinion depends on putting out the subversive ideas without revealing their source. They came to suspect that "prejudice" against foreign ideas is really a protective device of nature against mental food that may be

---

[1]**hyphenism:** The view that U.S. citizens of foreign ancestry were not loyal Americans but remained loyal to their country of origin.

indigestible. They saw, finally, that the alien leaders in America act on this theory, and that there is a steady flood of alien ideas being spread over the country, always carefully disguised as American.

As they learned all this the Nordic Americans have been gradually arousing themselves to defend their homes and their own kind of civilization. They have not known just how to go about it; the idealist philanthropy and good-natured generosity which led to the philosophy of the melting pot have died hard. Resistance to the peaceful invasion of the immigrant is no such simple matter as snatching up weapons and defending frontiers, nor has it much spectacular emotionalism to draw men to the colors.

The old-stock Americans are learning, however. They have begun to arm themselves for this new type of warfare. Most important, they have broken away from the fetters of the false ideals and philanthropy which put aliens ahead of their own children and their own race.

To do this they have had to reject completely—and perhaps for the moment the rejection is a bit too complete—the whole body of "Liberal" ideas which they had followed with such simple, unquestioning faith. The first and immediate cause of the break with Liberalism was that it had provided no defense against the alien invasion, but instead had excused it—even defended it against Americanism. Liberalism is today charged in the mind of most Americans with nothing less than national, racial and spiritual treason. . . .

We are a movement of the plain people, very weak in the matter of culture, intellectual support, and trained leadership. We are demanding, and we expect to win, a return of power into the hands of the everyday, not highly cultured, not overly intellectualized, but entirely unspoiled and not de-Americanized, average citizen of the old stock. Our members and leaders are all of this class—the opposition of the intellectuals and liberals who held the leadership, betrayed Americanism, and from whom we expect to wrest control, is almost automatic. . . .

Our critics have accused us of being merely a "protest movement," of being frightened; they say we fear alien competition, are in a panic because we cannot hold our own against the foreigners. That is partly true. We are a protest movement—protesting against being robbed. We are afraid of competition with peoples who would destroy our standard of living. We are suffering in many ways, we have been betrayed by our trusted leaders, we are half beaten already. But we are not frightened nor in a panic. We have merely awakened to the fact that we must fight for our own. We are going to fight—and win! . . .

QUESTIONS FOR READING AND DISCUSSION

1. What did Evans mean by "the American race"? How was such a "race" formed? Who composed it?

2. Why was "the Nordic American today . . . a stranger"? In what ways had a "moral breakdown" occurred, according to Evans? What part did World War I play?

3. Why was "hyphenism" important? In what sense was "the melting pot . . . a ghastly failure"? Why? How might an immigrant have responded to Evans's arguments?

4. Why did Evans believe "Liberalism" amounted to "national, racial and spiritual treason"? What was the significance of "false ideals and philanthropy"? How might a "Liberal" have replied to Evans's criticisms?

DOCUMENT 23–4

Mothers Seek Freedom from Unwanted Pregnancies

When birth control activist Margaret Sanger opened the first birth control clinic in the United States in Brooklyn in 1916, authorities arrested and jailed her for violating the Comstock Law of 1873, which outlawed the distribution of information about contraception. Undeterred, Sanger sponsored many other clinics and worked tirelessly to publicize birth control. During the 1920s more than 250,000 women wrote to Sanger, asking for information and help. Excerpted below, these letters revealed what Sanger termed the "bondage" of motherhood. Many women experienced the 1920s not as an era of flappers and sexual freedom but of overwhelming burdens of child rearing and family responsibilities.

Margaret Sanger
Motherhood in Bondage, 1928

Thousands of letters are sent to me every year by mothers in all parts of the United States and Canada.

All of them voice desperate appeals for deliverance from the bondage of enforced maternity. . . . [Here are] the confessions of these enslaved mothers. . . .

[MOTHER A]

I was married at the age of twelve years. One month before my thirteenth birthday I became the mother of my first child, and now at the age of thirty I am the mother of eleven children, ten of them living, the youngest now seven months old. My health has been poor the past two years now and I don't believe I could ever stand it to have any more. Please won't you send me information so I won't have to have more children, for we have more now that we can really take care of. . . .

[MOTHER B]

I am nineteen years old, have been married two and a half years and my second baby is just two months old. I love my babies, my husband and my home. Life and the work it brings would be nothing to me if I could only feel sure I would have no more children right away. I do not want another for a few years. But my babies are girls, and my husband wanted a son and I want to give him one, but I would like to wait until my little girls are better on their way in life and I am more mature and stronger. I can feel myself becoming weaker and if I had another baby within the next couple of years it would only be detrimental to the child and the rest of the family as well as myself. I left high school at the age of seventeen to marry a poor man and never have regretted it. I have done all my own work and borne my own children happily and with never a complaint, but I live in constant dread of another baby soon, and so does my husband. He has kept away from me for long periods but I cannot ask that of him forever. In the hospital where my babies were born every woman there was trying to find out the same thing. They asked

---

From Margaret Sanger, *Motherhood in Bondage*, 1928. Used with permission of the Ohio State University.

doctors, nurses and each other. They were all in constant dread of more children. Such a condition is deplorable in this age of freedom in everything else. . . .

[MOTHER C]

I was a high school girl of seventeen when I married a farmer, fourteen years ago. I am the mother of eight living children, one baby dead and a three months miscarriage. I am thirty-one years of age and have spent almost all of my married life nursing and carrying babies. I would like you to advise me what to do to prevent from having any more children. My oldest child is thirteen and my youngest five months. I love my children and would give my life for them. But what good would that do, who will teach and care and sacrifice for them as a mother will? I know it was my ignorance on this important subject that has put me where I am, but I must learn all I can for I have three little girls who will need to know about these things and it is them I must learn to care for and save from my fate. . . . I have always suffered and worked and never enjoyed myself without this fear of being pregnant again. I love my husband as much as ever and we never quarrel or have hard feelings. We both work hard to make an honest living for our children. I have hired help when I need them most, but I want my home, my husband and children to myself, to raise as we wish without being spoiled with hired help. I want to teach my girls and get advice for myself. My mother is old-fashioned and thinks children should not know too much and never told us girls what to expect at our sick times or when we were married. I have asked my doctor many times but never get any satisfaction from him. I think I have been down to the valley of death enough times. So please answer and give me some hope. . . .

[MOTHER D]

I have been married twelve years and am the mother of seven girls. The oldest is ten years old and you know what I suffered. We are poor. We can't care for what we got half the time for them to be healthy. I got one dead. My oldest one living has got heart trouble. My youngest one is seven months old. I'm just twenty-eight years old. We are working on the shares this year. My husband is a hard worker and tries to make an honest living. And let me tell you I have to work to make ends meet. I saw, chop wood, plow and have my little kids to tend to for they are not large enough to help me but a little. Oh, I have a hard time. We are never out of debt. I never get to go anywhere for I never got a dress nice enough to wear or I'm always in a family way. Oh, it is hard on poor women to be in my shape. It is just one baby after another. I can't stand it much longer and work like I do, trying to keep a little to eat and wear. I pray you to help me. If I could stop having babies long enough for these to get where they could walk, Lord, how glad I would be. I know little babies are sweet but when you can't clothe them like they are to be and then they are sick. Lord what trouble mothers do have. . . .

[MOTHER E]

I was married three years ago and have two children one two years old and the other almost a year. Before I was married there was no other girl in the community that was stronger or healthier than I—I did not know what it was to be sick. We rented a house and my husband intended working in the mill but then the mill shut down and he could get no work anywhere. I was in the family way and of course we tried to live as cheap as we possibly could, having no work I worried all day and couldn't sleep at nights. I would worry all the time. When my baby was born it only weighed three and a half pounds and cried lots. Then my husband still had no work. When baby was three months old we got a chance to work on a farm. I to keep house and him to work on the farm. I got up at four o'clock and went to bed at ten o'clock. I was in the family way again. Then last spring we came up to my father's house I to keep house and husband to work in the mill. I had lots of work, I get up at three o'clock and go to bed at nine; there is father and six brothers and sisters, myself and two children now. I don't want any more children. If I get in the family way again I don't know what I will do. . . . I seem to have lost all interest in life, I sometimes feel that I would be glad to die sooner than to have more children. . . .

[MOTHER F]

I am twenty-five years of age and a mother of three children and in less than five years. I had the three of them and it's very hard for me. I do be very sick and I have to take chloroform and roar like a lion with pains. So please help me, give me some good advice what to do to take care of myself as my dear mother is died and I didn't know any better so I married young and a poor man just like myself and so his mother was died also. So we went housekeeping for his father. Now there is five of them, who are all boys and a father-in-law and five of us: now there's eleven of us and only myself to take care of all those people and my three poor little ones are neglected and my baby one seventeen months old and a very mean father-in-law. He says throw the kid down on the floor and you do this and that and hurry up. So I would not want any more children for I can't give the care they ought to have and I have tried to do all the washing, ironing, cooking, baking bread and yet beside sewing for my children and myself as we can't afford to buy things ready made. Just think the work for eleven people! It is very hard for me and when evening comes I'm in and out all tired. Why when I go to bed I can't turn round and can't stand it any more and I work all day and cry beside and when they get home from work I don't even hear a kind word from any one. . . . My heart is broken. No one ever takes pity on me and I'm just tired of living and bringing those children into this world to suffer. . . .

[MOTHER G]

I am twenty-eight years old and the mother-to-be very soon of a sixth child. I am a farmer's wife. My husband is a drunkard and so very abusive. He tries to kill me and beats at my door. I have to hide the butcher- and paring knives and the guns. He calls me the vilest things a woman can be called before my children and threatens my aged parents and I don't dare tell the neighbors. They respect him. He don't say anything before them.

I have so much work to do. I raise garden enough for seven or eight people to eat all summer. I canned six hundred quarts of fruit last summer. Always do. I have to raise enough chickens to eat, some to sell and enough to supply our family in eggs and help keep up the table. I do all our washing for our family and I have been injured when my first baby was born until I can hardly stand on my feet and no one knows what I suffer. We own 114 acres of well-improved corn-belt land. I have it thrown in my face how dishonest I am, and what a liar I am. He never trusts me an inch and will ask the neighbors and children questions — to see if I am lying.

He calls me a liar and thief and other names fifty times a day. He says I am no wife if I don't like the way he does, how can I help myself, and a thousand other things. I can't please him no way, shape or manner. My baby will be born the last of April. I don't want it. . . .

[MOTHER H]

My mother is of the old German type and she said everybody could and should have all the children they could even if it kills them. She is a good mother, but I don't think it is right to raise children like cattle and then throw them to the street or poorhouse to be brought up or die. If I could get one good contraceptive that would not fail but would be sure so I would not become pregnant till I can get strong again I would surely be glad. Then I could give my husband my true love and do my children justice.

QUESTIONS FOR READING AND DISCUSSION

1. Sanger claimed that these mothers were "enslaved," that they sought "deliverance from the bondage of enforced maternity." Did the mothers see themselves in those terms? According to the mothers, who were their enslavers?

2. If these mothers sought to limit births, why didn't they just say "No"? Many claimed to be ignorant about birth control methods. Do you think that was true? Why or why not?

3. In these letters, how did mothers portray their relationship to their children? Why, according to Mother B, were they "all in constant dread of more children"?

4. To what degree did the husbands of these mothers share their desire to limit births? What do you think these mothers and their husbands believed about sexuality?

5. These mothers "have a hard time," as Mother D said. To what extent were their experiences typical? In what ways were their difficulties the result of poverty?

DOCUMENT 23–5

Marcus Garvey Explains the Goals of the Universal Negro Improvement Association

Ideals of racial pride and purity appealed to many African Americans. Tens of thousands joined Marcus Garvey's Universal Negro Improvement Association (UNIA) and many thousands more sympathized with Garvey's ideas. In this excerpt from an essay in a contemporary periodical, Garvey explained the origins of the UNIA and why he believed its program of racial purity, separatism, and nationalism represented the best hope for the future. His essay reveals both aspirations and frustrations common among many African Americans during the 1920s.

From Marcus Garvey, "The Negro's Greatest Enemy," *Current History* 18 (September 1923), 951–57.

The Negro's Greatest Enemy, 1923

I was born in the Island of Jamaica, British West Indies, on Aug. 17, 1887. My parents were black negroes. . . . I grew up with other black and white boys. I was never whipped by any, but made them all respect the strength of my arms. I got my education from many sources — through private tutors, two public schools, two grammar or high schools and two colleges. . . .

To me, at home in my early days, there was no difference between white and black. . . . We romped and were happy children playmates together. The little white girl whom I liked most knew no better than I did myself. We were two innocent fools who never dreamed of a race feeling and problem. As a child, I went to school with white boys and girls, like all other negroes. We were not called negroes then. I never heard the term negro used once until I was about fourteen.

At fourteen my little white playmate and I parted. Her parents thought the time had come to separate us and draw the color line. They sent her and another sister to Edinburgh, Scotland, and told her that she was never to write or try to get in touch with me, for I was a "nigger." It was then that I found for the first time that there was some difference in humanity, and that there were different races, each having its own separate and distinct social life. . . .

At maturity the black and white boys separated, and took different courses in life. I grew up then to see the difference between the races more and more. My schoolmates as young men did not know or remember me any more. Then I realized that I had to make a fight for a place in the world, that it was not so easy to pass on to office and position. Personally, however, I had not much difficulty in finding and holding a place for myself, for I was aggressive. At eighteen I had an excellent position as manager of a large printing establishment, having under my control several men old enough to be my grandfathers. But I got mixed up with public life. I started to take an interest in the politics of my country, and then I saw the injustice done to my race because it was black, and I became dissatisfied on that account. I went traveling to South and Central America and parts of the West Indies to find out if it was so elsewhere, and I found the same situation. I set sail for Europe to find out if it was different there, and again I found the same stumbling-block—"You are black." I read of the conditions in America. I read "Up From Slavery," by Booker T. Washington, and then my doom—if I may so call it—of being a race leader dawned upon me in London after I had traveled through almost half of Europe.

I asked, "Where is the black man's Government?" "Where is his King and his kingdom?" "Where is his President, his country, and his ambassador, his army, his navy, his men of big affairs?" I could not find them, and then I declared, "I will help to make them."

Becoming naturally restless for the opportunity of doing something for the advancement of my race, I was determined that the black man would not continue to be kicked about by all the other races and nations of the world, as I saw it in the West Indies, South and Central America and Europe, and as I read of it in America. My young and ambitious mind led me into flights of great imagination. I saw before me then, even as I do now, a new world of black men, not peons, serfs, dogs and slaves, but a nation of sturdy men making their impress upon civilization and causing a new light to dawn upon the human race. I could not remain in London any more. My brain was afire. There was a world of thought to conquer. I had to start ere it became too late and the work be not done. Immediately I boarded a ship at Southampton for Jamaica, where I arrived on July 15, 1914. The Universal Negro Improvement Association and African Communities

(Imperial) League was founded and organized five days after my arrival, with the program of uniting all the negro peoples of the world into one great body to establish a country and Government absolutely their own. . . .

I got in touch with Booker Washington and told him what I wanted to do. He invited me to America and promised to speak with me in the Southern and other States to help my work. Although he died in the Fall of 1915, I made my arrangements and arrived in the United States on March 23, 1916.

Here I found a new and different problem. I immediately visited some of the then so-called negro leaders, only to discover, after a close study of them, that they had no program, but were mere opportunists who were living off their so-called leadership while the poor people were groping in the dark. I traveled through thirty-eight States and everywhere found the same condition. I visited Tuskegee [Alabama] and paid my respects to the dead hero, Booker Washington, and then returned to New York, where I organized the New York division of the Universal Negro Improvement Association. . . .

The organization under my Presidency grew by leaps and bounds. I started *The Negro World*. Being a journalist, I edited this paper free of cost for the association, and worked for them without pay until November, 1920. I traveled all over the country for the association at my own expense, and established branches until in 1919 we had about thirty branches in different cities. By my writings and speeches we were able to build up a large organization of over 2,000,000 by June, 1919, at which time we launched the program of the Black Star Line. . . .

The first year of our activities for the Black Star Line added prestige to the Universal Negro Improvement Association. Several hundred thousand dollars worth of shares were sold. Our first ship, the steamship Yarmouth, had made two voyages to the West Indies and Central America. The white press had flashed the news all over the world. I, a young negro, as President of the corporation, had become famous. My name was discussed on five continents. The Universal Negro Improvement Association gained millions of followers all over the world. By August, 1920, over 4,000,000 persons had joined the movement. A convention of all the negro peoples of the world was called to meet in New York that month. Delegates came from all parts of the known world. Over 25,000 persons packed the Madison Square Garden on Aug. 1 to hear me speak to the first International Convention of Negroes. It was a record-breaking meeting, the first and the biggest of its kind. The name of Garvey had become known as a leader of his race.

Such fame among negroes was too much for other race leaders and politicians to tolerate. My downfall was planned by my enemies. They laid all kinds of traps for me. They scattered their spies among the employees of the Black Star Line and the Universal Negro Improvement Association. Our office records were stolen. Employees started to be openly dishonest; we could get no convictions against them. . . . The ships' officers started to pile up thousands of dollars of debts against the company without the knowledge of the officers of the corporation. Our ships were damaged at sea, and there was a general riot of wreck and ruin. Officials of the Universal Negro Improvement Association also began to steal and be openly dishonest. I had to dismiss them. They joined my enemies, and thus I had an endless fight on my hands to save the ideals of the association and carry out our program for the race. My negro enemies, finding that they alone could not destroy me, resorted to misrepresenting me to the leaders of the white race, several of whom, without proper investigation, also opposed me. . . .

The temporary ruin of the Black Star Line has in no way affected the larger work of the Universal Negro Improvement Association, which now has 900 branches with an approximate membership of 6,000,000. This organization has succeeded in organizing the negroes all over the world and we now look forward to a renaissance that will create a new people and bring about the restoration of Ethiopia's ancient glory.

Being black, I have committed an unpardonable offense against the very light colored negroes in America and the West Indies by making myself famous as a negro leader of millions. In their view, no black man must rise above them, but I still forge ahead determined to give to the world the truth about the new negro who is determined to make and hold for himself a place in the affairs of men. The Universal Negro Improvement Association has been misrepresented by my enemies. They have tried to make it appear that we are hostile to other races. This is absolutely false. We love all humanity. We are working for the peace of the world which we believe can only come about when all races are given their due.

We feel that there is absolutely no reason why there should be any differences between the black and white races, if each stop to adjust and steady itself. We believe in the purity of both races. We do not believe the black man should be encouraged in the idea that his highest purpose in life is to marry a white woman, but we do believe that the white man should be taught to respect the black woman in the same way as he wants the black man to respect the white woman. It is a vicious and dangerous doctrine of social equality to urge, as certain colored leaders do, that black and white should get together, for that would destroy the racial purity of both.

We believe that the black people should have a country of their own where they should be given the fullest opportunity to develop politically, socially and industrially. The black people should not be encouraged to remain in white people's countries and expect to be Presidents, Governors, Mayors, Senators, Congressmen, Judges and social and industrial leaders. We believe that with the rising ambition of the negro, if a country is not provided for him in another 50 or 100 years, there will be a terrible clash that will end disastrously to him and disgrace our civilization. We desire to prevent such a clash by pointing the negro to a home of his own. We feel that all well disposed and broad minded white men will aid in this direction. It is because of this belief no doubt that my negro enemies, so as to prejudice me further in the opinion of the public, wickedly state that I am a member of the Ku Klux Klan, even though I am a black man.

I have been deprived of the opportunity of properly explaining my work to the white people of America through the prejudice worked up against me by jealous and wicked members of my own race. My success as an organizer was much more than rival negro leaders could tolerate. They, regardless of consequences, either to me or to the race, had to destroy me by fair means or foul. The thousands of anonymous and other hostile letters written to the editors and publishers of the white press by negro rivals to prejudice me in the eyes of public opinion are sufficient evidence of the wicked and vicious opposition I have had to meet from among my own people, especially among the very lightly colored. . . . No wonder, therefore, that the great white population of this country and of the world has a wrong impression of the aims and objects of the Universal Negro Improvement Association and of the work of Marcus Garvey.

Having had the wrong education as a start in his racial career, the negro has become his own greatest enemy. Most of the trouble I have had in advancing the cause of the race has come from negroes. Booker Washington aptly described the race in one of his lectures by stating that we were like crabs in a barrel, that none would allow the other to climb over, but on any such attempt all would continue to pull back into the barrel the one crab that would make the effort to climb out. Yet, those of us with vision cannot desert the race, leaving it to suffer and die.

Looking forward a century or two, we can see an economic and political death struggle for the survival of the different race groups. Many of our present-day national centres will have become over-crowded with vast surplus populations. The fight for bread and position will be keen and severe. The weaker and unprepared group is bound to go under. That is why, visionaries as we are in the Universal Negro Improvement Association, we are fighting for the founding of a negro nation in Africa, so that there will be no clash between black and white and that each race will have a separate existence and civilization all its own without courting suspicion and hatred or eyeing each other with jealousy and rivalry within the borders of the same country.

White men who have struggled for and built up their countries and their own civilizations are not disposed to hand them over to the negro or any other race without let or hindrance. It would be unreasonable to expect this. Hence any vain assumption on the part of the negro to imagine that he will one day become President of the Nation, Governor of the State or Mayor of the city in the countries of white men, is like waiting on the devil and his angels to take up their residence in the Realm on High and direct there the affairs of Paradise.

QUESTIONS FOR READING AND DISCUSSION

1. What meanings did "race" have for Garvey? How did he envision the ideal relationship among races? Why was it "a vicious and dangerous doctrine" to urge that "black and white should get together"? How did his personal experience with racial segregation inform his view?
2. What goals did he have for the UNIA? How would "a new world of black men" be different from the world that existed?
3. How might a supporter of Booker T. Washington have responded to Garvey's arguments?
4. To what extent did Garvey's ideas reflect larger currents of thought during the 1920s? Were Garvey's ideas an expression of — or a challenge to — American ideals?

COMPARATIVE QUESTIONS

1. How did the army's transcontinental convoy illustrate the strengths and limitations of American society in the 1920s?
2. How did Reinhold Niebuhr's view of industrial society and spiritual progress compare with that of the mothers who wrote to Margaret Sanger?
3. How did Hiram Evans's characterization of America compare with Niebuhr's?
4. How did Evans's advocacy of the Ku Klux Klan compare with Marcus Garvey's promotion of the UNIA?
5. What arguments might the Republican presidents of the 1920s have made to respond to the views of Niebuhr, Evans, Garvey, and the mothers in bondage?
6. According to the documents in this chapter, what were the major divisions in American society, and what should be done, if anything, to repair them? Did the authors of these documents feel that they had the power, or the freedom, to change and improve their situations within the contemporary social and political structure?

24 The New Deal Experiment
1932–1939

The New Deal initiated an unprecedented array of government reforms in response to the unprecedented crisis of the Great Depression. Franklin D. Roosevelt had few specific plans other than to improvise constantly and experiment until something worked. The New Deal's willingness to identify problems and try to solve them represented a departure from the laissez-faire policies of Roosevelt's Republican predecessors. Working people appreciated the New Dealers' efforts to help, but by the end of the 1930s many remained mired in hard times. The following documents illustrate the hopes many working people had about what Roosevelt's government would do, as well as shortcomings and criticisms of New Deal programs from those who believed they went too far and those who faulted them for not going far enough.

DOCUMENT 24–1

Martha Gellhorn Reports on Conditions in North Carolina in 1934

To comprehend the needs of Americans impoverished by the Depression, President Franklin D. Roosevelt's key domestic advisor, Harry Hopkins, director of the Federal Emergency Relief Administration, sent reporters throughout the country to observe the struggles of ordinary citizens and report back. Martha Gellhorn, one of the reporters Hopkins hired, returned from a stint as a foreign correspondent in Europe to report on conditions in the United States. (Gellhorn later met and married the novelist Ernest Hemingway and had a distinguished career as a war correspondent during World War II.) Gellhorn's report from North Carolina, excerpted here, highlighted the widespread faith in President Roosevelt and the New Deal among poor people, amidst the grim realities of need and blight.

Martha Gellhorn to Harry Hopkins, November 11, 1934

All during this trip [to North Carolina] I have been thinking to myself about that curious phrase "red menace," and wondering where said menace hid itself. Every house I visited — [textile] mill worker or unemployed — had a picture of the President. These ranged from newspaper clippings (in destitute homes) to large colored prints, framed in gilt cardboard. The portrait holds the place of honour over the mantel; I can only compare this to the Italian peasant's Madonna. And the feeling of these people for the president is one of the most remarkable emotional phenomena I have ever met. He is at once God and their intimate friend; he knows them all by name, knows their little town and mill, their little lives and problems. And, though everything else fails, he is there, and will not let them down.

I have been seeing people who, according to almost any standard, have practically nothing in life and practically nothing to look forward to or hope for. But there is hope; confidence, something intangible and real: "the president isn't going to forget us."

Let me cite cases: I went to see a woman with five children who was living on relief ($3.40 a week). Her picture of the President was a small one, and she told me her oldest daughter had been married some months ago and had cried for the big, coloured picture as a wedding present. The children have no shoes and that woman is terrified of the coming cold as if it were a definite physical entity. There is practically no furniture left in the home, and you can imagine what and how they eat. But she said, suddenly brightening, "I'd give my heart to see the President. I know he means to do everything he can for us; but they make it hard for him; they won't let him." I note this case as something special; because here the faith was coupled with a feeling (entirely sympathetic) that the President was not entirely omnipotent.

I have been seeing mill workers; and in every mill when possible, the local Union president. There has been widespread discrimination in the south; and many mills haven't re-opened since the strike. Those open often run on such curtailment that workers are getting from 2 to 3 days work a week. The price of food has risen (especially the kind of food they eat: fat-back bacon, flour, meal, sorghum) as high as 100%. It is getting cold; and they have no clothes. The Union presidents are almost all out of work, since the strike. In many mill villages, evictions have been served; more threatened. These men are in a terrible fix. (Lord, how barren the language seems: these men are faced by hunger and cold, by the prospect of becoming dependent beggars — in their own eyes: by the threat of homelessness, and their families dispersed. What more can a man face, I don't know.) You would expect to find them maddened with fear; with hostility. I expected and waited for "lawless" talk; threats; or at least, blank despair. And I didn't find it. I found a kind of contained and quiet misery; fear for their families and fear that their children wouldn't be able to go to school. ("All we want is work and the chance to care for our families like a man should.") But what is keeping them sane, keeping them going on and hoping, is their belief in the President. . . .

These are the things they say to me; "We trust in the Supreme Being and Franklin Roosevelt." — "You heard him talk over the radio, ain't you? He's the only president who ever said anything about the forgotten man. We know he's going to stand by us." — "He's a man of his word and he promised us; we aren't

From Martha Gelhorn to Harry Hopkins, Report, Gaston County, North Carolina, November 11, 1934, Franklin D. Roosevelt Library, Harry Hopkins Papers, Box 66.

worrying as long as we got him" — "The president won't let these awful conditions go on." — "The president said no man was going to go hungry and cold;
he'll get us our jobs." . . .

I am going on and on about this because I think it has vast importance. These
people will be slow to give up hope; terribly slow to doubt the president. But if they
don't get their jobs; then what? If the winter comes on and they find themselves
on our below-subsistence relief; then what? I think they might strike again; hopelessly and apathetically. In very few places, there might be some violence speedily
crushed. But if they lose this hope, there isn't much left for them as a group. And
I feel [if] this class (whatever marvelous stock they are, too) loses its courage or
morale or whatever you want to call it, there will be an even worse social problem
than there now is. And I think that with time, adding disillusionment and suffering,
they might actually go against their own grain and turn into desperate people. As it
is, between them and fear, stands the President. But only the President. . . .

What has been constantly before me is the health problem. To write about it
is difficult only in that one doesn't know where to begin. Our relief people [who
receive relief from New Deal agencies] are definitely on below subsistence living
scales. (This is the unanimous verdict of anyone connected with relief; and a brief
study of budgets clinches the matter.)

The result is that dietary diseases abound. I know that in this area there has
always been pelagra [a serious vitamin deficiency disease caused by poor nutrition];
but that doesn't make matters better. In any case it is increasing; and I have seen it
ranging from scaly elbows in children to insanity in a grown man. Here is what
doctors say: "It's no use telling mothers what to feed their children; they haven't
the food to give" . . . "Conditions are really horrible here; it seems as if the people
were degenerating before your eyes: the children are worse mentally and physically than their parents." . . . "I've just come from seeing some patients who have
been living on corn bread and corn hominy, without seasoning, for two weeks. I
wonder how long it takes for pelagra to set in; just a question of days now." . . . "All
the mill workers I see are definite cases of undernourishment; that's the best breeding ground I know for disease." . . . "There's not much use prescribing medicine;
they haven't the money to buy it." . . . "You can't do anything with these people
until they're educated to take care of themselves; they don't know what to eat; they
haven't the beginning of an idea how to protect themselves against sickness." . . .

Every doctor says that syphilis is spreading unchecked and uncured. One
doctor even said that it had assumed the proportions of an epidemic and wouldn't
be stopped unless the government stepped in; and treated it like small-pox. . . .

Which brings us to birth control. Every social worker I saw, and every doctor,
and the majority of mill owners, talked about birth control as the basic need of
this class. I have seen three generations of unemployed (14 in all) living in one
room; and both mother and daughter were pregnant. Our relief people have a
child a year; large families are the despair of the social worker and the doctor. The
doctors say that the more children in a family[,] the lower the health rating. These
people regard children as something the Lord has seen fit to send them, and you
can't question the Lord even if you don't agree with him. There is absolutely no
hope for these children; I feel that our relief rolls will double themselves given
time. The children are growing up in terrible surroundings; dirt, disease, over-
crowding, undernourishment. Often their parents were farm people, who at least
had air and enough food. This cannot be said for the children. I know we could do
birth control in this area; it would be a slow and trying job beginning with education. (You have to fight superstition, stupidity and lack of hygiene.) But birth

control would be worked into prenatal clinics; and the grape vine telegraph is the best propaganda I know. I think if it isn't done that we may as well fold up; these people cannot be bettered under present circumstances. Their health is going to pieces; the present generation of unemployed will be useless human material in no time; their housing is frightful . . . ; they are ignorant and often below-par intelligence. What can we do: feed them—feed them pinto beans and corn bread and sorghum and watch the pelagra spread. And in twenty years, what will there be; how can a decent civilization be based on a decayed substrata, which is incapable physically and mentally to cope with life? . . .

[There is also] a problem of education. (Do you know that the highest paid teacher in a school in North Carolina gets $720 a year? This is not criticism of the teachers; it is a downright woe.) But the schooling is such awful nonsense. Teach the kids to recite the Gettysburg address by heart: somehow one is not impressed. And they don't know what to eat or how to cook it; they don't even know that their bodies can be maintained in health by protective measures; they don't know that one needn't have ten children when one can't feed one; they don't know that syphilis is destroying and contagious. And with all this, they are grand people. If there is any meaning in the phrase "American stock" it has some meaning here. They are sound and good humored; kind and loyal. I don't believe they are lazy; I believe they are mostly ill and ignorant. They have a strong family feeling; and one sees this in pitiful ways—for instance: if there is any means of keeping the children properly or prettily clothed, it is done; but the mother will be a prematurely aged, ugly woman who has nothing to put on her back. And the father's first comment will be: could we get shoes for the children so they can go to school (though the father himself may be walking on the ground). . . .

I hope you won't misunderstand this report. It's easy to see what the government is up against. What with a bunch of loathsome [anti–New Deal] ignoramuses talking about "lavish expenditure" and etc. And all right-minded [anti–New Deal] citizens virtuously protesting against anything which makes sense or sounds new. I'm writing this . . . report because you did send us out to look; and you ought to get as much as we see. It isn't all there is to see, by any means; and naturally I have been looking at the worst and darkest side. But it is a terribly frightening picture. Is there no way we can get it before the public, no way to make them realize that you cannot build a future on bad basic material? We are so proud of being a new people in a free land. And we have a serf class; a serf class which seems to me to be in as bad a state of degeneration maybe, in this area, worse than the low class European who has learned self-protection through centuries of hardship. It makes me raging mad to hear talk of "red revolution," the talk of cowards who would deserve what they got, having blindly and selfishly fomented revolution themselves. Besides I don't believe it; it takes time for all things including successful rebellion; time and a tradition for revolutions which does not exist in this country. But it's far more terrible to think that the basis of our race is slowly rotting, almost before we have had time to become a race.

QUESTIONS FOR READING AND DISCUSSION

1. According to Gellhorn, why was it important that the North Carolinians she met said, for example, "We trust in the Supreme Being and Franklin Roosevelt"? What did such statements say about their outlook?

2. What accounted for the serious health problems Gellhorn encountered, according to her report?

3. What did Gellhorn expect "loathsome ignoramuses" and "all right-minded citizens" would think about the conditions she saw in North Carolina and how they might be remedied?

4. Gellhorn observed that "a tradition for revolutions does not exist in this country." Why did she think that was important? Why did she think it was "more terrible" still that "the basis of our race is slowly rotting"?

5. Did Gellhorn believe the conditions she observed in North Carolina could be improved by the New Deal? If so, how? If not, why not?

DOCUMENT 24–2

Working People's Letters to New Dealers

President Roosevelt expressed sympathy for the plight of working people during the Great Depression. That sympathy, heard by millions in Roosevelt's fireside chats and frequent press conferences, helped to shape efforts to provide relief, to restore employment, and to regulate wages, hours, and working conditions. Feeling they had a friend in the White House, thousands of American working people wrote the president and other New Dealers, especially Secretary of Labor Frances Perkins. Those letters, excerpted here, illustrated the hard times many Americans continued to face long after the New Deal was under way.

Letter to Frances Perkins, January 27, 1935

Winston-Salem, North Carolina

Dear Miss Perkins:

Please allow me to state some of the facts concerning our wages paid in the Tobacco factories first I want to call your attention to the firm I am working for. The Brown & Williamson Co; We make 40 hours a week and we don't average $10.00 per week for semi skilled labor in my department where the plug tobacco is manufactured we that are doing semi skilled labor make less than those doing common labor. [T]hey make around $12.00 per week while we make from $7.00 to $10.00 and maybe some few of us might make $13.00 once and a while. Now how can we be considered in the Presidents spending program when we don't make enough to live on and pay our just and honest debts. Please take notice Meat advanced from 6 cents to 16 cents sugar from 5 to 6 cents flour has almost doubled and house rent and every thing but our wages the idea of men young and middle age making less than $2.00 while we are piling up millions for the firms we work and the sad part of it is the majority are afraid to make an out cry about conditions. Now I think our great trouble lies in the fact that no[body] ever investigates our working conditions and the greatest portion of us are colored people and I think every body hates a colored man. How can we support a family of 7 or 8 send our children to school and teach them citizen ship when capitalist choke us and make criminals out of some of us that might be a bit weak. Now Miss Perkins just think about our condition how hard it is to come up to the American Standard of living on less than $10.00 for 40 hours work and 7 or 8 in family or it seems

---

From Gerald Markowitz and David Rosner, *"Slaves of the Depression": Workers' Letters about Life on the Job* (Ithaca, NY: Cornell University Press, 1987), 21–167.

that my race of people are not considered in the American Standard of living. Now most of my people are afraid to complain because some few years ago the R. J. Reynolds Tobacco Co. discharged every one that joined a union they were trying to organize here and for reason you can't find any union workers in the R. J. Reynolds firm among the colored people. . . . It seems that some investigations should be made. Now how can we pay our debts educate our children and if we have to call a doctor we don't have the money to pay him for his visit. . . . How can we get a square deal as our case is continued to be pushed a side. Please consider these facts Miss Perkins We are up against a hard proposition.

O. G.

Letter to Frances Perkins, March 29, 1935

Brooklyn, New York

Dear Miss Perkins:

Reading about you as I do I have come to the understanding, that you are a fair and impartial observer of labor conditions in the United States. Well, I'll have to get a load off my chest, and tell you of the labor conditions in a place which is laughingly called a factory. We work in a Woolstock Concern. We handle discarded rags. We work, ten hours a day for six days. In the grime and dirt of a nation. We go home tired and sick—dirty—disgusted—with the world in general, work—work all day, low pay—average wage sixteen dollars. Tired in the train going home, sitting at the dinner table, too tired to even wash ourselves, what for—to keep body and souls together not to depend on charity. What of N.R.A.?[1] What of everything—? We handle diseased rags all day. Tuberculosis roaming loose, unsanitary conditions—, slaves—slaves of the depression! I'm even tired as I write this letter—, a letter of hope—. What am I? I am young—I am twenty, a high school education—no recreation—no fun—. Pardon ma'am—but I want to live—! Do you deny me that right—? As an American citizen I ask you—, what—what must we do? Please investigate this matter. I sleep now, yes ma'am with a prayer on my lips, hoping against hope—, that you will better our conditions. I'll sign my name, but if my boss finds out—, well—Give us a new deal, Miss Perkins. . . .

Yours hoping,
J. G.

Letter to Franklin D. Roosevelt, November 23, 1936

Paris, Texas

Dear President now that we have had a land Slide and done just what was best for our country & I will Say more done the only thing that could of bin done to Save this Country I do believe you Will Strain a point to help the ones who helped you mostly & that is the Working Class of People I am not smart or I

---

[1]**N.R.A.:** Here, the National Recovery Administration.

would be in a different line of work & better up in ever way yet I will Know you are the one & only President that ever helped a Working Class of People I have Writen you several letters & have always received a answer from Some of you officials clerks or Some one & I will know you have to much to think about to answer a little man letter like my Self yet I will Say I and thousands of men just like me were in the fight for you & I for one will go down for you any day I am a White Man American age, 47 married wife 2 children in high School am a Finishing room foreman I mean a Working foreman & am in a furniture Factory here in Paris Texas where thaire is 175 to 200 Working & when the NRA came in I was Proud to See my fellow workmen Rec 30 Per hour in Place of 8 cents to 20 cents Per hour yet the NRA did not make any allowance for Skilled labor or foreman unless they rec as much as 35.00 [dollars] Per Week & very few Furniture Makers rec Such a Price I have bin with this firm for 25 years & they have Surly reaped the harvest. . . . I can't see for my life President why a man must toil & work his life out in Such factories 10 long hours ever day except Sunday for a small sum of 15 cents to 35 cents per hour & pay the high cost of honest & deason living expences is thaire any way in the world to help this one class of Laboring People just a little I admit this class of Working People should form a union but ever time it talked the big boy owners say we will close down then it is more releaf workers to take care of more expence to our Government and more trouble to you what we need is a law passed to shorten our hours at a living & let live scal & take more men off the Government expense & put them in the factories & get things to running normal but if a co cuts hours & then tells Foreman shove & push them & keeps putting out as much with short hours & driving the men like convicts it will never help a bit you have had your load & I well know it but please see if something can be done to help this one Class of Working People the factories are a man killer not venelated or kept up just a bunch of Republickins Grafters 90/100 of them Please help us some way I Pray to God for relief. I am a christian . . . and a truthful man & have not told you wrong & am for you to the end.

Letter to Frances Perkins, July 27, 1937

Plaquemine, Louisiana

Dear Miss Perkins:

I am writing to you because I think you are pretty square to the average laboring man. but I am wondering if anyone has told you of the cruel and terrible condition that exist in this part of the country or the so called sugar cane belt in Louisiana. I am sure that it hasn't made any progress or improvement since slavery days and to many people here that toil the soil or saw mills as laboring men I am sure slavery days were much better for the black slaves had their meals for sure three times a day and medical attention at that. but if an American nowadays had that much he is a communist I am speaking of the labor not the ones that the government give a sugar bounty too but the real forgotten people for the ones the government give the sugar bounty too are the ones that really don't need it for those same people that has drawn the sugar bonus for two years has never gave an extra penny to their white and black slaves labor. I will now make an effort to give you an idea of the terrible inhuman condition.

I will first give you the idea of the sugar cane tenants and plantations poor laboring people. The bell rings at 2 a.m. in the morning when all should really be sleeping at rest. they work in the summer until 9 or 10 a.m. the reason they knock them off from the heat is not because of killing the labor from heat but they are afraid it kills the mule not the slave. Their wages runs from go 90¢ to $1.10 per day. Their average days per week runs from three to four days a week in other words people that are living in so called United States have to live on the about $4.00 per week standing of living in a so called American Community which is way below the Chinese standard of living for the Chinese at least have a cheaper food and clothing living but here one has to pay dear for food and clothing because these sugar cane slave owners not only give inhuman wages but the ones that work for them have to buy to their stores, which sells from 50 per cent to 60 per cent higher than the stores in town still these same people that are worst than the old time slave owners or yelling and hollering for more sugar protection, why should they get more when they don't pay their white and black slaves more. It is true they give the white and black slaves a place to live on. But Miss Perkins if you were to see these places they live on you'd swear that this is not our so call rich America with it high standing of living for I am sure that the lowest places in China or Mexico or Africa has better places to live in. These Southern Senators which are backed by the big shots will tell you it is cheaper to live in the South but have you investigated their living condition. Sometimes I don't wonder why some of these people don't be really communism but they are true Americans only they are living in such a low standing of living that one wouldn't believe they are living in the good old U.S.A.

Now regarding the saw mills of this town and other towns in this section but most particular this town they pay slightly more than the plantation but they get it back by charging more for food & clothing which they have to buy in their stores.

I am writing you this hoping that you will try to read it and understand the situation which if you think is not true you can send an investigator in this section of Louisiana that has American freedom of speech for some hasn't that speech in our so called free America. . . .

Thanking you for humanity sake.
R. J.

Letter to Franklin D. Roosevelt, November 27, 1939

Detroit, Michigan

President Roosevelt
Dear Honorable Sir:
     I am living in a city that should be one of the prized possessions of these United States of America but it isn't only to a small group of chiseling money mongers.

     I and my husband are and have been Americans for three generations and we are proud of what our parents did also our grandparents to help America progress. They were builders of our country not destructers as is now going on to make the rich man richer and the poor man poorer in fact try and starve them in a land of plenty. We have six growing children that are all separated each one pining for each other and our hearts nearly broken because we cannot keep them all together.

     We have tried so hard these past seven years we lost our furniture twice lost our car our insurance even my engagement ring and finally the wedding ring to buy groceries pay rent and for illness. Neither one of us are lazy he worked in steel mills auto factories painting dishwashing and anything he could get. I worked at waitress janitress selling to make a few dollars now my health is slowly ebbing. I was a widow when I married my present husband my first husband died shortly after the world war having served as a submarine chaser. I received a check for $1.00 for each day he served he died leaving me two lovely children. Why should descent American people be made suffer in this manner living in an attic room paying $5.00 per week and if its not paid out you go on the streets. Welfare has never solved these problems as there are far too many inefficient social workers also too much political graft for it to survive or even help survive. We are one family out of 100,000 that are in the same position right here in Detroit where the ones we labor for and help build up vast fortunes and estates do nothing but push us down farther. They cheat the government out of taxes hire foreign labor at lower rates and if we get discouraged and take some groceries to feed our family we must serve time.

They have 40 to 100 room houses with no children to make it even like a home while we are denied a small home and enough wages to provide for them. Barbara Hutton has herself exploited that she pays $650.00 to have one tooth pulled and the girls in her dime stores slave all week for $12 or $14 and must help provide for others out of it. I'll wager to say that the poor class were lucky to have roast pork @ 13¢ per lb on Thanksgiving Day while the rich people in this country probably throwed a lot out in there garbage cans. These so called intelligent rich men including the Congressmen and the Senators better wake up and pass some laws that will aid labor to make a living as they would have never accumulated their vast fortunes had it not been from the hard sweat that honest labor men brought them.

We read with horror of the war in Europe and of the blockade to starve the people into submission and right here in Detroit we have the same kind of a blockade. Do the intelligent men of America think we are going to stand for this much longer. I alone hear a lot of viewpoints and it will be very hard to get our men to fight another war to make more wealth for men that never had to labor and never appreciated where the real source of their wealth derived from. This country was founded on Thanksgiving day to get away from the brutal treatment the British gave them and us real true Americans intend keeping it so. We need men of wealth and men of intelligence but we also need to make labor healthy and self supporting or our nation will soon crumble and it is head on to a good start. Even prisoners will balk at an injustice and we are not prisoners. . . .

A true American mother & family
M. Q. L.

QUESTIONS FOR READING AND DISCUSSION

1. The authors of these letters assumed that the president and other New Dealers would listen to their grievances. Why did they appeal to such high, distant officials? If they did not like their jobs, why didn't they find another place to work or get a better education? Why didn't they ask their employers for better wages, hours, and working conditions?

2. What assumptions did the letter writers make about government? What did they want the government to do?

3. Several letters refer to the American standard of living. What defined that standard? In what ways did the authors of these letters believe they fell short of that standard? How could they achieve it?

4. To what extent had New Deal measures made a difference in their lives?

DOCUMENT 24–3

Oklahoma Tenant Farmer Leads His Family Down the Road, 1938

Tenant farmers, whites and blacks, made up about two-thirds of all farmers in Oklahoma in the 1930s, accounting for the highest rate of farm tenancy in the nation. The man shown here leading his family down a highway worked a tenant farm in the southeast corner of Oklahoma. He supplied his landlord a third of any grain he raised and a quarter of any cotton, the usual terms of Oklahoma tenants. In 1936, however, this farmer came down with pneumonia, was unable to work, and eventually lost the farm. He could not get hired on a Works Progress Administration job. The county where he and his family had lived for fifteen years refused to grant him relief since he had temporarily lived in another county shortly after recovering from pneumonia. When New Deal photographer Dorothea Lange took this photo, this man and his family were hauling their worldly possessions to a small town 120 miles away where they hoped to find work.

Dorothea Lange,
"Family Walking on Highway, five children," 1938

Library of Congress, 3c30176

QUESTIONS FOR READING AND DISCUSSION

1. How might this family obtain food, water, and shelter during their long walk to a possible job?
2. According to the photo, what resources does this family have to support themselves when they arrive at their destination?
3. To what extent are this man and his family helped or hindered by New Deal programs?
4. What values about family, work, community, and government are depicted in this photo?
5. How does this photo illustrate the agricultural crisis of the 1930s and the limitations of the New Deal?

DOCUMENT 24–4

Huey Long Proposes Redistribution of Wealth

The inadequacy of New Deal reforms to reduce the poverty and suffering of many Americans created support for more drastic measures. Huey Long, U.S. senator from Louisiana, organized the Share Our Wealth Society with the professed goal to guarantee a measure of security and well-being to all Americans. Long's proposals attracted a large following among the many people mired in the lingering depression. The popularity of Long's scheme pressured Roosevelt to consider more far-reaching efforts of relief and reform. Long's ideas, expressed in the following speech to a group of supporters in 1935, revealed the widespread perception that, while affluent people remained comfortable, the New Deal did not do enough to protect most Americans from economic misery and insecurity.

Speech to Members of the Share Our Wealth Society, 1935

For 20 years I have been in the battle to provide that, so long as America has, or can produce, an abundance of the things which make life comfortable and happy, that none should own so much of the things which he does not need and cannot use as to deprive the balance of the people of a reasonable proportion of the necessities and conveniences of life. The whole line of my political thought has always been that America must face the time when the whole country would shoulder the obligation which it owes to every child born on earth—that is, a fair chance to life, liberty, and happiness.

I had been in the United States Senate only a few days when I began my effort to make the battle for a distribution of wealth among all the people a national issue for the coming elections. On July 2, 1932, pursuant to a promise made, I heard Franklin Delano Roosevelt, accepting the nomination of the Democratic Party at the Chicago convention for President of the United States, use the following words:

"Throughout the Nation, men and women, forgotten in the political philosophy of the Government for the last years, look to us here for guidance and for a more equitable opportunity to share in the distribution of the national wealth."

From Congressional Record, 74th Cong., 2nd Sess., vol. 79 (no. 107) (Washington, D.C.: U.S. Government Printing Office, 1935), 8333–36.

It therefore seemed that all we had to do was to elect our candidate and that then my object in public life would be accomplished.

But a few nights before the Presidential election I listened to Mr. Herbert Hoover deliver his speech in Madison Square Garden, and he used these words:

"My conception of America is a land where men and women may walk in ordered liberty, where they may enjoy the advantages of wealth, not concentrated in the hands of a few, but diffused through the lives of all."

So it seems that so popular had become the demand for a redistribution of wealth in America that Mr. Hoover had been compelled to somewhat yield to that for which Mr. Roosevelt had previously declared without reservation.

It is not out of place for me to say that the support which I brought to Mr. Roosevelt to secure his nomination and election as President—and without which it was hardly probable he would ever have been nominated—was on the assurances which I had that he would take the proper stand for the redistribution of wealth in the campaign. He did that much in the campaign; but after his election, what then? I need not tell you the story. We have not time to cry over our disappointments, over promises which others did not keep, and over pledges which were broken.

We have not a moment to lose.

It was after my disappointment over the Roosevelt policy, after he became President, that I saw the light. I soon began to understand that, regardless of what we had been promised, our only chance of securing the fulfillment of such pledges was to organize the men and the women of the United States so that they were a force capable of action, and capable of requiring such a policy from the lawmakers and from the President after they took office. That was the beginning of the Share Our Wealth Society movement.

We now have enough societies and enough members, to say nothing of the well-wishers, who—if they will put their shoulders to the wheel and give us one-half of the time which they do not need for anything else—can force the principles of the Share Our Wealth Society to the fore-front, to where no person participating in national affairs can ignore them further.

We are calling upon people whose souls cannot be cankered by the lure of wealth and corruption. We are calling upon people who have at heart, above their own nefarious possessions, the welfare of this country and of its humanity. We are calling upon them, we are calling upon you, we are calling upon the people of America, upon the men and women who love this country, and who would save their children and their neighbors from calamity and distress, to call in the people whom they know, to acquaint them with the purpose of this society and secure organization and cooperation among everyone willing to lend his hand to this worthy work. Fear of ridicule? Fear of reprisal? Fear of being taken off of the starvation dole? It is too late for our people to have such fears. I have undergone them all. There is nothing under the canopy of heaven which has not been sent to ridicule and embarrass my efforts in this work. And yet, despite such ridicule, face to face in any argument I have yet to see the one of them who dares to gainsay the principle to share our wealth. On the contrary, when their feet are put to the fire, each and every one of them declare that they are in favor of sharing the wealth, and the redistribution of wealth. But then some get suddenly ignorant and say they do not know how to do it. Oh, ye of little faith! God told them how. Apparently they are too lazy in mind or body to want to learn, so long as their ignorance is for the benefit of the 600 ruling families of America who have forged chains of slavery around the wrists and ankles of 125,000,000 free-born citizens. Lincoln freed the black man, but today the white and the black are shackled far worse than any colored person in 1860.

The debt structure alone has condemned the American people to bondage worse than the Egyptians ever forged upon the Israelites. Right now America's debts, public and private, are $262,000,000,000, and nearly all of it has been laid on the shoulders of those who have nothing. It is a debt of more than $2,000 to every man, woman, or child. They can never pay it. They never have paid such debts. No one expects them to pay it. But such is the new form of slavery imposed upon the civilization of America; and the street-corner sports and hired political tricksters, with the newspapers whom they have perverted, undertake to laugh to scorn the efforts of the people to throw off this yoke and bondage; but we were told to do so by the Lord, we were told to do so by the Pilgrim Fathers, we were guaranteed such should be done by our Declaration of Independence and by the Constitution of the United States.

Here is the whole sum and substance of the Share Our Wealth movement:

1. Every family to be furnished by the Government a homestead allowance, free of debt, of not less than one-third the average family wealth of the country, which means, at the lowest, that every family shall have the reasonable comforts of life up to a value of from $5,000 to $6,000. No person to have a fortune of more than 100 to 300 times the average family fortune, which means that the limit to fortunes is between $1,500,000 and $5,000,000, with annual capital levy taxes imposed on all above $1,000,000.

2. The yearly income of every family shall not be less than one-third of the average family income, which means that, according to the estimates of the statisticians of the United States Government and Wall Street, no family's annual income would be less than from $2,000 to $2,500. No yearly income shall be allowed to any person larger than from 100 to 300 times the size of the average family income, which means that no person would be allowed to earn in any year more than from $600,000 to $1,800,000, all to be subject to present income-tax laws.

3. To limit or regulate the hours of work to such an extent as to prevent overproduction; the most modern and efficient machinery would be encouraged, so that as much would be produced as possible so as to satisfy all demands of the people, but to also allow the maximum time to the workers for recreation, convenience, education, and luxuries of life.

4. An old age pension to the persons over 60.

5. To balance agricultural production with what can be consumed according to the laws of God, which includes the preserving and storage of surplus commodities to be paid for and held by the Government for the emergencies when such are needed. Please bear in mind, however, that when the people of America have had money to buy things they needed, we have never had a surplus of any commodity. This plan of God does not call for destroying any of the things raised to eat or wear, nor does it countenance wholesale destruction of hogs, cattle, or milk.

6. To pay the veterans of our wars what we owe them and to care for their disabled.

7. Education and training for all children to be equal in opportunity in all schools, colleges, universities, and other institutions for training in the

professions and vocations of life, to be regulated on the capacity of children to learn, and not upon the ability of parents to pay the costs. Training for life's work to be as much universal and thorough for all walks in life as has been the training in the arts of killing.

8. The raising of revenue and taxes for the support of this program to come from the reduction of swollen fortunes from the top, as well as for the support of public works to give employment whenever there may be any slackening necessary in private enterprise.

QUESTIONS FOR READING AND DISCUSSION

1. Why did Long believe that people with wealth should share it with people who needed it? What was the "obligation" of the nation?
2. According to Long, what was wrong with the New Deal? In what ways were people "shackled far worse" than slaves in 1860?
3. How would wealth redistribution work, according to Long? How would it differ from existing New Deal programs? How did Long's program differ from "the starvation dole"?

DOCUMENT 24–5

Conservatives Criticize the New Deal

New Deal programs and goals outraged many conservative Americans. Herbert Hoover, often blamed for neglecting the suffering of poor Americans during his presidency, bitterly accused the New Deal of violating fundamental American ideals of liberty. Hoover's speech during the presidential campaign of 1936, excerpted here, expressed the deeply held beliefs of many conservatives that the New Deal undermined rather than exemplified the promise of America. The following letter to Eleanor Roosevelt from Minnie A. Hardin, a taxpayer from Columbus, Indiana, detailed conservatives' objections to the consequences of New Deal programs for struggling taxpayers and for those who received federal help. Both Hoover and Hardin disclosed assumptions about individuals and government common among the New Deal's conservative critics.

Herbert Hoover
Anti–New Deal Campaign Speech, 1936

Through four years of experience this New Deal attack upon free institutions has emerged as the transcendent issue in America.

All the men who are seeking for mastery in the world today are using the same weapons. They sing the same songs. They all promise the joys of Elysium[1] without effort.

From "This Challenge to Liberty," speech delivered in Denver, Colorado, October 30, 1936; published in Herbert Hoover, *Addresses upon the American Road, 1933–1938* (New York: Charles Scribner's Sons, 1938), pp. 216–27. Eleanor Roosevelt Papers, Series 190, Miscellaneous, 1937, Franklin D. Roosevelt Library.

[1]**Elysium**: In Greek mythology, the portion of the underworld reserved for the good.

But their philosophy is founded on the coercion and compulsory organization of men. True liberal government is founded on the emancipation of men. This is the issue upon which men are imprisoned and dying in Europe right now. . . .

Freedom does not die from frontal attack. It dies because men in power no longer believe in a system based upon liberty. . . .

I gave the warning against this philosophy of government four years ago from a heart heavy with anxiety for the future of our country. It was born from many years' experience of the forces moving in the world which would weaken the vitality of American freedom. It grew in four years of battle as President to uphold the banner of free men.

And that warning was based on sure ground from my knowledge of the ideas that Mr. Roosevelt and his bosom colleagues had covertly embraced despite the Democratic platform.

Those ideas were not new. Most of them had been urged upon me.

During my four years powerful groups thundered at the White House with these same ideas. Some were honest, some promising votes, most of them threatening reprisals, and all of them yelling "reactionary" at us.

I rejected the notion of great trade monopolies and price-fixing through codes. That could only stifle the little business man by regimenting him under the big brother. That idea was born of certain American Big Business and grew up to be the NRA.[2]

I rejected the schemes of "economic planning" to regiment and coerce the farmer. That was born of a Roman despot 1,400 years ago and grew up into the AAA.[3]

I refused national plans to put the government into business in competition with its citizens. That was born of Karl Marx.

I vetoed the idea of recovery through stupendous spending to prime the pump. That was born of a British professor [John Maynard Keynes].

I threw out attempts to centralize relief in Washington for politics and social experimentation. I defeated other plans to invade States' rights, to centralize power in Washington. Those ideas were born of American radicals.

I stopped attempts at currency inflation and repudiation of government obligation. That was robbery of insurance policy holders, savings bank depositors and wage-earners. That was born of the early Brain Trusters.[4]

I rejected all these things because they would not only delay recovery but because I knew that in the end they would shackle free men.

Rejecting these ideas we Republicans had erected agencies of government which did start our country to prosperity without the loss of a single atom of American freedom. . . .

Our people did not recognize the gravity of the issue when I stated it four years ago. That is no wonder, for the day Mr. Roosevelt was elected recovery was in progress, the Constitution was untrampled, the integrity of the government and the institutions of freedom were intact.

It was not until after the election that the people began to awake. Then the realization of intended tinkering with the currency drove bank depositors into the panic that greeted Mr. Roosevelt's inauguration.

---

[2]**NRA**: Here, the National Recovery Administration.

[3]**AAA**: Agricultural Adjustment Act.

[4]**Brain Trusters**: A group of economists and professors who advised Franklin D. Roosevelt.

Recovery was set back for two years, and hysteria was used as the bridge to reach the goal of personal government.

I am proud to have carried the banner of free men to the last hour of the term my countrymen entrusted it to me. It matters nothing in the history of a race what happens to those who in their time have carried the banner of free men. What matters is that the battle shall go on.

The people know now the aims of this New Deal philosophy of government.

We propose instead leadership and authority in government within the moral and economic framework of the American System.

We propose to hold to the Constitutional safeguards of free men.

We propose to relieve men from fear, coercion and spite that are inevitable in personal government.

We propose to demobilize and decentralize all this spending upon which vast personal power is being built.

We propose to amend the tax laws so as not to defeat free men and free enterprise.

We propose to turn the whole direction of this country toward liberty, not away from it.

The New Dealers say that all this that we propose is a worn-out system; that this machine age requires new measures for which we must sacrifice some part of the freedom of men. Men have lost their way with a confused idea that governments should run machines.

Man-made machines cannot be of more worth than men themselves. Free men made these machines. Only free spirits can master them to their proper use.

The relation of our government with all these questions is complicated and difficult. They rise into the very highest ranges of economics, statesmanship and morals.

And do not mistake. Free government is the most difficult of all government. But it is everlastingly true that the plain people will make fewer mistakes than any group of men no matter how powerful. But free government implies vigilant thinking and courageous living and self-reliance in a people.

Let me say to you that any measure which breaks our dikes of freedom will flood the land with misery.

Minnie Hardin

Letter to Eleanor Roosevelt, December 14, 1937

Mrs. Roosevelt:

I suppose from your point of view the work relief, old age pensions, slum clearance and all the rest seems like a perfect remedy for all the ills of this country, but I would like for you to see the results, as the other half see them.

We have always had a shiftless, never-do-well class of people whose one and only aim in life is to live without work. I have been rubbing elbows with this class for nearly sixty years and have tried to help some of the most promising and have seen others try to help them, but it can't be done. We cannot help those who will not try to help themselves and if they do try, a square deal is all they need, and by the way that is all this country needs or ever has needed: a square deal for all and then, let each paddle their own canoe, or sink.

There has never been any necessity for any one who is able to work, being on relief in this locality, but there have been many eating the bread of charity and they have lived better than ever before. I have had taxpayers tell me that their children came from school and asked why they couldn't have nice lunches like the children on relief. The women and children around here have had to work at the fields to help save the crops and several women fainted while at work and at the same time we couldn't go up or down the road without stumbling over some of the reliefers, moping around carrying dirt from one side of the road to the other and back again, or else asleep. I live alone on a farm and have not raised any crops for the last two years as there was no help to be had. I am feeding the stock and have been cutting the wood to keep my home fires burning. There are several reliefers around here now who have been kicked off relief but they refuse to work unless they can get relief hours and wages, but they are so worthless no one can afford to hire them.

As for the clearance of the real slums, it can't be done as long as their inhabitants are allowed to reproduce their kind. I would like for you to see what a family of that class can do to a decent house in a short time. Such a family moved into an almost new, neat, four-room house near here last winter. They even cut down some of the shade trees for fuel, after they had burned everything they could pry loose. There were two big idle boys in the family and they could get all the fuel they wanted, just for the cutting, but the shade trees were closer and it was taking a great amount of fuel, for they had broken out several windows and they had but very little bedding. There were two women there all the time and three part of the time and there was enough good clothing tramped in the mud around the yard to have made all the bedclothes they needed. It was clothing that had been given them and they had worn it until it was too filthy to wear any longer without washing, so they threw it out and begged more. I will not try to describe their filth for you would not believe me. They paid no rent while there and left between two suns owing everyone from whom they could get a nickels worth of anything. They are just a fair sample of the class of people on whom so much of our hard earned tax money is being squandered and on whom so much sympathy is being wasted.

As for the old people on beggars' allowances: the taxpayers have provided homes for all the old people who never liked to work, where they will be neither cold nor hungry: much better homes than most of them have ever tried to provide for themselves. They have lived many years through the most prosperous times of our country and had an opportunity to prepare for old age, but they spent their lives in idleness or worse and now they expect those who have worked like slaves, to provide a living for them and all their worthless descendants. Some of them are asking for from thirty to sixty dollars a month when I have known them to live on a dollar a week rather than go to work. There is many a little child doing without butter on its bread, so that some old sot can have his booze and tobacco: some old sot who spent his working years loafing around pool rooms and saloons, boasting that the world owed him a living.

Even the child welfare has become a racket. The parents of large families are getting divorces, so that the mothers and children can qualify for aid. The children have to join the ranks of the "unemployed" as they grow up, for no child that has been raised on charity in this community has ever amounted to anything.

You people who have plenty of this worlds goods and whose money comes easy, have no idea of the heart-breaking toil and self-denial which is the lot of the working people who are trying to make an honest living, and then to have to shoulder all these unjust burdens seems like the last straw. During the worst of the depression many of the farmers had to deny their families butter, eggs, meat, etc.

and sell it to pay their taxes and then had to stand by and see the dead-beats carry it home to their families by the arm load, and they knew their tax money was helping pay for it. One woman saw a man carry out eight pounds of butter at one time. The crookedness, selfishness, greed and graft of the crooked politicians is making one gigantic racket out of the new deal, and it is making this a nation of dead-beats and beggars and if it continues the people who will work will soon be nothing but slaves for the pampered poverty rats and I am afraid these human parasites are going to become a menace to the country unless they are disfranchised. No one should have the right to vote theirself a living at the expense of the taxpayers. They learned their strength at the last election and also learned that they can get just about what they want by "voting right." They have had a taste of their coveted life of idleness, and at the rate they are increasing, they will soon control the country. The twentieth child arrived in the home of one chronic reliefer near here some time ago.

Is it any wonder the taxpayers are discouraged by all this penalizing of thrift and industry to reward shiftlessness, or that the whole country is on the brink of chaos?

QUESTIONS FOR READING AND DISCUSSION

1. According to Hoover and Hardin, how did the New Deal "weaken the vitality of American freedom" and "shackle free men"?
2. What did Hoover believe were the most important sources of New Deal programs? How did Republican ideals differ from the New Deal, according to Hoover? What did Hoover believe was the proper relationship between individuals and the government?
3. What contrasts did Hardin note between her life and the lives of people who benefited from the New Deal? How did her notion of a "square deal" differ from the New Deal?
4. What solutions did Hardin propose to the problems of poverty? Why were "the people who . . . work . . . nothing but slaves for the pampered poverty rats"? What did Hardin believe the government should do about the unde-serving poor?

COMPARATIVE QUESTIONS

1. According to Martha Gellhorn, Herbert Hoover, and Minnie Hardin, those who favored the New Deal viewed the role of government differently than those who opposed the New Deal. How did their views on government differ? Why?
2. What might Huey Long have said about Lange's photo of the tenant farmer walking his family along the road in Oklahoma? How would Republican opponents of the New Deal have criticized Huey Long's plans? To what extent were Long's policies a departure from the New Deal or merely an extension of it? How might a New Dealer criticize Long's proposals?
3. How might the Oklahoma tenant farmer and the working people who talked with New Dealers or wrote to the Roosevelt administration have responded to Minnie Hardin's claims that people on relief were "human parasites" and "pampered poverty rats"?
4. The documents in this chapter express conflicting views about the relationship between individual freedom and government action. To what extent did the New Deal try to alter that relationship? To what extent did it succeed?

The United States and the Second World War

1939–1945

N othing in the previous history of the world compared with the conflagration of World War II. The entire globe became engulfed by fighting, preparing to fight, or supplying combatants. The high stakes of the conflict were made clear by the attack on Pearl Harbor and reports of Nazi anti-Semitism. Nearly all Americans enlisted in the war effort, whether or not they wore a uniform. The following documents illustrate some of the experiences, at home and overseas, shared by millions of Americans during World War II and suggest the long-term consequences of those experiences.

DOCUMENT 25–1

A Japanese American War Hero Recalls Pearl Harbor

Grant Hirabayashi was one of fourteen Japanese American soldiers who fought during World War II in an elite unit that drove Japanese occupiers out of Burma at a devastating cost: a casualty rate of more than 90 percent. Their efforts opened the way for supplies to flow to the Chinese nationalists, who were also battling Japanese invaders. In an oral history interview in 1999, Hirabayashi recalled his experiences in both the United States and Japan before the war and what happened to him and his parents after Pearl Harbor.

Grant Hirabayashi
Oral History, 1999

Hirabayashi: I was born in Kent, Washington. My birth date is 9 November, 1919. . . . My parents are from . . . northwest of Tokyo. . . . My father came to this country in 1907, and my mother in 1915.

From Grant Hirabayashi, video interview, 1999. Transcribed by Claire Cage. Go for Broke National Education Center, http://www.goforbroke.org/default.asp.

Interviewer: Do you know . . . why they came over or how they came?

H: Well, in the case of my father, he went to . . . a private institution where he studied, and the master of the school was . . . a Christian, and he did convert many of his students including my father. So my father was a Christian before he came to this country. He also was brought up with two brothers who had participated in the Russo–Japanese war in 1904. And, he heard about the horrors of war, and, I believe he became a conscientious objector. Well there were from the United States, a matter of fact there were about seventy students who graduated this [school] who did come to the United States. And they were getting feedback, and some were very favorable. And my father was adventurous, and he liked the idea that he would be able to be in a country where he would have the freedom of religion. He was a very religious man. . . .

[W]e were Methodist, and he was a very strict Methodist. So we were forbidden to do any of the things which our friends were privileged to do. But, it was a very close-knit family. We were very religious. We all went to church. . . . [T]here's eight of us. Six boys. Two girls. . . .

I was brought up on a farm—a truck farm. And the schooling, as I recall was 50-50 in these days. 50 percent Niseis[1] and 50 percent Caucasian. And at school we got along very well, but in our social activities we were separated.

I: During school was it, uh, was it mostly . . . did you guys intermingle a lot?

H: Yes, we did a lot at school but not after school. . . . Well, I do know that the parents wanted us to be exposed to the Japanese language and culture. We did attend [Japanese language school], and, uh. . . . Well, I enjoyed it because I was—I had an option to play baseball [*laughs*]. Perhaps I emphasized more on baseball than the language. . . .

Well, hmm, at the age of twelve I went to Japan. . . . So before the war, I did spend eight years schooling in Japan. And I came back in 1940, and fortunately the [Washington] school accepted all my credits which I took in Japan. So I was able to graduate in one year in Kent High School.

I: Did you go to Japan by yourself?

H: Yes.

I: Was that your choice?

H: Well, to make a long story short, there was three of us about the same height, same age, same class. And as a matter of fact, friends called us the three chipmunks, because we were small. But, we used to go fishing on weekends, and . . . the fishing was very poor. And so we started talking. Two of my friends talked about their experience in Japan. And, uh, which left me out. And I felt like the outsider. When I went home, I did talk to my father and he said, you know, I would like to go to Japan during the summer vacation. Well my father looked at me and he says, son, there's eight of you. I can't afford to send you on a summer vacation to Japan. But, I was very persistent . . . whenever I had a one-on-one situation with my father, I would bring up the question. And, one day, I think, at a haircut, I did say to my father: Father, if you're not going to send me, I'm going to swim across the Pacific Ocean. That impressed him very much, and he said if you're that determined . . . I'll have to come up with a deal. And he said the deal is this: I can't afford to send you for the summer vacation, but if you'll study for two years, the Japanese language, he said, that's something there that would be acceptable to him, to which I agreed. And that is how I got to Japan. . . .

---

[1]**Niseis**: U.S. born children of Japanese immigrants.

I: Do you ever look back . . . [and] reflect on what would have happened if you would have stayed there [Japan]?

H: Well, I was not a dual citizen. As a matter of fact, when I finished high school, I was offered what they call . . . [an appointment as] a military cadet. And, I told the officer that thanks, but no thanks. I was an American citizen. So if I were to have stayed, I'm sure I would have been treated as a foreigner, like many of my friends were.

I: . . . [C]ompare Washington growing up and Japan. What one did you think you fit in more?

H: Well, I think in Japan it was a little more full in that I was able to go to school together, also play after school together. The association was much closer. . . .

I: Did you feel any discrimination or tension between you and [kids in Washington] . . . ?

H: Well, I think, you know, when you're kids there's bound to be some, but I didn't take it seriously. . . . I personally have not felt any discrimination as such.

I: How about when you went to Japan, did you feel any?

H: Well, when I first went there, because of my inability to communicate, I did confront some . . . situations. I may have used some, um, my fist to get my point across, and, which was not [*laughs*] acceptable. But, when I first went there, the teachers gave me preferential treatment, in that they let me still wear my hair long and I also wore shoes as I entered the school, which was only for the teachers. So I did, for the first year, receive preferential treatment, and of course some of the students did object to that. But, during the second year, I was able to communicate, and I was ready to be one of them. So I had my hair cut as well as take my shoes off as I went to class. . . .

I: Before you graduated and before your brother told you about the situation did you consider staying in Japan?

H: I had some mixed feelings because I knew I was an American citizen, and if something were to happen I would be in a very difficult situation. At the same time, I said, after eight years in Japan, I may have some difficulty adjusting myself [to the United States]—but, I did the right thing. . . .

I: So you graduated from high school in '41? Ok, what happened then?

H: Well, I was . . . debating what I should do. And it was about that time that I got my draft notice. So I did report for draft, which was four days before Pearl Harbor. But in those days, you're able to enlist, and by enlisting you're able to choose your field of service. And I said to myself, if I'm going to serve, I might as well pick up . . . some work, a profession so to speak. So I decided to take, uh, so I decided to become an airplane mechanic. And I enlisted in the Army Air Corps.

I: What did your parents have to say about that?

H: Well before I left, my father took me aside. . . . He said, "these are very difficult times, but I want you to take care and do your utmost." . . .

Well, of course the war broke out shortly thereafter. And before I left Kent, my parents said they would visit me the following Sunday. And, I was waiting, and as I was about to go to the gate, I heard that Pearl Harbor was struck. And, of course, I didn't know where Pearl Harbor was. So I immediately went to the pay phone to tell them that perhaps it would be advisable to not make the trip. But the phone was already disconnected. Then word came out that all leaves were cancelled—that no one [was] able to visit you. But I did go to the gate. And I waited, and there were many people. And I was very fortunate; we were able to identify each other. We waved, and we parted.

But, the following day, it was a very scary experience for me. The sergeant told us to fall out and assemble in front of the barrack, and he said, "Men, this is a rifle. It is a Springfield rifle. We have none to distribute. They all have been sent to the Philippines." He said, "Men, this is a helmet." He said, "It will be distributed as soon as we receive the supply." . . . he said, "Men, this is a gas mask." He said, "We have none to issue. They were all sent to the Philippines." So one GI spoke up and said, "Sarge, what would we do if there were a gas attack?" He said, "Men, you take your helmet. You dig a hole in the ground. Stick your nose in it." And, of course, I was shaking in my boots [*laughs*], knowing what I had gone through training in Japan. . . . Well, the men had wooden rifles, and doing bang, bang, bang. And I said, oh my gosh [*laughs*] what am I . . . fighting a war with. . . .

Well, in Japan, we were compelled — we had military service, or military training, for five years, and during the — uh, we had a gun . . . , which was issued to . . . fourth- and fifth-graders. So between the two, we had one gun. And, in my case, I even had a saber. We had actual military training. We went on maneuvers. We had gas mask training. And, if they had drafted me, perhaps I would have been good as a soldier. . . .

I: . . . [W]hen you heard about Pearl Harbor — what were your thoughts . . . ?

H: That was also a very difficult moment. I said to myself, I had just taken [an] oath to serve my country. I'm in a war which I did not see and against an enemy which I did not choose. Now my parents were . . . classified as undesirable foreign aliens. The enemy was my blood relatives, my friends, and my classmates. And you can just imagine what went through my mind. But, this was war and subsequently the people were evacuated, and I had a chance after I graduated from the military intelligence to visit the Toluca Lake [internment camp]; that was just prior to the transfer [of the people in the camp] to Wyoming. Heart Mountain, Wyoming. And as I approached the desert, I did see the barbed-wire fences. And as I looked up, I saw the sentry armed with a rifle, but he was facing inward. Well, you know how I felt then. As I entered, I was taken to the barracks where my parents were. And when I saw them, placed in a quarter which was [to] me unfit for humans, it was very devastating. . . .

Well, I felt sorry for my parents. . . . As you recall that after they settled and had a farm, the farm was confiscated under the Land Law. And here again, they were being deprived of their livelihood and being deprived of their rights. It was a shock. . . .

Well, . . . we awaited overseas assignment. . . . But, one day, they asked for volunteers, and I responded. I understand there were about 200 who volunteered. And all I knew at the time was that they said it's a dangerous and a sacred, dangerous and hazardous mission. And out of approximately 200 volunteers they selected fourteen. And I happened to be one of them. The composition of the fourteen was seven from Hawaii and seven from the continental U.S. . . . It was not until after I was selected that I heard that, according to the War Department's projection, they had estimated eighty-five percent casualties.

QUESTIONS FOR READING AND DISCUSSION

1. According to Hirabayashi, why did he want to go to Japan to study? Why did he decide to return to the United States?

2. What did it mean to Hirabayashi to be "treated as a foreigner" in Japan? How did that compare to his treatment in the United States?

3. How did Pearl Harbor influence Hirabayashi and his family? What did Hirabayashi mean by saying, "The enemy was my blood relatives, my friends, and my classmates"?

4. How did Hirabayashi's military training in Japan compare to the situation in the United States shortly after Pearl Harbor?

5. What did Hirabayashi mean by the term "my country"? How did he determine what country was his? Why wasn't he taken to an internment camp like his parents?

DOCUMENT 25–2

American Jewish Leaders Notify FDR about the Holocaust

Nazi anti-Semitism was well known in the United States because Adolf Hitler had sponsored persecution of German Jews for more than a decade. But during World War II, many Americans and others among the Allied powers considered reports of Nazi policies of systematic annihilation of Europe's Jews utterly and completely incredible. In December 1942, leaders of major American Jewish organizations delivered a report to FDR, excerpted below, that summarized the Nazis' program of Jewish extermination. The report attempted to overturn the widespread disbelief about the Holocaust by citing evidence from reliable sources. Jewish leaders urged FDR and the Allies to take notice of the plight of European Jews and to warn the Nazis about the consequences of their mass murders.

Memorandum Submitted to the President of the United States at the White House on Tuesday, December 8, 1942

Almost two million Jews of Nazi Europe have been exterminated through mass murder, planned starvation, deportation, slave labor and epidemic[s] in disease-ridden ghettos, penal labor colonies and slave reservations created for their destruction by the German Government and its satellites. The five million Jews who may still be alive inside Nazi-occupied territory are threatened with total extermination under the terms of an official order by Hitler calling for the compete annihilation of the Jews of Europe by December 31, 1942.

Confirmation of the existence of this program of extermination is offered in (a) depositions made to representatives of the United States Government abroad and transmitted through the State Department to American Jewish agencies, (b) official German admissions as well as confidential German reports, (c) eye-witness accounts received by Jewish agencies in free countries, (d) first-hand reports appearing in the underground press of Poland and other occupied lands and (e) corroborative evidence received by the Governments-in-Exile through their underground channels.

"Memorandum Submitted to the President of the United States at the White House on Tuesday, December 8, 1942 at Noon by a Delegation of Representatives of Jewish Organizations . . ." The Yiddish Scientific Institute/YIVO, The Institution for Research and Training in the Jewish Social Studies, New York.

The dual process of outright slaughter and slow death began for the Jews of Germany when Hitler came to power and for the Jews of other lands whenever the German army moved in or wherever countries joined the Axis. During the past six months, the organized destruction of the Jews has increased tremendously in its ruthless tempo. . . .

The Hitler order calling for the extermination of the Jews by December 1942 was issued in the late Summer. . . . Under the plan, all Jews living in Germany and German occupied and controlled countries should, after deportation to certain regions in Eastern Europe, be exterminated at one stroke in order to solve once and for all the Jewish question in Europe. . . . Immediately following the adoption of the plan, pogroms [massacres] and mass executions on a large scale began. Those unfit for work were killed. Those engaged in slave labor were worked to death.

Deportation has become one of the deliberate forms of exterminating the Jews. Thirty per cent among those deported fail to reach their destination. These figures were offered in an official report . . . to Gestapo Chief Heinrich Himmler last Summer. Since that time "resettlement in the East" has become a Gestapo euphemism [a polite word] for cold blooded murder. . . .

WRN, a leading Polish underground paper, reports: "During the recent transfer of Jews from the villages in the vicinity of Warsaw to the city ghetto, all who were unable to keep pace with the German guards, whether they were adults, old people or children, were indiscriminately shot on the spot.". . .

The miserable remnants of Jews who are still in segregated areas and concentration camps in Western and Central Europe are being rapidly transported to the East. This technique serves a double purpose:

1. Jews are thereby removed from the half light which still filters into the streets of Paris, Brussels, Antwerp and Amsterdam and from the eyes of the population of Western and Central Europe, to the utter desolation and darkness of devastated Eastern Europe.
2. Here their extermination is carried out without attracting notice. . . .

The method of accomplishing death by deportation is described in the November 24th report of the Polish Government in London. The report describes how masses of Jews were loaded into freight cars in batches of 150 when there were accommodations for less than one-third of that number. The floors were covered with a thick layer of lime or chlorine, sprinkled with water. The doors are sealed. When the trains reach their destination, half the occupants are dead from suffocation and starvation. Survivors are sent to special campus in Southeastern Poland, where the mass murder of all but those capable of slave labor takes place. Of 250,000 thus "resettled" only about 4,000 reached labor gangs. . . .

Centers have been established in various parts of Eastern Europe for the scientific and cold blooded mass murder of Jews. Polish Christian workers, eye-witnesses, have confirmed reports that concrete buildings, on the former Russian frontiers, are used by the Germans as gas chambers in which thousands of Jews have been put to death.

The slaughter of trainloads of Jewish adults and children in great crematoriums at [Auschwitz] near Cracow is confirmed by eye-witnesses in reports which recently reached Jerusalem. . . .

In the interval between the outbreak of the war and the launching of the all-out extermination drive against the Jews, some 500,000 Jews had already been massacred in pogroms. . . .

At the Jewish cemetery in Kiev, great masses of Jews were mowed down with automatics and sub-machine guns, their bodies hastily covered with earth, and a new batch of victims quickly lined up for slaughter. These were in turn followed by a third layer of murdered Jews. According to Soviet Foreign Commissar Molotov, 52,000 men, women and children were killed during the Kiev massacres, of whom a very large proportion was Jewish. Comparable pogroms took place . . . in every area seized by German troops and their Rumanian Hungarian and Slovak allies. . . .

In Nazi camps holding Soviet prisoners of war, great numbers of Jews have been singled out from the rest, stripped of their clothes and butchered.

In line with the policy of immediate liquidation of those who cannot work as slave laborers for the Axis war machine, the Germans have, in recent months, been systematically rounding up and killing Jewish children between 1 and 12 years of age, as well as the aged and the infirm. . . .

Long before the campaign of wholesale assassination of the Jews was launched, the groundwork was laid by a policy of systematic persecutions and cold terror which (a) destroyed the right of Jews as men and citizens; (b) reduced them to the status of paupers; (c) segregated them in disease-ridden ghettos; and (d) subjected them to carefully planned starvation.

Jews who are temporarily spared from "resettlement in the East" and extermination before machine-gun squads and in gas chambers, are being slowly starved to death by a racial food ration system which has no parallel in history. The Germans, as Marshal Herman Goering pointed out some time ago, have decided the order in which the people of Europe shall eat — and starve. According to this plan, Jews may obtain only the last crumbs.

In Poland, the bread ration of the Jews is only one-third of that allotted to the Poles, and only about one-fourth of the Belgian, Norwegian, Dutch, and French bread rations. Furthermore, in all lands under Nazi control, (a) Jews cannot purchase the few unrationed articles still available; (b) they are denied access to many rationed products; (c) they are compelled to make their purchases at such hours when stocks are either depleted or entirely gone; (d) they receive no supplementary rations for heavy manual labor such as other workers obtain; and (e) being confined under the pain of death to ghettos and other urban areas of concentration, they cannot go to the countryside in search of food. Finally, (f) pregnant Jewish women, mothers and small children are denied milk rations. . . .

In all, some 550,000 Jews had already perished between September 1939 and the Summer of 1942 as the result of planned starvation, forced labor and other "bloodless" forms of extermination. . . .

The so-called able-bodied Jews, now concentrated in Eastern Europe, are mainly employed as slave labor in construction gangs under conditions which hold little hope for their survival over any long period of time. In Poland alone there are known to have been at least 85 Jewish labor camps as of last Summer. Here workers were quartered in unheated barracks, barns or stables where elementary hygienic facilities were unknown. A typical day's diet consisted of black coffee and bread for breakfast and supper, bread and potato soup for dinner. Jews were laboring in stone quarries, on river canals; they were working on reclamation projects and repairing bomb-blasted bridges under the eyes of the German army and the Gestapo. The turn-over in such camps is very great because conditions are so intolerable that swift physical breakdown is almost inevitable. According to the most recent reports, Jewish slave laborers who are absent on sick leave for more than two days are taken out and shot as useless. . . .

In their efforts to destroy the spirit as well as the body of their Jewish victims, the Germans and their satellites have accomplished the following:

1. The destruction of the leading synagogues of Europe or their conversion into public latrines, garages, stables and similar uses.
2. The prohibition of public worship.
3. The wholesale and deliberate desecration of the Torah, scrolls of Law, the most sacred of the Jewish religious symbols.
4. The systematic destruction of ancient Jewish tombstones which constitute the evidence of the organic place of the Jews in the history of civilized Germany.
5. The destruction and plunder of Jewish religious libraries involving millions of volumes of historic Jewish writing.
6. The prohibition of the observance of the Sabbath by the Jews who were the first to give to the world the idea of a universal day of rest.
7. The dissolution of the Jewish religious communities.
8. The liquidation of the institutions of Jewish religious education which served as the source as well for secular education for hundreds of thousands of Jews. . . .

The process of mass extermination by combined methods of murder and slow death has not followed a uniform course. There have been times when little was heard of massacres. The grinding process of slow, but nonetheless inexorable, extermination has never abated. Nevertheless, the Nazi regime has sometimes retreated in the face of energetic and clearcut warnings on the part of President Roosevelt and Prime Minister Churchill. The lull in the slaughter of hostages which followed such warnings is an example of this. On the other hand, reverses suffered by the Nazis either through the bombardment of their cities or by setbacks on the Russian front have almost invariably resulted in a new outburst of mass murders of Jews.

Ultimate German plans, as they are already being tested upon the Jews, spell a depopulated and dehabilitated Europe where the process of elimination would make Germans the master race. With the apparent turn of the tide of battle, most of the oppressed peoples have reason to hope that long before this occurs, Germany will go down to utter defeat. But the Jews of Europe, whom Hitler has marked out as the first to suffer utter extinction, have no assurance at present that a United Nations victory will come in time to save them from complete annihilation.

Questions for Reading and Discussion

1. According to the report, how did the Germans and their allies carry out their policies of "outright slaughter and slow death"?
2. Why was "resettlement in the East" such an important part of Nazis' attacks on Jews?
3. How did the war influence Nazi policies, according to the report?
4. How did the report seek to provide evidence of the Holocaust that might persuade skeptics?
5. What might FDR and the Allies have done in response to this report?

DOCUMENT 25–3

Rosies the Riveter Recall
Working in War Industries

The all-out mobilization of the American economy to build ships, tanks, airplanes, weaponry, and every other form of military equipment created millions of jobs, and women rushed to fill them. Industries eagerly hired women for work previously done only by men. Popularly dubbed Rosies the Riveter, these women made a major contribution to the war effort. Wartime industrial work was also a new experience for the women and it often changed their lives, as the following brief memoirs demonstrate.

Rosie the Riveter Memoirs, ca. 2004

Susan E. Page, Journeyman Welder

I was born . . . in San Francisco, the second child of Danish immigrants. . . . I was attending San Mateo [California] High School when the war broke out. I was 14 years old. I had come down the stairs that morning and I saw my mother, father & brother huddled around the radio in the kitchen. I could hear the familiar voice of our President, Franklin D. Roosevelt saying that the Japanese had just attacked Pearl Harbor. Where was Pearl Harbor, I wondered? And why were they attacking us?

My brother was saying quietly that he would enlist and hopefully be accepted as a pilot. I was full of questions, but not yet realizing what this would mean to our little family and our nation. Right away most of his friends and mine . . . began talking about the war and the service, knowing that they would be called to serve our country. They did not want to wait for that call and a group of them agreed to sign up as soon as possible. Events happened so fast after that—they were all leaving their homes and families, including my dear brother. They were sent to different boot camps all over the country. . . .

It seemed that our lives had changed overnight. My father was trying to get into the service even though he was in his forties. I was losing interest in school. It somehow didn't feel as important as it once had. I begged my father to give his release for me to leave school. He was finally convinced by my promise to find a job right away. Dad persevered in his efforts to join up until, at last, he was accepted into the Navy, and was soon gone. My mother was working long hours and our house felt so empty. I began working as a waitress in a creamery. But I knew this was not what I wanted to do. I was just marking time.

One night my friend Bonnie called me and said she had heard that Western Pipe and Steel in South San Francisco was hiring and she was going there in the morning. I said I wanted to go with her and apply for a job there also. We met the next morning to figure out how to get there. Neither of us had a car, so we decided to hitch hike. We were both hired that very day. Oh my, we really lied about our ages! We put down that we were 18 years old, but I was not quite 17 yet! No one raised an eyebrow!

From "Rosie the Riveter: Women Working during World War II," http://www.nps .gov/pwro/collection/website/story.htm.

My friend was sent to class to learn how to become a "Burner." I went to welding classes, held right across the street from the shipyards. Completing the required two-week classes, I became a "tacker" for a shipfitter named "Pucinelli." His English was not perfect, but we worked well together and his sense of humor helped the long days pass quickly. After a couple of months working with Pucinelli, I became a journeyman welder. That involved more complicated and challenging work, but I loved it. I felt like I was finally doing something that would bring my brother and others home again. I went to work every day with enthusiasm and dedication. . . .

Donna Jean Harvey, Riveter and Radar Installer

I was born in Casper Wyoming . . . [and] was raised and educated there. . . . I married Lewis Early Harvey in January 1941. He was drafted when the war broke out. . . .

Labor force was critical at that time so I went to United Modification Plant and learned how to rivet, [and] do installations of various kinds. . . . When the "new" radar system was implemented, I asked to be put on that crew. The F.B.I. investigated me and found me to be worthy and I proceeded to install radar along with my riveting duties, while waiting for the next shipment of planes to come in. They were sent here from the factory, literally as "shells" and we put them together and sent them on their way to Europe and other points where the B-17's were needed. I installed relief tubes occasionally, did some aerial installations, loaded the shells in the magazines, installed Plexiglass for the rear gunners and etc. When the next shipment came in we had plenty of riveting to do and a time allotment to get them ready. I was awarded the Army-Navy E Award and was presented with a pin. I've always been very proud of that!!! I certainly got educated in more ways than I ever expected, being a very young girl. . . .

My feeling about the war in most instances was a conglomerate of mixed emotions. I had lived a fairly sheltered life, but I listened and learned and managed to survive, but I must admit, it left a scar on my memory that can never be erased. . . .

The government was asking for rubber donations so my mother and I gave them our rubber girdles!! We liked to think that our girdles helped win the war!!!

My life took on a totally new perspective the longer I worked there. I saw many tragic accidents, none of which I care to talk about which haunt me to this day.

I couldn't do much socializing as I had a small infant at home to care for when off work and besides I was really pooped. Those midnight shifts were "killers." . . . I tried to write weekly letters to my husband in between my other duties. . . . I did enjoy sharing stories with my co-workers as most of them were "war widows" also and we gave each other a shoulder to cry on when needed and a hug whether we needed it or not just to get ourselves through the shift.

Our community gathered together and collected scrap metals and such to help in the war effort and thanks to a good neighbor, who was growing a victory garden; we managed to get gifts of potatoes and lettuce etc. The government issued coupon books that allowed us two bananas a week, one pound of sugar and so many gallons of gas. We traded back and forth depending on our individual needs. . . .

The day the war was over, I gathered up my young son and my parents and we went to town and danced in the streets with everybody else, waved our flags and just generally whooped it up!!! Praised the Lord, it was over!! And yes, the war changed my life. . . . It also taught me that war is hell, pure hell. . . . I pray that once and for all . . . people will learn to live in peace and respect each other for who they are and just get along. . . .

Delana Jensen Close, Machinist

I spent two years of the war in a small town in the San Francisco Bay Area, at the Yuba Manufacturing Company, making 155 millimeter howitzer field guns. . . . When I arrived in California from Utah, I was told that a war plant had opened up in the town of Benecia and was hiring women, so . . . I applied for work. After a battery of tests I was put to work operating one of the large boring lathes. . . .

I was later told that when I applied for a job, the plant had been testing women to find out if they were capable of running one of the big machines. I was hired and was the only woman to ever operate one of them, and in six months time I was training men for the job.

My machine was thirty-five feet long and rested in an oil pan that was thirty-eight feet long. The oil constantly lubricated and cooled the machine as it bored the metal. I spent the war years standing on the rim of that oil pan so I could look down on the section of the barrel that I was working on and be able to reach the part of the operation which I performed. My job was to bore out the inside of the barrel where the breach lock fit. It had to be perfect, the measurement within 1/1,000th of an inch.

While my girl friends worked in the shipyards at Vallejo for 65 cents an hour, I was among the elite: I made guns at Yuba, and was a machinist second class. I joined the union, paid my dues, and earned $1.31 an hour. And on that grand amount, with the help of three housemates, I bought a house and furnished it. . . .

But we were living in a special time and place. There was an energy in the air and in the people. We were wanted and needed and important to the war effort.

V-E Day, on May 8, 1945 was a day of celebration, but one of mixed emotions for us. We lost our jobs. Yuba would no longer make guns. We said our good byes, and when the foreman of my section shook my hand and said goodbye, he added, "You were the best man I had."

Loucille Ramsey Long, Sheet Metal Mechanic and Riveter

It was on December 7, 1941. Our family . . . heard on the radio . . . President Roosevelt sadly gave the news of Japan's attack on Pearl Harbor. I went outside and looked up at the stars with a thought of how can I help? I was 18 years old, I was one of the eleven children of my parents who were farmers in Oklahoma.

In two months I took a bus to California to live with my sister in Clovis, California. I worked in a dime store a short time, then I heard that the government wanted women to sign up to be trained to work at ship building and aircraft repairs to replace men who were being called to services. My friend and I went to Fresno and signed up for training.

We were sent to Santa Barbara and lived in a big house with many other women, daily we were taken to a shop and were taught how to use tools in sheet metal work in ship building. . . .

About two months later we were told we were to be taken to Sacramento. We arrived and stayed in old Army barracks. We had an Army cook and lived there and were bussed to the Fairgrounds to learn our trade in a big shop. We took lessons on both sheet metals for aircraft and ship building.

Our instructor, Mr. Lloyd told me and my friend, Maxine Landtrip, he wanted us to go to Mather Field and to do repairs on airplanes, he was boss of all civilian workers there. . . .

The guys at Mather pulled many tricks on us such as being sent to a tool room for female and male tools, but we did fine. At first there were only trainer planes, later came the bombers. . . . We worked shift work all days and hours. . . .

We noted the crew would look real anxious when they saw girls working on their plane. They looked like "We don't know if we will make it to our destination," sometimes one of the crew would wait and watch what we were doing, we understood! We riveted in many tight spots with space only for a hand and a metal bucking block. It took both of us one to run the rivet gun and one to buck the rivets. . . .

We worked on B-24's, B 17's, and many others. One day we had a meeting of all workers, we were told that Mather had been chosen . . . to receive, check, and work on the new bombers, the B-29's. We were told it was to be a secret and kept that way for the rest of the war with Japan. If we told anyone other than our people at the base we would be put in jail.

We were very excited one day to see many B-29's hitting the runways, taxied up and formed a long line. Each plane was assigned a guard with a high powered rifle. When we got assigned a job on a B-29 the guard was to check our tool box and see each tool taken in and out of the plane. . . .

One day I was in the shop working and I looked across the hanger I saw a B-29 taxi up to the hanger and turn around on the side of the plane its name printed as the "Enola Gay." . . . We didn't know at that time the mission of the "Enola Gay" until recently I read a book that said it was to drop the atom bomb.

QUESTIONS FOR READING AND DISCUSSION

1. What motivated these women to work in war industries?
2. Donna Jean Harvey reported that, "my life took on a totally new perspective the longer I worked." What new perspectives did she and the other women mention?
3. Delana Jensen Close recalled that "we were wanted and needed and important to the war effort." Do you think the many women who did not work in war industries had such attitudes?
4. According to these memoirs, how did working in war industries influence Rosies, their coworkers, and their home lives?

DOCUMENT 25–4

Soldiers Send Messages Home

At home, Americans built a war economy. Thousands of tanks, airplanes, and ships came off American assembly lines. Millions of uniforms, bombs, and bullets funneled from civilian plants into military warehouses. Vital and compelling as all this military production was, probably no domestic activity was more important to Americans on the home front than the post office. Letters from loved ones in uniform overseas—"V mail"—were treasured. News of the war was always welcome, but news that the soldier was still alive was even better. The following correspondence illustrates what home-front Americans learned when they opened V mail.

Sergeant Irving Strobing

Radio Address from Corregidor, Philippines, May 5 or 6, 1942

They are not yet near. We are waiting for God only knows what. How about a chocolate soda? Not many. Not here yet. Lots of heavy fighting going on. We've only got about one hour, twenty minutes before. . . . We may have to give up by noon. We don't know yet. They are throwing men and shells at us and we may not be able to stand it. They have been shelling us faster than you can count. . . .

We've got about fifty-five minutes and I feel sick at my stomach. I am really low down. They are around us now smashing rifles. They bring in the wounded every minute. We will be waiting for you guys to help. This is the only thing I guess that can be done. General Wainwright is a right guy and we are willing to go on for him, but shells are dropping all night, faster than hell. Damage terrific. Too much for guys to take.

Enemy heavy cross-shelling and bombing. They have got us all around and from skies. From here it looks like firing ceased on both sides. Men here all feeling bad, because of terrific nervous strain of the siege. Corregidor used to be a nice place, but it's haunted now. Withstood a terrific pounding. Just made broadcast to Manila to arrange meeting for surrender. Talk made by General Beebe. I can't say much.

I can hardly think. Can't think at all. Say, I have sixty pesos you can have for this weekend. The jig is up. Everyone is bawling like a baby. They are piling dead and wounded in our tunnel. Arms weak from pounding [radio] key long hours, no rest, short rations. Tired. I know now how a mouse feels. Caught in a trap waiting for guys to come along finish it. Got a treat. Can pineapple. Opening it with a Signal Corps knife.

My name Irving Strobing. Get this to my mother. Mrs. Minnie Strobing, 605 Barbey Street, Brooklyn, New York. They are to get along O.K. Get in touch with them soon as possible. Message, My love to Pa, Joe, Sue, Mac, Carrie, Joy and Paul. Also to all family and friends. God bless 'em all, hope they be here when I come home. Tell Joe wherever he is to give 'em hell for us. My love to all. God bless you and keep you. Love.

Sign my name and tell Mother how you heard from me. Stand by. . . . Strobing

---

From Annette Tapert, ed., *Lines of Battle: Letters from American Servicemen, 1941– 1945* (New York: Times Books, 1987), 20–286.

John Conroy
Letter, December 24, 1942

Mare Island Naval Hospital, San Francisco

Dear Mother and Dad:

... You keep asking so I'll tell you. I have been shell-shocked and bomb-shocked. My memory is very dim regarding my civilian days. They feel that sudden shock in action now would affect my sanity. All the boys back here have received the same diagnosis. Injury to my back helps to make further combat service for me impossible. It's so very difficult for me to explain, to say the things I want to, my thoughts are so disconnected.

Of course I'm not insane. But I've been living the life of a savage and haven't quite got used to a world of laws and new responsibilities. So many of my platoon were wiped out, my old Parris Island buddies, that it's hard to sleep without seeing them die all over again. Our living conditions on Guadalcanal had been so bad—little food or hope—fighting and dying each day—four hours sleep out of 72—the medicos here optimistically say I'll pay for it the rest of my life. My bayonet and shrapnel cuts are all healed up, however. Most of us will be fairly well in six months, but none of us will be completely cured for years. My back is in bad condition. I can't stand or walk much. The sudden beat of a drum or any sharp, resonant noise has a nerve-ripping effect on us.

Ah, well, let's not think, but just be happy that we'll all be together soon.

Loads and loads of love,
John

Allen Spach
Letter, February 1943

[February 1943]

Dear Dad,

I think you will find this letter quite different than the others which you've received from me. My health is well as could be expected as most of us boys in the original outfit that left the States together about [CENSORED] of us are still here. The other are replacements. The missing have either been killed, wounded or from other various sources mainly malaria fever.

On May 16 '42 we left New River N.C., and went to the docks at Norfolk. On the 20th at midnight we hit the high seas with 7,000 marines aboard the U.S.S. Wakefield. We went down through the Panama Canal and past Cuba. On the 29th we crossed the international date line. . . . Was continually harassed by submarines as we had no convoy whatsoever.

We landed in New Zealand 28 days later and they were wonderful to us as we were the first Americans to arrive there. We lived aboard ship at the dock for about a month loading equipment on incoming ships getting ready for "The Day." After working day and night we left and went to one of the Fiji Islands for four days. I was aboard the U.S.S. Fuller picked up in New Zealand. In our convoy were about 100 ships including 3 aircraft carriers and the battleship,

North Carolina. We also had air protection from Flying Fortresses coming from Australia. On August 6 we had our last dinner aboard ship and they gave us all we wanted with ice cream and a pack of cigarettes. Just like a man doomed for the electric chair he got any kind of food for this last meal. That was our last for a while. Each one of us received a letter from our commanding officer, the last sentence reading Good Luck, God Bless You and to hell with the japs. On the morning of the 7th I went over the side with the first wave of troops as Rifle Grenadier, just another chicken in the infantry. With naval bombardment and supreme control of the air we hit the beach at 9.47. All hell broke loose. Two days later our ships left taking our aircraft with them, never to have any sea and air protection for the next two [CENSORED]. In the meantime the Japanese navy and air force took the advantage and gave us hell from sea and air. I won't say what the ground troops had to offer us yet. I can say we never once retreated but kept rushing forward taking the airport first thing.

Left to do or die we fought hard with one purpose in mind to do, kill every slant eyed bastard within range of rifle fire or the bayonet which was the only thing left to stop their charge. We were on the front lines 110 days before we could drop back for a shave, wash up. Don't many people know it but we were the first allied troops to be on the lines that long, either in this war or the last. We have had to face artillery both naval and field, mortar bombings sometimes three or four times a day, also at night, flame throwers, hand grenades, tanks, booby traps, land mines, everything I guess except gas. The most common headache caused by machine gun fire, snipers, rifle fire, and facing sabers, bayonet fighting, the last most feared by all. A war in five offensive drives and also in defense of our own lines. I've had buddies shot down on both sides of me, my closest calls being a shot put through the top of my helmet by a sniper. Once I had to swim a river when we were trapped by the enemy.

With no supplies coming in we had to eat coconuts, captured rice, crab meat, fish heads. We also smoked their dopey cigarettes. We also captured a warehouse full of good Saba Beer, made in Tokyo. Didn't shave or have hair cut for nearly four months, looked rather funny too. Wore Jap clothing such as underwear, socks, shoes. Had plenty of thrills watching our boys in the air planes dog fighting after they sent us some planes to go on the newly finished field that they had built. . . . What few of the old fellows here are scarred by various wounds and 90% have malaria. I've been down with it several times but I dose heavy with quinine till I feel drunk. . . . We want to come home for a while before seeing action again which is in the very near future, but they won't do it even though the doctors want us to. We were continually bombed and strafed but took it pretty good. The average age of the boys was 21 and were around 18 to 20. When we were finally relieved by the army who were all larger and older they were surprised to find us kids who had done such a good job. My best buddie at the time was caught in the face by a full blast of machine gun fire and when the hole we were laying in became swamped by flies gathering about him and being already dead, I had to roll him out of the small hole on top of the open ground and the dirty SOBs kept shooting him full of holes. Well anyway God spared my life and I am thankful for it. I know that your and dear Mama's prayers helped bring me safely through the long months of it. I hope that you will forgive me of my misdoings as it had to take this war to bring me to my senses. Only then did I realize how much you both had done for me and Dear God, maybe I can come through the next to see you and my friends again. . . .

God bless the whole world and I'm looking forward to the days when Italy and Germany are licked so that the whole might of the allied nations can be thrown in to crush Japan and the swines that are her sons, fighting to rule the white race. I heard an English speaking Nip say that if he didn't die fighting, that is if he didn't win or if he was captured and later came to Japan, he would be put in prison for 17 years and that all his property would be taken over by the government. That's his point of view. Where ever we go us boys will do our best always till the end when we don't have the strength to press a trigger.

Love always,
Your son,
Allen

James McMahon
Letter, March 10, 1944

March 10, 1944

My Dear Parents:
    This letter will introduce my best buddy Bill Nelson. I was on Captain DeMont's crew with him. . . .

    10.18.43. My first raid was a diversion over the North Sea. We had no fighter escort and got lost and ended up over Holland (Friesian Islands). I saw my first enemy fighters, four ME-109s, and they shot down a B-24. It went into a dive and no one got out. The next raid was Wilhelmshaven on Nov. 3rd (1943). The sky was overcast, but we bombed anyway and did a good job. I only saw one other B-24 go down. My next raid was Bremen on November 13th. About 10 minutes from the target I noticed our waist gunner was unconscious and appeared to be dying (which he was). Immediately Captain DeMont dropped down to 5,000 feet and headed for home. The waist gunner (Erderly) was dying from lack of oxygen and frostbite (57 below). On the way home he came to and when we landed he went into the hospital. That day Freddie's ship and two others from our squadron went down. One of the waist gunners on his crew is safe but we believe all others are dead. It was over the North Sea they went down and you can't live more than 10 minutes in that water.
    Well, my next raid was Kjeller, Norway, November 18th. It was cold as hell and Bill will go more into detail for you. No flack but coming out we were about 50 miles from land and the Jerry [German] fighters jumped us. There was about 25 or 30 (maybe more) twin engine jobs. . . . Well, Bill got the first one, and then things popped. Our tail gunner Ray Russell got the next one and then (I was on the right waist gun) one popped up out of a cloud and tried to draw a bead on us. I shot his left engine off and killed the pilot and it went down in flames, its wing falling off. Bill in the meantime is having a party for himself. I looks over to see how he's going and he is firing so long at one of the bastards that his bullets are coming out red hot. He kills the pilot of this one and shoots the left wing off, and down goes number four in flames. In the meantime 12 B-24s get shot down, but then the fighters leave us and we pat each other on the back. Boy what a day. Man did we have fun. Well on my next raid, Kiel Dec. 13th, I was engineer riding

the top turret. The flack was bad, but again the cloud cover was with us and we didn't get any holes. . . .

Dec. 31st. St. Angeley. Again I went to Kiel. This time as a waist gunner. My ship was in the low element flying in "Coffin Corner." The weather was perfect over the target and we didn't even see any flack till we opened our bomb bay doors. Then all hell broke loose. The sky turned black with flack. Our control cables were shot out on the left hand side, and our 4 engine was also shot out. The top turret got about 20 holes in it, and also the nose turret. The bombardier was hit in the throat (he recovered). All at once I was knocked down as something hit me in the back. A piece of flack was sticking out of my jacket. I was so scared by now that I could hardly stand up and I couldn't see as the sweat was running into my eyes. The temperature was 45 below too. Well, we went into a crazy spin and I was halfway out of the window when he pulled it out and we headed for home. We almost didn't make it. The fighters stayed a way out and didn't attack us. After this raid my nerves were so shot I could hardly write. We were under artillery (flack) fire for 12 minutes that time. It is the most terrible experience you can have. It is just like going "over the top" into an artillery barrage. I saw 2 ships blow up this day, and one go down by fighters. It makes a guy so damned mad and you can't do anything about it. . . .

2.20.44. Well my next raid was Gotha. It's a wonderful trip. I was in the nose turret and I didn't even see a burst of flack. This raid is a milk run. Too bad they can't all be like that. Well now comes the next one. This one will slay you.

BERLIN! on the 6th March. I was in the tail turret and we were high element and "coffin corner." The sky was perfect, no clouds, which meant the fighters were going to come up and the flack would be accurate. On this raid I should have been as nervous as hell, but I thought of Thom, Henn, Fred, and all the fellows I had seen go down. I figured if I came back, O.K., but if I went down it would be for Thom. Gee I felt glad. Well, all the way in to the target the flack was bad, and the Jerry fighters sure played hell. Our fighters sure gave them hell too. Well I didn't get any more shots at fighters till the target. I saw one FW-190 shoot down one of our planes which went into a dive and went straight down. Then all hell broke loose. The flack was terrible and the fighters everywhere. The group right behind us was catching hell with fighters (FW-190s) and I got in about 10 squirts at them. We kept flying through the flack and made two runs on the target which took about 20 minutes. All this time I can see Berlin, and man there are 24's and 17's all over the place. I see our bombs hit smack on the target and my heart bleeds for those damned Krauts down there. Well after that for 100 miles I can see the fires and smoke. It looks like all Berlin is on fire. Boy do I feel good. I'm laughing like hell for some reason. I guess it is because I am still there. Well after I get back to base (after squirting those Jerry fighters all the way home) I go to sleep and dream of Thom. All the time over the target I was thinking about him and Dad and Mom and Sis and . . . [e]verything was going through my mind at once. I sure feel good, 'cause we knocked the hell out of them. We didn't even get a scratch on the plane either. And that sure is something for the books. By the time you get this letter, I will probably have 5 or 6 more raids in, but I will explain them to you myself. I want you to promise that you will not tell about anything in this letter. Except maybe that I've been to Berlin. I am sure proud of my record. 9 times over the target and 7 times deep into Germany.

I want you to know that if anything ever happens to me that I think I have the most wonderful and courageous parents in the world, and the most beautiful and wonderful sister on this earth. I am proud of you all and my brother Thom. . . . God Bless you all and keep you safe. I'll come back. I can't say I know I will, but I have as good a chance as anyone. Give my pal Bill the best you've got, 'cause he's the best the E.T.O.[1] has. Let Joe take him down to Eddie's and give him plenty Scotch. He was raised on the stuff. God bless you. I hope this letter gives you an idea of what Bill and I have been through. So long. Hope I see you soon.

Your loving son,
Jimmie

David Mark Olds
Letter, July 12, 1945

Rosenheim
July 12, 1945

Dear family:
    . . . Dad, you ask for my opinion and reactions and those of the GI in general about several things. . . . For one thing everybody is mostly concerned with getting his own skin back to the States and home, regardless of what he leaves here and in what condition it is. I think this is a pretty universal feeling anyway — leave it to the next fellow or the politicians to worry about the world. I wanna go home and get some small measure of happiness out of life. There are many of us who feel that not much good will be done with all these noble efforts. First of all, the death of President Roosevelt was almost a mortal blow. Second the regrowth of national selfishness which we can plainly see in France, where we are no longer the saviors but annoying foreigners who interfere with their life. Thirdly, the turmoil in England, and finally the pathetic shortsightedness of those who keep hinting at and whooping up talk of war with Russia. Everywhere we hear how terrible the occupying Russian forces are, how barbaric, how savage, how primitive, etc. etc., and I blush to say, many who say this are wearing the American uniform, men who should realize that without Russia's help we would have surely been beaten. . . . [S]ooner or later . . . the disarming friendliness and cleverness of the Germans will make us doubt if they are so bad. "After all they are a civilized nation, they have great men, etc. etc." My own solution . . . would have a very liberal policy of passes so that men could get out of this accursed country say once a month or so, to breathe the freer air of the Allied countries. Let them change the occupying personnel every six months or so. Let the German PWs be kept in the Army and used as labor of all kinds, farm, factory, etc., instead of discharging them here while we poor bastards have

---

[1]**E.T.O.**: European Theater of Operations.

to sit and sweat in the Army in a foreign hated land. I would crush every vestige of military or industrial might in Germany. Let them be a pauper nation. They deserve it. Let the Russians take over, they have shown how to handle them — be rough with them. Of course some innocent and some helpless will suffer — too bad — in the Army you learn callousness. It is impossible I know, but I would love to personally shoot all young Hitlerites, say between the ages of 10 and 30, and have a rigidly supervised program of education for the young. I don't know if that gives you any better idea of how I feel. . . .

You also asked about the concentration camps and the mass grave victims. It is hard for me to convey all of it to you. You drive through the surrounding towns where there are happy little children at play, and people going about their business, looking like any townspeople the world over, yet within two miles of them, its charged fences harsh against the plains, its chimneys belching smoke from cremating ovens — within two miles is a concentration camp whose very existence is such a horrible thought that a man may doubt that any good can exist in the same world, let alone area, with them. The humans who, though long dead, are yet physically alive with their stick like limbs and vacant faces are so terrible a blasphemy on civilization — yet the German civilians nearby either pretend not to realize them, or what is worse, see no wrong. God, how can people be like that. The concentration camp is even worse when it is empty, and just stands there, a mute testimonial to a brutality beyond comprehension. The gas chambers, as neat and as clean as shower rooms, the cremating ovens where the odor of human flesh is yet ingrained in the bricks, the pitiful barracks and grounds enclosed by the deadly barbed wire and guarded walls. I have seen soldiers get sick standing in the empty desolate chambers, thinking of the horror the walls have seen.

The mass graves and reburials are, for brutality, even worse. Is your stomach strong? Let me tell you about Volarv. The SS troopers and the civilians of the town, including some women, when the Germans were falling back in April, rounded up some 200 Jews with about 50 women in the lot. The men were emasculated, disembowelled and shot. The women were killed very simply. A bayonet was run into their reproductive organs and into their bowels. Pretty, isn't it. When they were being dug up from the ditch where they had been thrown, placed in rude but honorable wooden coffins, and being reburied in plots dug by German civilians and soldiers, American officers and men called all the people out of the town to witness the burial, to see the bodies, to touch the bodies, to have that memory printed on their minds of what a horrible thing they had done, only a few of them showed either remorse or sickness. They stood there, hard and sullen-faced, muttering and obstinate. They would turn away and be forced to turn back and look. These same people would have cried in anguish had this been done to their own, to Germans, but what if it happened to inferior people, to Jews, and Russians, and Poles? A shrug of the shoulders, too bad, it had to be done. And yet how quickly these things can be forgotten here. . . . I want to get out of this country while I still hate it. Forgive me if this picture seems too pessimistic — I have been here longer than I want to, and it is all getting on my nerves.

Love,
David

1. How did the war affect these soldiers? Did it change their attitudes toward themselves, their families, and the meaning of the war?

2. What did these soldiers think about their fellow soldiers and their enemy?

3. How might reading these and other such letters from Americans in the service have influenced the views of people on the home front? To what degree did these private letters reinforce or qualify official, public accounts of the war?

DOCUMENT 25–5

U.S. Generals Inspect Ohrdruf Concentration Camp, 1945

As American GIs advanced deeper into Germany in April 1945, they encountered a Nazi concentration camp at Ohrdruf. The camp had housed nearly 12,000 prisoners used by the Nazis for slave labor. Before the Americans arrived, more than three thousand prisoners had died of torture, starvation, and disease, many of whom the Nazis buried in a shallow mass grave. Two days before the U.S. Army liberated the camp, Nazi officials forced most of the prisoners still alive to march to Buchenwald. Nazis shot prisoners considered too weak for the march. Before fleeing, Nazi officials tried to hide evidence of their atrocities by cremating about 1,600 of the corpses on a crude pyre, shown in the following photo. About a week after Ohrdruf was liberated, General Eisenhower (front row, third from left) toured the camp along with Generals Bradley (next to Eisenhower on the right), Patton (front row, first on the right), and others. The man on Bradley's right is Captain Alois Liethen (with mustache) who had arrived with the first Americans and was conducting the tour for the generals. The man next to Liethen (on the right, with a scarf) claimed to be a prisoner and helped direct the generals' tour. In reality the man was an Ohrdruf prison guard who had failed to escape and disguised himself as a prisoner; the day after the photo, according to Patton, a "prisoner beat his brains out with a rock." Eisenhower wrote his boss General George C. Marshall in Washington that he "made the visit deliberately, in order to be in a position to give first-hand evidence of these things if ever, in the future, there develops a tendency to charge these allegations merely to 'propaganda.'" Eisenhower invited important Americans and British legislators and newspaper people to come to Ohrdruf as quickly as possible because, he wrote, "the evidence should be immediately placed before the American and British publics in a fashion that would leave no room for cynical doubt." Eisenhower also ordered every nearby soldier not at the front to tour Ohrdruf, saying, "We are told that the American soldier does not know what he is fighting for. Now, at least, he will know what he is fighting against."

U.S. Generals Inspect Ohrdruf
Concentration Camp, April 12, 1945

Eisenhower Presidential Library

QUESTIONS FOR READING AND DISCUSSION

1. How does the photo reveal the motivations of the Nazi officials who ran Ohrdruf and governed Germany?

2. What does the crudely built cremation pyre suggest about the Nazis who fled and forced thousands of prisoners to march to Buchenwald?

3. What evidence is there in this photo that Ohrdruf was in an active war zone?

4. What did Eisenhower's insistence that Ohrdruf be toured by GIs suggest about his views of the morale of American soldiers?

5. What did Eisenhower's eagerness to publicize Ohrdruf suggest about support for the war effort?

6. How might Ohrdruf have helped American soldiers understand what they were fighting for and against?

COMPARATIVE QUESTIONS

1. How did the experience of the Hirabayashi family compare with the policies of the governments the United States fought against?

2. To what extent did soldiers' letters home contain evidence of the meaning of official wartime goals in their own daily experiences? How did their

letters compare with the Holocaust atrocities reported by Jewish leaders and displayed at the Ohrdruf concentration camp visited by Eisenhower and other generals?

3. How did the soldiers' concerns about the home front compare to the experiences of Rosies the Riveter?

4. In what ways did the war intensify racial and gender identities and stereotyping, according to the documents in this chapter? Who were the exceptions to these stereotypes?

5. Judging from the documents in this chapter, was World War II a just war? Why or why not?

26 The New World of the Cold War
1945–1960

After World War II, the United States and the Soviet Union—former allies—squared off as antagonists. Their confrontation escalated to a Cold War within months after the surrender of Germany and Japan. The Cold War shaped American foreign and domestic policy for nearly half a century. American policymakers maneuvered to maintain military strength in order to contain Soviet influence in the world, while many politicians worried about internal subversion by Communist agents or dupes. GIs returning from Europe or the Pacific found a home front transformed by American power and prosperity, which the Korean War soon tested. The following documents reveal the crosscurrents of victory and continued warfare, of confidence and anxiety, and of possibilities and threats that characterized the postwar years.

DOCUMENT 26–1

General Marshall Summarizes the Lessons of World War II

In November 1945, General George C. Marshall, one of the nation's most distinguished military leaders, outlined the lessons of World War II. Marshall argued that America could no longer afford to be ill-prepared for the next major conflict. The nature of modern warfare required careful military planning if the Allies' hard-won victory was to make possible a lasting peace. Marshall outlined an influential plan to make military readiness a major feature of postwar American society. Marshall's plan, in the report excerpted here, expressed both the immense sacrifices that brought victory in World War II and the persistent fear that, in a dangerous world, only systematic military preparedness for the entire society could reduce the need for future sacrifices.

For the Common Defense, 1945

To fulfill its responsibility for protecting this nation against foreign enemies, the Army must project its planning beyond the immediate future. In this connection I feel that I have a duty, a responsibility, to present publicly at this time my conception, from a military point of view, of what is required to prevent another international catastrophe.

For years men have been concerned with individual security. Modern nations have given considerable study and effort to the establishment of social security systems for those unable or unwise enough to provide for themselves. But effective insurance against the disasters which have slaughtered millions of people and leveled their homes is long overdue.

We finish each bloody war with a feeling of acute revulsion against this savage form of human behavior, and yet on each occasion we confuse military preparedness with the causes of war and then drift almost deliberately into another catastrophe. This error of judgment was defined long ago by [George] Washington. He proposed to endow this nation at the outset with a policy which should have been a reasonable guarantee of our security for centuries. The cost of refusing his guidance is recorded in the sacrifice of life and in the accumulation of mountainous debts. We have continued [being] impractical. We have ignored the hard realities of world affairs. We have been purely idealistic.

We must start, I think, with a correction of the tragic misunderstanding that a security policy is a war policy. War has been defined by a people who have thought a lot about it — the Germans. They have started most of the recent ones. The German soldier-philosopher Clausewitz described war as a special violent form of political action. Frederic of Prussia, who left Germany the belligerent legacy which has now destroyed her, viewed war as a device to enforce his will whether he was right or wrong. He held that with an invincible offensive military force he could win any political argument. This is the doctrine [Adolf] Hitler carried to the verge of complete success. It is the doctrine of Japan. It is a criminal doctrine, and like other forms of crime, it has cropped up again and again since man began to live with his neighbors in communities and nations. There has long been an effort to outlaw war for exactly the same reason that man has outlawed murder. But the law prohibiting murder does not of itself prevent murder. It must be enforced. The enforcing power, however, must be maintained on a strictly democratic basis. There must not be a large standing army subject to the behest of a group of schemers. The citizen-soldier is the guarantee against such a misuse of power.

In order to establish an international system for preventing wars, peace-loving peoples of the world are demonstrating an eagerness to send their representatives to such conferences as those at Dumbarton Oaks and San Francisco[1] with the fervent hope that they may find a practical solution. Yet, until it is proved that such a solution has been found to prevent wars, a rich nation which lays down its arms as we have done after every war in our history, will court disaster. The existence of the complex and fearful instruments of destruction now available make this a simple truth which is, in my opinion, undebatable.

From General George C. Marshall, "For the Common Defense: Biennial Report of the Chief of Staff, July 1, 1943 to June 30, 1945," *The War Reports* (Philadelphia: J. B. Lippincott, 1947), 289–96.

[1]These conferences built the foundation of what became the United Nations.

So far as their ability to defend themselves and their institutions was concerned, the great democracies were sick nations when Hitler openly massed his forces to impose his will on the world. As sick as any was the United States of America. We had no field army. There were the bare skeletons of three and one-half divisions scattered in small pieces over the entire United States. It was impossible to train even these few combat troops as divisions because motor transportation and other facilities were lacking and funds for adequate maneuvers were not appropriated. The air forces consisted of a few partially equipped squadrons serving continental United States, Panama, Hawaii, and the Philippines; their planes were largely obsolescent and could hardly have survived a single day of modern aerial combat. We lacked modern arms and equipment. When President Roosevelt proclaimed, on 8 September 1939, that a limited emergency existed for the United States we were, in terms of available strength, not even a third-rate military power. Some collegians had been informing the world and evidently convincing the Japanese that the young men of America would refuse to fight in defense of their country.

The German armies swept over Europe at the very moment we sought to avoid war by assuring ourselves that there could be no war. The security of the United States of America was saved by sea distances, by Allies, and by the errors of a prepared enemy. For probably the last time in the history of warfare those ocean distances were a vital factor in our defense. We may elect again to depend on others and the whim and error of potential enemies, but if we do we will be carrying the treasure and freedom of this great Nation in a paper bag.

Returning from France after the last war, with General Pershing, I participated in his endeavors to persuade the nation to establish and maintain a sound defense policy. Had his recommendations been accepted, they might have saved this country the hundreds of billions of dollars and the more than a million casualties it has cost us again to restore the peace. We might even have been spared this present world tragedy. General Pershing was asked against whom do we prepare. Obviously that question could not be answered specifically until nearly 20 years later when Adolf Hitler led the replenished armies of defeated Germany back into world conflict. Even as late as 1940 I was asked very much the same question before a committee of Congress. Not even then could I say definitely exactly where we might have to fight, but I did recall that in past wars the United States forces had fought in Latin America, in France, in Belgium, in Germany, in Russia, in Siberia, in Africa, in the Philippines, and in China, but I did not anticipate that in the near future American soldiers would fight in the heart of Burma and in the islands of the vast Pacific, and would be garrisoning areas across the entire land and water masses of the earth. From this lesson there is no alternative but that this nation must be prepared to defend its interest against any nation or combination of nations which might sometime feel powerful enough to attempt the settlement of political arguments or gain resources or territory by force of arms.

Twice in recent history the factories and farms and people of the United States have foiled aggressor nations; conspirators against the peace would not give us a third opportunity.

Between Germany and America in 1914 and again in 1939 stood Great Britain and the U.S.S.R., France, Poland, and the other countries of Europe. Because the technique of destruction had not progressed to its present peak, these nations had to be eliminated and the Atlantic Ocean crossed by ships before our factories could be brought within the range of the enemy guns. At the close of the German war in Europe they were just on the outer fringes of the range of fire from an enemy in Europe. Goering[2] stated after his capture that it was a certainty the eastern American cities would have been under rocket bombardment had Germany remained undefeated for two more years. The first attacks would have started much sooner. The technique of war has brought the United States, its homes and factories into the front line of world conflict. They escaped destructive bombardment in the second World War. They would not in a third.

It no longer appears practical to continue what we once conceived as hemispheric defense as a satisfactory basis for our security. We are now concerned with the peace of the entire world. And the peace can only be maintained by the strong.

What then must we do to remain strong and still not bankrupt ourselves on military expenditures to maintain a prohibitively expensive professional army even if one could be recruited? President Washington answered that question in recommendations to the first Congress to convene under the United States Constitution. He proposed a program for the peacetime training of a citizen army. At that time the conception of a large professional Regular Army was considered dangerous to the liberties of the Nation. It is still so today. But the determining factor in solving this problem will inevitably be the relation between the maintenance of military power and the cost in annual appropriations. No system, even if actually adopted in the near future, can survive the political pressure to reduce the military budget if the costs are high—and professional armies are very costly.

There is now another disadvantage to a large professional standing army. Wars in the twentieth century are fought with the total resources, economic, scientific, and human of entire nations. Every specialized field of human knowledge is employed. Modern war requires the skills and knowledge of the individuals of a nation.

Obviously we cannot all put on uniforms and stand ready to repel invasion. The greatest energy in peacetime of any successful nation must be devoted to productive and gainful labor. But all Americans can, in the next generations, prepare themselves to serve their country in maintaining the peace or against the tragic hour when peace is broken, if such a misfortune again overtakes us. This is what is meant by Universal Military *Training*. It is not universal military *service*—the actual induction of men into the combatant forces. Such forces would be composed during peacetime of volunteers. The trainees would be in separate organizations maintained for training purposes only. Once trained, young men would be freed from further connection with the Army unless they chose, as they now may, to enroll in the National Guard or an organized reserve unit, or to volunteer for service in the small professional army. When the Nation is in jeopardy they could be called, just as men are now called, by a committee of local neighbors, in an order of priority and under such conditions as directed at that time by the Congress. . . .

Out of our entire military mobilization of 14,000,000 men, the number of infantry troops was less than 1,500,000 Army and Marine.

The remainder of our armed forces, sea, air, and ground, was largely fighting a war of machinery. Counting those engaged in war production there were probably 75,000,000 to 80,000,000 Americans directly involved in prosecution of the war. To technological warfare we devoted 98 percent of our entire effort.

---

[2]**Goering**: Hermann Göring (1893–1946), commander of the Luftwaffe and leading member of the Nazi Party.

Nor is it proposed now to abandon this formula which has been so amazingly successful. The harnessing of the basic power of the universe will further spur our efforts to use brain for brawn in safeguarding the United States of America.

However, technology does not eliminate the need for men in war. The air forces, which were the highest developed technologically of any of our armed forces in this war, required millions of men to do their job. Every B-29 that winged over Japan was dependent on the efforts of 12 officers and 73 men in the immediate combat area alone.

The number of men that were involved in the delivery of the atomic bomb on Hiroshima was tremendous. First we had to have the base in the Marianas from which the plane took off. This first required preliminary operations across the vast Pacific, thousands of ships, millions of tons of supply, the heroic efforts of hundreds of thousands of men. Further, we needed the B-20's and their fighter escort which gave us control of the air over Japan. This was the result of thousands of hours of training and preparation in the U.S., and the energies of hundreds of thousands of men.

The effect of technology on the military structure is identical to its effect on the national economy. Just as the automobile replaced the horse and made work for millions of Americans, the atomic explosives will require the services of millions of men if we are compelled to employ them in fighting our battles.

This war has made it clear that the security of the Nation, when challenged by an armed enemy, requires the services of virtually all able-bodied male citizens within the effective military age group.

QUESTIONS FOR READING AND DISCUSSION

1. Why was the United States "sick," unprepared for World War II, according to Marshall? What did Marshall mean by saying that Americans "have been purely idealistic"?

2. How did modern warfare require different methods and different preparations and bring American "homes and factories into the front line of world conflict"?

3. What did Marshall believe were the advantages and disadvantages of universal military training? What were the social and economic implications of using "brain for brawn" to safeguard the United States?

4. What assumptions was Marshall arguing against? What did he perceive as the principal dangers confronting postwar American society?

DOCUMENT 26–2

George F. Kennan Outlines Containment

For American policymakers, no problem loomed larger in the postwar world than relations with the Soviet Union. Soviet armies had been decisive in the defeat of Nazi Germany and currently occupied most of Eastern Europe. Soviet leaders were Communists who professed their hatred of capitalism and the political institutions of the United States and other Western democracies. George F. Kennan, a diplomat in the U.S. Embassy in Moscow, sent a long, secret telegram to the State Department early in 1946 that was the embryo of what became the American policy of containment. Excerpts from that telegram follow.

The Long Telegram, February 22, 1946

. . . BASIC FEATURES OF POST-WAR SOVIET OUTLOOK, AS PUT FORWARD BY OFFICIAL PROPAGANDA MACHINE, ARE AS FOLLOWS:

(A) USSR still lives in antagonistic "capitalist encirclement" with which in the long run there can be no permanent peaceful coexistence. . . .

(B) Capitalist world is beset with internal conflicts, inherent in nature of capitalist society. . . .

(C) Internal conflicts of capitalism inevitably generate wars. . . .

(D) Intervention against USSR, while it would be disastrous to those who undertook it, would cause renewed delay in progress of Soviet socialism and must therefore be forestalled at all costs.

(E) Conflicts between capitalist states, though likewise fraught with danger for USSR, nevertheless hold out great possibilities for advancement of socialist cause, particularly if USSR remains militarily powerful, ideologically monolithic and faithful to its present brilliant leadership. . . .

So much for premises. To what deductions do they lead from standpoint of Soviet policy? To following:

(A) Everything must be done to advance relative strength of USSR as factor in international society. Conversely, no opportunity must be missed to reduce strength and influence, collectively as well as individually, of capitalist powers.

(B) Soviet efforts, and those of Russia's friends abroad, must be directed toward deepening and exploiting of differences and conflicts between capitalist powers. . . .

(C) "Democratic-progressive" elements abroad are to be utilized to maximum to bring pressure to bear on capitalist governments along lines agreeable to Soviet interests. . . .

Before examining ramifications of this party line in practice there are certain aspects of it to which I wish to draw attention.

First, it does not represent natural outlook of Russian people. Latter are, by and large, friendly to outside world, eager for experience of it, eager to measure against it talents they are conscious of possessing, eager above all to live in peace and enjoy fruits of their own labor. Party line only represents thesis which official propaganda machine puts forward with great skill and persistence to a public often remarkably resistant in the stronghold of its innermost thoughts. But party line is binding for outlook and conduct of people who make up apparatus of power-party, secret police and government—and it is exclusively with these that we have to deal.

Second, please note that premises on which this party line is based are for most part simply not true. Experience has shown that peaceful and mutually profitable coexistence of capitalist and socialist states is entirely possible. Basic internal conflicts in advanced countries are no longer primarily those arising out of capitalist ownership of means of production, but are ones arising from advanced urbanism and industrialism as such, which Russia has thus far been spared not by socialism but only by her own backwardness. . . .

From *Foreign Relations of the United States*, 1946, vol. 6 (Washington, DC: U.S. Government Printing Office).

At bottom of Kremlin's neurotic view of world affairs is traditional and instinctive Russian sense of insecurity. Originally, this was insecurity of a peaceful agricultural people trying to live on vast exposed plain in neighborhood of fierce nomadic peoples. To this was added, as Russia came into contact with economically advanced west, fear of more competent, more powerful, more highly organized societies in that area. But this latter type of insecurity was one which afflicted rather Russian rulers than Russian people; for Russian rulers have invariably sensed that their rule was relatively archaic in form, fragile and artificial in its psychological foundation, unable to stand comparison or contact with political systems of western countries. For this reason they have always feared foreign penetration, feared direct contact between western world and their own, feared what would happen if Russians learned truth about world without or if foreigners learned truth about world within. And they have learned to seek security only in patient but deadly struggle for total destruction of rival power, never in compacts and compromises with it. . . .

This thesis provides justification for that increase of military and police power of Russian state, for that isolation of Russian population from outside world, and for that fluid and constant pressure to extend limits of Russian police power which are together the natural and instinctive urges of Russian rulers. Basically this is only the steady advance of uneasy Russian nationalism, a centuries old movement in which conceptions of offense and defense are inextricably confused. But in new guise of international Marxism, with its honeyed promises to a desperate and war torn outside world, it is more dangerous and insidious than ever before. . . .

In summary, we have here a political force committed fanatically to the belief that with US there can be no permanent modus vivendi,[1] that it is desirable and necessary that the internal harmony of our society be disrupted, our traditional way of life be destroyed, the international authority of our state be broken, if Soviet power is to be secure. This political force has complete power of disposition over energies of one of world's greatest peoples and resources of world's richest national territory, and is borne along by deep and powerful currents of Russian nationalism. In addition, it has an elaborate and far flung apparatus for exertion of its influence in other countries, an apparatus of amazing flexibility and versatility, managed by people whose experience and skill in underground methods are presumably without parallel in history. Finally, it is seemingly inaccessible to considerations of reality in its basic reactions. For it, the vast fund of objective fact about human society is not, as with us, the measure against which outlook is constantly being tested and re-formed, but a grab bag from which individual items are selected arbitrarily and tendenciously to bolster an outlook already preconceived. This is admittedly not a pleasant picture. Problem of how to cope with this force is undoubtedly greatest task our diplomacy has ever faced and probably greatest it will ever have to face. . . . It should be approached with same thoroughness and care as solution of major strategic problem in war, and if necessary, with no smaller outlay in planning effort. I cannot attempt to suggest all answers here. But I would like to record my conviction that problem is within our power to solve—and that without recourse to any general military conflict. And in support of this conviction there are certain observations of a more encouraging nature I should like to make:

---

[1]**modus vivendi**: An agreement of peaceful coexistence between warring parties.

(One) Soviet power, unlike that of Hitlerite Germany, is neither schematic nor adventuristic. It does not work by fixed plans. It does not take unnecessary risks. Impervious to logic of reason, and it is highly sensitive to logic of force. For this reason it can easily withdraw — and usually does — when strong resistance is encountered at any point. Thus, if the adversary has sufficient force and makes clear his readiness to use it, he rarely has to do so. . . .

(Two) Gauged against western world as a whole, Soviets are still by far the weaker force. Thus, their success will really depend on degree of cohesion, firmness and vigor which western world can muster. And this is factor which it is within our power to influence.

(Three) Success of Soviet system, as form of internal power, is not yet finally proven. It has yet to be demonstrated that it can survive supreme test of successive transfer of power from one individual or group to another. Lenin's death was first such transfer, and its effects wracked Soviet state for 15 years after. Stalin's death or retirement will be second. But even this will not be final test. Soviet internal system will now be subjected, by virtue of recent territorial expansions, to series of additional strains which once proved severe tax on Tsardom. We here are convinced that never since termination of civil war have mass of Russian people, been emotionally farther removed from doctrines of communist party than they are today. In Russia, party has now become a great and — for the moment — highly successful apparatus of dictatorial administration, but it has ceased to be a source of emotional inspiration. Thus, internal soundness and permanence of movement need not yet be regarded as assured.

(Four) All Soviet propaganda beyond Soviet security sphere is basically negative and destructive. It should therefore be relatively easy to combat it by any intelligent and really constructive program.

For these reasons I think we may approach calmly and with good heart problem of how to deal with Russia. As to how this approach should be made, I only wish to advance, by way of conclusion, following comments:

(One) Our first step must be to apprehend, and recognize for what it is, the nature of the movement with which we are dealing. We must study it with same courage, detachment, objectivity, and same determination not to be emotionally provoked or unseated by it, with which doctor studies unruly and unreasonable individual.

(Two) We must see that our public is educated to realities of Russian situation. I cannot over-emphasize importance of this. Press cannot do this alone. It must be done mainly by government, which is necessarily more experienced and better informed on practical problems involved. . . . I am convinced that there would be far less hysterical anti-Sovietism in our country today if realities of this situation were better understood by our people. There is nothing as dangerous or as terrifying as the unknown. It may also be argued that to reveal more information on our difficulties with Russia would reflect unfavorably on Russian American relations. I feel that if there is any real risk here involved, it is one which we should have courage to face, and sooner the better. But I cannot see what we would be risking. Our stake in this country, even coming on heels of tremendous demonstrations of our friendship for Russian people, is remarkably small. We have here no investments to guard, no actual trade to lose, virtually no citizens to protect, few cultural contacts to preserve. Our only stake lies in what we hope rather than what we have; and I am convinced we have better chance of realizing those hopes if our public is enlightened and if our dealings with Russians are placed entirely on realistic and matter of fact basis.

(Three) Much depends on health and vigor of our own society. World communism is like malignant parasite which feeds only on diseased tissue. This is point at which domestic and foreign policies meet. Every courageous and incisive measure to solve internal problems of our own society, to improve self-confidence, discipline, morale and community spirit of our own people, is a diplomatic victory over Moscow worth a thousand diplomatic notes and joint communiqués. If we cannot abandon fatalism and indifference in face of deficiencies of our own society, Moscow will profit. . . .

(Four) We must formulate and put forward for other nations a much more positive and constructive picture of sort of world we would like to see than we have put forward in past. It is not enough to urge people to develop political processes similar to our own. Many foreign peoples, in Europe at least, are tired and frightened by experiences of past, and are less interested in abstract freedom than in security. They are seeking guidance rather than responsibilities. We should be better able than Russians to give them this. And unless we do, Russians certainly will.

(Five) Finally we must have courage and self-confidence to cling to our own methods and conceptions of human society. After all, the greatest danger that can befall us in coping with this problem of Soviet Communism, is that we shall allow ourselves to become like those with whom we are coping.

QUESTIONS FOR READING AND DISCUSSION

1. According to Kennan, why did the official Soviet view of the United States emphasize that "there can be no permanent modus vivendi"?
2. What policies were the leaders of the Soviet Union likely to follow? Did the Russian people share their leaders' perspectives?
3. What policies did Kennan recommend that the United States adopt toward the Soviets? What did the United States have to fear from the Russians?
4. How did Kennan recommend that the U.S. government build support for its policy toward the Soviets? Why did he warn that "the greatest danger that can befall us in coping with . . . Soviet Communism, is that we shall allow ourselves to become like those with whom we are coping"?

DOCUMENT 26–3

Cold War Blueprint

In 1950, the National Security Council advised President Harry S. Truman in a top-secret memorandum titled NSC-68 that "the survival of the free world is at stake" in the Cold War between the United States and the Soviet Union. NSC-68 provided a blueprint for American foreign policy in the Cold War, complete with moral and political justifications for understanding "that the cold war is in fact a real war." The proposals and reasoning of NSC-68 governed American policy during the Cold War, outlining the framework for what some scholars have termed "the national security state."

NSC-68: U.S. Objectives and Programs for National Security, 1950

Within the past thirty-five years the world has experienced two global wars of tremendous violence. It has witnessed two revolutions — the Russian and the Chinese — of extreme scope and intensity. It has also seen the collapse of five empires — the Ottoman, the Austro-Hungarian, German, Italian, and Japanese — and the drastic decline of two major imperial systems, the British and the French. During the span of one generation, the international distribution of power has been fundamentally altered. . . .

Two complex sets of factors have now basically altered this historic distribution of power. First, the defeat of Germany and Japan and the decline of the British and French Empires have interacted with the development of the United States and the Soviet Union in such a way that power increasingly gravitated to these two centers. Second, the Soviet Union, unlike previous aspirants to hegemony, is animated by a new fanatic faith, antithetical to our own, and seeks to impose its absolute authority over the rest of the world. Conflict has, therefore, become endemic and is waged, on the part of the Soviet Union, by violent or non-violent methods in accordance with the dictates of expediency. With the development of increasingly terrifying weapons of mass destruction, every individual faces the ever-present possibility of annihilation should the conflict enter the phase of total war.

On the one hand, the people of the world yearn for relief from the anxiety arising from the risk of atomic war. On the other hand, any substantial further extension of the area under the domination of the Kremlin[1] would raise the possibility that no coalition adequate to confront the Kremlin with greater strength could be assembled. It is in this context that this Republic and its citizens in the ascendancy of their strength stand in their deepest peril.

The issues that face us are momentous, involving the fulfillment or destruction not only of this Republic but of civilization itself. They are issues which will not await our deliberations. With conscience and resolution this Government and the people it represents must now take new and fateful decisions. . . .

The Kremlin regards the United States as the only major threat. . . . The implacable purpose of the slave state to eliminate the challenge of freedom has placed the two great powers at opposite poles. It is this fact which gives the present polarization of power the quality of crisis.

The free society values the individual as an end in himself, requiring of him only that measure of self-discipline and self-restraint which make the rights of each individual compatible with the rights of every other individual. The freedom of the individual has as its counterpart, therefore, the negative responsibility of the individual not to exercise his freedom in ways inconsistent with the freedom of other individuals and the positive responsibility to make constructive use of his freedom in the building of a just society.

From this idea of freedom with responsibility derives the marvelous diversity, the deep tolerance, the lawfulness of the free society. This is the explanation of the strength of free men. It constitutes the integrity and the vitality of a free and democratic system. The free society attempts to create and maintain an environment

---

From U.S. Department of State, *Foreign Relations of the United States*, 1950, vol. I.

[1]**Kremlin:** The government headquarters of the Soviet Union in Moscow.

in which every individual has the opportunity to realize his creative powers. It also explains why the free society tolerates those within it who would use their freedom to destroy it. By the same token, in relations between nations, the prime reliance of the free society is on the strength and appeal of its idea, and it feels no compulsion sooner or later to bring all societies into conformity with it. . . .

The idea of freedom is the most contagious idea in history, more contagious than the idea of submission to authority. For the breadth of freedom cannot be tolerated in a society which has come under the domination of an individual or group of individuals with a will to absolute power. Where the despot holds absolute power . . . all other wills must be subjugated in an act of willing submission, a degradation willed by the individual upon himself under the compulsion of a perverted faith. It is the first article of this faith that he finds and can only find the meaning of his existence in serving the ends of the system. The system becomes God, and submission to the will of God becomes submission to the will of the system. . . .

The same compulsion which demands total power over all men within the Soviet state without a single exception, demands total power over all Communist Parties and all states under Soviet domination. . . . By the same token the "peace policy" of the Soviet Union, described at a Party Congress as "a more advantageous form of fighting capitalism," is a device to divide and immobilize the non-Communist world, and the peace the Soviet Union seeks is the peace of total conformity to Soviet policy.

The antipathy of slavery to freedom explains the iron curtain, the isolation, the autarchy of the society whose end is absolute power. The existence and persistence of the idea of freedom is a permanent and continuous threat to the foundation of the slave society; and it therefore regards as intolerable the long continued existence of freedom in the world. What is new, what makes the continuing crisis, is the polarization of power which now inescapably confronts the slave society with the free.

The assault on free institutions is world-wide now, and in the context of the present polarization of power a defeat of free institutions anywhere is a defeat everywhere. . . .

Thus unwillingly our free society finds itself mortally challenged by the Soviet system. No other value system is so wholly irreconcilable with ours, so implacable in its purpose to destroy ours, so capable of turning to its own uses the most dangerous and divisive trends in our own society, no other so skillfully and powerfully evokes the elements of irrationality in human nature everywhere, and no other has the support of a great and growing center of military power. . . .

A more rapid build-up of political, economic, and military strength and thereby of confidence in the free world. . . . is the only course which is consistent with progress toward achieving our fundamental purpose. The frustration of the Kremlin design requires the free world to develop a successfully functioning political and economic system and a vigorous political offensive against the Soviet Union. These, in turn, require an adequate military shield under which they can develop. It is necessary to have the military power to deter, if possible, Soviet expansion, and to defeat, if necessary, aggressive Soviet or Soviet-directed actions of a limited or total character. The potential strength of the free world is great; its ability to develop these military capabilities and its will to resist Soviet expansion will be determined by the wisdom and will with which it undertakes to meet its political and economic problems.

1. Military aspects. . . . The history of war . . . indicates that a favorable decision can only be achieved through offensive action. Even a defensive strategy, if it is to be successful, calls not only for defensive forces to hold vital positions while mobilizing and preparing for the offensive, but also for offensive forces to attack the enemy and keep him off balance. . . .

In the broadest terms, the ability to perform these tasks requires a build-up of military strength by the United States and its allies to a point at which the combined strength will be superior for at least these tasks, both initially and throughout a war, to the forces that can be brought to bear by the Soviet Union and its satellites. In specific terms, . . . [we must] provide an adequate defense against air attack on the United States and Canada and an adequate defense against air and surface attack on the United Kingdom and Western Europe, Alaska, the Western Pacific, Africa, and the Near and Middle East, and on the long lines of communication to these areas. Furthermore, it is mandatory that in building up our strength, we enlarge upon our technical superiority by an accelerated exploitation of the scientific potential of the United States and our allies.

Forces of this size and character are necessary not only for protection against disaster but also to support our foreign policy. . . . [I]t is clear that a substantial and rapid building up of strength in the free world is necessary to support a firm policy intended to check and to roll back the Kremlin's drive for world domination. . . .

2. Political and economic aspects. The immediate objectives . . . are a renewed initiative in the cold war and a situation to which the Kremlin would find it expedient to accommodate itself, first by relaxing tensions and pressures and then by gradual withdrawal. The United States cannot alone provide the resources required for such a build-up of strength. The other free countries must carry their part of the burden, but their ability and determination to do it will depend on the action the United States takes to develop its own strength and on the adequacy of its foreign political and economic policies. . . .

At the same time, we should take dynamic steps to reduce the power and influence of the Kremlin inside the Soviet Union and other areas under its control. The objective would be the establishment of friendly regimes not under Kremlin domination. Such action is essential to engage the Kremlin's attention, keep it off balance, and force an increased expenditure of Soviet resources in counteraction. In other words, it would be the current Soviet cold war technique used against the Soviet Union.

A program for rapidly building up strength and improving political and economic conditions will place heavy demands on our courage and intelligence; it will be costly; it will be dangerous. But half-measures will be more costly and more dangerous, for they will be inadequate to prevent and may actually invite war. Budgetary considerations will need to be subordinated to the stark fact that our very independence as a nation may be at stake. . . .

The threat to the free world involved in the development of the Soviet Union's atomic and other capabilities will rise steadily and rather rapidly. For the time being, the United States possesses a marked atomic superiority over the Soviet Union which, together with the potential capabilities of the United States and other free countries in other forces and weapons, inhibits aggressive Soviet action. This provides an opportunity for the United States, in cooperation with other free countries, to launch a build-up of strength which will support a firm policy directed to the frustration of the Kremlin design. . . .

In particular, the United States now faces the contingency that within the next four or five years the Soviet Union will possess the military capability of delivering a surprise atomic attack of such weight that the United States must have substantially increased general air, ground, and sea strength, atomic capabilities, and air and civilian defenses to deter war and to provide reasonable assurance, in the event of war, that it could survive the initial blow and go on to the eventual attainment of its objectives. In return, this contingency requires the intensification of our efforts in the fields of intelligence and research and development. . . .

The whole success of the proposed program hangs ultimately on recognition by this Government, the American people, and all free peoples, that the cold war is in fact a real war in which the survival of the free world is at stake.

QUESTIONS FOR READING AND DISCUSSION

1. According to NSC-68, how had the distribution of international power been altered and why was the present situation a "crisis"? What made "the cold war . . . in fact a real war"?

2. Why did the "free society" find itself "mortally challenged by the Soviet system"? Why was the Soviet Union different from, for example, American enemies in World War II, Germany and Japan?

3. Why was "a defeat of free institutions anywhere . . . a defeat everywhere"?

4. To what extent did the proposed plan employ "the current Soviet cold war technique used against the Soviet Union" itself?

5. In what ways were the institution of a "slave society" and the loss of freedom "at stake"?

DOCUMENT 26–4

Civilians Prepare for Nuclear Attack

To protect Americans from a nuclear attack by the Soviet Union, the federal government urged people to build bomb shelters in their backyards. Edward Teller, a leading scientist who helped develop the hydrogen bomb, declared "it is necessary to provide every person in the U.S. with a shelter." Teller and federal officials acknowledged that a fallout shelter could not survive a direct hit, but it could shield people from dangerous radioactive debris for a few weeks. Since Congress did not agree to pay for the construction of fallout shelters, it was up to individual property owners to dig a hole in their backyards and build a shelter. Many Americans did not have a backyard, of course, and many who did could not afford a shelter. Still, contractors hustled to meet the demand for home fallout shelters. To promote the 22-ton steel and concrete model shown here, a Miami contractor arranged in 1959 for newlyweds Maria Rodriguez and Melvin Minnison to spend their two-week honeymoon twelve feet underground in this eight by fourteen foot shelter. After their subterranean honeymoon, Maria and Melvin received a two-week vacation in Mexico from the contractor.

Miami Couple Honeymoons in Fallout Shelter, 1959

Bettmann/Getty Images

QUESTIONS FOR READING AND DISCUSSION

1. What message does the photo of this newlywed couple convey about fallout shelters? What dangers does the shelter appear ready to protect them from? What dangers might still threaten them?
2. How are Maria and Melvin expected to carry out the activities of daily life inside the shelter? What might happen to people without shelters during a nuclear attack?
3. If Maria and Melvin had entered the shelter to escape a genuine nuclear attack, how might the photo have been different?
4. What political messages does the photo send about the potential dangers of nuclear warfare during the Cold War?
5. How did federal encouragement of shelter-building reflect and perhaps help shape Americans' attitudes about Cold War policies?

DOCUMENT 26–5

A Veteran Recalls Combat in the Korean War

Marine Staff Sergeant Donald M. Griffith was a squad leader in a racially integrated platoon that landed behind North Korean lines at Inchon in September 1950. Griffith remained in combat until December when he was captured during a massive Chinese attack at Chosin Reservoir that overran American defenders. In an interview in 2003, excerpted below, Griffith recalled his wartime experience, including the thirty-three months he spent as a prisoner of war (POW). Griffith's memoir illustrates the brutal military conflict in Korea inflamed by the global tensions of the Cold War.

Donald M. Griffith Interview, 2003

And the next morning we woke up and all you could see was ships all around. . . . I never seen so many ships at one time. And about this time . . . our airplane started rocketing . . . these [concrete] walls to tear them down because we were going to go in and make the landing there. . . . That's Inchon. And I went in on the second wave at Inchon, and they were shooting at us going in. And we got on the shoreline, and I was really upset because the first wave was supposed to get in and move out, and I started really losing my temper and swearing quite a bit. . . . And about that time, they started dropping mortars in on us, and one of my kids, a black kid, got hit with a mortar. And, oh, what I forgot to tell you is when we were going in I went out first and I had my carbine up like this, and they shot the front handguard off my carbine. So when Baker, the black kid that got hit there from the mortar, when he got hit I picked up his M1 rifle, and I carried that until the firing pin broke on it when I got captured. . . .

So we're in there and finally we get within Inchon, inside the city, and troops are still coming in, landing craft are still coming in, and our planes had hit some of the warehouses, and they were burning, that's all the light that we had. . . . I made it a policy to every night be in the fox hole with a different man in my squad. I was the squad leader there. And as it so happened, we had an experimental platoon. Our platoon was one of the first Marine platoons that had blacks, whites, Spanish, Indians, and even a Polish DP [displaced person] was in my squad. . . .

So the next morning things kind of quieted down. We had taken the city of Inchon. So we started marching, we were going to capture Kimpo airfield. . . . [A]ll of a sudden a runner comes back, and he said, There's three Russian tanks coming in towards us. So they told us all to get on the high ground. So we got on top of these mountains and we're watching — we're looking down, and sure enough, here comes the first tank around the corner there. And our bazooka man, he fires one round and, boom, he knocks the old tank out with one round. And the soldiers, we usually called them gooks, were bailing out of the tank. And when they did, why, our machine gunners had crossfire, and they annihilated them, you know. And here comes the second tank, and one round, boom. He missed. Second round, boom, he got it. And the same thing happened, they bailed out. And then the third tank came around and one round, he got it. So he got three tanks with four rounds. And he did a heck of a job. He got the Medal of Honor, and he went back to the states, and didn't have to finish the war out.

. . . [W]e got on tanks, and . . . when we got just outside of Kimpo, we run into some . . . weapons fire . . . and we went into the attack. And when we arrived there, why, here's all these civilians, and they had the North Koreans behind them pushing them toward us yelling bonsai, bonsai, you know, and we didn't have any choice because we had to get at those North Korean soldiers. So we had to

---

From *30 Below on Christmas Eve: Interviews with Northwest Ohio Veterans of the Korean War* (Toledo: University of Toledo Press, 2011).

open fire, and it wasn't pleasant, you know. But that was war. And we took the airfield. . . . And after we took Kimpo airfield, why, then we headed toward the city of Seoul. . . . And we had to cross the Hahn River. . . . So we went down and we got on these . . . amtracks. They can go in water or on the land, you know. And we went across [the river] on the amtracks. And we went into the attack, on Hill 51. We hit the main line of resistance going into Seoul. And our platoon strength was — we had 39 men, that includes the platoon leader, the platoon sergeant, and squad leaders and fire team leaders, and three Navy corpsmen. And when we hit that main line of resistance, when we come out of there, there was only ten of us left: The platoon leader, platoon sergeant, myself, and a couple corporals, fire team leaders. But that's all that was left out of the 39. And then we went back to Inchon from there. We secured Seoul. . . .

[A]fter Thanksgiving, we moved . . . to the western side [of the Chosin Reservoir], and we went into the attack immediately because the Chinese had moved in. And I remember this day vividly because it was cold. The temperatures had gone down as low as 30 and 40 below zero, and that's not chill factor. . . . And when we went into the attack, why, of course the Chinese are shooting at us, and we're running up this mountainside, . . . and there goes my sleeping bag down the hill. I said oh, no. And I wasn't about to go down there because they were shooting at us down there. So we finally took the hill. There was a pill box there, and we cleaned that out, and went on up. And we could see the Chinese coming in. I mean, there was boucous [many] of them, you know. So that night I nearly froze to death, because I didn't have a sleeping bag and that temperature must have got down to 40 below. . . . So finally . . . the Chinese hit that night and they got down in with our headquarters, and we couldn't shoot down there because we were afraid of shooting our own people. But they broke through on, well, beyond our flank. . . . And they had quite a battle down there. . . .

Well, then the next day I was called down to go to a meeting with the company commander. And I went down, and he's telling us that things are bad, and we're going to be fighting in a different direction. He said, We're not retreating, he said, Some people will say we're retreating but we're not. He said, We're just fighting in a different direction. I said, Sir, I said, You know, our rations are getting kind of low, and our ammo is getting kind of low. I said, When will we have some airdrops? You know, we were getting airdrops during all the time that we were up there. He said, Sergeant, I want to tell you something. He said, We're 24th on the priority list for an airdrop. I said, excuse me? And he said, We're 24th on the priority list for an airdrop. I said, Now wait a minute. I said, . . . You mean that they've got all of us surrounded? He said, We're not the only ones surrounded, he said, They've got 23 other outfits that are surrounded. . . .

By the Chinese. Of course, . . . our numbers were about 11,000; their numbers were 110,000. So we started moving back. And our platoon was the last platoon; we were the ones that stayed last. And everybody was going through us back, leapfrogging back, you know. And on this particular night . . . [o]ne o'clock in the morning, bugles started blowing, whistles started — they [Chinese soldiers] started yelling and screaming, and they hit us. I mean they hit us hard, too. And I had two grenades, and I threw them, and I started firing my M1 and the firing pin broke. It was so cold, you know, the firing pin broke. So I took the trigger housing out and threw that away, and threw the rest of the rifle away. And I had — Romero was an Indian boy in my fox hole with me. And the grenade went off in front, and it hit me in the eye, and cut my nose down here, and my lip, and I got a chunk in my muscle, my calf, you know. And I told him, I said, Romero, you go back to tell the company commander what's happening here. So he made it back, but he had this finger and thumb shot off, and he was bayonetted in the neck, but he made it back. . . .

November. That's when they [the Chinese] started coming across the Yalu River. . . . On December the 1st, I'm . . . out here on this ledge. I've got my squad around here. . . . And that's one of the few nights we didn't have any machine guns attached to us because we were supposed to move out and they had already moved out. But they hit. And when they threw that grenade and got me, it kind of dazed me, and I had my fur-lined parka on with a hood, and I had my metal helmet on, and I had the hood up over my helmet. And this chinaman that came in first, he hit me in the head with the stock of his rifle. And thank God I had that helmet on, because he really rung my bell even though I . . . had the hood and the helmet on, you know. And then he took off. And I'm laying there, and I'm bleeding, but the blood is starting to freeze on my face, you know. So I'm thinking, boy, what if the next one jumps down in and sticks me with his bayonet, you know. So the next guy, he jumped down in the hole, and when he jumped down I jumped up and I scared the hell out of him. But they—he let out a yell and about ten of them came over, and the first thing they did was take my fur-lined parka away from me. And man, I was cold. . . . I myself and the two brothers, the two Dowling brothers started—they took us down the mountain. They marched us for two days and three nights without any food, no water, or nothing, getting us out of there. And we would fall down and grab a handful of snow and put that in our mouth for moisture, you know. And if they caught us they would knock it out of our hands, you know. . . .

My wounds, I still had my wounds. They never did a thing for my wounds in all the time that I was a POW. I was blind in the right eye, and the scabs would fall off. Well, we never even got to wash. . . . They took us to this village, which we called Death Valley. And while there I . . . escaped. . . . And they got me back there, and they made sure that the other POWs in the Death Valley seen that they recaptured me. So . . . this North Korean kid [who captured me], he couldn't have been more than 17, but he was a big deal.

And then he threw me in the pig pen. I was in the pig pen for about 33 days and there was a GI in there, a guy from the Army, and he went insane. He kept saying that the pig manure was steak, and he was eating that he was so hungry. And I woke up one morning and rigor mortis had set in, he had died during the night. . . . And eventually after a while I—after 33 days they put me back in with the rest of the guys. Meantime, the guys are dying. Boy, three or four a night were dying, you know. And . . . they had a big hole dug, and it was a mass grave really. . . . We never covered it up because there was more guys dying, you know.

We lost 51 percent of our prisoners that were over there.

QUESTIONS FOR READING AND DISCUSSION

1. In what sense was Griffith's platoon "experimental"? What was the significance of the experiment?
2. To what extent did the conditions of combat permit Griffith's squad to distinguish between unarmed civilians and North Koreans and Chinese soldiers?
3. How did China's entry into the Korean conflict affect Griffith?
4. Why do you think Griffith and his men fought with determination and courage, despite high casualties?

COMPARATIVE QUESTIONS

1. To what degree was General Marshall's plan for military readiness consistent with Kennan's proposal for confronting the Soviet threat? Did Marshall perceive the Soviet Union as the major danger facing the United States, as Kennan and NSC-68 did?

2. How did George F. Kennan's views of Communists and of the internal dangers of the Cold War differ from those in NSC-68?

3. How did fallout shelters and other civil defense measures influence U.S. public attitudes and political support for the Cold War?

4. To what extent did Donald Griffith's experiences confirm Kennan's and NSC-68's views about the threat of communism?

5. How were the views of the individuals in these documents shaped by what they perceived as the lessons of World War II? What were those lessons, according to the documents in this chapter? Did the Cold War suggest new lessons?

27 | Postwar Culture and Politics

1945–1960

During the 1950s, Americans bought homes, refrigerators, cars, television sets, and other goods at an unprecedented pace. People could not seem to get enough of anything. Many worried that prosperity had a dark side that threatened to undermine traditional values. In the Cold War climate, raising questions about the role of women, the conformity of social and cultural expectations, the justice of segregation, or the Cold War itself seemed subversive to many people. The numerous achievements of the nation during the 1950s seemed to be creating new, unsettling problems. The documents that follow illustrate Americans' often conflicting faith in both the new and the tried and true.

DOCUMENT 27–1

Edith M. Stern Attacks the Domestic Bondage of Women

The prosperity of the 1950s made it possible for a home to be a castle in new ways, and most Americans assumed that each castle would have its queen. Edith Stern, a college-educated writer living in Washington, D.C., ridiculed the assumption that women lived queenly lives of domestic bliss. Men, industrial workers, and even slaves had advantages housewives lacked, Stern declared. Her description of household bondage, written for a magazine in 1949 and excerpted here, expressed the frustrations and the aspirations of many American women and raised questions about why such bondage existed and how it might be changed.

Women Are Household Slaves, 1949

HELP WANTED: DOMESTIC: FEMALE. All cooking, cleaning, launder-ing, sewing, meal planning, shopping, weekday chauffeuring, social secretarial service, and complete care of three children. Salary at employer's option. Time off if possible.

No one in her right senses would apply for such a job. No one in his right senses, even a desperate widower, would place such an advertisement. Yet it cor-rectly describes the average wife and mother's situation, in which most women remain for love, but many because they have no way out.

A nauseating amount of bilge is constantly being spilled all over the public press about the easy, pampered existence of the American woman. Actually, the run of the mill, not gainfully employed female who is blessed with a husband and from two to four children leads a kind of life that theoretically became passé with the Emancipation Proclamation. Its confinement makes her baby's play pen seem like the great open spaces. Its hours—at least fourteen a day, seven days a week—make the well known sunup to sundown toil of sharecroppers appear, in comparison, like a union standard. Beside the repetitious, heterogeneous mass of chores endlessly bedeviling the housewife, an executive's memorandum of unfin-ished business is a virgin sheet.

Housewifery is a complex of housekeeping, household management, house-work and childcare. Some of its elements, such as budgeting, dietetics, and above all, the proper upbringing of children, involve the higher brain centers; indeed, home economics has quite as respectable an academic status as engineering, and its own laboratories, dissertations and hierarchy of degrees. Other of its facets, and those the most persistent and time-consuming, can be capably handled by an eight-year-old child. The role of the housewife is, therefore, analogous to that of the president of a corporation who would not only determine policies and make over-all plans but also spend the major part of his time and energy in such activi-ties as sweeping the plant and oiling machines.

Industry, of course, is too thrifty of the capacities of its personnel to waste them in such fashion. Likewise, organized labor and government afford workers certain standardized legal or customary protections. But in terms of enlightened labor practice, the housewife stands out blackly as the Forgotten Worker.

She is covered by no minimum wage law; indeed, she gets no wages at all. Like the bondservant of another day, or the slave, she receives maintenance; but anything beyond that, whether in the form of a regular "allowance" or sporadic largesse, is ruggedly individualistic. . . .

No state or county health and sanitation inspectors invade the privacy of the home, as they do that of the factory; hence kitchens and domestic dwellings may be ill-ventilated, unsanitary and hazardous without penalty. That many more accidents occur in homes than in industry is no coincidence. Furthermore, when a disability is incurred, such as a bone broken in a fall off a ladder or legs scalded by the overturning of a kettle of boiling water, no beneficent legislation provides for the housewife's compensation.

Rest periods are irregular, about ten to fifteen minutes each, a few times during the long day; night work is frequent and unpredictably occasioned by a wide

From Edith M. Stern, "Women Are Household Slaves," American Mercury 68 (January 1949), 71–76.

variety of factors such as the mending basket, the gang gathering for a party, a sick child, or even more pressing, a sick husband. The right to a vacation, thoroughly accepted in business and industry, is non-existent in the domestic sphere. When families go to beach bungalows or shacks in the woods Mom continues on almost the same old treadmill; there are still little garments to be buttoned and unbuttoned, three meals a day to prepare, beds to be made and dishes to be washed. Even on jolly whole-family motor trips with the blessings of life in tourist camps or hotels, she still has the job considered full time by paid nurses and governesses.

Though progressive employers make some sort of provision for advancement, the housewife's opportunities for advancement are nil; the nature and scope of her job, the routines of keeping a family fed, clothed and housed remain always the same. If the male upon whom her scale of living depends prospers, about all to which she can look forward is a larger house—and more work. Once, under such circumstances, there would have been less, thanks to servants. Currently, however, the jewel of a general houseworker is virtually extinct and even the specialists who smooth life for the wealthy are rarities.

Industry has a kind of tenderness toward its women workers that is totally lacking towards women workers in the home. Let a plant employee be known to be pregnant, and management and foremen, who want to experience no guilt feelings toward unborn innocents, hasten to prevent her doing any kind of work that might be a strain upon her. In the home, however, now as for centuries, a "normal" amount of housework is considered "healthy"—not to mention, since no man wants to do it, unavoidable. There may be a few proscriptions against undue stretching and heavy lifting, but otherwise, pregnant or not, the housewife carries on, turning mattresses, lugging the vacuum cleaner up and down stairs, carrying winter overcoats to the attic in summer and down from it in the fall, scrubbing kitchen and bathroom floors, washing woodwork if that is indicated by the season, and on her feet most of the time performing other such little chores beside which sitting at an assembly line or punching a typewriter are positively restful.

Despite all this, a good many arguments about the joys of housewifery have been advanced, largely by those who have never had to work at it. One much stressed point is that satisfaction every good woman feels in creating a home for her dear ones. Well, probably every good woman does feel it, perhaps because she has had it so drummed into her that if she does not, she is not a good woman; but that satisfaction has very little to do with housewifery and housework. It is derived from intangibles, such as the desirable wife-husband and mother-child relationships she manages to effect, the permeating general home atmosphere of joviality or hospitality or serenity or culture to which she is the key, or the warmth and security she gives to the home by way of her personality, not her broom, stove or dishpan. For a woman to get a rewarding sense of total creation by way of the multiple, monotonous chores that are her daily lot would be as irrational as for an assembly line worker to rejoice that he had created an automobile because he tightens a bolt. It is difficult to see how clearing up after meals three times a day and making out marketing lists (three lemons, two packages of soap powder, a can of soup), getting at the fuzz in the radiators with the hard rubber appliance of the vacuum cleaner, emptying wastebaskets and washing bathroom floors day after day, week after week, year after year, add up to a sum total of anything except minutiae that laid end to end reach nowhere.

According to another line of reasoning, the housewife has the advantage of being "her own boss" and unlike the gainfully employed worker can arrange her own schedules. This is pure balderdash. . . . If there is anything more inexorable than children's needs, from an infant's yowls of hunger and Junior's shrieks that he has just fallen down the stairs to the subtler need of an adolescent for a good listener during one of his or her frequent emotional crises, it is only the pressure of Dad's demand for supper as soon as he gets home. . . . What is more, not her own preferences as to hours, but those set by her husband's office or plant, by the schools, by pediatricians and dentists, and the children's homework establish when the housewife rises, when she goes forth, and when she cannot get to bed.

Something else makes a mockery of self-determined routines; interruptions from the outside world. Unprotected by butler or doorman, the housewife is at the mercy of peddlers, plain or fancy Fuller brush; odd-job seekers; gas and electric company men who come to read meters; the Salvation Army in quest of newspapers; school children hawking seeds or tickets or chances; and repair men suggesting that the roof is in a hazardous condition or household machinery needs overhauling. Unblessed with a secretary, she answers telephone calls from insurance and real estate agents who "didn't want to bother your husband at his office." . . . All such invasions have a common denominator: the assumption that the housewife's time, like that of all slave labor, has no value.

In addition to what housewifery has in common with slavery, there are factors making it even less enviable as a way of life. The jolly gatherings of darkies with their banjos in the Good Old Days Befoh de Wah may be as mythical as the joys of housewifery, but at any rate we can be sure that slaves were not deprived of social intercourse throughout their hours of toil; field hands worked in gangs, house servants in teams. The housewife, however, carries through each complex operation of cooking, cleaning, tidying and laundering solo; almost uniquely among workers since the Industrial Revolution, she does not benefit by division of labor. Lunch time, ordinarily a pleasant break in the working day, for her brings no pleasant sociability with the girls in the cafeteria, the hired men in the shade of the haystack, or even the rest of the household staff in the servants' dining room. From the time her husband departs for work until he returns, except for an occasional chat across the back fence or a trek to market with some other woman as childbound, housebound, and limited in horizons as herself, she lacks adult company; and even to the most passionately maternal, unbroken hours of childish prattle are no substitute for the conversation of one's peers, whether that be on a high philosophical plane or on the lower level of neighborhood gossip. The Woman's Club, happy hunting ground of matrons in their forties, is perhaps a reaction against this enforced solitude during earlier married life.

Something else enjoyed by slaves, but not by housewives, was work in some measure appropriate to their qualifications. The more intelligent were selected as house servants; the huskier as field hands. Such crude vocational placement has been highly refined in industry, with its battery of intelligence and aptitude tests, personnel directors and employment counselors. Nothing of the kind is even attempted for unpaid domestic workers. When a man marries and has children, it is assumed that he will do the best work along lines in which he has been trained or is at least interested. When a woman marries and has children, it is assumed that she will take to housewifery. But whether she takes to it or not, she does it.

Such regimentation, for professional or potentially professional women, is costly both for the individual and society. For the individual, it brings about conflicts and frustrations. The practice of housewifery gives the lie to the theory of almost every objective of higher education. The educated individual should have a community, a national, a world viewpoint; but that is pretty difficult to get and hold when you are continually involved with cleaning toilets, ironing shirts, peeling potatoes, darning socks and minding children. The educated should read widely; but reading requires time and concentration and besides, the conscientious housewife has her own five-foot shelf of recipes and books on child psychology to occupy her. Most frustrating of all, education leads one to believe that a project attempted should be systematically carried through to completion. In housewifery there is inevitable hopping from one unrelated, unfinished task to another; start the dinner—get at the mending—collect the baby—take down the laundry—finish the dinner is about the maximum height of efficiency. This innate incoherence of housewifery is like a mental patient's flight of ideas; nothing leads quite logically from one thing to another; and the woman schooled like her husband to think generally and in sequence, has a bad time of it intellectually and emotionally as a result.

Perhaps even more deplorable is the loss to society when graduate nurses, trained teachers, lawyers, physicians, artists and other gifted women are unable to utilize their prolonged and expensive educations for the common good. Buried in the homemade cakes the family loves, lost among the stitches of patches, sunk in the suds of the week's wash, are incalculable skilled services.

But just as slaves were in the service of individual masters, not of the community or state or nation in general, so are housewives bound to the service of individual families. That it devolves upon a mother to tend her children during helpless infancy and childhood—or at any rate, to see that they are tended by someone—is undeniable. But only a psychology of slavery can put women at the service of grown men. Ironically, the very gentlemen scrupulous about opening a door for a lady, carrying her packages, or helping her up onto a curb, take it for granted that at mealtime, all their lives long, ladies should carry their food to them and never sit through a meal while they never get up. A wife, when she picks up the soiled clothing her husband has strewn on the floor, lugs his garments to the tailor, makes his twin bed, or sews on his buttons, acts as an unpaid body-servant. If love is the justification for this role, so was love a justification for antebellum Mammies. Free individuals, in a democracy, perform personal services for themselves or, if they have the cash, pay other free individuals to wait on them. It is neither freedom nor democracy when such service is based on color or sex.

As long as the institution of housewifery in its present form persists, both ideologically and practically it blocks any true liberation of women. The vote, the opportunity for economic independence, and the right to smoke cigarettes are all equally superficial veneers over a deep-rooted, ages-old concept of keeping woman in her place. Unfortunately, however, housewives not only are unorganized, but also, doubtless because of the very nature of their brain-dribbling, spirit-stifling vocation, conservative. There is therefore little prospect of a Housewives' Rebellion. There is even less, in the light of men's comfortable setup under the present system, of a male-inspired movement for Abolition!

Questions for Reading and Discussion

1. Why did housewives accept their chores and confinements, according to Stern? How did their experiences differ from the "nauseating . . . bilge" in the press?

2. To what extent was "the housewife . . . the Forgotten Worker"? Why were housewives different from industrial workers?

3. Why did Stern believe housewives were comparable to slaves? Did her comparison fail to mention important differences between housewives and workers or slaves?

4. How might a woman who worked in a factory have responded to Stern's arguments? What might an African American woman who worked as a domestic servant in a white household have said about Stern's statements?

5. In what ways did housewifery block "any true liberation of women"? How could women liberate themselves from housewifery? Why did Stern believe that there was "little prospect of a Housewives' Rebellion"?

DOCUMENT 27–2

Vance Packard Analyzes the Age of Affluence

Material abundance and mass consumption undermined class differences and created equality, many commentators declared in the 1950s. In his book The Status Seekers, *sociologist Vance Packard argued instead that seeking status through consumption masked persistent and increasingly rigid stratification in American society. He raised questions about the social and political consequences of the postwar culture of abundance and striving celebrated during the 1950s.*

The Status Seekers, 1959

What happens to class distinctions among people when most of them are enjoying a long period of material abundance?

Suppose for example that most of the people are able to travel about in their own gleaming, sculptured coaches longer than the average living room and powered by the equivalent of several hundred horses. Suppose that they are able to wear a variety of gay-colored apparel made of miraculous fibers. Suppose they can dine on mass-merchandised vichyssoise[1] and watch the wonders of the world through electronic eyes in their own air-conditioned living rooms.

In such a climate, do the barriers and humiliating distinctions of social class evaporate? Do anxieties about status—and strivings for evidences of superior status—ease up notably? And do opportunities for leadership roles become more available to all who have natural talent?

The recent experience of the people of the United States is instructive. In the early 1940s an era of abundance began which by 1959 had reached proportions fantastic by any past standards. Nearly a half-trillion dollars' worth of goods and services—including television, miracle fibers, and vichyssoise—were being produced.

Before this era of fabled plenty began, it was widely assumed that prosperity would eliminate, or greatly reduce, class differences. If everybody could enjoy the

---

[1]**vichyssoise**: A cold leek and potato soup.

good things of life—as defined by mass merchandisers—the meanness of class distinctions would disappear.

Such a view seemed reasonable to most of us in those pinched pre-plenty days of the thirties because, then, differences in status were all too plainly visible. You could tell who was who—except for a few genteel poor—by the way people dressed, ate, traveled, and—if they were lucky—by the way they worked. The phrase "poor people" then had an intensely vivid meaning. A banker would never be mistaken for one of his clerks even at one hundred feet.

What, actually, has happened to social class in the United States during the recent era of abundance?

A number of influential voices have been advising us that whatever social classes we ever had are now indeed withering away. We are being told that the people of our country have achieved unparalleled equality. Listen to some of the voices.

Some months ago, a national periodical proclaimed the fact that the United States had recently achieved the "most truly classless society in history." A few weeks later, a publisher hailed the disappearance of the class system in America as "the biggest news of our era." Still later, the director of a market-research organization announced his discovery that America was becoming "one vast middle class." Meanwhile, a corporation in paid advertisements was assuring us that "there are more opportunities in this country than ever before." Whatever else we are, we certainly are the world's most self-proclaimed equalitarian people.

The rank-and-file citizens of the nation have generally accepted this view of progress toward equality because it fits with what we would like to believe about ourselves. It coincides with the American Creed and the American Dream, and is deeply imbedded in our folklore.

Such a notion unfortunately rests upon a notable lack of perception of the true situation that is developing. Class lines in several areas of our national life appear to be hardening. And status straining has intensified. . . .

Webster defines status as the "position; rank; standing" of a person. (The word can be pronounced either "stay-tus" or "stat-us.") Although present-day Americans in this era of material abundance are not supposed to put differential labels of social status on fellow citizens, many millions of them do it every day. And their search for appropriate evidences of status for themselves appears to be mounting each year. There is some evidence that wives, generally speaking, tend to be more status conscious than their husbands.

The majority of Americans rate acquaintances and are themselves being rated in return. They believe that some people rate somewhere above them, that some others rate somewhere below them, and that still others seem to rate close enough to their own level to permit them to explore the possibility of getting to know them socially without fear of being snubbed or appearing to downgrade themselves.

When any of us moves into a new neighborhood—and 33,000,000 Americans now do this every year—we are quickly and critically appraised by our new neighbors and business acquaintances before being accepted or rejected for their group. We, in turn, are appraising them and in many cases attempt not to commit what some regard as the horrid error of getting in with the wrong crowd.

Furthermore, most of us surround ourselves, wittingly or unwittingly, with status symbols we hope will influence the raters appraising us, and which we hope will help establish some social distance between ourselves and those we consider below us. The vigorous merchandising of goods as status symbols by advertisers is playing a major role in intensifying status consciousness. Emotionally insecure people are most vulnerable. Others of us, less expert in the nuances of status symbols or more indifferent to them, persist in modes of behavior and in displays of taste that themselves serve as barriers in separating us from the group to which we may secretly aspire. They can keep us in our place. If we aspire to rise in the world but fail to take on the coloration of the group we aspire to—by failing to discard our old status symbols, friends, club memberships, values, behavior patterns, and acquiring new ones esteemed by the higher group—our chances of success are diminished. . . .

Many people are badly distressed, and scared, by the anxieties, inferiority feelings, and straining generated by this unending process of rating and status striving. The status seekers, as I use the term, are people who are continually straining to surround themselves with visible evidence of the superior rank they are claiming. The preoccupation of millions of Americans with status is intensifying social stratification in the United States. . . .

[W]hy is it that so many opinion molders have been announcing their conclusion that classes are disappearing?

The discrepancy arises partly as a result of a generalized desire on the part of United States adults—particularly businessmen—to support the American Dream. Also it arises from the widespread assumption that the recent general rise in available spending money in this country is making everybody equal. Class, in fact, has several faces and income is just one of them. With the general diffusion of wealth, there has been a crumbling of visible class lines now that such one-time upper-class symbols as limousines, power boats, and mink coats are available to a variety of people. Coincidentally, there has been a scrambling to find new ways to draw lines that will separate the elect from the non-elect.

A working-class man, however, does not move up into another social class just by being able to buy a limousine, either by cash or installment, and he knows it. In terms of his productive role in our society—in contrast to his consuming role—class lines in America are becoming more rigid, rather than withering away.

In truth, America, under its gloss of prosperity, is undergoing a significant hardening of the arteries of its social system at some critical points.

As I perceive it, two quite sharply divided major groupings of social classes are emerging, with the old middle class being split into two distinct classes in the process. At the places where most Americans work . . . we are seeing a new emphasis on class lines and a closing-in of the opportunities available to make more than a minor advance. In modern big business, it is becoming more and more difficult to start at the bottom and reach the top. Any leaping aspiration a non-college person has after beginning his career in big business in a modest capacity is becoming less and less realistic.

Furthermore, stratification (formalized inequality of rank) is becoming built-in as our increasingly bureaucratized society moves at almost every hand toward bigness: Big Business, Big Government, Big Labor, Big Education. Bigness is one of the really major factors altering our class system. . . . In the hierarchy of the big corporation, stratification is being carried to exquisite extremes. Employees are usually expected to comport themselves in conformity with their rank, and generally do so. Industrialists are noting that the military experience millions of our younger generation have had has made them more accepting of rank. . . . Employees in big offices, as well as big plants, are finding their work roles fragmentized and impersonalized. There has been, perhaps unwittingly, a sealing-off of contact between big and little people on the job. And there has been a startling rise in the number of people who are bored with their work and feel no pride of initiative or creativity. They must find their satisfactions outside their work. Many do it by using their paychecks to consume flamboyantly. . . .

In brief, the American Dream is losing some of its luster for a good many citizens who would like to believe in it. . . . It is my impression that status lines are more carefully observed in the East and South than in most of the other parts of the country. Californians, with their yeasty social climate, seem the least status-conscious people I've encountered in the nation. . . .

A society that encourages status striving produces, in contrast, a good deal of bruising, disappointment, and ugly feelings. If a society promotes the idea that success is associated with upward mobility, those who can't seem to get anywhere are likely to be afflicted with the feeling that they are personal failures, even though the actual situation may be pretty much beyond their control or capacity to change. . . . [An] educational psychologist . . . has asked . . . this blunt question: "How much should the school urge children to be ambitious and mobile, in a society where most of them will find jobs calling for little skill?" And one of America's leading ministers . . . has in sermons admonished his listeners to be realistic about ambition. It is an admirable quality, he said, but added that we are not all equal in native capacity. "Most of us," he said, "are modestly endowed and we shall not achieve effectiveness or happiness until we recognize it."

The person standing still in a culture that glorifies upward progress often suffers hurts. The greater menace to society, however, is the person moving downward. Any society that has a good deal of upward circulation is bound to have some downward circulation too. We can't all stay at the high level our elders or we ourselves achieve. The person being declassed is, as previously indicated, almost invariably in an ugly mood. He is seething with humiliation and apprehension. If society has not developed a mechanism for quickly and gently helping him find a new, more humble niche, then he becomes a bigot, a searcher for scapegoats, and an eager recruit for almost any demagogue who promises to set up a completely new social order. . . .

We confront in America a historical situation that cries out for a society of achieved status. We are badly maladjusted to our environment and are becoming more maladjusted every month. . . . [W]e need to draw upon all the talent and intelligence we can muster. We need to encourage by every means possible the discovery and advancement of people of unusual potential. . . . In a rigidly stratified society, such people are not even considered.

The challenge to us is to recognize the realities of our current class situation. The main reality is our tendency toward greater rigidity in our stratification while pretending that precisely the opposite is occurring. We are consigning tens of millions of our people to fixed roles in life where aspiration is futile, and yet we keep telling them that those who have the stuff will rise to the top. We don't even allow them the satisfaction of feeling secure, dignified, and creative in their low status. And, socially, we look down upon them.

QUESTIONS FOR READING AND DISCUSSION

1. According to Packard, what happened to "the barriers and humiliating distinctions of social class" during the 1950s? To what extent did they "evaporate"? How did the 1950s compare to the 1930s?

2. What did Packard mean by "status symbols"? To what extent did they create "anxieties [and] inferiority feelings" among many people? Why?

3. Why did Packard suppose that "preoccupation" with status intensified "social stratification in the United States"?

4. What political and social consequences did status seeking have, according to Packard? To what extent did it influence "the American Dream"?

5. How did status seeking hinder the creation of "a society of achieved status"? What role should ambition play in American society? How should it be identified and expressed?

DOCUMENT 27–3

George E. McMillan Reports on Racial Conditions in the South in 1960

The Supreme Court's decision in Brown v. Board of Education *that racial segregation in public schools was unconstitutional created a passionate backlash among southern whites, while engendering anger among African Americans about the glacial pace of racial change. George E. McMillan, a white reporter from Tennessee, surveyed the mood of the South in 1960, six years after the* Brown *decision. McMillan's essay, excerpted below, highlighted the bitter conflict between whites and blacks, analyzed attitudes among both groups, and explained why gradual change was not the answer.*

Sit-Downs: The South's New Time Bomb, 1960

I have just made a trip through the [South]. Everywhere I went, I felt the current raw, ugly temper of the South. Although I live in a small Southern town myself, what astonished me most during my survey was how rigidly and inflexibly the "sides" have lined up. The mood of the South today is frequently compared with what it was 100 years ago — as the South stood at the threshold of a civil war.

The most frightening thing now is the air of resignation with which Southerners of both races view the inevitability of violence.

On my trip, I talked with many kinds of Southerners. I interviewed police chiefs, sheriffs, highway patrolmen, state and city safety directors, mayors and city managers. I also talked with Negro students, Negro school principals, Negro college teachers and administrators. And I talked with many white and Negro people who were not immediately involved in the [civil rights] demonstrations, but whose interest in and knowledge of Southern race relations is immediate and extensive.

It is not so much that anyone wants violence, I discovered, as it is that nobody sees any alternative to it.

The Negroes are infused with a new determination, and are ready to risk violence to get some of the gains they believe are due them.

From George E. McMillan, "Sit-Downs: The South's New Time Bomb," *Look*, July 5, 1960, 21–25.

The middle-class whites seem hopelessly committed to violence. They've said so long, "there'll be trouble," if the old balance between the races is disturbed, that they now find themselves almost counting on trouble as a solution to their problem.

Even the Southern "liberals," an almost professionally hopeful group in the past, are today saying, as one of them did to me, "I don't see how this thing can be settled without slugging it out right down the line." . . .

Elsewhere throughout the South, violence has coursed through community after community. . . . In Biloxi, Miss., whites used dog chains and, later, shotguns on Negroes who showed up at a segregated public beach; in Portsmouth, Va., they armed themselves with hammers; in Montgomery, Ala., they swung baseball bats.

The crisis of law and order is so real, so immediate, that it calls for a new look at what has been the nation's approach to, and its responsibility in, the Southern racial problem.

That approach has been gradualism: slow and evolutionary change. But when looked at against today's urgencies, gradualism shapes up as a failure. . . .

When the evidence is weighed today, gradualism not only looks wrong, but also appears to have been mistaken in intent.

Gradualism is deeply ingrained in the American tradition, and Americans outside the South, recent surveys show, are reluctant to believe that gradual social change isn't the best way to solve the South's problems.

But the simple logic of the future of Southern race relations is that somebody outside the South is going to have to intervene. That intervention will almost certainly have to come from the Federal Government.

The question that remains is whether the Government will intervene after damage is done, including perhaps serious international damage to America's prestige, or whether national public opinion will support positive and constructive steps of prevention.

The persistent American image of the South's situation is that there are two extreme sides, with a happy middle ground between them and that this middle ground must be occupied in the South, as it is almost everywhere else in the U.S., by people who are essentially moral and law-abiding.

Almost exactly this view has been expressed by President Eisenhower.

"The South is full of people of good will," he told a press conference in 1956, after the riots in Clinton, Tenn., "but they are not the ones we now hear. We hear the people who are adamant, and are so filled with prejudice that they can't keep still—they even resort to violence; and the same way on the other side of the thing, the people who want to have the whole matter settled today. This is a question of leading and training and teaching people, and it takes some time, unfortunately."

The President's view seems to be similar to the present mood and temper of the country. . . . [A *Newsweek* poll] concluded, "The prevailing view among opinion leaders is one of understanding and sympathy. From California to Maine, men recognize that decades of strict social custom in the South cannot be overturned quickly." . . .

But the answer from the young Negro college students in the South is plain. "Mr. Local Custom Must Die," read a placard carried by one of them in a recent demonstration.

If there is a lesson in the current racial crisis, it is that the Southern climate is not democratic, and that gradualism will not work there because the essentials of gradualism—a flexible society in which competing claims are freely heard and fairly adjusted—do not exist.

In the first place, the Negro's claims for his legal and constitutional rights, not to mention economic opportunity and personal dignity, have run into a stone wall of denial and defiance from the white South.

In the decade and a half since World War II, the Southern Negro has pressed his claims through the courts, in the democratic tradition, only to win his suits and lose his case. Today, he is fed up with legalism. . . .

The crowning disappointment to the Negro, and the most disastrous failure of moderation, lies in the six-year history of enforcement, or lack of enforcement, of the 1954 U.S. Supreme Court decision on the schools.

In the spring of 1960, six years after the Court handed down its ruling that racial segregation in schools is illegal, 94 per cent of the South's Negro students were still attending segregated classes, according to the authoritative Southern Education Reporting Service. . . .

Behind the question of tactics and speed lies another source of disillusionment for the Negro. In a society whose keynote is its chance for individual economic advancement, the Negro is not even standing still; he is losing ground. . . . In 1950, America's Negro families earned about 54 per cent as much as whites, but in 1958, the ratio had dropped to 51 per cent. Negroes in the South fared even worse. In 1958 . . . family income for Southern Negroes was $2,014, or 44 per cent of the white income. Gradualism clearly has not helped at all in that area.

"You can't argue," said one Negro, "that there's any question of time in giving a man a job. You either hire a man or you don't. You can't hire a leg today and an arm tomorrow."

There is almost no hope for a Negro, no matter what his skills or training, to land professional employment in the South outside of rigidly segregated facilities—and very little there. In private industry, there is nothing but "the mop and the broom," and little more in state and municipal governments. . . .

If the Negro's spectrum is dark almost everywhere he looks, the classic failure of legalism and gradualism seems to have been the Supreme Court decision. Gradualism, the democratic way, assumes that leadership groups will lead, and lead in the right direction, if they have the facts and the moment of opportunity. The school decision was designed to give moderation a fair chance to work.

In allowing the South a year's breathing spell after its initial decision, and in leaving implementation to Federal district judges, the Court showed that it believed the South deserved time, and would use the time well. But it didn't work out that way.

A perceptive Southern newspaperman described what happened:

"Everybody was in shock for a few weeks immediately after the decision. Many people concerned with government or schools were convinced the time had come. They thought they were going to have to comply. Many school superintendents went right ahead with plans for integration. If the Court had ordered Southern school systems to submit plans within 12 months, all, or all but a few, would have done so." Then, legislatures erected new legal barriers and delay followed delay. . . .

The pertinent question today is not whether there are any white "people of good will" so much as it is: Under what conditions would the white people who normally play leadership roles in the South take positive and constructive leadership on the racial question?

Do they need time? Would they do more if they had more time?

One of the least understood facts about the South is that there is a wider atmosphere of professed acquiescence there than few people outside the region realize. In the country clubs, on the terraces, in the new ranch-house living rooms where middle- and upper-class Southerners gather, there is general agreement that "the Negro's got to make some progress," or "something has got to give" or "someday we've got to integrate the schools." It has almost become a matter of class status to say: "As far as I'm concerned, I wouldn't care if they integrated tomorrow." Thus, the upper-class Southerner distinguishes himself from the lower-class white person—whose principal characteristic in the past has always been his overt hatred for the Negro.

Middle-class whites—ministers, teachers, professionals—say it is not prejudice that holds them back but practicality. "There'd be trouble," they say. What they do not say, and would not admit, is that they are as much in bondage as the Negro himself. In the past, when members of this class have let their consciences guide them into attempts to change the status quo, reprisal has been visited on them just as effectively, if not as violently, as it has on the Negro himself.

Time has little to do with their attitudes or their behavior.

They are simply disenfranchised, caught in the grip of an archaic, rigid and oversimplified power structure welded long ago specifically to fight off all changes in the racial situation. . . .

The South is in the midst of a deep economic as well as social conflict. It is torn between the values of an almost feudalistic agricultural society and a modern industrial one. Much of its new industry has been attracted to the region by low taxes and no unions. But the bargain that the textile mills made with their workers years ago still seems to hold for the plant that came to town yesterday: "We'll keep the niggers out if you'll keep the unions out."

Thus, despite all the signs of a "new" South, despite hundreds of new factories lining Southern highways, despite the prosperous suburbs that stretch around the big cities like Atlanta and Charlotte, the political energy of the region is still single-mindedly devoted to an anachronistic cause.

The banks, the large corporations, the utilities and the rural landowners—the people who hold economic and political power in the South—are not yet convinced that it is not best to let the traditional people handle the traditional problem in the traditional way. . . .

The question of how much time the South should be allowed in which to drop its "strict customs" is in some ways a very complicated problem; in others, a very simple one. It involves prejudice, taboos, culture, folklore and mores. But change can be made.

Ironically, every day throughout the deepest recesses of the Deep South, some Southern whites are peacefully working with, living with and eating with Negroes on an integrated basis. In military camps all over the South, Southern boys are serving uneventfully in completely integrated military units, and have been doing so for several years. . . .

The rule seems to be that Southerners will abandon their customs more rapidly when it is a matter of economic necessity, but insist on them when they can get by with it. . . .

Much evidence suggests that . . . the best way to handle integration is the quickest way, giving the South's long-nurtured irrationalities the shortest possible shrift.

From my own observations . . . , three realities must be faced: that racial discrimination is the number-one social problem of this decade in American life; that the situation is now in a deadly and dangerous stalemate and that the only agency that can do anything meaningful at this juncture is the Federal Government.

QUESTIONS FOR READING AND DISCUSSION

1. What led McMillan to conclude there was a "crisis of law and order" in the South? What accounted for the "air of resignation" about the "inevitability of violence"?

2. Why did McMillan come to believe that "gradualism shapes up as a failure"? What alternative did he propose?

3. What was the meaning of the sign carried by the black civil rights demonstrator, "Mr. Local Custom Must Die"?

4. What was the significance of the "bargain" between employers and their workers that "We'll keep the niggers out if you'll keep the unions out"?

5. Do you agree with McMillan's statement that "racial discrimination is the number-one social problem of this decade in American life"? Why or why not?

DOCUMENT 27–4

Youth Culture and the Draft

During the 1950s, American teenagers listened to music more often than ever before. Music blared on radios in cars and in many teenagers' bedrooms. They bought countless records and played them over and over with friends. Pop megastars of the 1940s, like crooner Frank Sinatra, no longer captivated young people. Instead, they became fans of emerging rock and roll legends like Chuck Berry, Little Richard, Jerry Lee Lewis, and—especially—Elvis Presley. Elvis rocketed to superstardom between 1954 and 1958 with hit after hit, and performed with gyrations that led critics to label him "Elvis the Pelvis." His performances thrilled his young fans, but guardians of mainstream culture denounced Elvis as a talentless goon and his music as little more than degenerate groans that made young people lose their self-control and refuse to obey their parents.

At the height of his popularity in 1958, Elvis was drafted into the Army. By then, he had starred in four major movies, performed numerous times on network television, toured throughout the nation, and sold millions of recordings. The following photo shows Elvis and other draftees being sworn into the Army near Fort Smith, Arkansas, in March 1958. The photo captures a moment when Elvis was forced to set aside his rock and roll life and, like so many other young Americans in the 1950s, conform to established institutions and hierarchies.

Elvis Presley Joins the Army, 1958

Hulton Archive/Getty Images

QUESTIONS FOR READING AND DISCUSSION

1. In what ways does the photo suggest that Elvis is not like the other draftees? In what ways is he similar to the others?
2. Given Elvis's status as the nation's iconic rock and roll star at that time, what might fans and critics think about his taking the Oath of Enlistment? How might this photo have affected Elvis's public image?
3. How do the draftees in the photo illustrate changes adopted by the American military after World War II?
4. In what ways does the induction ceremony shown in the photo reflect the ability of established institutions and hierarchies to require conformity?

DOCUMENT 27–5

President Dwight D. Eisenhower Warns about the Military-Industrial Complex

After eight years as president and a lifetime of service at the highest levels of the U.S. military, Dwight D. Eisenhower delivered his farewell address on nationwide television. In his address, excerpted here, Eisenhower surveyed American achievements during the 1950s and identified threats posed by those achievements. His assessment suggests the qualms that, for many Americans, mingled with confidence about the future.

Farewell Address, January 1961

This evening I come to you with a message of leave-taking and farewell, and to share a few final thoughts with you, my countrymen. . . .

We now stand ten years past the midpoint of a century that has witnessed four major wars among great nations. Three of these involved our own country. Despite these holocausts America is today the strongest, the most influential and most productive nation in the world. Understandably proud of this pre-eminence, we yet realize that America's leadership and prestige depend, not merely upon our unmatched material progress, riches and military strength, but on how we use our power in the interests of world peace and human betterment.

Throughout America's adventure in free government, our basic purposes have been to keep the peace; to foster progress in human achievement, and to enhance liberty, dignity and integrity among people and among nations. To strive for less would be unworthy of a free and religious people. Any failure traceable to arrogance, or for lack of comprehension or readiness to sacrifice would inflict upon us grievous hurt both at home and abroad.

Progress toward these noble goals is persistently threatened by the conflict now engulfing the world. It commands our whole attention, absorbs our very beings. We face a hostile ideology global in scope, atheistic in character, ruthless in purpose, and insidious in method. Unhappily the danger it poses promises to be of indefinite duration. To meet it successfully, there is called for, not so much the emotional and transitory sacrifices of crisis, but rather those which enable us to carry forward steadily, surely, and without complaint the burdens of a prolonged and complex struggle—with liberty the stake. Only thus shall we remain, despite every provocation, on our charted course toward permanent peace and human betterment.

Crises there will continue to be. In meeting them, whether foreign or domestic, great or small, there is a recurring temptation to feel that some spectacular and costly action could become the miraculous solution to all current difficulties. A huge increase in newer elements of our defense; development of unrealistic programs to cure every ill in agriculture; a dramatic expansion in basic and applied research—these and many other possibilities, each possibly promising in itself, may be suggested as the only way to the road we wish to travel.

But each proposal must be weighed in the light of a broader consideration: the need to maintain balance in and among national programs—balance between the private and the public economy, balance between cost and hoped for advantage—balance between the clearly necessary and the comfortably desirable; balance between our essential requirements as a nation and the duties imposed by the nation upon the individual; balance between actions of the moment and the national welfare of the future. Good judgment seeks balance and progress; lack of it eventually finds imbalance and frustration.

The record of many decades stands as proof that our people and their government have, in the main, understood these truths and have responded to them well, in the face of stress and threat. But threats, new in kind or degree, constantly arise. I mention two only.

A vital element in keeping the peace is our military establishment. Our arms must be mighty, ready for instant action, so that no potential aggressor may be tempted to risk his own destruction.

From *Public Papers of the Presidents of the United States: Dwight D. Eisenhower, 1960–61* (1961).

Our military organization today bears little relation to that known by any of my predecessors in peacetime, or indeed by the fighting men of World War II or Korea. Until the latest of our world conflicts, the United States had no armaments industry. American makers of plowshares could, with time and as required, make swords as well. But now we can no longer risk emergency improvisation of national defense; we have been compelled to create a permanent armaments industry of vast proportions. Added to this, three and a half million men and women are directly engaged in the defense establishment. We annually spend on military security more than the net income of all United States corporations.

This conjunction of an immense military establishment and a large arms industry is new in the American experience. The total influence — economic, political, even spiritual — is felt in every city, every State house, every office of the Federal government. We recognize the imperative need for this development. Yet we must not fail to comprehend its grave implications. Our toil, resources and livelihood are all involved; so is the very structure of our society.

In the councils of government, we must guard against the acquisition of unwarranted influence, whether sought or unsought, by the military-industrial complex. The potential for the disastrous rise of misplaced power exists and will persist.

We must never let the weight of this combination endanger our liberties or democratic processes. We should take nothing for granted. Only an alert and knowledgeable citizenry can compel the proper meshing of the huge industrial and military machinery of defense with our peaceful methods and goals, so that security and liberty may prosper together.

Akin to, and largely responsible for the sweeping changes in our industrial-military posture, has been the technological revolution during recent decades.

In this revolution, research has become central; it also becomes more formalized, complex, and costly. A steadily increasing share is conducted for, by, or at the direction of, the Federal government.

Today, the solitary inventor, tinkering in his shop, has been overshadowed by task forces of scientists in laboratories and testing fields. In the same fashion, the free university, historically the fountainhead of free ideas and scientific discovery, has experienced a revolution in the conduct of research. Partly because of the huge costs involved, a government contract becomes virtually a substitute for intellectual curiosity. For every old blackboard there are now hundreds of new electronic computers.

The prospect of domination of the nation's scholars by Federal employment, project allocations, and the power of money is ever present — and is gravely to be regarded.

Yet, in holding scientific research and discovery in respect, as we should, we must also be alert to the equal and opposite danger that public policy could itself become the captive of a scientific-technological elite.

It is the task of statesmanship to mold, to balance, and to integrate these and other forces, new and old, within the principles of our democratic system — ever aiming toward the supreme goals of our free society.

Another factor in maintaining balance involves the element of time. As we peer into society's future, we — you and I, and our government — must avoid the impulse to live only for today, plundering, for our own ease and convenience, the precious resources of tomorrow. We cannot mortgage the material assets of our grandchildren without risking the loss also of their political and spiritual heritage. We want democracy to survive for all generations to come, not to become the insolvent phantom of tomorrow.

Down the long lane of the history yet to be written America knows that this world of ours, ever growing smaller, must avoid becoming a community of dreadful fear and hate, and be, instead, a proud confederation of mutual trust and respect.

Such a confederation must be one of equals. The weakest must come to the conference table with the same confidence as do we, protected as we are by our moral, economic, and military strength. That table, though scarred by many past frustrations, cannot be abandoned for the certain agony of the battlefield. Disarmament, with mutual honor and confidence, is a continuing imperative. Together we must learn how to compose differences, not with arms, but with intellect and decent purpose. Because this need is so sharp and apparent I confess that I lay down my official responsibilities in this field with a definite sense of disappointment. As one who has witnessed the horror and the lingering sadness of war—as one who knows that another war could utterly destroy this civilization which has been so slowly and painfully built over thousands of years—I wish I could say tonight that a lasting peace is in sight.

Happily, I can say that war has been avoided. Steady progress toward our ultimate goal has been made. But, so much remains to be done. As a private citizen, I shall never cease to do what little I can to help the world advance along that road....

You and I—my fellow citizens—need to be strong in our faith that all nations, under God, will reach the goal of peace with justice. May we be ever unswerving in devotion to principle, confident but humble with power, diligent in pursuit of the Nation's great goals.

QUESTIONS FOR READING AND DISCUSSION

1. What did Eisenhower identify as basic American goals and what was required to achieve them?
2. Why did he urge Americans to "guard against the acquisition of unwarranted influence . . . by the military-industrial complex"? What dangers did the military-industrial complex pose?
3. To what extent did Eisenhower's address reflect the major historical legacies of the 1950s? Do you think his concerns are still relevant in the twenty-first century? Why or why not?

COMPARATIVE QUESTIONS

1. How do Edith M. Stern's notions about women's enslavement compare with George E. McMillan's observations about racial discrimination? What might account for the differences in their ideas?
2. How did Vance Packard's view of the American dream compare with that of the fans of Elvis Presley? Would Elvis's fans view his being drafted as a blow to the American dream? How might Packard respond?
3. How did Dwight D. Eisenhower's views about the dangers confronting the nation compare with those of Packard, Stern, and McMillan?
4. How did the era's relative economic abundance shape the ideas and experiences described in these documents?
5. How did the events of World War II continue to impact Americans' lives during the 1950s? What changes that occurred during the war were reversed during peacetime? Why?

28 Rights, Rebellion, and Reaction

1960–1974

D uring the 1960s, many Americans sought to make changes that many other Americans resisted. To those who wanted change, the times seemed right and the causes just. Presidents sympathetic to change occupied the Oval Office for most of the period. Civil rights demonstrators confronted Jim Crow laws, black power advocates called for racial pride and revolution, women's rights leaders outlined proposals for gender equality, and anti-war activists sought to end the Vietnam war. The possibilities for change seemed extraordinary to many and dangerous—even anti-American—to many others. The widespread sense that the American dream could be more fully realized, as well as the lingering obstacles to achieving that goal, are revealed in the following documents.

DOCUMENT 28–1

Martin Luther King Jr. Explains Nonviolent Resistance

Participants in the civil rights demonstrations that swept across the South during the 1960s used tactics of nonviolent resistance. Many white Americans, North and South, condemned the demonstrators as extremists and lawbreakers whose ends may have been admirable but whose means were deplorable. Martin Luther King Jr. responded to those views in 1963 in a letter he wrote while in jail in Birmingham, Alabama, where he had been arrested for participating in demonstrations. King's letter, excerpted here, was directed to a group of white clergymen who had criticized the Birmingham demonstrations. King's letter set forth the ideals of nonviolence embraced by many civil rights activists.

Letter from Birmingham City Jail, 1963

My dear Fellow Clergymen,

While confined here in the Birmingham city jail, I came across your recent statement calling our present activities "unwise and untimely." . . . [S]ince I feel that you are men of genuine good will and your criticisms are sincerely set forth, I would like to answer your statement in what I hope will be patient and reasonable terms.

I think I should give the reason for my being in Birmingham, since you have been influenced by the argument of "outsiders coming in." I have the honor of serving as president of the Southern Christian Leadership Conference, an organization operating in every southern state, with headquarters in Atlanta, Georgia. We have some eighty-five affiliate organizations all across the South. . . . Several months ago our local affiliate here in Birmingham invited us to be on call to engage in a nonviolent direct-action program if such were deemed necessary. . . .

Beyond this, I am in Birmingham because injustice is here. . . . I cannot sit idly by in Atlanta and not be concerned about what happens in Birmingham. Injustice anywhere is a threat to justice everywhere. . . .

You deplore the demonstrations that are presently taking place in Birmingham. But I am sorry that your statement did not express a similar concern for the conditions that brought the demonstrations into being. . . .

Birmingham is probably the most thoroughly segregated city in the United States. Its ugly record of police brutality is known in every section of this country. Its injust treatment of Negroes in the courts is a notorious reality. There have been more unsolved bombings of Negro homes and churches in Birmingham than any city in this nation. These are the hard, brutal and unbelievable facts. . . .

You may well ask, "Why direct action? Why sit-ins, marches, etc.? Isn't negotiation a better path?" You are exactly right in your call for negotiation. Indeed, this is the purpose of direct action. Nonviolent direct action seeks to create such a crisis and establish such creative tension that a community that has constantly refused to negotiate is forced to confront the issue. It seeks so to dramatize the issue that it can no longer be ignored. . . . So the purpose of the direct action is to create a situation so crisis-packed that it will inevitably open the door to negotiation. . . .

One of the basic points in your statement is that our acts are untimely. . . . My friends, I must say to you that we have not made a single gain in civil rights without determined legal and nonviolent pressure. History is the long and tragic story of the fact that privileged groups seldom give up their privileges voluntarily. . . .

We know through painful experience that freedom is never voluntarily given by the oppressor; it must be demanded by the oppressed. Frankly, I have never yet engaged in a direct action movement that was "well-timed," according to the timetable of those who have not suffered unduly from the disease of segregation. For years now I have heard the words "Wait!" It rings in the ear of every Negro with a piercing familiarity. This "Wait" has almost always meant "Never." . . . We have waited for more than 340 years for our constitutional and God-given rights. The nations of Asia and Africa are moving with jetlike speed toward the goal of political independence, and we still creep at horse and buggy pace toward the gaining of a cup of coffee at a lunch counter. I guess it is easy for those who have never felt the stinging darts of segregation to say, "Wait." But when you have seen vicious mobs lynch your mothers and fathers at will and drown your sisters and brothers at whim; when you have seen hate-filled policemen curse, kick, brutalize and even kill your black brothers and sisters with impunity; when you see the vast majority of your twenty million Negro brothers smothering in an airtight cage of poverty in the midst of an affluent society; when you suddenly find your tongue twisted and your speech stammering as you seek to explain to your six-year-old daughter why she can't go to the public amusement park that has just been advertised on television, and see tears welling up in her little eyes when she is told that Funtown is closed to colored children, and see the depressing clouds of inferiority begin to form in her little mental sky, and see her begin to distort her little personality by unconsciously developing a bitterness toward white people; when you have to concoct an answer for a five-year-old son asking in agonizing pathos: "Daddy, why do white people treat colored people so mean?"; when you take a cross-country drive and find it necessary to sleep night after night in the uncomfortable corners of your automobile because no motel will accept you; when you are humiliated day in and day out by nagging signs reading "white" and "colored"; when your first name becomes "nigger" and your middle name becomes "boy" (however old you are) and your last name becomes "John," and when your wife and mother are never given the respected title "Mrs."; when you are harried by day and haunted by night by the fact that you are a Negro, living constantly at tiptoe stance never quite knowing what to expect next, and plagued with inner fears and outer resentments; when you are forever fighting a degenerating sense of "nobodiness"; then you will understand why we find it difficult to wait. There comes a time when the cup of endurance runs over, and men are no longer willing to be plunged into an abyss of injustice where they experience the blackness of corroding despair. I hope, sirs, you can understand our legitimate and unavoidable impatience.

You express a great deal of anxiety over our willingness to break laws. This is certainly a legitimate concern. Since we so diligently urge people to obey the Supreme Court's decision of 1954 outlawing segregation in the public schools, it is rather strange and paradoxical to find us consciously breaking laws. One may well ask, "How can you advocate breaking some laws and obeying others?" The answer is found in the fact that there are two types of laws: there are *just* and there are *unjust* laws. I would agree with Saint Augustine that "An unjust law is no law at all."

Now what is the difference between the two? How does one determine when a law is just or unjust? A just law is a man-made code that squares with the moral law or the law of God. An unjust law is a code that is out of harmony with the moral law. To put it in the terms of Saint Thomas Aquinas, an unjust law is a human law that is not rooted in eternal and natural law. Any law that uplifts human personality is just. Any law that degrades human personality is unjust. All segregation statutes are unjust because segregation distorts the soul and damages the personality. It gives the segregator a false sense of superiority, and the segregated a false sense of inferiority. . . . So segregation is not only politically, economically and sociologically unsound, but it is morally wrong and sinful. . . . So I can urge men to disobey segregation ordinances because they are morally wrong. . . .

I hope you can see the distinction I am trying to point out. In no sense do I advocate evading or defying the law as the rabid segregationist would do. This would lead to anarchy. One who breaks an unjust law must do it *openly, lovingly* . . . and with a willingness to accept the penalty. I submit that an individual who breaks a law that conscience tells him is unjust, and willingly accepts the penalty by staying in jail to arouse the conscience of the community over its injustice, is in reality expressing the very highest respect for law.

Of course, there is nothing new about this kind of civil disobedience. . . . It was practiced superbly by the early Christians who were willing to face hungry lions and the excruciating pain of chopping blocks, before submitting to certain unjust laws of the Roman Empire. . . .

I must make two honest confessions to you, my Christian and Jewish brothers. First, I must confess that over the last few years I have been gravely disappointed with the white moderate. I have almost reached the regrettable conclusion that the Negro's great stumbling block in the stride toward freedom is not the White Citizen's Counciler or the Ku Klux Klanner, but the white moderate who is more devoted to order than to justice; who prefers a negative peace which is the absence of tension to a positive peace which is the presence of justice; who constantly says, "I agree with you in the goal you seek, but I can't agree with your methods of direct action"; who paternalistically feels that he can set the timetable for another man's freedom; who lives by the myth of time and who constantly advised the Negro to wait until a "more convenient season." Shallow understanding from people of good will is more frustrating than absolute misunderstanding from people of ill will. Lukewarm acceptance is much more bewildering than outright rejection.

I had hoped that the white moderate would understand that law and order exist for the purpose of establishing justice, and that when they fail to do this they become dangerously structured dams that block the flow of social progress. I had hoped that the white moderate would understand that the present tension of the South is merely a necessary phase of the transition from an obnoxious negative peace, where the Negro passively accepted his unjust plight, to a substance-filled positive peace, where all men will respect the dignity and worth of human personality. Actually, we who engage in nonviolent direct action are not the creators of tension. We merely bring to the surface the hidden tension that is already alive. We bring it out in the open where it can be seen and dealt with. . . .

In your statement you asserted that our actions, even though peaceful, must be condemned because they precipitate violence. But can this assertion be logically made? Isn't this like condemning the robbed man because his possession of money precipitated the evil act of robbery? . . .

You spoke of our activity in Birmingham as extreme. At first I was rather disappointed that fellow clergymen would see my nonviolent efforts as those of the extremist. I started thinking about the fact that I stand in the middle of two opposing forces in the Negro community. One is a force of complacency made up of Negroes who, as a result of long years of oppression, have been so completely drained of self-respect and a sense of "somebodiness" that they have adjusted to segregation, and, of a few Negroes in the middle class who, because of a degree of academic and economic security, and because at points they profit by segregation, have unconsciously become insensitive to the problems of the masses. The other force is one of bitterness and hatred, and comes perilously close to advocating violence. It is expressed in the various black nationalist groups that are springing up over the nation, the largest and best known being Elijah Muhammad's Muslim movement. This movement is nourished by the contemporary frustration over the continued existence of racial discrimination. It is made up of people who have lost faith in America, who have absolutely repudiated Christianity, and who have concluded that the white man is an incurable "devil." I have tried to stand between these two forces, saying that we need not follow the "do-nothingism" of the complacent or the hatred and despair of the black nationalist. There is the more excellent way of love and nonviolent protest. I'm grateful to God that, through the Negro church, the dimension of nonviolence entered our struggle. If this philosophy had not emerged, I am convinced that by now many streets of the South would be flowing with floods of blood. And I am further convinced that if our white brothers dismiss as "rabble-rousers" and "outside agitators" those of us who are working through the channels of nonviolent direct action and refuse to support our nonviolent efforts, millions of Negroes, out of frustration and despair, will seek solace and security in black nationalist ideologies, a development that will lead inevitably to a frightening racial nightmare.

Oppressed people cannot remain oppressed forever. The urge for freedom will eventually come. This is what happened to the American Negro. . . .

But as I continued to think about the matter I gradually gained a bit of satisfaction from being considered an extremist. Was not Jesus an extremist in love—"Love your enemies, bless them that curse you, pray for them that despitefully use you." . . . Was not Abraham Lincoln an extremist—"This nation cannot survive half slave and half free." Was not Thomas Jefferson an extremist—"We hold these truths to be self-evident, that all men are created equal." So the question is not whether we will be extremist but what kind of extremist will we be. Will we be extremists for hate or will we be extremists for love? Will we be extremists for the preservation of injustice—or will we be extremists for the cause of justice? . . .

But before closing I am impelled to mention one other point in your statement that troubled me profoundly. You warmly commended the Birmingham police force for keeping "order" and "preventing violence." I don't believe you would have so warmly commended the police force if you had seen its angry violent dogs literally biting six unarmed, nonviolent Negroes. I don't believe you would so quickly commend the policemen if you would observe their ugly and inhuman treatment of Negroes here in the city jail; if you would watch them push and curse old Negro women and young Negro girls; if you would see them slap and kick old Negro men and young boys; if you will observe them, as they did on two occasions, refuse to give us food because we wanted to sing our grace together. I'm sorry that I can't join you in your praise for the police department. . . .

I wish you had commended the Negro sit-inners and demonstrators of Birmingham for their sublime courage, their willingness to suffer and their amazing discipline in the midst of the most inhuman provocation. One day the South will recognize its real heroes. They will be the James Merediths,[1] courageously and with a majestic sense of purpose facing jeering and hostile mobs and the agonizing loneliness that characterizes the life of the pioneer. They will be old, oppressed, battered Negro women, symbolized in a seventy-two-year-old woman of Montgomery, Alabama, who rose up with a sense of dignity and with her people decided not to ride the segregated buses, and responded to one who inquired about her tiredness with ungrammatical profundity: "My feet is tired, but my soul is rested." They will be the young high school and college students, young ministers of the gospel and a host of their elders courageously and nonviolently sitting-in at lunch counters and willingly going to jail for conscience's sake. One day the South will know that when these disinherited children of God sat down at lunch counters they were in

---

[1]**James Meredith**: The first black student to attend the University of Mississippi, Meredith had to be escorted by U.S. marshals to protect him from a rioting mob of segregationists in 1962.

reality standing up for the best in the American dream and the most sacred values in our Judeo-Christian heritage, and thusly, carrying our whole nation back to those great wells of democracy which were dug deep by the Founding Fathers in the formulation of the Constitution and the Declaration of Independence.

QUESTIONS FOR READING AND DISCUSSION

1. In what ways did segregation generate a "sense of 'nobodiness'" and "a false sense of superiority"? Why?

2. King distinguished between just and unjust laws. How could one tell whether segregation was just or unjust? What was the difference between "civil disobedience" and criminal activity? Why did civil disobedience express "the very highest respect for law"?

3. Why did white moderates disappoint King? What historical and religious examples did he invoke as admirable? Would white moderates have found King's arguments persuasive? Why or why not?

4. Where did King position himself and his followers along the spectrum of black society? What alternatives to nonviolence were advocated by others? Why did he gain "a bit of satisfaction from being considered an extremist"?

5. King intended to reach an audience far beyond Birmingham with his letter. What groups did he hope to appeal to with his arguments, and why were they important to the civil rights movement?

DOCUMENT 28–2

George C. Wallace Denounces the Civil Rights Movement

Alabama governor George C. Wallace declared in his 1963 inaugural address, "segregation today, segregation tomorrow, segregation forever." He won a large regional and national following for his hard-line opposition to racial change. He entered Democratic presidential primaries in 1964 and ran as the presidential nominee of the American Independent Party in 1968. In a 1964 speech in Atlanta about civil rights, Wallace outlined arguments that appealed to many people who opposed the changes under way in American society during the 1960s.

The Civil Rights Movement: Fraud, Sham, and Hoax, July 4, 1964

We come here today in deference to the memory of those stalwart patriots who on July 4, 1776, pledged their lives, their fortunes, and their sacred honor to establish and defend the proposition that governments are created by the people, empowered by the people, derive their just powers from the consent of the people, and must forever remain subservient to the will of the people. . . .

From George C. Wallace, "The Civil Rights Movement: Fraud, Sham, and Hoax," Speech in Atlanta, July 4, 1964.

It is therefore a cruel irony that the President of the United States has only yesterday signed into law the most monstrous piece of legislation [the 1964 Civil Rights Act] ever enacted by the United States Congress.

It is a fraud, a sham, and a hoax.

This bill will live in infamy. To sign it into law at any time is tragic. To do so upon the eve of the celebration of our independence insults the intelligence of the American people.

It dishonors the memory of countless thousands of our dead who offered up their very lives in defense of principles which this bill destroys.

Never before in the history of this nation have so many human and property rights been destroyed by a single enactment of the Congress. It is an act of tyranny. It is the assassin's knife stuck in the back of liberty.

With this assassin's knife and a blackjack in the hand of the Federal force-cult, the left-wing liberals will try to force us back into bondage. Bondage to a tyranny more brutal than that imposed by the British monarchy which claimed power to rule over the lives of our forefathers under sanction of the Divine Right of kings.

Today, this tyranny is imposed by the central government which claims the right to rule over our lives under sanction of the omnipotent black-robed despots who sit on the bench of the United States Supreme Court.

This bill is fraudulent in intent, in design, and in execution. It is misnamed. . . .

To illustrate the fraud — it is not a Civil Rights Bill. It is a Federal Penal Code. It creates Federal crimes which would take volumes to list and years to tabulate because it affects the lives of 192 million American citizens. Every person in every walk and station of life and every aspect of our daily lives becomes subject to the criminal provisions of this bill.

It threatens our freedom of speech, of assembly, or association, and makes the exercise of these Freedoms a [F]ederal crime under certain conditions.

It affects our political rights, our right to trial by jury, our right to the full use and enjoyment of our private property, the freedom from search and seizure of our private property and possessions, the freedom from harassment by Federal police and, in short, all the rights of individuals inherent in a society of free men.

Ministers, lawyers, teachers, newspapers, and every private citizen must guard his speech and watch his actions to avoid the deliberately imposed booby traps put into this bill. It is designed to make Federal crimes of our customs, beliefs, and traditions. Therefore, under the fantastic powers of the Federal judiciary to punish for contempt of court and under their fantastic powers to regulate our most intimate aspects of our lives by injunction, every American citizen is in jeopardy and must stand guard against these despots. . . .

Yet a Federal judge may still try one without a jury under the provisions of this bill. It was the same persons who said it was a good bill before the amendment pretending to forbid busing of pupils from neighborhood schools. Yet a Federal judge may still order busing from one neighborhood school to another. They have done it, they will continue to do it. . . .

It was left-wing radicals who led the fight in the Senate for the so-called civil rights bill now about to enslave our nation. . . .

I am not about to be a party to anything having to do with the law that is going to destroy individual freedom and liberty in this country.

I am having nothing to do with enforcing a law that will destroy our free enterprise system.

I am having nothing to do with enforcing a law that will destroy neighborhood schools.

I am having nothing to do with enforcing a law that will destroy the rights of private property.

I am having nothing to do with enforcing a law that destroys your right—and my right—to choose my neighbors—or to sell my house to whomever I choose.

I am having nothing to do with enforcing a law that destroys the labor seniority system.

I am having nothing to do with this so-called civil rights bill. . . .

It would have been impossible for the American people to have been deceived by the sponsors of this bill had there been a responsible American press to tell the people exactly what the bill contained. If they had had the integrity and the guts to tell the truth, this bill would never have been enacted. . . .

We couldn't get the truth to the American people. You and I know that that's extremely difficult to do where our newspapers are owned by out-of-state interests. Newspapers which are run and operated by left-wing liberals, Communist sympathizers, and members of the Americans for Democratic Action and other Communist front organizations with high sounding names.

However, we will not be intimidated by the vultures of the liberal left-wing press. We will not be deceived by their lies and distortions of truth. We will not be swayed by their brutal attacks upon the character and reputation of any honest citizen who dares stand up and fight for liberty. . . .

Nor would we have had a bill had it not been for the United States Supreme Court. . . .

Now on the subject of the court let me make it clear that I am not attacking any member of the United States Supreme Court as an individual. However, I do attack their decisions, I question their intelligence, their common sense and their judgment, I consider the Federal Judiciary system to be the greatest single threat to individual freedom and liberty in the United States today, and I'm going to take off the gloves in talking about these people.

There is only one word to describe the Federal judiciary today. That word is "lousy."

They assert more power than claimed by King George III, more power than Hitler, Mussolini, or Khrushchev ever had. They assert the power to declare unconstitutional our very thoughts. To create for us a system of moral and ethical values. To outlaw and declare unconstitutional, illegal, and immoral the customs, traditions, and beliefs of the people, and furthermore they assert the authority to enforce their decrees in all these subjects upon the American people without their consent. . . .

The court today, just as in 1776, is deaf to the voices of the people and their repeated entreaties: they have become arrogant, contemptuous, highhanded, and literal despots. . . .

Today, 188 years later, we have actually witnessed the invasion of the State[s] of Arkansas, Mississippi, and Alabama by the armed forces of the United States and maintained in the state against the will of the people and without consent of state legislatures.

It is a form of tyranny worse than that of King George III who had sent mercenaries against the colonies because today the Federal Judicial tyrants have sanctioned the use of brother against brother and father against son by federalizing the National Guard. . . .

Today, we have absolute proof that the Federal Department of Justice has planned, supervised, financed and protected acts of insurrection in the southern states, resulting in vandalism, property damage, personal injury, and staggering expense to the states. . . .

Today, the Federal judiciary asserts the power not only to dissolve state legislatures but to create them and to dissolve all state laws and state judicial decrees, and to punish a state governor by trial without jury. . . .

The United States Supreme Court is guilty of each and every one of these acts of tyranny. . . .

It is perfectly obvious from the left-wing liberal press and from the left-wing law journals that what the court is saying behind all the jargon is that they don't like our form of government.

They think they can establish a better one. In order to do so it is necessary that they overthrow our existing form, destroy the democratic institutions created by the people, change the outlook, religion, and philosophy, and bring the whole area of human thought, aspiration, action and organization, under the absolute control of the court. Their decisions reveal this to be the goal of the liberal element on the court which is in a majority at present.

It has reached the point where one may no longer look to judicial decisions to determine what the court may do. However, it is possible to predict with accuracy the nature of the opinions to be rendered. One may find the answer in the Communist Manifesto.

The Communists are dedicated to the overthrow of our form of government. They are dedicated to the destruction of the concept of private property. They are dedicated to the object of destroying religion as the basis of moral and ethical values.

The Communists are determined that all natural resources shall be controlled by the central government, that all productive capacity of the nation shall be under the control of the central government, that the political sovereignty of the people shall be destroyed as an incident to control of local schools. It is their objective to capture the minds of our youth in order to indoctrinate them in what to think and not how to think.

I do not call the members of the United States Supreme Court Communists. But I do say, and I submit for your judgment the fact that every single decision of the court in the past ten years which related in any way to each of these objectives has been decided against freedom and in favor of tyranny. . . .

The record reveals, for the past number of years, that the chief, if not the only beneficiaries of the present court's rulings, have been duly and lawfully convicted criminals, Communists, atheists, and clients of vociferous left-wing minority groups. . . .

Let us look at the record further with respect to the court's contribution to the destruction of the concept of God and the abolition of religion.

The Federal court rules that your children shall not be permitted to read the bible in our public school systems.

Let me tell you this, though. We still read the bible in Alabama schools and as long as I am governor we will continue to read the bible no matter what the Supreme Court says. . . .

So, let me say to you today. Take heart. Millions of Americans believe just as we in this great region of the United States believe.

I shall never forget last spring as I stood in the midst of a great throng of South Milwaukee supporters at one of the greatest political rallies I have ever witnessed.

A fine-looking man grabbed my hand and said:

"Governor, I've never been south of South Milwaukee, but I am a South-erner!" Of course, he was saying he believed in the principles and philoso-phy of the southern people . . . of you here today and the people of my state of Alabama.

He was right.

Being a southerner is no longer geographic. It's a philosophy and an attitude.

One destined to be a national philosophy — embraced by millions of Amer-icans — which shall assume the mantle of leadership and steady a governmental structure in these days of crises.

Certainly I am a candidate for President of the United States.

If the left-wingers do not think I am serious — let them consider this.

I am going to take our fight to the people — the court of public opinion — where truth and common sense will eventually prevail.

QUESTIONS FOR READING AND DISCUSSION

1. Why did George Wallace believe the civil rights legislation of 1964 was "a fraud, a sham, and a hoax"? Why did he think it was "an act of tyranny"?

2. How did civil rights laws "destroy individual freedom and liberty in this country," according to Wallace? Why did Wallace believe the federal judiciary was "lousy"?

3. According to Wallace, what was the relation between civil rights and commu-nism? How might civil rights supporters respond to Wallace's arguments?

4. What was the significance of the Wisconsin man telling Wallace, "I've never been south of South Milwaukee, but I am a Southerner!"? Why do you think Wallace's ideas appealed to this man and many others like him?

5. Why do you think Wallace did not specifically emphasize racial segregation in his speech? Did he ignore segregation?

DOCUMENT 28–3

Equal Rights for Women

Justice and equality for women had far-reaching implications for social change. In 1966, the newly formed National Organization for Women (NOW) adopted a statement of pur-pose — excerpted here — that identified the changes demanded by women's rights activists. The statement, drafted by feminist leader Betty Friedan, revealed the concerns of many American women in the 1960s.

National Organization for Women
Statement of Purpose, October 29, 1966

We, men and women who hereby constitute ourselves as the National Orga-nization for Women, believe that the time has come for a new movement toward true equality for all women in America, and toward a fully equal partnership of

---

National Organization for Women Statement of Purpose (1966). Reprinted by permission.

the sexes, as part of the world-wide revolution of human rights now taking place within and beyond our national borders.

The purpose of NOW is to take action to bring women into full participation in the mainstream of American society now, exercising all the privileges and responsibilities thereof in truly equal partnership with men.

We believe the time has come to move beyond the abstract argument, discussion and symposia over the status and special nature of women which has raged in America in recent years; the time has come to confront, with concrete action, the conditions that now prevent women from enjoying the equality of opportunity and freedom of choice which is their right as individual Americans, and as human beings.

NOW is dedicated to the proposition that women first and foremost are human beings, who, like all other people in our society, must have the chance to develop their fullest human potential. We believe that women can achieve such equality only by accepting to the full the challenges and responsibilities they share with all other people in our society, as part of the decision-making mainstream of American political, economic and social life.

We organize to initiate or support action, nationally or in any part of this nation, by individuals or organizations, to break through the silken curtain of prejudice and discrimination against women in government, industry, the professions, the churches, the political parties, the judiciary, the labor unions, in education, science, medicine, law, religion and every other field of importance in American society.

Enormous changes taking place in our society make it both possible and urgently necessary to advance the unfinished revolution of women toward true equality, now. With life span lengthened to nearly seventy-five years it is no longer either necessary or possible for women to devote the greater part of their lives to child-rearing; yet childbearing and rearing—which continues to be a most important part of most women's lives—still is used to justify barring women from equal professional and economic participation and advance.

Today's technology has reduced most of the productive chores which women once performed in the home and in mass-production industries based upon routine unskilled labor. This same technology has virtually eliminated the quality of muscular strength as a criterion for filling most jobs, while intensifying America's need for creative intelligence. In view of this new industrial revolution created by automation in the mid-twentieth century, women can and must participate in old and new fields of society in full equality—or become permanent outsiders. . . .

There is no civil rights movement to speak for women, as there has been for Negroes and other victims of discrimination. The National Organization for Women must therefore begin to speak.

WE BELIEVE that the power of American law, and the protection guaranteed by the U.S. Constitution to the civil rights of all individuals, must be effectively applied and enforced to isolate and remove patterns of sex discrimination, to ensure equality of opportunity in employment and education, and equality of civil and political rights and responsibilities on behalf of women, as well as for Negroes and other deprived groups.

We realize that women's problems are linked to many broader questions of social justice; their solution will require concerted action by many groups. Therefore, convinced that human rights for all are indivisible, we expect to give active support to the common cause of equal rights for all those who suffer discrimination and deprivation, and we call upon other organizations committed to such goals to support our efforts toward equality for women.

WE DO NOT ACCEPT the token appointment of a few women to high-level positions in government and industry as a substitute for a serious continuing effort to recruit and advance women according to their individual abilities. To this end, we urge American government and industry to mobilize the same resources of ingenuity and command with which they have solved problems of far greater difficulty than those now impeding the progress of women.

WE BELIEVE that this nation has a capacity at least as great as other nations, to innovate new social institutions which will enable women to enjoy true equality of opportunity and responsibility in society, without conflict with their responsibilities as mothers and homemakers. In such innovations, America does not lead the Western world, but lags by decades behind many European countries. We do not accept the traditional assumption that a woman has to choose between marriage and motherhood, on the one hand, and serious participation in industry or the professions on the other. We question the present expectation that all normal women will retire from job or profession for ten or fifteen years, to devote their full time to raising children, only to reenter the job market at a relatively minor level. This in itself is a deterrent to the aspirations of women, to their acceptance into management or professional training courses, and to the very possibility of equality of opportunity or real choice, for all but a few women. Above all, we reject the assumption that these problems are the unique responsibility of each individual woman, rather than a basic social dilemma which society must solve. True equality of opportunity and freedom of choice for women requires such practical and possible innovations as a nationwide network of child-care centers, which will make it unnecessary for women to retire completely from society until their children are grown, and national programs to provide retraining for women who have chosen to care for their own children full time.

WE BELIEVE that it is as essential for every girl to be educated to her full potential of human ability as it is for every boy — with the knowledge that such education is the key to effective participation in today's economy and that, for a girl as for a boy, education can only be serious where there is expectation that it will be used in society. We believe that American educators are capable of devising means of imparting such expectations to girl students. Moreover, we consider the decline in the proportion of women receiving higher and professional education to be evidence of discrimination. This discrimination may take the form of quotas against the admission of women to colleges and professional schools; lack of encouragement by parents, counselors and educators; denial of loans or fellowships; or the traditional or arbitrary procedures in graduate and professional training geared in terms of men, which inadvertently discriminate against women. We believe that the same serious attention must be given to high school dropouts who are girls as to boys.

WE REJECT the current assumptions that a man must carry the sole burden of supporting himself, his wife, and family, and that a woman is automatically entitled to lifelong support by a man upon her marriage, or that marriage, home and family are primarily woman's world and responsibility — hers, to dominate, his to support. We believe that a true partnership between the sexes demands a different concept of marriage, an equitable sharing of the responsibilities of home and children and of the economic burdens of their support. We believe that proper recognition should be given to the economic and social value of homemaking and child care. To these ends, we will seek to open a reexamination of laws and mores governing marriage and divorce, for we believe that the current state of "half-equality" between the sexes discriminates against both men and women, and is the cause of much unnecessary hostility between the sexes.

WE BELIEVE that women must now exercise their political rights and responsibilities as American citizens. They must refuse to be segregated on the basis of sex into separate-and-not-equal ladies' auxiliaries in the political parties, and they must demand representation according to their numbers in the regularly constituted party committees—at local, state, and national levels—and in the informal power structure, participating fully in the selection of candidates and political decision-making, and running for office themselves.

IN THE INTERESTS OF THE HUMAN DIGNITY OF WOMEN, we will protest and endeavor to change the false image of women now prevalent in the mass media, and in the texts, ceremonies, laws, and practices of our major social institutions. Such images perpetuate contempt for women by society and by women for themselves. We are similarly opposed to all policies and practices—in church, state, college, factory, or office—which, in the guise of protectiveness, not only deny opportunities but also foster in women self-denigration, dependence, and evasion of responsibility, undermine their confidence in their own abilities and foster contempt for women.

NOW WILL HOLD ITSELF INDEPENDENT OF ANY POLITICAL PARTY in order to mobilize the political power of all women and men intent on our goals. We will strive to ensure that no party, candidate, President, senator, governor, congressman, or any public official who betrays or ignores the principle of full equality between the sexes is elected or appointed to office. If it is necessary to mobilize the votes of men and women who believe in our cause, in order to win for women the final right to be fully free and equal human beings, we so commit ourselves.

WE BELIEVE THAT women will do most to create a new image of women by acting now, and by speaking out in behalf of their own equality, freedom, and human dignity—not in pleas for special privilege, nor in enmity toward men, who are also victims of the current half-equality between the sexes—but in an active, self-respecting partnership with men. By so doing, women will develop confidence in their own ability to determine actively, in partnership with men, the conditions of their life, their choices, their future and their society.

QUESTIONS FOR READING AND DISCUSSION

1. Why did NOW reject the assumption that the solution to the inequality of women was "the unique responsibility of each individual woman, rather than a basic social dilemma"?

2. What social changes permitted advancing the "unfinished revolution"?

3. What goals did NOW seek, and what tactics did they intend to use? Who did they consider allies and enemies? What were the major barriers to achieving their goals?

4. How might men benefit if NOW's goals were realized?

DOCUMENT 28–4
Black Power

To some activists, the doctrines of nonviolence seemed self-defeating and dangerous. The violence that civil rights demonstrators repeatedly suffered convinced many younger activists that the strength of white racism made racial integration hopeless. In 1967, the Chicago office of the Student Non-Violent Coordinating Committee (SNCC) published a manifesto calling for black power. The SNCC leaflet, excerpted here, embodied ideas that appealed to many African Americans and other activists in the later 1960s.

Chicago Student Non-Violent Coordinating Committee Leaflet, 1967

BLACK MEN OF AMERICA ARE A CAPTIVE PEOPLE

The black man in America is in a perpetual state of slavery no matter what the white man's propaganda tells us.

The black man in America is exploited and oppressed the same as his black brothers are all over the face of the earth by the same white man. . . .

We are not alone in this fight, we are a part of the struggle for self-determination of all black men everywhere. We here in America must unite ourselves to be ready to help our brothers elsewhere.

We must first gain BLACK POWER here in America. Living inside the camp of the leaders of the enemy forces, it is our duty to our Brothers to revolt against the system and create our own system so that we can live as MEN.

We must take over the political and economic systems where we are in the majority in the heart of every major city in this country as well as in the rural areas. We must create our own black culture to erase the lies the white man has fed our minds from the day we were born.

THE BLACK MAN IN THE GHETTO WILL LEAD THE BLACK POWER MOVEMENT

The black Brother in the ghetto will lead the Black Power Movement and make the changes that are necessary for its success.

The black man in the ghetto has one big advantage that the bourgeois Negro does not have despite his "superior" education. He is already living outside the value system white society imposes on all black Americans.

He has to look at things from another direction in order to survive. He is ready. He received his training in the streets, in the jails, from the ADC[1] check his mother did not receive in time and the head-beatings he got from the cop on the corner.

Once he makes that first important discovery about the great pride you feel inside as a BLACK MAN and the great heritage of the mother country, Africa,

---

From Chicago Office of SNCC, *We Want Black Power* (1967); reprinted in *Black Protest Thought in the Twentieth Century*, 2d ed., eds. August Meier, Elliott Rudwick, and Frances L. Broderick (Indianapolis: Bobbs-Merrill, 1971), 484–90.

[1]**ADC**: Aid to Dependent Children.

there is no stopping him from dedicating himself to fight the white man's system.

This is why the Black Power Movement is a true revolutionary movement with the power to change men's minds and unmask the tricks the white man has used to keep black men enslaved in modern society.

THE BOURGEOIS NEGRO CANNOT BE A PART OF THE BLACK POWER MOVEMENT

The bourgeois Negro has been force-fed the white man's propaganda and has lived too long in the half-world between white and phony black bourgeois society. He cannot think for himself because he is a shell of a man full of contradictions he cannot resolve. He is not to be trusted under any circumstances until he has proved himself to be "cured." There are a minute handful of these "cured" bourgeois Negroes in the Black Power Movement and they are most valuable but they must not be allowed to take control. They are aware intellectually but under stress will react emotionally to the pressures of white society in the same way a white "liberal" will expose an unconscious prejudice that he did not even realize he possessed.

WHAT BROTHER MALCOLM X TAUGHT US ABOUT OURSELVES

Malcolm X was the first black man from the ghetto in America to make a real attempt to get the white man's fist off the black man. He recognized the true dignity of man—without the white society prejudices about status, education and background that we all must purge from our minds.

Even today, in the Black Power Movement itself we find Brothers who look down on another Brother because of the conditions that life has imposed upon him. The most beautiful thing that Malcolm X taught us is that once a black man discovers for himself a pride of his blackness, he can throw off the shackles of mental slavery and become a MAN in the truest sense of the word. We must move on from the point our Great Black Prince had reached.

WE MUST BECOME LEADERS FOR OURSELVES

We must not get hung-up in the bag of having one great leader who we depend upon to make decisions. This makes the Movement too vulnerable to those forces the white man uses to keep us enslaved, such as the draft, murder, prison or character assassination.

We have to all learn to become leaders for ourselves and remove all white values from our minds. When we see a Brother using a white value through error it is our duty to the Movement to point it out to him. We must thank our Brothers who show us our own errors. We must discipline ourselves so that if necessary we can leave family and friends at a moment's notice, maybe forever, and know our Brothers have pledged themselves to protect the family we have left behind.

As a part of our education, we must travel to other cities and make contracts with the Brothers in all the ghettos in America so that when the time is right we can unite as one under the banner of BLACK POWER.

LEARNING TO THINK BLACK AND REMOVE WHITE THINGS FROM OUR MINDS

We have got to begin to say and understand with complete assuredness what black is. Black is an inner pride that the white man's language hampers us from expressing. Black is being a complete fanatic, who white society considers insane. We have to learn that black is so much better than belonging to the white race with the blood of millions dripping from their hands that it goes far beyond any prejudice or resentment. We must fill ourselves with hate for all white things. This is not vengeance or trying to take the white oppressors' place to become new black oppressors but is a oneness with a worldwide black brotherhood.

We must regain respect for the lost religion of our fathers, the spirits of the black earth of Africa. The white man has so poisoned our minds that if a Brother told you he practiced Voodoo you would roll around on the floor laughing at how stupid and superstitious he was.

We have to learn to roll around on the floor laughing at the black man who says he worships the white Jesus. He is truly sick.

We must create our own language for these things that the white man will not understand because a Black Culture exists and it is not the wood-carvings or native dancing it is the black strength inside of true men.

IDEAS ON PLANNING FOR THE FUTURE OF BLACK POWER

We must infiltrate all government agencies. This will not be hard because black clerks work in all agencies in poor paying jobs and have a natural resentment of the white men who run these jobs.

People must be assigned to seek out these dissatisfied black men and women and put pressure on them to give us the information we need. Any man in overalls, carrying a tool box, can enter a building if he looks like he knows what he is doing.

Modern America depends on many complex systems such as electricity, water, gas, sewerage and transportation and all are vulnerable. Much of the government is run by computers that must operate in air conditioning. Cut off the air conditioning and they cannot function.

We must begin to investigate and learn all of these things so that we can use them if it becomes necessary. We cannot train an army in the local park but we can be ready for the final confrontation with the white man's system.

Remember your Brothers in South Africa and do not delude yourselves that it could not happen here. We must copy the white man's biggest trick, diversion, (Hitler taught them that) and infiltrate all civil rights groups, keep them in confusion so they will be neutralized and cannot be used as a tool of the white power structure.

The civil rights, integrationist movement says to the white man, "If you please, Sir, let us, the 10 percent minority of Americans have our rights. See how nice and nonviolent we are?"

This is why SNCC calls itself a Human Rights Organization. We believe that we belong to the 90 percent majority of the people on earth that the white man oppresses and that we should not beg the white man for anything. We want what belongs to us as human beings and we intend to get it through BLACK POWER.

HOW TO DEAL WITH BLACK TRAITORS

Uncle Tom is too kind of a word. What we have are black traitors, quislings, collaborators, sell-outs, white Negroes.

We have to expose these people for once and for all for what they are and place them on the side of the oppressor where they belong. Their black skin is a lie and their guilt the shame of all black men. We must ostracize them and if necessary exterminate them.

We must stop fighting a "fair game." We must do whatever is necessary to win BLACK POWER. We have to hate and disrupt and destroy and blackmail and lie and steal and become blood-brothers like the Mau-Mau.[2]

We must eliminate or render ineffective all traitors. We must make them fear to stand up like puppets for the white men, and we must make the world understand that these so-called men do not represent us or even belong to the same black race because they sold out their birthright for a mess of white society pottage. Let them choke on it.

PITFALLS TO AVOID ON THE PATH TO BLACK POWER

We must learn how close America and Russia are politically. The biggest lie in the world is the cold-war. Money runs the world and it is controlled completely by the white man.

Russia and America run the two biggest money systems in the world and they intend to keep it under their control under any circumstances. Thus, we cannot [ac]cept any help from Communism or any other "ism."

We must seek out poor peoples movements in South America, Africa and Asia and make our alliances with them. We must not be fooled into thinking that there is a ready-made doctrine that will solve all our problems.

There are only white man's doctrines and they will never work for us. We have to work out our own systems and doctrines and culture.

WHY PROPAGANDA IS OUR MOST IMPORTANT TOOL

The one thing that the white man's system cannot stand is the TRUTH because his system is all based on lies.

There is no such thing as "justice" for a black man in America. The white man controls everything that is said in every book, newspaper, magazine, TV and radio broadcast.

Even the textbooks used in the schools and the bible that is read in the churches are designed to maintain the system for the white man. Each and every one of us is forced to listen to the white man's propaganda every day of our lives.

The political system, economic system, military system, educational system, religious system and anything else you name is used to preserve the status quo of white America getting fatter and fatter while the black man gets more and more hungry.

We must spend our time telling our Brothers the truth.

We must tell them that any black woman who wears a diamond on her finger is wearing the blood of her Brothers and Sisters in slavery in South Africa where

---

[2]**Mau-Mau**: A revolutionary tribal society in Kenya in the 1950s that engaged in terrorism in an effort to rid the country of Europeans.

one out of every three black babies die before the age of one, from starvation, to make the white man rich.

We must stop wearing the symbols of slavery on our fingers.

We must stop going to other countries to exterminate our Brothers and Sisters for the white man's greed.

We must ask our Brothers which side they are on.

Once you know the truth for yourself it is your duty to dedicate your life to recruiting your Brothers and to counteract the white man's propaganda.

We must disrupt the white man's system to create our own. We must publish newspapers and get radio stations. Black Unity is strength—let's use it now to get BLACK POWER.

QUESTIONS FOR READING AND DISCUSSION

1. According to this Chicago SNCC leaflet, why was "the Black Power Movement" a "true revolutionary movement"? What tactics would bring about the revolution?
2. Who was the Great Black Prince, and what did he teach? How did his teachings differ from nonviolence? Why? Who were black power's most important allies? Why?
3. What "white things" should be hated? Why was it necessary to be "a complete fanatic"? How did "white things" differ from "Black Culture"?
4. This SNCC document repeatedly declares the importance of black men. Where did women fit into the goals and tactics of the black power movement? Was the emphasis on men significant? If so, why?

DOCUMENT 28–5

Students Protest the Vietnam War

The growing need for soldiers made the Vietnam War an intensely personal issue for Americans. The draft forced every young man to confront what he should do: volunteer for military service; seek a deferment to avoid being drafted; or take one's chances in the draft and hope for the best. College campuses became hubs of anti-war protests fed by U.S. military escalation in Vietnam and the possibility of being drafted to fight in an undeclared, bloody war against enemies who posed no visible threat to the United States.

In May 1970, in response to President Nixon's expansion of the war into Cambodia, hundreds of demonstrators at Kent State University in northeast Ohio gathered to express their opposition to this latest escalation of the war. The governor of Ohio referred to the protestors as "the worst type of people we harbor in America," and called out the National Guard, armed with M-1 rifles and bayonets, to disperse the unarmed demonstrators. On May 4, when National Guard soldiers, most of them about the age of the students, threw tear gas canisters and charged, the demonstrators threw the tear gas back along with some rocks. Suddenly, twenty-nine of the soldiers, claiming later that their lives were in danger, fired more than sixty shots in less than fifteen seconds. The gunfire killed four students and wounded nine others.

The following photo was taken immediately after the shooting by John Filo, a photographer for the student newspaper. Mary Ann Vecchio screams in horror over the body of protester Jeffrey Miller, who was killed instantly by a shot through the mouth. Miller was 265 feet from the soldiers when he was killed, much farther than he could have thrown anything that posed a threat to the soldiers. Allison Krause, another protester who was killed, was almost three hundred and fifty feet from the soldiers. The other two students killed—William Schroeder and Sandra Lee Scheuer—were even farther from the soldiers. They were not protesters. They were simply walking across campus on their way to their next class. Several of the wounded students were shot in the back.

The Kent State shootings sparked massive anti-war demonstrations at hundreds of college campuses throughout the nation. According to a Gallup poll taken soon after the shootings, 58 percent of Americans blamed students for the Kent State massacre, 11 percent blamed the National Guard soldiers, and the rest had no opinion. The photo below depicts the war at home—the searing domestic conflict created by the Vietnam War.

National Guard Soldiers Shoot Kent State University Students, 1970

John Filo/Getty Images

QUESTIONS FOR READING AND DISCUSSION

1. The students in the photo were near Jeffrey Miller when he was killed. Mary Ann Vecchio is shown kneeling near the body. How does her reaction compare to that of the other students shown in the photo? Why is she the only person in the photo gesturing in outrage toward the soldiers?

2. Why might soldiers shoot at student protestors like those in the photo? Were the soldiers' claims that their own lives were in danger credible, based on the evidence in this photo? Do the demonstrators appear in the photo to be "the worst type of people we harbor in America"?

3. How does the word "SLAVE" on Mary Ann Vecchio's shirt suggest connections between the women's rights movement, the civil rights movement, and the anti-war movement?

4. What arguments might be used by the large majority of Americans who blamed the students for the massacre? In contrast, what arguments might be used by the small minority who blamed the soldiers? Given the evidence in this photo, does one set of arguments seem stronger than the other?

5. In what ways does the photo illustrate the war at home in 1970?

COMPARATIVE QUESTIONS

1. Why did the aspirations for a just American society expressed by Martin Luther King Jr., the Chicago SNCC, and NOW outrage George C. Wallace and fuel the shootings by the National Guard soldiers at Kent State?

2. Judging from the documents in this chapter, how would King have responded to the arguments for Black Power? How did the ideas expressed by advocates of Black Power differ from King's?

3. In what ways did NOW's call for the reeducation of women compare with SNCC's advocacy of black culture and King's belief in nonviolence? How might the challenges faced by NOW have been different from the adversity faced by SNCC and Martin Luther King Jr.? What accounts for the differences?

4. Each of the documents in this chapter makes assumptions about the state of American society and what it means to be an American. To what extent do the documents agree and disagree about these matters? Did the documents also advocate changes in what it meant to be an American? If so, what changes did they seek? Why?

29 Confronting Limits
1961–1979

T he war in Vietnam began almost unnoticed by most Americans, but by the mid-1960s it had become the dominating fact of American political life. American views of the war conflicted profoundly. Presidents justified American involvement in Vietnam in public speeches while policymakers tried to devise a military strategy that would also win domestic political support for the war. Officers struggled with maintaining military discipline in an unpopular war while soldiers encountered the horrifying realities of combat. At home Richard M. Nixon's Watergate scandal revealed a presidential administration that violated the law and the Constitution, rather than upheld them. Meanwhile stubborn inflation combined with alarming oil shortages caused many to wonder if Americans' way of life could not be sustained without making fundamental changes. The following documents illustrate some of the limits of American power and confidence in the 1960s and 1970s.

DOCUMENT 29–1

A Secret Government Assessment of the Vietnam War

Policymakers in Washington, D.C., directed the military operations of the Vietnam War more closely than any previous war in American history. Advanced technology made it possible for politicians and generals to communicate readily and to gather and analyze vast quantities of information. The political sensitivity of the war made that communication necessary. In October 1966, Secretary of Defense Robert S. McNamara drafted a secret memorandum for President Lyndon B. Johnson about the current status of the war in Vietnam. McNamara's memorandum, excerpted here, expressed the misgivings of one of the most influential political managers of the war—misgivings that remained confined to secret documents until the Pentagon Papers *were published in 1971.*

Robert S. McNamara
Actions Recommended for Vietnam, October 14, 1966

1. EVALUATION OF THE SITUATION.

In the report of my last trip to Vietnam almost a year ago, I stated that the odds were about even that, even with the then-recommended deployments, we would be faced in early 1967 with a military stand-off at a much higher level of conflict and with "pacification" still stalled. I am a little less pessimistic now in one respect. We have done somewhat better militarily than I anticipated. We have by and large blunted the communist military initiative—any military victory in South Vietnam the Viet Cong [VC] may have had in mind 18 months ago has been thwarted by our emergency deployments and actions. And our program of bombing the North has exacted a price.

My concern continues, however, in other respects. This is because I see no reasonable way to bring the war to an end soon. Enemy morale has not broken—he apparently has adjusted to our stopping his drive for military victory and has adopted a strategy of keeping us busy and waiting us out (a strategy of attriting our national will). He knows that we have not been, and he believes we probably will not be, able to translate our military successes into the "end products"—broken enemy morale and political achievements by the GVN [government of Vietnam].

The one thing demonstrably going for us in Vietnam over the past year has been the large number of enemy killed-in-action resulting from the big military operations. Allowing for possible exaggeration in reports, the enemy must be taking losses—deaths in and after battle—at the rate of more than 60,000 a year. The infiltration routes would seem to be one-way trails to death for the North Vietnamese. Yet there is no sign of an impending break in enemy morale and it appears that he can more than replace his losses by infiltration from North Vietnam and recruitment in South Vietnam.

Pacification is a bad disappointment. We have good grounds to be pleased by the recent elections, by Ky's[1] 16 months in power, and by the faint signs of development of national political institutions and of a legitimate civil government. But none of this has translated itself into political achievements at Province level or below. Pacification has if anything gone backward. As compared with two, or four, years ago, enemy full-time regional forces and part-time guerrilla forces are larger; attacks, terrorism and sabotage have increased in scope and intensity; more railroads are closed and highways cut; the rice crop expected to come to market is smaller; we control little, if any, more of the population; the VC political infrastructure thrives in most of the country, continuing to give the enemy his enormous intelligence advantage; full security exists nowhere (not even behind the U.S. Marines' lines and in Saigon); in the countryside, the enemy almost completely controls the night.

From Robert S. McNamara, "Actions Recommended for Vietnam," October 14, 1966; reprinted in *The Pentagon Papers,* ed. George C. Herring (New York: McGraw-Hill, 1971), 554–72.

[1]**Ky**: Nguyen Cao Ky was premier of the Republic of South Vietnam from 1965 to 1967.

Nor has the ROLLING THUNDER program of bombing the North either significantly affected infiltration or cracked the morale of Hanoi. There is agreement in the intelligence community on these facts. . . .

In essence, we find ourselves . . . no better, and if anything worse off. This important war must be fought and won by the Vietnamese themselves. We have known this from the beginning. But the discouraging truth is that, as was the case in 1961 and 1963 and 1965, we have not found the formula, the catalyst, for training and inspiring them into effective action.

2. RECOMMENDED ACTIONS.

In such an unpromising state of affairs, what should we do? We must continue to press the enemy militarily; we must make demonstrable progress in pacification; at the same time, we must add a new ingredient forced on us by the facts. Specifically, we must improve our position by getting ourselves into a military posture that we credibly would maintain indefinitely—a posture that makes trying to "wait us out" less attractive. I recommend a five-pronged course of action to achieve those ends.

A. STABILIZE U.S. FORCE-LEVELS IN VIETNAM.

It is my judgment that, barring a dramatic change in the war, we should limit the increase in U.S. forces . . . in 1967 to 70,000 men and we should level off at the total of 470,000. . . . It is my view that this is enough to punish the enemy at the large-unit operations level and to keep the enemy's main forces from interrupting pacification. I believe also that even many more than 470,000 would not kill the enemy off in such numbers as to break their morale so long as they think they can wait us out. It is possible that such a 40 percent increase over our present level of 325,000 will break the enemy's morale in the short term; but if it does not, we must, I believe, be prepared for and have under way a long-term program premised on more than breaking the morale of main force units. A stabilized U.S. force level would be part of such a long-term program. It would put us in a position where negotiations would be more likely to be productive, but if they were not we could pursue the all-important pacification task with proper attention and resources and without the spectre of apparently endless escalation of U.S. deployments.

B. INSTALL A BARRIER.

A portion of the 470,000 troops—perhaps 10,000 to 20,000—should be devoted to the construction and maintenance of an infiltration barrier. Such a barrier would lie near the 17th parallel—would run from the sea, across the neck of South Vietnam (choking off the new infiltration routes through the DMZ [demilitarized zone]) and across the trails in Laos. . . .

C. STABILIZE THE ROLLING THUNDER
PROGRAM AGAINST THE NORTH.

Attack sorties in North Vietnam have risen from about 4,000 per month at the end of last year to 6,000 per month in the first quarter of this year and 12,000 per month at present. Most of our 50 percent increase of deployed attack-capable aircraft has been absorbed in the attacks on North Vietnam. In North Vietnam, almost 84,000 attack sorties have been flown (about 25 percent against fixed targets), 45 percent during the past seven months.

Despite these efforts, it now appears that the North Vietnamese-Laotian road network will remain adequate to meet the requirements of the Communist forces in South Vietnam — this is so even if its capacity could be reduced by one-third and if combat activities were to be doubled. North Vietnam's serious need for trucks, spare parts and petroleum probably can, despite air attacks, be met by imports. The petroleum requirement for trucks involved in the infiltration movement, for example, has not been enough to present significant supply problems, and the effects of the attacks on the petroleum distribution system, while they have not yet been fully assessed, are not expected to cripple the flow of essential supplies. Furthermore, it is clear that, to bomb the North sufficiently to make a radical impact upon Hanoi's political, economic and social structure, would require an effort which we could make but which would not be stomached either by our own people or by world opinion; and it would involve a serious risk of drawing us into open war with China. . . .

At the proper time . . . I believe we should consider terminating bombing in all of North Vietnam, or at least in the Northeast zones, for an indefinite period in connection with covert moves toward peace.

D. PURSUE A VIGOROUS PACIFICATION PROGRAM.

As mentioned above, the pacification (Revolutionary Development) program has been and is thoroughly stalled. The large-unit operations war, which we know best how to fight and where we have had our successes, is largely irrelevant to pacification as long as we do not lose it. By and large, the people in rural areas believe that the GVN when it comes will not stay but that the VC will; that cooperations with the GVN will be punished by the VC; that the GVN is really indifferent to the people's welfare; that the low-level GVN are tools of the local rich; and that the GVN is ridden with corruption.

Success in pacification depends on the interrelated functions of providing physical security, destroying the VC apparatus, motivating the people to cooperate and establishing responsive local government. An obviously necessary but not sufficient requirement for success of the Revolutionary Development cadre and police is vigorously conducted and adequately prolonged clearing operations by military troops, who will "stay" in the area, who behave themselves decently and who show some respect for the people.

This elemental requirement of pacification has been missing.

In almost no contested area designated for pacification in recent years have ARVN [Army of the Republic of Vietnam] forces actually "cleared and stayed" to a point where cadre teams, if available, could have stayed overnight in hamlets and survived, let alone accomplish their mission. VC units of company and even battalion size remain in operation, and they are more than large enough to overrun anything the local security forces can put up.

Now that the threat of a Communist main-force military victory has been thwarted by our emergency efforts, we must allocate far more attention and a portion of the regular military forces (at least half of the ARVN and perhaps a portion of the U.S. forces) to the task of providing an active and permanent security screen behind which the Revolutionary Development teams and police can operate and behind which the political struggle with the VC infrastructure can take place.

The U.S. cannot do this pacification security job for the Vietnamese. All we can do is "Massage the heart." For one reason, it is known that we do not intend to stay; if our efforts worked at all, it would merely postpone the eventual confrontation of the VC and GVN infrastructures. The GVN must do the job; and I am convinced that drastic reform is needed if the GVN is going to be able to do it.

The first essential reform is in the attitude of GVN officials. They are generally apathetic, and there is corruption high and low. Often appointments, promotions, and draft deferments must be bought; and kickbacks on salaries are common. Cadre at the bottom can be no better than the system above them.

The second needed reform is in the attitude and conduct of the ARVN. The image of the government cannot improve unless and until the ARVN improves markedly. They do not understand the importance (or respectability) of pacification nor the importance to pacification of proper, disciplined conduct. Promotions, assignments and awards are often not made on merit, but rather on the basis of having a diploma, friends or relatives, or because of bribery. The ARVN is weak in dedication, direction and discipline. . . .

E. PRESS FOR NEGOTIATIONS.

I am not optimistic that Hanoi or the VC will respond to peace overtures now. . . . The ends sought by the two sides appear to be irreconcilable and the relative power balance is not in their view unfavorable to them. But three things can be done, I believe, to increase the prospects:

(1) Take steps to increase the credibility of our peace gestures in the minds of the enemy. There is considerable evidence both in private statements by the Communists and in the reports of competent Western officials who have talked with them that charges of U.S. bad faith are not solely propagandistic, but reflect deeply held beliefs. Analyses of Communists' statements and actions indicate that they firmly believe that American leadership really does not want the fighting to stop, and, that we are intent on winning a military victory in Vietnam and on maintaining our presence there through a puppet regime supported by U.S. military bases.

As a way of projective U.S. bona fides, I believe that we should consider two possibilities with respect to our bombing program against the North, to be undertaken, if at all, at a time very carefully selected with a view to maximizing the chances of influencing the enemy and world opinion and to minimizing the chances that failure would strengthen the hand of the "hawks" at home: First, without fanfare, conditions, or avowal, whether the stand-down was permanent or temporary, stop bombing all of North Vietnam. It is generally thought that Hanoi will not agree to negotiations until they can claim that the bombing has stopped unconditionally. We should see what develops, retaining freedom to resume the bombing if nothing useful was forthcoming. . . . [A footnote:] Any limitation on the bombing of North Vietnam will cause serious psychological problems among the men who are risking their lives to help achieve our political objectives; among their commanders up to and including the JCS [Joint Chiefs of Staff]; and among those of our people who cannot understand why we should withhold punishment from the enemy. General Westmoreland, as do the JCS, strongly believes in the military value of the bombing program. Further, Westmoreland reports that the morale of his Air Force personnel may already be showing signs of erosion—an erosion resulting from current operational restrictions.

To the same end of improving our credibility, we should seek ways—through words and deeds—to make believable our intention to withdraw our forces once the North Vietnamese aggression against the South stops. In particular, we should avoid any implication that we will stay in South Vietnam with bases or to guarantee any particular outcome to a solely South Vietnamese struggle. . . .

3. THE PROGNOSIS.

The prognosis is bad that the war can be brought to a satisfactory conclusion within the next two years. The large-unit operations probably will not do it; negotiations probably will not do it. *While we should continue to pursue both of these routes in trying for a solution in the short run, we should recognize that success from them is a mere possibility, not a probability.*

The solution lies in girding, openly, for a longer war and in taking actions immediately which will in 12 to 18 months give clear evidence that the continuing costs and risks to the American people are acceptably limited, that the formula for success has been found, and that the end of the war is merely a matter of time.

QUESTIONS FOR READING AND DISCUSSION

1. Why did McNamara "see no reasonable way to bring the war to an end soon"? What was the difference, if any, between ending the war and winning the war?
2. To what extent could McNamara's assessment be said to reflect the success of the North Vietnamese "strategy of attriting our national will"?
3. What goals did McNamara hope to achieve? What actions did he recommend? To what extent were those actions within the capability of American military forces?
4. What assumptions did McNamara make about the support for the war among the South Vietnamese, American military personnel, and Americans at home?

DOCUMENT 29–2

Military Discipline in an Unpopular War

Soldiers in Vietnam knew that they were fighting in a controversial war—one that did not have overwhelming public support at home, that seemed confusing and deadly in the field, and that seemed to be poorly supported by the Vietnamese army, government, and general population. The perceptions and experiences of American soldiers had important consequences for military discipline. In 1971, Colonel Robert D. Heinl Jr., a twenty-seven-year veteran of the Marine Corps, cataloged in an army publication the state of military discipline among troops in Vietnam. Heinl's article, excerpted here, illustrates the demoralization within the armed forces while peace negotiators huddled with representatives of North Vietnam and the fighting continued.

Robert D. Heinl Jr.
The Collapse of the Armed Forces, June 7, 1971

The morale, discipline and battleworthiness of the U.S. Armed Forces are, with a few salient exceptions, lower and worse than at any time in this century and possibly in the history of the United States.

From Colonel Robert D. Heinl Jr., "The Collapse of the Armed Forces," *Armed Forces Journal*, June 7, 1971.

By every conceivable indicator, our army that now remains in Vietnam is in a state approaching collapse, with individual units avoiding or having refused combat, murdering their officers and noncommissioned officers, drug-ridden, and dispirited where not near-mutinous. . . .

Intolerably clobbered and buffeted from without and within by social turbulence, pandemic drug addiction, race war, sedition, civilian scapegoatise, draftee recalcitrance and malevolence, barracks theft and common crime, unsupported in their travail by the general government, in Congress as well as the executive branch, distrusted, disliked, and often reviled by the public, the uniformed services today are places of agony for the loyal, silent professionals who doggedly hang on and try to keep the ship afloat. . . .

While no senior officer (especially one on active duty) can openly voice any such assessment, the foregoing conclusions find virtually unanimous support in numerous non-attributable interviews with responsible senior and midlevel officers, as well as career noncommissioned officers and petty officers in all services.

Historical precedents do exist for some of the services' problems, such as desertion, mutiny, unpopularity, seditious attacks, and racial troubles. Others, such as drugs, pose difficulties that are wholly new. Nowhere, however, in the history of the Armed Forces have comparable past troubles presented themselves in such general magnitude, acuteness, or concentrated focus as today. . . .

To understand the military consequences of what is happening to the U.S. Armed Forces, Vietnam is a good place to start. It is in Vietnam that the rear-guard of a 500,000-man army, in its day (and in the observation of the writer) the best army the United States ever put into the field, is numbly extricating itself from a nightmare war the Armed Forces feel they had foisted on them by bright civilians who are now back on campus writing books about the folly of it all.

"They have set up separate companies," writes an American soldier from Cu Chi, . . . "for men who refuse to go out into the field. It is no big thing to refuse to go. If a man is ordered to go to such and such a place he no longer goes through the hassle of refusing; he just packs his shirt and goes to visit some buddies at another base camp. Operations have become incredibly ragtag. Many guys don't even put on their uniforms any more. . . . The American garrisons on the larger bases are virtually disarmed. The lifers have taken our weapons from us and put them under lock and key. . . . There have also been quite a few frag incidents in the battalion."

Can all this really be typical or even truthful? Unfortunately the answer is yes.

"Frag incidents" or just "fragging" is current soldier slang in Vietnam for the murder or attempted murder of strict, unpopular, or just aggressive officers and NCOs [noncommissioned officers]. With extreme reluctance (after a young West Pointer from Senator Mike Mansfield's Montana was fragged in his sleep) the Pentagon has now disclosed that fraggings in 1970 (209) have more than doubled those of the previous year (96).

Word of the deaths of officers will bring cheers at troop movies or in bivouacs of certain units. In one such division . . . fraggings during 1971 have been authoritatively estimated to be running about one a week. . . .

Bounties, raised by common subscription in amounts running anywhere from $50 to $1,000, have been widely reported put on the heads of leaders whom the privates . . . want to rub out.

Shortly after the costly assault on Hamburger Hill in mid-1969, the GI underground newspaper in Vietnam, GI Says, publicly offered a $10,000 bounty on LCol Weldon Honeycutt, the officer who ordered (and led) the attack. Despite several attempts, however, Honeycutt managed to live out his tour and return Stateside.

"Another Hamburger Hill" (i.e., toughly contested assault), conceded a veteran major, "is definitely out."

The issue of "combat refusal," an official euphemism for disobedience of orders to fight—the soldier's gravest crime—has only recently been again precipitated on the frontier of Laos. . . .

"Search and evade" (meaning tacit avoidance of combat by units in the field) is now virtually a principle of war, vividly expressed by the GI phrase, "CYA (cover your ass) and get home!"

That "search-and-evade" has not gone unnoticed by the enemy is underscored by the Viet Cong delegation's recent statement at the Paris Peace Talks that communist units in Indochina have been ordered not to engage American units which do not molest them. The same statement boasted—not without foundation in fact—that American defectors are in the VC ranks.

Symbolic antiwar fasts (such as the one at Pleiku where an entire medical unit, led by its officers, refused Thanksgiving turkey), peace symbols, "V"-signs not for victory but for peace, booing and cursing of officers and even of hapless entertainers such as Bob Hope, are unhappily commonplace.

As for drugs and race, Vietnam's problems today not only reflect but reinforce those of the Armed Forces as a whole. In April, for example, members of a Congressional investigating subcommittee reported that 10 to 15% of our troops in Vietnam are now using high-grade heroin, and that drug addiction there is "of epidemic proportions."

Only last year an Air Force major and command pilot for Ambassador Bunker was apprehended at Tan Son Nhut air base outside Saigon with $8-million worth of heroin in his aircraft. This major is now in Leavenworth. . . .

It is a truism that national armies closely reflect societies from which they have been raised. It would be strange indeed if the Armed Forces did not today mirror the agonizing divisions and social traumas of American society, and of course they do.

For this very reason, our Armed Forces outside Vietnam not only reflect these conditions but disclose the depths of their troubles in an awful litany of sedition, disaffection, desertion, race, drugs, breakdowns of authority, abandonment of discipline, and, as a cumulative result, the lowest state of military morale in the history of the country.

Sedition—coupled with disaffection within the ranks, and externally fomented with an audacity and intensity previously inconceivable—infests the Armed Services:

At best count, there appear to be some 144 underground newspapers published on or aimed at U.S. military bases in this country and overseas. Since 1970 the number of such sheets has increased 40% (up from 103 last fall). These journals are not mere gripe-sheets that poke soldier fun . . . at the brass and the sergeants. "In Vietnam," writes the Ft. Lewis-McChord Free Press, "the Lifers, the Brass, are the true Enemy, not the enemy." Another West Coast sheet advises readers: "Don't desert. Go to Vietnam and kill your commanding officer."

At least 14 GI dissent organizations (including two made up exclusively of officers) now operate more or less openly. Ancillary to these are at least six antiwar veterans' groups which strive to influence GIs. . . .

By present count at least 11 (some go as high as 26) off-base antiwar "coffee houses" ply GIs with rock music, lukewarm coffee, antiwar literature, how-to-do-it tips on desertion, and similar disruptive counsels. . . .

Internally speaking, racial conflicts and drugs—also previously insignificant—are tearing the services apart today. . . .

Racial conflicts (most but not all sparked by young black enlisted men) are erupting murderously in all services.

At a recent high commanders' conference, General Westmoreland and other senior generals heard the report from Germany that in many units white soldiers are now afraid to enter barracks alone at night for fear of "head-hunting" ambushes by blacks. . . . All services are today striving energetically to cool and control this ugly violence which in the words of one noncommissioned officer, has made his once taut unit divide up "like two street gangs." . . .

The drug problem — like the civilian situation from which it directly derives — is running away with the services. In March, Navy Secretary John H. Chafee, speaking for the two sea services, said bluntly that drug abuse in both the Navy and Marines is out of control.

In 1966, the Navy discharged 170 drug offenders. Three years later (1969), 3,800 were discharged. Last year in 1970, the total jumped to over 5,000.

Drug abuse in the Pacific Fleet — with Asia on one side, and kinky California on the other — gives the Navy its worst headaches. To cite one example, a destroyer due to sail from the West Coast last year for the Far East nearly had to postpone deployment when, five days before departure, a ring of some 30 drug users (over 10 percent of the crew) was uncovered. . . .

What those statistics say is that the Armed Forces (like their parent society) are in the grip of a drug pandemic—a conclusion underscored by the one fact that, just since 1968, the total number of verified drug addiction cases throughout the Armed Forces has nearly doubled. One other yardstick: according to military medical sources, needle hepatitis now poses as great a problem among young soldiers as VD. . . .

With conditions what they are in the Armed Forces, and with intense efforts on the part of elements in our society to disrupt discipline and destroy morale the consequences can be clearly measured in two ultimate indicators: manpower retention (reenlistments and their antithesis, desertions); and the state of discipline.

In both respects the picture is anything but encouraging. . . . Desertion rates are going straight up. . . .

In 1970, the Army had 65,643 deserters, or roughly the equivalent of four infantry divisions. This desertion rate (52.3 soldiers per thousand) is well over twice the peak rate for Korea (22.5 per thousand). It is more than quadruple the 1966 desertion-rate (14.7 per thousand) of the then well-trained, high-spirited professional Army. . . .

Admiral Elmo R. Zumwalt, Jr., Chief of Naval Operations, minces no words. "We have a personnel crisis," he recently said, "that borders on disaster." . . .

The trouble of the services — produced by and also in turn producing the dismaying conditions described in this article — is above all a crisis of soul and backbone. It entails — the word is not too strong — something very near a collapse of the command authority and leadership George Washington saw as the soul of military forces. This collapse results, at least in part, from a concurrent collapse of public confidence in the military establishment.

QUESTIONS FOR READING AND DISCUSSION

1. According to Robert Heinl, why was the army in Vietnam "in a state approaching collapse"? What caused fragging, bounties, combat refusal, and search and evade?
2. What did Heinl believe were the sources of sedition, racial strife, and drug abuse? How did such problems influence the military effort in Vietnam?
3. What did Heinl mean by saying, "The trouble of the services . . . is above all a crisis of soul and backbone"?

DOCUMENT 29–3

The Evacuation of Saigon Exposes the Limits of U.S. Military Power

Nothing dramatized more vividly the limits of American military power than the panicked evacuation of Saigon on April 30, 1975. North Vietnamese forces overwhelmed South Vietnamese defenses much more rapidly than had been expected by military and intelligence experts. South Vietnamese soldiers stripped off their uniforms and boots and disappeared into the civilian population rather than trying to stop the North Vietnamese advance. Americans had little time to organize evacuation of American officials and their South Vietnamese allies. Unable to defend the major Saigon airport from enemy attack, Americans resorted to helicopters that landed in the compound of the U.S. embassy and loaded up with evacuees who were then ferried to warships off shore. In this famous photo by a Dutch journalist, people desperate to evacuate climb a dangerous stairway to the roof of the American embassy where a CIA agent helps them board a rescue helicopter. In the end, over twenty thousand people were evacuated, but tens of thousands of others were left behind. Despite American promises and massive military might, they could not be rescued or protected.

Evacuation of Saigon, April 30, 1975

Hugh Fan Es/UPI/Newscom

QUESTIONS FOR READING AND DISCUSSION

1. As shown in the photograph, helicopters could only hold a relatively small number of evacuees. What does the use of helicopters suggest about the situation in Saigon? Why weren't other methods of evacuation used?

2. The people shown in the photo were the lucky ones who managed to get a helicopter ride to safety. Unseen in the photo are thousands of other people clamoring to get on the roof. What might have been going on outside the frame of the photo? What might explain how the people shown managed to get a helping hand from the CIA agent?

3. What does the absence of soldiers and military weapons from the photo suggest about the failure of American policy and the success of the North Vietnamese?

4. In what specific ways does the photo illustrate the limits of America's Vietnam policy and U.S. military power in general in the spring of 1975?

DOCUMENT 29–4

The Watergate Tapes: Nixon, Dean, and Haldeman Discuss the Cancer within the Presidency

President Richard M. Nixon used the powers of the presidency to violate the law and spy on political opponents. When the burglars who broke into the office of the Democratic National Committee in the Watergate building on June 17, 1972, were caught and arrested, they quickly began to demand financial help from their employers in the Republican Party. They also threatened to tell what they knew about their other dirty tricks. On March 21, 1973, John Dean, the president's counsel, met with Nixon in the Oval Office to inform him of the demands of the Watergate burglars and the dangers they posed to his presidency. Secret tape recordings of that meeting and others were made public in April 1974 by President Nixon. He announced in an address to the nation that "I know in my own heart that, through the long painful and difficult process revealed in these transcripts, I was trying in that period to discover what was right and to do what was right." The transcript of the March 21 meeting, excerpted here, demonstrates instead deep involvement in criminal activities by Nixon and leading members of his administration. The transcripts of the Watergate tapes provided all Americans with a detailed, word-by-word portrait of the inner workings of the Nixon White House.

Transcript from Tape-Recorded Meeting, March 21, 1973

D[ean]: The reason that I thought we ought to talk this morning is because in our conversations, I have the impression that you don't know everything I know and it makes it very difficult for you to make judgments that only you can make on some of these things and I thought that —

P[resident]: In other words, I have to know why you feel that we shouldn't unravel something?

D: Let me give you my overall first.

P: In other words, your judgment as to where it stands, and where we will go,

From *Submission of Recorded Presidential Conversations to the Committee on the Judiciary of the House of Representatives* by President Richard M. Nixon, April 1974.

D: I think that there is no doubt about the seriousness of the problem we've got. We have a cancer within, close to the Presidency, that is growing. It is growing daily. It's compounded, growing geometrically now, because it compounds itself. That will be clear if I, you know, explain some of the details of why it is. Basically, it is because (1) we are being blackmailed; (2) people are going to start perjuring themselves very quickly that have not had to perjure themselves to protect other people in the line. And there is no assurance —

P: That that won't bust?

D: That that won't bust. So let me give you the sort of basic facts, talking first about the Watergate; and then about Segretti;[1] and then about some of the peripheral items that have come up. First of all on the Watergate: how did it all start, where did it start? OK! It started with an instruction to me from Bob Haldeman[2] to see if we couldn't set up a perfectly legitimate campaign intelligence operation over at the Re-Election Committee. . . . That is when I came up with Gordon Liddy.[3] They needed a lawyer. Gordon had an intelligence background from his FBI service. I was aware of the fact that he had done some extremely sensitive things for the White House while he had been at the White House and he had apparently done them well. Going out into Ellsberg's[4] doctor's office —

P: Oh, yeah.

D: And things like this. He worked with leaks. He tracked these things down. So the report that I got . . . was that he was a hell of a good man and not only that a good lawyer and could set up a proper operation. . . . Magruder[5] called me in January and said I would like to have you come over and see Liddy's plan.

P: January of '72?

D: January of '72.

D: . . . So I came over and Liddy laid out a million dollar plan that was the most incredible thing I have ever laid my eyes on: all in codes, and involved black bag operations, kidnapping, providing prostitutes to weaken the opposition, bugging, mugging teams. It was just an incredible thing. . . .

So there was a second meeting. . . . I came into the tail end of the meeting. . . . [T]hey were discussing again bugging, kidnapping and the like. At this point I said right in front of everybody, very clearly, I said, "These are not the sort of things (1) that are ever to be discussed in the office of the Attorney General of the United States—that was where he still was—and I am personally incensed." And I am trying to get Mitchell[6] off the hook. . . . So I let it be known, I said, "You all pack that stuff up and get it the hell out of here. You just can't talk this way in this office and you should re-examine your whole thinking."

---

[1]**Segretti**: Donald Segretti, a staff member of the Committee to Re-elect the President.

[2]**Bob Haldeman**: H. Robert Haldeman, Nixon's chief of staff.

[3]**Gordon Liddy**: A former FBI agent who led a secret unit set up by the Nixon administration and nicknamed the "plumbers" because their mission was to stop the kind of "leaks" that had led to the publication of the *Pentagon Papers*.

[4]**Ellsberg**: Daniel Ellsberg, a former aide who had leaked the *Pentagon Papers* to the *New York Times* in 1971. In an attempt to discredit Ellsberg, the Nixon administration hired men to break into Ellsberg's psychiatrist's office, steal confidential records, and leak them to the press.

[5]**Magruder**: Jeb Magruder, who worked for the Committee to Re-elect the President.

[6]**Mitchell**: John Mitchell, Nixon's former attorney general, who ran the Committee to Re-elect the President, the organization that authorized the Watergate break-in.

P: Who all was present?

D: It was Magruder, Mitchell, Liddy and myself. I came back right after the meeting and told Bob, "Bob, we have a growing disaster on our hands if they are thinking this way," and I said, "The White House has got to stay out of this and I, frankly, am not going to be involved in it." He said, "I agree, John." I thought at that point that the thing was turned off. That is the last I heard of it and I thought it was turned off because it was an absurd proposal. . . . I think Bob was assuming that they had something that was proper over there, some intelligence gathering operation that Liddy was operating. . . . They were going to infiltrate, and bug, and do this sort of thing to a lot of these targets. This is knowledge I have after the fact. Apparently after they had initially broken in and bugged the DNC [Democratic National Committee] they were getting information. . . .

P: They had never bugged Muskie,[7] though, did they?

D: No, they hadn't, but they had infiltrated it by a secretary.

P: By a secretary?

D: By a secretary and a chauffeur. There is nothing illegal about that. So the information was coming over here. . . . The next point in time that I became aware of anything was on June 17th when I got the word that there had been this break-in at the DNC and somebody from our Committee had been caught in the DNC. And I said, "Oh, (expletive deleted)." You know, eventually putting the pieces together —

P: You knew what it was.

D: I knew who it was. . . .

P: Why at that point in time I wonder? I am just trying to think. We had just finished the Moscow trip. The Democrats had just nominated [George] McGovern — I mean, (expletive deleted), what in the hell were these people doing? I can see their doing it earlier. I can see the pressures, but I don't see why all the pressure was on then.

D: I don't know, other than the fact that they might have been looking for information about the conventions.

P: That's right. . . .

P: What did they say in the Grand Jury?

D: They said, as they said before the trial in the Grand Jury, that . . . we knew [Liddy] had these capacities to do legitimate intelligence. We had no idea what he was doing. . . . We had no knowledge that he was going to bug the DNC.

P: The point is, that is not true?

D: That's right.

P: Magruder did know it was going to take place?

D: Magruder gave the instructions to be back in the DNC.

P: He did?

D: Yes.

P: You know that?

D: Yes.

P: I see. OK.

---

[7]**Muskie**: Edmund Muskie, a Democratic senator from Maine who had hoped to run against Nixon in the 1972 election. Watergate hearings in 1973 revealed that his bid for the Democratic nomination had been sabotaged by the Committee to Re-elect the President.

D: I honestly believe that no one over here knew that. I know that as God is my maker, I had no knowledge that they were going to do this.

P: Bob didn't either, or wouldn't have known that either. You are not the issue involved. Had Bob known, he would be.

D: Bob—I don't believe specifically knew that they were going in there.

P: I don't think so.

D: I don't think he did. I think he knew that there was a capacity to do this but he was not given the specific direction. . . .

D: So, those people are in trouble as a result of the Grand Jury and the trial. . . . Now what has happened post June 17? I was under pretty clear instructions not to investigate this, but this could have been disastrous on the electorate if all hell had broken loose. I worked on a theory of containment —

P: Sure.

D: To try to hold it right where it was.

P: Right.

D: There is no doubt that I was totally aware of what the Bureau was doing at all times. I was totally aware of what the Grand Jury was doing. I knew what witnesses were going to be called. I knew what they were asked, and I had to. . . . Now post June 17th: These guys . . . started making demands. "We have to have attorneys fees. We don't have any money ourselves, and you are asking us to take this through the election." Alright, so arrangements were made through Mitchell, initiating it. And I was present in discussions where these guys had to be taken care of. Their attorneys fees had to be done. Kalmbach[8] was brought in. Kalmbach raised some cash.

P: They put that under the cover of a Cuban Committee,[9] I suppose?

D: Well, they had a Cuban Committee and . . . some of it was given to Hunt's[10] lawyer, who in turn passed it out. . . .

P: (unintelligible)—but I would certainly keep that cover for whatever it is worth. . . .

D: . . . Here is what is happening right now. . . . One, this is going to be a continual blackmail operation by Hunt and Liddy and the Cubans. No doubt about it. And McCord,[11] . . . Hunt has now made a direct threat against Ehrlichman,[12] . . . He says, "I will bring John Ehrlichman down to his knees and put him in jail. I have done enough seamy things for he and Krogh,[13] they'll never survive it."

P: Was he talking about Ellsberg?

D: Ellsberg, and apparently some other things. I don't know the full extent of it.

P: I don't know about anything else.

D: I don't know either, and I hate to learn some of these things. So that is that situation. Now, where are we at the soft points? How many people know about

---

[8]**Kalmbach**: Herbert Kalmbach, a fund-raiser for the Committee to Re-elect the President.

[9]**Cuban Committee**: A group opposed to Cuban president Fidel Castro.

[10]**Hunt**: E. Howard Hunt, a former CIA agent who, along with Liddy, led the "plumbers."

[11]**"Cubans. . . . McCord"**: Refers to the four Cuban Americans who, together with former CIA agent James McCord, were arrested in the Watergate break-in.

[12]**Ehrlichman**: John Ehrlichman, a top Nixon aide.

[13]**Krogh**: Egil Krogh, Nixon aide.

this? Well, let me go one step further in this whole thing. The Cubans that were used in the Watergate were also the same Cubans that Hunt and Liddy used for this California Ellsberg thing, for the break-in out there. So they are aware of that. How high their knowledge is, is something else. Hunt and Liddy, of course, are totally aware of it, of the fact that it is right out of the White House.

P: I don't know what the hell we did that for!

D: I don't know either. . . . So that is it. That is the extent of the knowledge. So where are the soft spots on this? Well, first of all, there is the problem of the continued blackmail which will not only go on now, but it will go on while these people are in prison, and it will compound the obstruction of justice situation. It will cost money. It is dangerous. People around here are not pros at this sort of thing. This is the sort of thing Mafia people can do: washing money, getting clean money, and things like that. We just don't know about those things, because we are not criminals and not used to dealing in that business.

P: That's right.

D: It is a tough thing to know how to do.

P: Maybe it takes a gang to do that.

D: That's right. There is a real problem as to whether we could even do it. Plus there is a real problem in raising money. Mitchell has been working on raising some money. He is one of the ones with the most to lose. But there is no denying the fact that the White House, in Ehrlichman, Haldeman and Dean are involved in some of the early money decisions.

P: How much money do you need?

D: I would say these people are going to cost a million dollars over the next two years.

P: We could get that. On the money, if you need the money you could get that. You could get a million dollars. You could get it in cash. I know where it could be gotten. It is not easy, but it could be done. But the question is who the hell would handle it? Any ideas on that? . . .

D: Now we've got Kalmbach. Kalmbach received, at the close of the '68 campaign in January of 1969, he got a million $700,000 to be custodian for. That came, down from New York, and was placed in safe deposit boxes here. Some other people were on the boxes. And ultimately, the money was taken out to California. Alright, there is knowledge of the fact that he did start with a million seven. Several people know this. Now since 1969, he has spent a good deal of this money and accounting for it is going to be very difficult for Herb [Kalmbach]. For example, he has spent close to $500,000 on private polling. That opens up a whole new thing. It is not illegal, but more of the same thing.

P: Everybody does polling.

D: That's right. There is nothing criminal about it. It's private polling. . . . I don't know of anything that Herb has done that is illegal. . . . What really bothers me is this growing situation. As I say, it is growing because of the continued need to provide support for the Watergate people who are going to hold us up for everything we've got, and the need for some people to perjure themselves as they go down the road here. If this thing ever blows, then we are in a cover up situation. I think it would be extremely damaging to you and the —

P: Sure. The whole concept of Administration justice. Which we cannot have! . . .

D: That's right. I am coming down to what I really think, is that Bob and John and John Mitchell and I can sit down and spend a day, or however long, to figure out one, how this can be carved away from you, so that it does not damage you or the Presidency. It just can't! You are not involved in it and it is something you shouldn't —

P: That is true! . . .

D: What really troubles me is one, will this thing not break some day and the whole thing — domino situation — everything starts crumbling, fingers will be pointing. Bob will be accused of things he has never heard of and deny and try to disprove it. It will get real nasty and just be a real bad situation. And the person who will be hurt by it most will be you and the Presidency, and I just don't think —

P: First, because I am an executive I am supposed to check these things.

D: That's right.

P: Let's come back to this problem. What are your feelings yourself, John? You know what they are all saying. What are your feelings about the chances?

D: I am not confident that we can ride through this. I think there are soft spots. . . .

P: . . . But just looking at it from a cold legal standpoint: you are a lawyer, you were a counsel — doing what you did as counsel. You were not — What would you go to jail for?

D: The obstruction of justice.

P: The obstruction of justice?

D: That is the only one that bothers me.

P: Well, I don't know. I think that one. I feel it could be cut off at the pass, maybe, the obstruction of justice. . . . Talking about your obstruction of justice, though, I don't see it.

D: Well, I have been a conduit for information on taking care of people out there who are guilty of crimes.

P: Oh, you mean like the blackmailers?

D: The blackmailers. Right.

P: Well, I wonder if that part of it can't be — I wonder if that doesn't — let me put it frankly: I wonder if that doesn't have to be continued? Let me put it this way: let us suppose that you get the million bucks, and you get the proper way to handle it. You could hold that side?

D: Uh, huh.

P: It would seem to me that would be worthwhile. . . .

D: There are two routes. One is to figure out how to cut the losses and minimize the human impact and get you up and out and away from it in any way. In a way it would never come back to haunt you. That is one general alternative. The other is to go down the road, just hunker down, fight it at every corner, every turn, don't let people testify — cover it up is what we really are talking about. Just keep it buried, and just hope that we can do it, hope that we make good decisions at the right time, keep our heads cool, we make the right moves.

P: And just take the heat?

D: And just take the heat. . . .

[H. R. Haldeman joins the meeting.]

P: . . . You see, John is concerned, as you know, about the Ehrlichman situation. It worries him a great deal because, and this is why the Hunt problem is so serious, because it had nothing to do with the campaign. It has to do with the Ellsberg case. I don't know what the hell the — (unintelligible)

H[aldeman]: But what I was going to say —

P: What is the answer on this? How you keep it out, I don't know. You can't keep it out if Hunt talks. You see the point is irrelevant. It has gotten to this point —

D: You might put it on a national security basis.

H: It absolutely was.

D: And say that this was —

H: (unintelligible) — CIA —

D: Ah —

H: Seriously.

P: National Security. We had to get information [from Ellsberg's psychiatrist's office] for national security grounds.

D: Then the question is, why didn't the CIA do it or why didn't the FBI do it?

P: Because we had to do it on a confidential basis.

H: Because we were checking them.

P: Neither could be trusted.

H: It has basically never been proven. There was reason to question their position.

P: With the bombing thing coming out and everything coming out, the whole thing was national security.

D: I think we could get by on that.

P: On that one I think we should simply say this was a national security investigation that was conducted. And on that basis, I think . . . Krogh could say he feels he did not perjure himself. He could say it was a national security matter. That is why —. . . You really only have two ways to go. You either decide that the whole (expletive deleted) thing is so full of problems with potential criminal liabilities, which most concern me. I don't give a damn about the publicity. We could rock that through that if we had to let the whole damn thing hang out, and it would be a lousy story for a month. But I can take it. The point is, that I don't want any criminal liabilities. That is the thing that I am concerned about for members of the White House staff, and I would trust for members of the Committee. . . .

H: Well, the thing we talked about yesterday. You have a question where you cut off on this. There is a possibility of cutting it at Liddy, where you are now.

P: Yeah.

D: But to accomplish that requires a continued perjury by Magruder and requires —

P: And requires total commitment and control over all of the defendants which — in other words when they are let down —. . . Another way to do it then Bob, and John realizes this, is to continue to try to cut our losses. Now we have to take a look at that course of action. First it is going to require approximately a million dollars to take care of the jackasses who are in jail. That can be arranged. That could be arranged. But you realize that after we are gone, and assuming we can expend this money, then they are going to crack and it would be an unseemly story. Frankly, all the people aren't going to care that much.

D: That's right.

P: People won't care, but people are going to be talking about it, there is no question. . . . And my point is that I think it is good, frankly, to consider these various options. And then, once you decide on the right plan, you say, "John," you say, "No doubts about the right plan before the election. You handled it just right. You contained it. And now after the election we have to have another plan. Because we can't for four years have this thing eating away." We can't do it.

H: We should change that a little bit. John's point is exactly right. The erosion here now is going to you, and that is the thing that we have to turn off at whatever cost. We have to turn it off at the lowest cost we can, but at whatever cost it takes.

D: That's what we have to do.

P: Well, the erosion is inevitably going to come here, apart from anything and all the people saying well the Watergate isn't a major issue. It isn't. But it will be. It's bound to. (Unintelligible) has to go out. Delaying is the great danger to the White House area. We don't, I say that the White House can't do it. Right?

D: Yes, Sir.

Questions for Reading and Discussion

1. What "cancer within" did Dean worry about? Why did Nixon and Dean believe they were being blackmailed, and how did they plan to respond? What were the "soft spots" that worried Dean?

2. Did Dean and Attorney General Mitchell entertain plans to break the law? Did Nixon?

3. How did President Nixon obtain information about political opponents? How did Nixon hope to use arguments about "national security"?

4. Did Nixon declare his opposition to a cover-up? Did he demand that all members of his administration strictly adhere to the law? Why or why not?

5. Nixon knew the conversations in his office were being taped, but none of the other officials were aware that their remarks were being recorded. To what extent might this knowledge have influenced what Nixon said?

DOCUMENT 29-5

President Carter Declares Energy Conservation the Moral Equivalent of War, 1977

The rampant inflation of the 1970s, caused in part by the huge costs of the Vietnam War, caused many Americans to worry whether they could make ends meet as prices ballooned and wages lagged. With interest rates topping the unheard of level of twenty percent, Americans wondered how the spiral of inflation could be contained without compromising consumers' desires to buy still more. Shrinking energy resources also boosted inflation. Few people could continue to drive big, heavy gas guzzlers without thinking about the escalating price of gas at the pump. Only a few months after his inauguration, President Jimmy Carter called for a full-scale government attack on the energy crisis. He asked Americans to change their wasteful habits of consumption and to support new government policies to encourage conservation. His speech was an effort to confront a crisis that he believed other presidents and most Americans had refused to recognize, at the nation's peril.

Address to the Nation on Proposed National Energy Policy, April 18, 1977

Tonight I want to have an unpleasant talk with you about a problem unprecedented in our history. With the exception of preventing war, this is the greatest challenge our country will face during our lifetimes.

Jimmy Carter, Address to the Nation on Proposed National Energy Policy, April 18, 1977. The American Presidency Project, University of California, Santa Barbara. https://www.presidency.ucsb.edu/documents/address-the-nation-energy

The energy crisis has not yet overwhelmed us, but it will if we do not act quickly. It's a problem we will not solve in the next few years, and it's likely to get progressively worse through the rest of this century.

We must not be selfish or timid if we hope to have a decent world for our children and grandchildren.

We simply must balance our demand for energy with our rapidly shrinking resources. By acting now, we can control our future instead of letting the future control us.

Two days from now, I will present my energy proposals to the Congress. . . . Many of these proposals will be unpopular. Some will cause you to put up with inconveniences and to make sacrifices.

The most important thing about these proposals is that the alternative may be a national catastrophe. Further delay can affect our strength and our power as a nation.

Our decision about energy will test the character of the American people and the ability of the President and the Congress to govern. This difficult effort will be the "moral equivalent of war"—except that we will be uniting our efforts to build and not destroy. . . .

The oil and natural gas we rely on for 75 percent of our energy are running out. In spite of increased effort, domestic production has been dropping steadily at about six percent a year. Imports have doubled in the last five years. Our nation's independence of economic and political action is becoming increasingly constrained. Unless profound changes are made to lower oil consumption, we now believe that early in the 1980s the world will be demanding more oil than it can produce.

The world now uses about 60 million barrels of oil a day and demand increases each year about 5 percent. This means that just to stay even we need the production of a new Texas every year, an Alaskan North Slope every nine months, or a new Saudi Arabia every three years. Obviously, this cannot continue.

We must look back in history to understand our energy problem. Twice in the last several hundred years there has been a transition in the way people use energy.

The first was about 200 years ago, away from wood—which had provided about 90 percent of all fuel—to coal, which was more efficient. This change became the basis of the Industrial Revolution.

The second change took place in this century, with the growing use of oil and natural gas. They were more convenient and cheaper than coal, and the supply seemed to be almost without limit. They made possible the age of automobile and airplane travel. Nearly everyone who is alive today grew up during this age and we have never known anything different.

Because we are now running out of gas and oil, we must prepare quickly for a third change, to strict conservation and to the use of coal and permanent renewable energy sources, like solar power.

The world has not prepared for the future. During the 1950s, people used twice as much oil as during the 1940s. During the 1960s, we used twice as much as during the 1950s. And in each of those decades, more oil was consumed than in all of mankind's previous history.

World consumption of oil is still going up. If it were possible to keep it rising during the 1970s and 1980s by 5 percent a year as it has in the past, we could use up all the proven reserves of oil in the entire world by the end of the next decade. . . .

But we do have a choice about how we will spend the next few years. Each American uses the energy equivalent of 60 barrels of oil per person each year. Ours is the most wasteful nation on earth. We waste more energy than we import. With about the same standard of living, we use twice as much energy per person as do other countries like Germany, Japan and Sweden.

One choice is to continue doing what we have been doing before. We can drift along for a few more years.

Our consumption of oil would keep going up every year. Our cars would continue to be too large and inefficient. Three-quarters of them would continue to carry only one person — the driver — while our public transportation system continues to decline. We can delay insulating our houses, and they will continue to lose about 50 percent of their heat in waste. . . .

We can't substantially increase our domestic production, so we would need to import twice as much oil as we do now. Supplies will be uncertain. The cost will keep going up. Six years ago, we paid $3.7 billion for imported oil. Last year we spent $37 billion — nearly ten times as much — and this year we may spend over $45 billion.

Unless we act, we will spend more than $550 billion for imported oil by 1985 — more than $2,500 a year for every man, woman, and child in America. Along with that money we will continue losing American jobs and becoming increasingly vulnerable to supply interruptions.

Now we have a choice. But if we wait, we will live in fear of embargoes. We could endanger our freedom as a sovereign nation to act in foreign affairs. Within ten years we would not be able to import enough oil — from any country, at any acceptable price.

If we wait, and do not act, then our factories will not be able to keep our people on the job with reduced supplies of fuel. Too few of our utilities will have switched to coal, our most abundant energy source.

We will not be ready to keep our transportation system running with smaller, more efficient cars and a better network of buses, trains and public transportation.

We will feel mounting pressure to plunder the environment. We will have a crash program to build more nuclear plants, strip-mine and burn more coal, and drill more offshore wells than we will need if we begin to conserve now. Inflation will soar, production will go down, people will lose their jobs. Intense competition will build up among nations and among the different regions within our own country.

If we fail to act soon, we will face an economic, social and political crisis that will threaten our free institutions.

But we still have another choice. We can begin to prepare right now. We can decide to act while there is time. . . .

Our national energy plan is based on ten fundamental principles.

The first principle is that we can have an effective and comprehensive energy policy only if the government takes responsibility for it and if the people understand the seriousness of the challenge and are willing to make sacrifices.

The second principle is that healthy economic growth must continue. Only by saving energy can we maintain our standard of living and keep our people at work. An effective conservation program will create hundreds of thousands of new jobs.

The third principle is that we must protect the environment. Our energy problems have the same cause as our environmental problems — wasteful use of resources. Conservation helps us solve both at once.

The fourth principle is that we must reduce our vulnerability to potentially devastating embargoes. We can protect ourselves from uncertain supplies by reducing our demand for oil, making the most of our abundant resources such as coal, and developing a strategic petroleum reserve.

The fifth principle is that we must be fair. Our solutions must ask equal sacrifices from every region, every class of people, every interest group. Industry will have to do its part to conserve, just as the consumers will. The energy producers deserve fair treatment, but we will not let the oil companies profiteer.

The sixth principle, and the cornerstone of our policy, is to reduce the demand through conservation. . . . Conservation is the quickest, cheapest, most practical source of energy. . . .

The seventh principle is that prices should generally reflect the true replacement costs of energy. We are only cheating ourselves if we make energy artificially cheap and use more than we can really afford.

The eighth principle is that government policies must be predictable and certain. Both consumers and producers need policies they can count on so they can plan ahead. . . . I am working with the Congress to create a new Department of Energy, to replace more than 50 different agencies that now have some control over energy.

The ninth principle is that we must conserve the fuels that are scarcest and make the most of those that are more plentiful. We can't continue to use oil and gas for 75 percent of our consumption when they make up seven percent of our domestic reserves. We need to shift to plentiful coal while taking care to protect the environment, and to apply stricter safety standards to nuclear energy.

The tenth principle is that we must start now to develop the new, unconventional sources of energy we will rely on in the next century. . . .

Our energy plan will also include a number of specific goals, to measure our progress toward a stable energy system.

These are the goals we set for 1985:

— Reduce gasoline consumption by ten percent below its current level.
— Cut in half the portion of United States oil which is imported, from a potential level of sixteen million barrels to six million barrels a day.
— Establish a strategic petroleum reserve of one billion barrels, more than six months' supply.
— Increase our coal production by about two thirds to more than one billion tons a year.
— Insulate 90 percent of American homes and all new buildings.
— Use solar energy in more than two and one-half million houses. . . .
— Reduce the annual growth rate in our energy demand to less than two percent.

I can't tell you that these measures will be easy, nor will they be popular. But I think most of you realize that a policy which does not ask for changes or sacrifices would not be an effective policy.

This plan is essential to protect our jobs, our environment, our standard of living, and our future.

Whether this plan truly makes a difference will be decided not here in Washington, but in every town and every factory, in every home and on every highway and every farm.

I believe this can be a positive challenge. There is something especially American in the kinds of changes we have to make. We have been proud, through our history of being efficient people . . .

We have been proud of our leadership in the world. Now we have a chance again to give the world a positive example.

And we have been proud of our vision of the future. We have always wanted to give our children and grandchildren a world richer in possibilities than we've had. They are the ones we must provide for now. They are the ones who will suffer most if we don't act. . . .

QUESTIONS FOR READING AND DISCUSSION

1. Why did Carter believe his talk would be unpleasant and unpopular?
2. Why did Carter claim that the nation faced "a problem unprecedented in our history"?
3. In what ways was "conservation the quickest, cheapest, and most practical source of energy"? What conservation methods does Carter specifically suggest? Why might he identify these methods in particular?
4. Why would it fall to every town, factory, home, and farm to decide whether Carter's proposals made a difference? Why couldn't the decision be made by the U.S. government or the president alone?
5. What made the energy crisis the "moral equivalent of war," according to Carter? Who were the enemies in the war? Who were the allies?

COMPARATIVE QUESTIONS

1. How did Robert S. McNamara's assessment of the war influence American policy in Vietnam and eventually the evacuation of Saigon?
2. Robert Heinl and McNamara both stressed the importance of morale, but differed sharply on what morale problems they believed existed and why. What accounts for these differences? How might Heinl have interpreted the evacuation of Saigon? How would McNamara's interpretation of the same event differ from Heinl's?
3. In what ways did McNamara's secret assessment of the Vietnam War compare to President Nixon's secret illegal activities in the Watergate scandal? How did each source illustrate the scope and limits of presidential power?
4. How did the energy crisis described by President Carter compare to America's struggle in Vietnam? How does the national energy policy Carter proposed compare to U.S. military policy in Vietnam?
5. Judging from the documents in this chapter, what fundamental American values were called into question or reaffirmed during this age of limits?

30 Divisions at Home and Abroad in a Conservative Era

1980–2000

The powerful currents of change that swept the nation during the 1960s created even stronger countercurrents that dominated the politics of subsequent decades. Most of the activist groups that had worked for social change succumbed to bitter in-fighting, fracturing their unity and sapping their political vitality. Their opponents mobilized effectively to redirect power, so they claimed, from the government to the people and to stymie what they regarded as further decay in American values. The following documents illustrate that the crosscurrents of the time raised questions about the nation's basic values and institutions: What role should religion play in American politics? Should the Supreme Court decide whether abortions were legal? What did America mean to new immigrants and the rest of the world? Did conservative demands for law and order contribute to racial injustice?

DOCUMENT 30–1

President Ronald Reagan Defends American Morality

President Ronald Reagan portrayed America as the embodiment of morality. He attributed American morality to traditional values he associated with Christianity. Reagan believed his views represented 100 percent Americanism and that those who differed were either deluded or suspect. Millions of Americans agreed with him and voted for him. Reagan drew upon his ideas of American morality in his speech—excerpted here—to the annual convention of the National Association of American Evangelicals in Orlando, Florida, in 1983. The speech illustrates Reagan's concept of history as a struggle between good and evil and his certainty that America was on the side of good.

Address to the National Association of American Evangelicals, 1983

Those of you in the National Association of Evangelicals are known for your spiritual and humanitarian work. And I would be especially remiss if I didn't discharge right now one personal debt of gratitude. Thank you for your prayers. . . .

So I tell you there are a great many God-fearing, dedicated, noble men and women in public life, present company included. And yes, we need your help to keep us ever mindful of the ideas and the principles that brought us into the public arena in the first place. The basis of those ideals and principles is a commitment to freedom and personal liberty that, itself, is grounded in the much deeper realization that freedom prospers only where the blessings of God are avidly sought and humbly accepted.

The American experiment in democracy rests on this insight. . . .

Well, I'm pleased to be here today with you who are keeping America great by keeping her good. Only through your work and prayers and those of millions of others can we hope to survive this perilous century and keep alive this experiment in liberty, this last, best hope of man.

I want you to know that this administration is motivated by a political philosophy that sees the greatness of America in you, her people, and in your families, churches, neighborhoods, communities—the institutions that foster and nourish values like concern for others and respect for the rule of law under God.

Now, I don't have to tell you that this puts us in opposition to, or at least out of step with, a prevailing attitude of many who have turned to a modern-day secularism, discarding the tried and time-tested values upon which our very civilization is based. No matter how well intentioned, their value system is radically different from that of most Americans. And while they proclaim that they're freeing us from superstitions of the past, they've taken upon themselves the job of superintending us by government rule and regulation. Sometimes their voices are louder than ours, but they are not yet a majority.

An example of that vocal superiority is evident in a controversy now going on in Washington. And since I'm involved, I've been waiting to hear from the parents of young America. How far are they willing to go in giving to government their prerogatives as parents?

Let me state the case as briefly and simply as I can. An organization of citizens, sincerely motivated and deeply concerned about the increase in illegitimate births and abortions involving girls well below the age of consent, some time ago established a nationwide network of clinics to offer help to these girls and, hopefully, alleviate this situation. Now, again, let me say, I do not fault their intent. However, in their well-intentioned effort, these clinics have decided to provide advice and birth control drugs and devices to underage girls without the knowledge of their parents. . . .

Well, we have ordered clinics receiving federal funds to notify the parents such help has been given. . . . I've watched TV panel shows discuss this issue, seen columnists pontificating on our error, but no one seems to mention morality as playing a part in the subject of sex.

From Ronald Reagan, "Remarks at the Annual Convention of the National Association of Evangelicals," The Public Papers of President Ronald Reagan, The Reagan Library, http://voicesofdemocracy.umd.edu/reagan-evil-empire-speech-text/.

Is all of Judeo-Christian tradition wrong? Are we to believe that something so sacred can be looked upon as a purely physical thing with no potential for emotional and psychological harm? . . .

Many of us in government would like to know what parents think about this intrusion in their family by government. We're going to fight in the courts. The right of parents and the rights of family take precedence over those of Washington-based bureaucrats and social engineers.

But the fight against parental notification is really only one example of many attempts to water down traditional values and even abrogate the original terms of American democracy. Freedom prospers when religion is vibrant and the rule of law under God is acknowledged. When our Founding Fathers passed the First Amendment, they sought to protect churches from government interference. They never intended to construct a wall of hostility between government and the concept of religious belief itself.

The evidence of this permeates our history and our government. The Declaration of Independence mentions the Supreme Being no less than four times. "In God We Trust" is engraved on our coinage. The Supreme Court opens its proceedings with a religious invocation. And the members of Congress open their sessions with a prayer. I just happen to believe the schoolchildren of the United States are entitled to the same privileges as Supreme Court justices and congressmen.

Last year, I sent the Congress a constitutional amendment to restore prayer to public schools. Already this session, there's growing bipartisan support for the amendment, and I am calling on the Congress to act speedily to pass it and to let our children pray. . . .

More than a decade ago, a Supreme Court decision literally wiped off the books of fifty states statutes protecting the rights of unborn children. Abortion on demand now takes the lives of up to one and a half million unborn children a year. Human life legislation ending this tragedy will someday pass the Congress, and you and I must never rest until it does. Unless and until it can be proven that the unborn child is not a living entity, then its right to life, liberty, and the pursuit of happiness must be protected. . . .

Now, I'm sure that you must get discouraged at times, but you've done better than you know, perhaps. There's a great spiritual awakening in America, a renewal of the traditional values that have been the bedrock of America's goodness and greatness.

One recent survey by a Washington-based research council concluded that Americans were far more religious than the people of other nations; 95 percent of those surveyed expressed a belief in God and a huge majority believed the Ten Commandments had real meaning in their lives. And another study has found that an overwhelming majority of Americans disapprove of adultery, teenage sex, pornography, abortion, and hard drugs. And this same study showed a deep reverence for the importance of family ties and religious belief.

I think the items that we've discussed here today must be a key part of the nation's political agenda. For the first time the Congress is openly and seriously debating and dealing with the prayer and abortion issues—and that's enormous progress right there. I repeat: America is in the midst of a spiritual awakening and a moral renewal. . . .

Now, obviously, much of this new political and social consensus I've talked about is based on a positive view of American history, one that takes pride in our country's accomplishments and record. But we must never forget that no government schemes are going to perfect man. We know that living in this world means dealing with what philosophers would call the phenomenology of evil or, as theologians would put it, the doctrine of sin.

There is sin and evil in the world, and we're enjoined by Scripture and the Lord Jesus to oppose it with all our might. Our nation, too, has a legacy of evil with which it must deal. The glory of this land has been its capacity for transcending the moral evils of our past. For example, the long struggle of minority citizens for equal rights, once a source of disunity and civil war, is now a point of pride for all Americans. We must never go back. There is no room for racism, anti-Semitism, or other forms of ethnic and racial hatred in this country.

I know that you've been horrified, as have I, by the resurgence of some hate groups preaching bigotry and prejudice. Use the mighty voice of your pulpits and the powerful standing of your churches to denounce and isolate these hate groups in our midst. The commandment given us is clear and simple: "Thou shalt love thy neighbor as thyself."

But whatever sad episodes exist in our past, any objective observer must hold a positive view of American history, a history that has been the story of hopes fulfilled and dreams made into reality. Especially in this century, America has kept alight the torch of freedom, but not just for ourselves but for millions of others around the world.

And this brings me to my final point today. During my first press conference as president, in answer to a direct question, I pointed out that, as good Marxist-Leninists, the Soviet leaders have openly and publicly declared that the only morality they recognize is that which will further their cause, which is world revolution. . . .

Well, I think the refusal of many influential people to accept this elementary fact of Soviet doctrine illustrates a historical reluctance to see totalitarian powers for what they are. We saw this phenomenon in the 1930s. We see it too often today.

This doesn't mean we should isolate ourselves and refuse to seek an understanding with them. I intend to do everything I can to persuade them of our peaceful intent, to remind them that it was the West that refused to use its nuclear monopoly in the forties and fifties for territorial gain and which now proposes a 50-percent cut in strategic ballistic missiles and the elimination of an entire class of land-based, intermediate-range nuclear missiles.

At the same time, however, they must be made to understand we will never compromise our principles and standards. We will never give away our freedom. We will never abandon our belief in God. And we will never stop searching for a genuine peace. But we can assure none of these things America stands for through the so-called nuclear freeze solutions proposed by some.

The truth is that a freeze now would be a very dangerous fraud, for that is merely the illusion of peace. The reality is that we must find peace through strength. . . .

A number of years ago, I heard a young father, a very prominent young man in the entertainment world, addressing a tremendous gathering in California. It was during the time of the cold war, and communism and our own way of life were very much on people's minds. And he was speaking to that subject. And suddenly . . . I heard him saying, "I love my little girls more than anything." . . . He went on: "I would rather see my little girls die now, still believing in God, than have them grow up under communism and one day die no longer believing in God."

There were thousands of young people in that audience. They came to their feet with shouts of joy. They had instantly recognized the profound truth in what he had said, with regard to the physical and the soul and what was truly important.

Yes, let us pray for the salvation of all of those who live in that totalitarian darkness—pray they will discover the joy of knowing God. But until they do, let us be aware that while they preach the supremacy of the state, declare its omnipotence over individual man, and predict its eventual domination of all peoples on the earth, they are the focus of evil in the modern world. . . .

But if history teaches anything, it teaches that simpleminded appeasement or wishful thinking about our adversaries is folly. It means the betrayal of our past, the squandering of our freedom.

So, I urge you to speak out against those who would place the United States in a position of military and moral inferiority. . . . I urge you to beware the temptation of pride—the temptation of blithely declaring yourselves above it all and label both sides equally at fault, to ignore the facts of history and the aggressive impulses of an evil empire, to simply call the arms race a giant misunderstanding and thereby remove yourself from the struggle between right and wrong and good and evil.

I ask you to resist the attempts of those who would have you withhold your support for our efforts, this administration's efforts, to keep America strong and free, while we negotiate real and verifiable reductions in the world's nuclear arsenals and one day, with God's help, their total elimination.

While America's military strength is important, let me add here that I've always maintained that the struggle now going on for the world will never be decided by bombs or rockets, by armies or military might. The real crisis we face today is a spiritual one; at root, it is a test of moral will and faith. . . .

I believe we shall rise to the challenge. I believe that communism is another sad, bizarre chapter in human history whose last pages even now are being written. I believe this because the source of our strength in the quest for human freedom is not material, but spiritual. And because it knows no limitation, it must terrify and ultimately triumph over those who would enslave their fellow man.

QUESTIONS FOR READING AND DISCUSSION

1. According to Reagan, why did freedom prosper "only where the blessings of God are avidly sought and humbly accepted"? What evidence did he cite that the Founders "never intended to construct a wall of hostility between government and the concept of religious belief"?

2. Reagan identified his opponents as advocates of "modern-day secularism." What did they believe, and why did their views threaten the "Judeo-Christian tradition"?

3. Why did Reagan call the Soviet Union "the focus of evil in the modern world"? What did he think the United States should do to oppose the Soviets?

4. Reagan advocated "a positive view of American history." What view was Reagan arguing against? What did he believe made the United States different from other nations? Who was Reagan arguing against?

DOCUMENT 30–2

Norma McCorvey Explains How She Became *"Roe"* of Roe v. Wade

Norma McCorvey, who became the "Roe" of Roe v. Wade, grew up in Houston, Texas. After giving birth to two children when she was in her late teens—both given up for adoption—she sought an abortion when she was 21 and pregnant with her third child. Since abortions were illegal in Texas, she was directed to a Dallas attorney who filed the legal case that resulted in Roe v. Wade in 1973. In a legal affidavit of 2000, excerpted below, McCorvey described her involvement in the case and accused her attorneys and the Supreme Court of misleading her and other American women about the realities of abortion. By the time she filed the affidavit, McCorvey had lived in Dallas for many years in a long-term lesbian relationship, converted to Christianity, become active in the antiabortion (or pro-life) movement, converted to Roman Catholicism, and renounced lesbianism. McCorvey's affidavit highlights the personal story behind the famous Supreme Court case and describes some of the issues that generated passionate debate between pro-choice and pro-life advocates, that is, between supporters and opponents of Roe v. Wade.

Affidavit, United States District Court, District of New Jersey, 2000

My name is Norma McCorvey, and I reside in Dallas, Texas. I was the woman designated as "Jane Roe" as plaintiff in *Roe v. Wade*, the United States Supreme Court decision that legalized abortion in the United States. . . .

Because of my role in *Roe v. Wade*, how that decision came about, and my experiences working at abortion clinics, I can provide the Court with information and a perspective unavailable from other sources. . . . My case was wrongfully decided and has caused great harm to the women and children of our nation. . . .

Virtually the entire basis for *Roe v. Wade* was built upon false assumptions. No meaningful trial to determine the real facts was ever held. The misrepresentations and deceptions that plagued *Roe v. Wade* . . . show why there is a dire necessity for a trial to ensure that the true facts regarding the nature of abortion and the interests of women are heard. . . . [W]e obtained a decision in Roe v. Wade based upon what abortion advocates wanted women to be able to do, not what women were truly capable of. . . .

While the experience of being Jane Roe over the past twenty-seven years has been very difficult, my life has been filled with hardship from the beginning. Although I was an emotionally abused child, and a sexually abused teenager, I believe the worst abuse was inflicted by the judicial system. In retrospect, I was exploited by two self-interested attorneys. Worse, the courts, without looking into my true circumstances and taking the time to decide the real impact abortion would have upon women, I feel used me to justify legalization of terminating the lives [of] over thirty-five million babies. Although on an intellectual level I know I was exploited, the responsibility I feel for this tragedy is overwhelming.

From Norma McCorvey Affidavit, United States District Court, District of New Jersey, March 15, 2000.

Because the courts allowed my case to proceed without my testimony, without ever explaining to me the reality of abortion, without being cross-examined on my erroneous perception of what . . . abortion really is, a tragic mistake was made by the courts. . . .

Prior to my pregnancy with the "Roe" baby, I gave birth to two other children. My first, a daughter, was adopted by my mother. It is difficult to part with my child, yet I have always been comforted by the fact that my daughter is alive and cared for. My second daughter was raised by her father, a young intern at Baylor Methodist Medical School. He was kind enough to want to get married and make a home, but I wasn't ready for that kind of commitment. Later, when I became pregnant with the "Roe" baby, I was really in a predicament. My mother expressed her disapproval of my having given birth out of wedlock. She told me how irresponsible I had been. My mother made it clear that she was not going to take care of another baby.

Certain that I was pregnant, I waited for a while before I went to the doctor. While I was waiting to be examined, I questioned the ladies there about whether they knew where a woman could go to have an abortion. A lady told me where an illegal clinic was located and told me that it would cost $250.00. Following our discussion, I told the doctor that I wanted to have an abortion, but he refused stating that abortion was illegal. He didn't believe in abortion and gave me the phone number of an adoption attorney.

When I had saved about two hundred dollars, I took a cross-town bus to the illegal clinic, which turned out to be a dentist's office that had been closed down the previous week. For some reason, I felt relieved yet angry at the same time. All my emotions were peaking; first, I was angry, then I was happy, and then I'd cry. From the abortion clinic, I took the bus to my dad's apartment and decided to speak with the adoption attorney. The adoption attorney set up the meeting and referred me to Sarah Weddington, the attorney who represented me in *Roe v. Wade*.

Although Weddington and I were about the same age, our lives were quite different. She was a young attorney, and I was homeless and lived in a park. Unconcerned about politics, I sold flowers and an underground newspaper describing the types and availability of illegal narcotics. I am not proud of my jobs. At the time I sought simply to survive.

Following the adoption attorney's introduction, Weddington invited me out to dinner. I agreed. At our initial meeting, I met with Sarah Weddington and Linda Coffee, her friend. Both Weddington and Coffee had recently finished law school and they wanted to bring a class action suit against the State of Texas to legalize abortion, not nationally. We discussed the case over a few pitchers of beer and pizza at a small restaurant in Dallas.

Weddington, Coffee, and I were drinking beer and trying to come up with a pseudonym for me. I had heard that whenever women were having illegal abortions, they wouldn't carry any identification with them. An unidentifiable woman was often referred to as Jane Doe. So we were trying to come up with something that would rhyme with "Doe." After three or four pitchers of beer, we started with the letter "a" and eventually we reached "r" and agreed on "Roe." Then I asked "What about Jane for the first name?" Janie used to be my imaginary friend as a child. I told them about her and how she always wanted to do good things for people, and it was decided — I became Jane Roe, by the stroke of a pen.

The young lawyers told me that they had spoken with two or three other women about being in the case, but they didn't fit their criteria. Although I did know what "criteria" meant, I asked them if I had what it is that it took to be in their suit. They said yes, "You're white. You're young, pregnant, and you want an abortion." At that time, I didn't know their full intent. Only that they wanted to make abortion legal and they thought I'd be a good plaintiff. I came for the food, and they led me to believe that they could help me get an abortion.

During our meeting, they questioned me, "Norma don't you think that abortion should be legal?" Unsure, I responded that I did not know. In fact, I did not know what the term "abortion" really meant. Back in 1970, no one discussed abortion. It was taboo, and so too was the subject of abortion. . . . "Abortion," to me, meant "going back" to the condition of not being pregnant. I never looked the word up in the dictionary until after I had already signed the affidavit. I was very naive. For their part, my lawyers lied to me about the nature of abortion. Weddington convinced me that "It's just a piece of tissue. You just missed your period." I didn't know during the *Roe v. Wade* case that the life of a human being was terminated. . . .

My lawyers never discussed what an abortion is, other than to make the misrepresentation that "it's only tissue." I never understood that the child was already in existence. I never understood that the child was a complete separate human being. I was under the false impression that abortion somehow reversed the process and prevented the child from coming into existence. In the two to three years during the case no one, including my lawyers told me that an abortion is actually terminating the life of an actual human being. The courts never took any testimony about this and I heard nothing which shed light on what abortion really was.

In 1972, Sarah Weddington argued in the courts, presumptuously on my behalf, that women should be allowed to obtain a legal abortion. The courts did not ask whether I knew what I was asking for. . . . Weddington and the other supporters of abortion used me and my circumstance to urge the courts to legalize abortion without any meaningful trial which addressed the humanity of the baby, and what abortion would do to women. At that time, I was a street person. I lived, worked, and panhandled out on the streets. My totally powerless circumstance made it easy for them to use me. My presence was a necessary evil. My real interests were not their concern.

As the class action plaintiff in the most controversial U.S. Supreme Court case of the twentieth century, I only met with the attorneys twice. Once over pizza and beer, when I was told that my baby was only "tissue." The other time at Coffee's office to sign the affidavit. No other personal contacts. I was never invited into court. I never testified. I was never present before any court on any level, and I was never at any hearing on my case. The entire case was an abstraction. The facts about abortion were never heard. Totally excluded from every aspect and every issue of the case, I found out about the decision from the newspaper just like the rest of the country. In a way my exclusion, and the exclusion of real meaningful findings of fact in *Roe v. Wade*, is symbolic of the way the women of the nation and their experiences with abortion have been ignored in a national debate by the abortion industry. . . .

My personal involvement in *Roe v. Wade* was not my only experience with abortion. Unskilled and uneducated, with alcohol and drug problems, finding and holding a job was always a problem for me. But with my notoriety, abortion facilities, usually paying a dollar an hour more than minimum wage, were always willing to add Jane Roe to their ranks. . . .

I worked in several abortion facilities over the years . . . and they were all the same with respect to the condition of the facilities and the "counseling" the women receive. One clinic where I worked in 1995 was typical: Light fixtures and plaster falling from the ceiling; rat droppings over the sinks; backed up sinks; and blood splattered on the walls. But the most distressing room in the facility was the "parts room." Aborted babies were stored here. There were dead babies and baby parts stacked like cordwood. . . . Veterinary clinics I have seen are cleaner and more regulated than the abortion clinics I worked in.

While all the facilities were much the same, the abortion doctors in the various clinics where I worked were very representative of abortionists in general. The abortionists I knew were usually of foreign descent with the perception that the lax abortion laws in the United States present a fertile money-making opportunity. One abortionist, in particular, would sometimes operate bare-chested, and sometimes shoeless with his shirt off, and earned a six-figure income. . . .

The lack of counseling provided the women was perhaps the greatest tragedy. Early in my abortion career, it became evident that the "counselors" and the abortionists were there for only one reason—to sell abortions. The extent of the abortionists' counseling was, "Do you want an abortion? Ok, you sign here and we give you abortion." . . . There was nothing more. There was never an explanation of the procedure. No one even explained to the mother that the child already existed and the life of a human was being terminated. No one ever explained that there were options to abortion, that financial help was available, or that the child was . . . unique and irreplaceable. No one ever explained that there were psychological and physical risks of harm to the mother. There was never time for the mother to reflect or to consult with anyone who could offer her help or an alternative. There was no informed consent. In my opinion, the only thing the abortion doctors and clinics cared about was making money. No abortion clinic cared about the women involved. As far as I could tell, every woman had the name of Jane Roe.

QUESTIONS FOR READING AND DISCUSSION

1. Why did McCorvey believe her "case was wrongfully decided"? How did she counter the arguments of the Supreme Court?

2. Why, according to McCorvey, was she "exploited by two self-interested attorneys"? Do you agree with her? Why or why not?

3. What, according to McCorvey's affidavit, was her understanding of abortion at the time she agreed with her lawyers to become a plaintiff? To what degree do you think her subsequent activity in the antiabortion movement might have influenced her account in 2000 of her decision more than thirty years earlier?

4. According to McCorvey, "the only thing the abortion doctors and clinics cared about was making money." To what extent did McCorvey's experiences working in abortion clinics influence her views? To what extent, if at all, did her experiences raise issues not considered by the Supreme Court?

5. How might a pro-choice supporter of *Roe v. Wade* respond to the arguments in McCorvey's affidavit?

DOCUMENT 30–3

A Vietnamese Immigrant on the West Coast

Following the Vietnam War, hundreds of thousands of immigrants came to the United States from Vietnam and elsewhere in Southeast Asia. The following interview, conducted in 1983, describes the experiences of one immigrant, a man from central Vietnam who preferred to remain anonymous. His statements reflect the experiences of millions of new immigrants who came to America seeking political asylum, reunion with family members, and, above all, a better life.

Anonymous Man
Oral History, 1983

On our third attempt, my wife, children, and I escaped by boat from Vietnam and arrived in Hong Kong, where we remained for three months. Then my brother, who came to America in 1975, sponsored us, and we arrived in America in 1978.

We stayed with my brother and his family for five months. Neither I nor anyone in our family spoke any English before our arrival in America. I realized that I must study to communicate. Even though my brother was in one place, I decided to move to the West Coast. For nine months we lived in one town, where my children went to school. My wife and I also attended school to learn English. Although we received public assistance, we were always short each month by $20, $30, or even $40. If the situation continued like this, we'd have no money for clothes for the family. Even then, what we bought were old clothes that cost 20 or 25 cents apiece.

We made a visit to one of my sisters who lived in a small city that was surrounded by a lot of farmland. I saw that many of the people worked as farmers. I thought, "Maybe it's better for us to move here because I am used to working hard. God made me a hard-working man."

In 1980 we moved to that farming town. As soon as we arrived, I started to grow vegetables in the small backyard of the house we rented. In the meantime, I also worked as a farm laborer. We earned $35 to $45 a day, and that made me feel at ease. During the day I worked outside; in the evening I worked in my backyard. We began to sell what we grew, and from this we earned $200 a month. We liked to have our portion of land to do something, but we did not have enough money to buy.

We received help from the Public Housing Authority. The new house we moved into has four bedrooms. Each month we pay $50. The rest . . . is paid for by the government. The owner who rents us the house likes me very much because we keep the house very clean. . . . I moved all of the fruit trees from the old to the new house, and also planted a larger garden of vegetables and herbs. We have very good relations with our neighbors. They like us very much. They hire us to work on their backyards. That's the reason our income has increased. I grew too much to sell only to our neighbors. I needed to find a market.

From James M. Freeman, *Hearts of Sorrow: Vietnamese-American Lives* (Stanford, CA: Stanford University Press, 1989), 382–90.

One day I went to the farmer's market. I didn't know how to do it. I brought my vegetables there but they chased me away. . . . The second time I went back, they chased me away again. But that time I asked, "Can you help me so I can sell vegetables like other people?"

That man told me, "Okay, you come with me; I'll show you how."

He gave me an application form, his business card, and an appointment. He explained to me during the appointment how I should do it and what kind of product I should have. He told me, "I want to come and see your garden, if it fulfills the requirements."

I agreed. He came down to inspect everything and wrote down on a piece of paper all the vegetables I grew. Then he gave me a permit. I brought my vegetables to the market, and nobody chased me any more. We earned some more money. . . .

After two years of this, we can save some [a lot]. Then we decided to have a fish truck. I borrowed some from my brother because it costs $4,000 to $5,000 to have a fish truck. During my work as a fish merchant our income was better. . . .

I am very happy in America for three reasons. First, I am very proud that I can do many things that other people could not do. Even though I do not know English very well, I did not bother anyone in dealing with paperwork or with translations. I myself did everything. I am very pleased by that. My English is not fluent, but when I speak with American people, they understand me, even though my grammar is not very good.

Second, I am at ease about living in America. Americans treat Vietnamese very well. I suppose if Americans had to live in Vietnam as refugees, the Vietnamese would not help them as much as the Americans helped me. We are very happy to live in America. I have received letters from Vietnamese refugees living in other countries. I am able to compare my life with theirs. Life in the United States is much better than in other countries of the Free World.

Third, what I like most is freedom, to move, to do business, and the freedom to work. I have freedom for myself, to work, to live, freedom to do everything you want. You can apply for a job or you can do a small business. You can apply for a license for a small business with no difficulties, no obstacles.

Although in America we live with everything free, to move, to do business, we still have the need to return to Vietnam one day. This is our dream. In Vietnam, before the Communists came, we had a sentimental life, more . . . comfortable and cozy, more joyful. To go out on the street, in the market in Vietnam, makes us more comfortable in our minds, spiritually.

Here in America, we have all the material comforts, very good. But the joy and sentiment are not like we had in Vietnam. There, when we went out from the home, we laughed, we jumped. And we had many relatives and friends to come to see us at home. Here in America, I only know what goes on in my home; my neighbor knows only what goes on in his home. We have a saying, "One knows only one's home." In America, when we go to work, we go in our cars. When we return, we leave our cars and enter our homes. . . . We do not need to know what goes on in the houses of our neighbors. That's why we do not have the kind of being at ease that we knew in Vietnam. . . .

When my sister came to America, she did as I am doing now. She and her family grew vegetables. Now they have two Vietnamese grocery stores and are the most successful Vietnamese refugees in their area. . . .

Another sister lives in the same town as I do. She and her husband are old, but their children are doing very well too. So four of my mother's children are now in America; four remain in Vietnam.

To live in America means that our life has changed. In Vietnam my family was very poor. We had to work very hard. We didn't have enough food or clothes. Under the Communist regime we were not free to do anything. If we made more than we needed, then the rest belonged to the revolutionary government. They did not want us to become rich. We needed to use old clothes. If we had new clothes, that's not good under the new regime because it showed that we had the capitalistic spirit.

My family living in America has everything complete and happy, and a new chance. I hope that my children become new people. My daughter in the eighth grade is the smartest of my children; she always gets A's. My youngest boy, who is eight years old, always is first in math in his class. My two oldest sons are not so good, but are above average and are preparing for electronics careers.

But the children are different here in America when compared with Vietnam. There is this big difference. Children growing up in Vietnam are afraid of their parents. Even when they marry, they still have respect and fear of their parents. In America, when they become 18, they lose their fear. They depend on the law of the land and go out of the house.

The one most difficult problem is the American law, and the American way to educate children. This is a big obstacle for the Vietnamese family. In Vietnam, in educating our children, if we cannot get success telling them what to do, we would punish them with a beating. By doing so, they would become good people. Here we cannot beat the children. That's the reason there's a big obstacle for us. When a child doesn't want to study, but likes to play with friends, if they want to smoke marijuana, when they do such bad things and parents tell them not to do so, the first, second, and third time, if they still don't listen, then parents *put them on the floor and beat them*. By doing so, this is the best way to prevent them from doing bad things, to get them to become good people. But here we cannot do that.

In my opinion, the Vietnamese have a lot of bad children because of American law, which is not like Vietnamese law. There are so many Vietnamese teenagers who came to America and who became not good people because of American law. When parents beat the child, the police come and arrest the parent. In the Vietnamese view, this is *the most dangerous and difficult obstacle*.

This is the *one most important thing* I want Americans to realize about the Vietnamese. The problem with educating and rearing the children is difficult because of American law. There's a second important point. Vietnamese life is not like American life. The Vietnamese have *villages, neighbors, and sentiment*. The father-child and mother-child relationship lasts forever, until the parents are very old. Children have the duty to take care of their parents. When the children were young, parents had the duty to raise and educate them. When the parents are old, duty is reversed: children take care of the parents. This is not like in America, where adult children leave the home, and old parents go to the nursing home. I'd like Americans to know that. I have met and talked with a lot of old American people. They have said to me, "When we become old, we . . . live together. When we become sick, nobody knows. When the postman comes, makes a surprise visit, only then does someone know we are sick. Sometimes our children aren't close by, or they live in a different state."

I ask the old people, "Do your children give you money?"

They reply, "No." These children do not think very much about their parents. This is very different from Vietnam; when children are married, they stay at home. When the parents become old, the children are together and take care of them.

But there are good lessons to be learned in America, such as *public sanitation*. That is what I have learned from America. At home, everything is arranged orderly and clean. Also, my American friends say what they think. This is different from what a Vietnamese would do. The American way, that's what I want my children to do. When we have one, we say "one." When we have two, we say "two." If that is a cow, we say it is a cow; if it's a goat, we say it's a goat. Vietnamese can learn this from Americans. I don't want to say what Americans can learn from the Vietnamese.

QUESTIONS FOR READING AND DISCUSSION

1. How did this Vietnamese immigrant come to the United States? What kind of work did he do after arriving?

2. Why was he "very happy in America"? How did his life in America differ from that in Vietnam and the experiences of other Vietnamese immigrants "in other countries of the Free World"?

3. Why did he believe the "most difficult" problems were "the American law, and the American way to educate children"?

4. This man hinted that "Americans can learn from the Vietnamese." What lessons do you think he might urge Americans to learn?

DOCUMENT 30–4

President Bush Announces a New World Order, *September 11, 1990*

When Iraq invaded its southern neighbor Kuwait in August 1990, President George Bush summoned support from the United Nations and a coalition of allies — including America's old Cold War foe, the Soviet Union — to enact sanctions against Iraq and ultimately to launch a full scale assault — Operation Desert Storm — to crush Iraqi forces in Kuwait. In an address to Congress, Bush announced that the U.S. would not tolerate Iraq's invasion of Kuwait for reasons of both principle and national interest. Bush proclaimed that defense of Kuwait and other Persian Gulf allies, especially Saudi Arabia, displayed American leadership in a new world order that would guide the nation's foreign policy and help achieve world peace and harmony. Bush's speech, followed by Operation Desert Storm, reflected the growing importance of the Middle East in American foreign policy in the aftermath of the Cold War. In the new world order, according to Bush, America would police the world in defense of oil reserves and national boundaries, while fighting terrorists who threatened both.

Address Before a Joint Session of the Congress, September 11, 1990

We gather tonight, witness to events in the Persian Gulf as significant as they are tragic. In the early morning hours of August 2, following negotiations and promises by Iraq's dictator Saddam Hussein not to use force, a powerful Iraqi Army invaded its trusting and much weaker neighbor, Kuwait. Within three days, 120,000 Iraqi troops with 850 tanks had poured into Kuwait and moved south to threaten Saudi Arabia. It was then that I decided to act to check that aggression.

At this moment, our brave servicemen and women stand watch in that distant desert and on distant seas, side by side with the forces of more than 20 other distant nations. They are some of the finest men and women of the United States of America. And they're doing one terrific job.

These valiant Americans were ready at a moment's notice to leave their spouses and their children, to serve on the front line halfway around the world. They remind us who keeps America strong. They do. . . . Let me just say . . . , America is proud of [and] . . . grateful to every soldier, sailor, Marine and airman serving the cause of peace in the Persian Gulf. . . .

I wish I could say their work is done. But we all know it's not.

So if ever there was a time to put country before self and patriotism before party, the time is now. . . . I want to talk to you about what's at stake — what we must do together to defend civilized values around the world and maintain our economic strength at home.

Our objectives in the Persian Gulf are clear, our goals defined and familiar:

Iraq must withdraw from Kuwait completely, immediately and without condition.

Kuwait's legitimate government must be restored.

The security and stability of the Persian Gulf must be assured.

And American citizens abroad must be protected.

These goals are not ours alone. They've been endorsed by the U.N. Security Council five times in as many weeks. Most countries share our concern for principle, and many have a stake in the stability of the Persian Gulf. This is not, as Saddam Hussein would have it, the United States against Iraq. It is Iraq against the world. . . .

Clearly, no longer can a dictator count on East-West confrontation to stymie concerted United Nations action against aggression.

A new partnership of nations has begun, and we stand today at a unique and extraordinary moment. The crisis in the Persian Gulf, as grave as it is, also offers a rare opportunity to move toward an historic period of cooperation. Out of these troubled times, our fifth objective — a new world order — can emerge: A new era — freer from the threat of terror, stronger in the pursuit of justice and

---

George Bush, Address Before a Joint Session of the Congress, September 11, 1990, The American Presidency Project, University of California, Santa Barbara, https://www.presidency.ucsb.edu/documents/address-before-joint-session-the-congress-the-persian-gulf-crisis-and-the-federal-budget.

more secure in the quest for peace. An era in which the nations of the world, east and west, north and south, can prosper and live in harmony.

A hundred generations have searched for this elusive path to peace, while a thousand wars raged across the span of human endeavor, and today that new world is struggling to be born. A world quite different from the one we've known. A world where the rule of law supplants the rule of the jungle. A world in which nations recognize the shared responsibility for freedom and justice. A world where the strong respect the rights of the weak.

This is the vision that I shared with [Soviet] President Gorbachev in Helsinki. He and the other leaders from Europe, the [Persian] gulf and around the world understand that how we manage this crisis today could shape the future for generations to come.

The test we face is great and so are the stakes. This is the first assault on the new world that we seek, the first test of our mettle. Had we not responded to this first provocation with clarity of purpose; if we do not continue to demonstrate our determination, it would be a signal to actual and potential despots around the world.

America and the world must defend common vital interests. And we will.

America and the world must support the rule of law. And we will.

America and the world must stand up to aggression. And we will.

And one thing more: in the pursuit of these goals, America will not be intimidated.

Vital issues of principle are at stake. Saddam Hussein is literally trying to wipe a country off the face of the Earth.

We do not exaggerate. Nor do we exaggerate when we say: Saddam Hussein will fail.

Vital economic interests are at risk as well. Iraq itself controls some 10 percent of the world's proven oil reserves. Iraq plus Kuwait controls twice that. An Iraq permitted to swallow Kuwait would have the economic and military power, as well as the arrogance, to intimidate and coerce its neighbors — neighbors who control the lion's share of the world's remaining oil reserves. We cannot permit a resource so vital to be dominated by one so ruthless. And we won't.

Recent events have surely proven that there is no substitute for American leadership. In the face of tyranny, let no one doubt American credibility and reliability. Let no one doubt our staying power. We will stand by our friends. One way or another, the leader of Iraq must learn this fundamental truth.

From the outset, acting hand-in-hand with others, we've sought to fashion the broadest possible international response to Iraq's aggression. The level of world cooperation and condemnation of Iraq is unprecedented.

Armed forces from countries spanning four continents are there at the request of King Fahd of Saudi Arabia to deter and, if need be, to defend against attack. Muslims and non-Muslims, Arabs and non-Arabs, soldiers from many nations, stand shoulder-to-shoulder, resolute against Saddam Hussein's ambitions.

And we can now point to five United Nations Security Council resolutions that condemn Iraq's aggression. They call for Iraq's immediate and unconditional withdrawal, the restoration of Kuwait's legitimate government and categorically reject Iraq's cynical and self-serving attempt to annex Kuwait. . . .

[The U.N.] Security Council has imposed mandatory economic sanctions on Iraq, designed to force Iraq to relinquish the spoils of its illegal conquest. The Security Council has also taken the decisive step of authorizing the use of all means necessary to ensure compliance with these sanctions.

Together with our friends and allies, ships of the United States Navy are today patrolling Mideast waters, and they've already intercepted more than 700 ships to enforce the sanctions. Three regional leaders I spoke with just yesterday told me that these sanctions are working. Iraq is feeling the heat.

We continue to hope that Iraq's leaders will recalculate just what their aggression has cost them. They are cut off from world trade, unable to sell their oil, and only a tiny fraction of goods gets through. . . .

There's an energy-related cost to be borne as well. Oil-producing nations are already replacing lost Iraqi and Kuwaiti output. More than half of what was lost has been made up, and we're getting superb cooperation. If producers, including the United States, continue steps to expand oil and gas production, we can stabilize prices and guarantee against hardship. Additionally, we and several of our allies always have the option to extract oil from our strategic petroleum reserves, if conditions warrant. As I've pointed out before, conservation efforts are essential to keep our energy needs as low as possible. We must then take advantage of our energy sources across the board: coal, natural gas, hydro and nuclear. Our failure, our failure to do these things has made us more dependent on foreign oil than ever before. And finally, let no one even contemplate profiteering from this crisis. We will not have it.

I cannot predict just how long it'll take to convince Iraq to withdraw from Kuwait. Sanctions will take time to have their full intended effect. We will continue to review all options with our allies, but let it be clear: We will not let this aggression stand.

Our interest, our involvement in the gulf, is not transitory. It pre-dated Saddam Hussein's aggression and will survive it. Long after all our troops come home, and we all hope it's soon, very soon, there will be a lasting role for the United States in assisting the nations of the Persian Gulf. Our role then is to deter future aggression. Our role is to help our friends in their own self-defense. And something else: to curb the proliferation of chemical, biological, ballistic missile and, above all, nuclear technologies.

And let me also make clear that the United States has no quarrel with the Iraqi people. Our quarrel is with Iraq's dictator and with his aggression. Iraq will not be permitted to annex Kuwait. And that's not a threat. It's not a boast. That's just the way it's going to be. . . .

In the final analysis, our ability to meet our responsibilities abroad depends upon political will and consensus at home. It's never easy in democracies, for we govern only with the consent of the governed. And although free people in a free society are bound to have their differences, Americans traditionally come together in times of adversity and challenge.

Once again, Americans have stepped forward to share a tearful goodbye with their families before leaving for a strange and distant shore. At this very moment, they serve together with Arabs, Europeans, Asians and Africans in defense of principle and the dream of a new world order. That is why they sweat and toil in the sand and the heat and the sun.

If they can come together under such adversity; if old adversaries like the Soviet Union and the United States can work in common cause, then surely we who are . . . Democrats, Republicans, liberals, [and] conservatives can come together to fulfill our responsibilities here.

QUESTIONS FOR READING AND DISCUSSION

1. According to President Bush, what were the goals of the "new world order"?
2. How did the Iraqi invasion of Kuwait undermine the new world order? Who was threatened by the invasion and why?
3. How did the invasion raise "vital issues of principle" and "vital economic interests"? Were principles and economic interests equally important? Were they in conflict?
4. What did the "dream of a new world order" require from the American people? What arguments might be used by opponents or critics of the new world order?

DOCUMENT 30–5

Police Brutality and Los Angeles Riots, 1992

In March 1991, Rodney King, a black construction worker, was pulled over by California Highway Patrol officers after a high-speed chase on a Los Angeles freeway in the middle of the night. King had been drinking and was on probation after serving a year in prison for armed robbery. Finally stopping in a residential neighborhood, King jumped out of his car and tried to flee but was apprehended by five white Los Angeles police officers who proceeded to beat him. The police inflicted more than thirty blows with metal batons and kicked King six times, even though he was face down on the ground. King's beating happened to be captured on video by a local resident. It was soon broadcast on a local television station and then seen throughout the world. King was hospitalized with broken bones and teeth in addition to many cuts and bruises. All charges against him were dropped. The video, however, eventually caused four of the Los Angeles policemen to be charged with assault and the use of excessive force. A little over a year after King's beating, a jury in a mostly white suburb of Los Angeles acquitted the policemen. The jury's verdict was condemned by the black mayor of Los Angeles and even by President George Bush.

The political cartoonist Pat Oliphant satirized the verdict with the drawing below. Shortly after the verdict was announced, black and Latino neighborhoods in the city erupted in violent outrage that lasted for six days. More than 3,000 stores were broken into and looted and more than 7,000 buildings and cars were set on fire, with losses totaling about a billion dollars. Los Angeles police reinforced by some 20,000 soldiers from the National Guard, Army, and Marines made more than 16,000 arrests. In all, more than 60 people were killed and over 2,300 were injured in the most prolonged incident of racial violence in the nation's history. The King beating, the jury verdict, the violence of black and Latino rioters, and the counter-violence by police officers and soldiers demonstrated the simmering bitterness and hatred among minority victims and forces of law and order.

Pat Oliphant
"Free at Last," 1992

QUESTIONS FOR READING AND DISCUSSION

1. Why are the Los Angeles policemen depicted proclaiming, "Free at last!"? What did "free" mean for them, according to the cartoon?

2. The little bird at the lower right says, "The president would like you to remain calm." Who should remain calm, according to the cartoon? Why is one party seen as more responsible for remaining calm in this situation than the other?

3. According to the cartoon, why were the policemen beating Rodney King, the man on the ground? What threat did King pose to the police or to society?

4. How did the cartoon call into question the meaning of law and order?

5. How might the cartoon have been different if it had been drawn after the riots that engulfed Los Angeles for six days following the jury verdict?

COMPARATIVE QUESTIONS

1. How did Ronald Reagan's vision of America compare with the experiences of the Vietnamese immigrant, Rodney King, and the uniformed and civilian participants in the Los Angeles violence?

2. How did George Bush's concept of a new world order compare with Reagan's view of America's global mission?

3. To what extent did Norma McCorvey's criticisms of the Supreme Court's decision in *Roe v. Wade* draw upon ideas found in the speeches by Reagan and Bush?

4. How do the documents in this chapter provide evidence of pronounced social, political, and racial divisions during the 1980s and 1990s?

America in a New Century

Since 2000

W hen the Soviet Union collapsed, the appeal of communism in most of the world collapsed with it. The dominance of the United States was now undisputed, but the foreign policy implications of American supremacy remained unclear. This supremacy was challenged on September 11, 2001, when President George W. Bush confronted the terrible realities of terrorism. The religious and political impulses motivating Islamic terrorists became the focus of worldwide attention and led the United States to announce a new national security strategy. Meanwhile, the Religious Right, which had gained strength since the Reagan years, played a crucial role in the rise of conservativism in the first decades of the twenty-first century. The election of President Barack Obama in 2008 partially reversed conservative trends and renewed hope for peaceful relations between the United States and the Muslim world. Donald J. Trump's election in 2016 reasserted conservative policies with renewed emphasis on putting America first, at least in theory.

DOCUMENT 31–1

National Security of the United States Requires Preemptive War

A year after the terrorist attacks of September 11, 2001, the Bush administration announced a national security strategy that asserted the doctrine of preemptive war against possible threats to the United States and declared the goal of making the nation the world's greatest military power for the indefinite future. The excerpts that follow document the explanations for such policies.

The National Security Strategy of the United States, September 2002

The United States of America is fighting a war against terrorists of global reach. The enemy is not a single political regime or person or religion or ideology. The enemy is terrorism—premeditated, politically motivated violence perpetrated against innocents.

In many regions, legitimate grievances prevent the emergence of a lasting peace. Such grievances deserve to be, and must be, addressed within a political process. But no cause justifies terror. The United States will make no concessions to terrorist demands and strike no deals with them. We make no distinction between terrorists and those who knowingly harbor or provide aid to them.

The struggle against global terrorism is different from any other war in our history. It will be fought on many fronts against a particularly elusive enemy over an extended period of time. Progress will come through the persistent accumulation of successes—some seen, some unseen.

Today our enemies have seen the results of what civilized nations can, and will, do against regimes that harbor, support, and use terrorism to achieve their political goals. Afghanistan has been liberated; coalition forces continue to hunt down the Taliban and al-Qaida. But it is not only this battlefield on which we will engage terrorists. Thousands of trained terrorists remain at large with cells in North America, South America, Europe, Africa, the Middle East, and across Asia.

Our priority will be first to disrupt and destroy terrorist organizations of global reach and attack their leadership; command, control, and communications; material support; and finances. This will have a disabling effect upon the terrorists' ability to plan and operate. . . .

We will disrupt and destroy terrorist organizations by:

- direct and continuous action using all the elements of national and international power. Our immediate focus will be those terrorist organizations of global reach and any terrorist or state sponsor of terrorism which attempts to gain or use weapons of mass destruction (WMD) or their precursors;
- defending the United States, the American people, and our interests at home and abroad by identifying and destroying the threat before it reaches our borders. While the United States will constantly strive to enlist the support of the international community, we will not hesitate to act alone, if necessary, to exercise our right of self defense by acting preemptively against such terrorists, to prevent them from doing harm against our people and our country; and
- denying further sponsorship, support, and sanctuary to terrorists by convincing or compelling states to accept their sovereign responsibilities.

We will also wage a war of ideas to win the battle against international terrorism. This includes:

- using the full influence of the United States, and working closely with allies and friends, to make clear that all acts of terrorism are illegitimate

From "The National Security Strategy of the United States of America," September 2002, https://www.state.gov/documents/organization/63562.pdf.

so that terrorism will be viewed in the same light as slavery, piracy, or genocide: behavior that no respectable government can condone or support and all must oppose;

- supporting moderate and modern government, especially in the Muslim world, to ensure that the conditions and ideologies that promote terrorism do not find fertile ground in any nation;

- diminishing the underlying conditions that spawn terrorism by enlisting the international community to focus its efforts and resources on areas most at risk; and

- using effective public diplomacy to promote the free flow of information and ideas to kindle the hopes and aspirations of freedom of those in societies ruled by the sponsors of global terrorism. . . .

The nature of the Cold War threat required the United States — with our allies and friends — to emphasize deterrence of the enemy's use of force, producing a grim strategy of mutual assured destruction. With the collapse of the Soviet Union and the end of the Cold War, our security environment has undergone profound transformation.

Having moved from confrontation to cooperation as the hallmark of our relationship with Russia, the dividends are evident: an end to the balance of terror that divided us; an historic reduction in the nuclear arsenals on both sides; and cooperation in areas such as counterterrorism and missile defense that until recently were inconceivable.

But new deadly challenges have emerged from rogue states and terrorists. None of these contemporary threats rival the sheer destructive power that was arrayed against us by the Soviet Union. However, the nature and motivations of these new adversaries, their determination to obtain destructive powers hitherto available only to the world's strongest states, and the greater likelihood that they will use weapons of mass destruction against us, make today's security environment more complex and dangerous.

In the 1990s we witnessed the emergence of a small number of rogue states that, while different in important ways, share a number of attributes. These states:

- brutalize their own people and squander their national resources for the personal gain of the rulers;

- display no regard for international law, threaten their neighbors, and callously violate international treaties to which they are party;

- are determined to acquire weapons of mass destruction, along with other advanced military technology, to be used as threats or offensively to achieve the aggressive designs of these regimes;

- sponsor terrorism around the globe; and

- reject basic human values and hate the United States and everything for which it stands.

At the time of the Gulf War, we acquired irrefutable proof that Iraq's designs were not limited to the chemical weapons it had used against Iran and its own people, but also extended to the acquisition of nuclear weapons and biological agents. In the past decade North Korea has become the world's principal purveyor of ballistic missiles, and has tested increasingly capable missiles while developing its own WMD arsenal. Other rogue regimes seek nuclear, biological, and chemical weapons as well. These states' pursuit of, and global trade in, such weapons has become a looming threat to all nations.

We must be prepared to stop rogue states and their terrorist clients before they are able to threaten or use weapons of mass destruction against the United States and our allies and friends. Our response must take full advantage of strengthened alliances, the establishment of new partnerships with former adversaries, innovation in the use of military forces, modern technologies, including the development of an effective missile defense system, and increased emphasis on intelligence collection and analysis.

Our comprehensive strategy to combat WMD includes:

- *Proactive counterproliferation efforts.* We must deter and defend against the threat before it is unleashed. We must ensure that key capabilities — detection, active and passive defenses, and counterforce capabilities — are integrated into our defense transformation and our homeland security systems. . . . It has taken almost a decade for us to comprehend the true nature of this new threat. Given the goals of rogue states and terrorists, the United States can no longer solely rely on a reactive posture as we have in the past. The inability to deter a potential attacker, the immediacy of today's threats, and the magnitude of potential harm that could be caused by our adversaries' choice of weapons, do not permit that option. We cannot let our enemies strike first.
- In the Cold War, especially following the Cuban missile crisis, we faced a generally status quo, risk-averse adversary. Deterrence was an effective defense. But deterrence based only upon the threat of retaliation is less likely to work against leaders of rogue states more willing to take risks, gambling with the lives of their people, and the wealth of their nations.
- In the Cold War, weapons of mass destruction were considered weapons of last resort whose use risked the destruction of those who used them. Today, our enemies see weapons of mass destruction as weapons of choice. For rogue states these weapons are tools of intimidation and military aggression against their neighbors. These weapons may also allow these states to attempt to blackmail the United States and our allies to prevent us from deterring or repelling the aggressive behavior of rogue states. Such states also see these weapons as their best means of overcoming the conventional superiority of the United States.
- Traditional concepts of deterrence will not work against a terrorist enemy whose avowed tactics are wanton destruction and the targeting of innocents; whose so-called soldiers seek martyrdom in death and whose most potent protection is statelessness. The overlap between states that sponsor terror and those that pursue WMD compels us to action.

For centuries, international law recognized that nations need not suffer an attack before they can lawfully take action to defend themselves against forces that present an imminent danger of attack. Legal scholars and international jurists often conditioned the legitimacy of preemption on the existence of an imminent threat — most often a visible mobilization of armies, navies, and air forces preparing to attack.

We must adapt the concept of imminent threat to the capabilities and objectives of today's adversaries. Rogue states and terrorists do not seek to attack us using conventional means. They know such attacks would fail. Instead, they rely on acts of terror and, potentially, the use of weapons of mass destruction—weapons that can be easily concealed, delivered covertly, and used without warning.

The targets of these attacks are our military forces and our civilian population, in direct violation of one of the principal norms of the law of warfare. As was demonstrated by the losses on September 11, 2001, mass civilian casualties is the specific objective of terrorists and these losses would be exponentially more severe if terrorists acquired and used weapons of mass destruction.

The United States has long maintained the option of preemptive actions to counter a sufficient threat to our national security. The greater the threat, the greater is the risk of inaction—and the more compelling the case for taking anticipatory action to defend ourselves, even if uncertainty remains as to the time and place of the enemy's attack. To forestall or prevent such hostile acts by our adversaries, the United States will, if necessary, act preemptively.

The United States will not use force in all cases to preempt emerging threats, nor should nations use preemption as a pretext for aggression. Yet in an age where the enemies of civilization openly and actively seek the world's most destructive technologies, the United States cannot remain idle while dangers gather.

We will always proceed deliberately, weighing the consequences of our actions. . . .

The purpose of our actions will always be to eliminate a specific threat to the United States or our allies and friends. The reasons for our actions will be clear, the force measured, and the cause just. . . .

It is time to reaffirm the essential role of American military strength. We must build and maintain our defenses beyond challenge. Our military's highest priority is to defend the United States. . . .

The unparalleled strength of the United States armed forces, and their forward presence, have maintained the peace in some of the world's most strategically vital regions. However, the threats and enemies we must confront have changed, and so must our forces. A military structured to deter massive Cold War–era armies must be transformed to focus more on how an adversary might fight rather than where and when a war might occur. . . .

The presence of American forces overseas is one of the most profound symbols of the U.S. commitments to allies and friends. Through our willingness to use force in our own defense and in defense of others, the United States demonstrates its resolve to maintain a balance of power that favors freedom. . . .

The United States must and will maintain the capability to defeat any attempt by an enemy—whether a state or non-state actor—to impose its will on the United States, our allies, or our friends. We will maintain the forces sufficient to support our obligations, and to defend freedom. Our forces will be strong enough to dissuade potential adversaries from pursuing a military build-up in hopes of surpassing, or equaling, the power of the United States. . . .

In exercising our leadership, we will respect the values, judgment, and interests of our friends and partners. Still, we will be prepared to act apart when our interests and unique responsibilities require.

Questions for Reading and Discussion

1. Are the doctrines of preemptive war and military supremacy new in American foreign policy, according to the national security strategy? How has the United States previously dealt with the "imminent danger of attack"?

2. To what extent is the national security strategy described in the excerpt a response to the September 11, 2001, terrorist attacks in the United States? To what extent is it a response to the end of the Cold War?

3. Do you think this policy influenced the Bush administration's war on Iraq? Why or why not? To what extent does the plan depend on weapons of mass destruction in the hands of terrorists? What weapons of mass destruction did the 9/11 terrorists employ?

4. Do you believe this national security strategy protects the "interests and unique responsibilities" of the American people? Why or why not?

5. What are the limits to the strategy of preemptive war? Should America be the world's police force, according to the strategy? Do you agree? Why or why not?

DOCUMENT 31–2

A Captured 9/11 Terrorist Confesses

In 2003, terrorist leader Khalid Sheikh Muhammad was captured in Pakistan and held in Central Intelligence Agency secret prisons for three years where he was interrogated and tortured. The CIA transferred him in 2006 to the U.S. military prison at Guantánamo Bay, Cuba, where he later confessed, "I was responsible for the 9/11 operation, from A to Z." He also confessed to planning and helping carry out thirty other global acts of terrorism. The Department of Defense released the secret transcript of his confession, excerpted below. Born in Pakistan in 1966, Muhammad grew up in Kuwait and graduated from a North Carolina university in 1986. His oral statement to the court, most of which he chose to deliver in English, reveals his thinking after years of confinement, interrogation, and torture. It raises questions about the motivations of the terrorists and the quality of the information provided by such confessions.

Khalid Sheikh Muhammad

Confession, 2007

[KSM speaks in Arabic; translator translates to English] In the name of God the most compassionate, the most merciful . . . if any fail to judge by the light of Allah has revealed, they are no better than wrongdoers, unbelievers, and the unjust.

[KSM speaks in English] For this verse, I take not the oath. Take an oath is a part of your Tribunal and I'll not accept it. To be or accept the Tribunal as to be, I'll accept it. That I'm accepting American constitution, American law or whatever you are doing here. This is why religiously I cannot accept anything you do. Just to explain for this one, does not mean I'm not saying that I'm lying. When I not take oath does not mean I'm lying. You know very well peoples take oath and they will lie. . . . So sometimes when I'm not making oath does not mean I'm lying. . . .

What I wrote here, is not I'm making myself hero, when I said I was responsible for this or that. But your are military man. You know very well there are

From "Confession of Khalid Sheikh Muhammad," http://i.a.cnn.net/cnn/2007/images/03/14/transcript_ISN10024.pdf.

language for any war. So, there are, we are when I admitting these things I'm not saying I'm not did it. I did it but this the language of any war. If America they want to invade Iraq they will not send for Saddam roses or kisses then send for a bombardment. This is the best way if I want. If I'm fighting for anybody admit to them I'm American enemies. For sure, I'm American enemies. Usama bin Laden, he did his best press conference in American media . . . when he made declaration against Jihad, against America . . . mostly he said about American military presence in Arabian peninsula and aiding Israel and many things. So when we made any way against America we are jackals fighting in the nights. I consider myself, for what you are doing, a religious thing as you consider us the fundamentalist. So, we derive from religious leading that we consider we and George Washington doing same thing. As consider George Washington as hero. Muslims many of them are considering Usama bin Laden. He is doing same thing. He is just fighting. He needs his independence. Even we think that, or not me only. Many Muslims, that al Qaida or Taliban they are doing. They have been oppressed by America. This is the feeling of the prophet. So when we say we are enemy combatant, that right. We are. But I'm asking you again to be fair with many Detainees which are not enemy combatant. Because many of them have been unjustly arrested. Many, not one or two or three. Cause the definition you which wrote even from my view it is not fair. Because if I was in the first Jihad times Russia. So I have to be Russian enemy. But America supported me in this because I'm their alliances when I was fighting Russia. Same job I'm doing. I'm fighting. I was fighting there Russia now I'm fighting America. So, many people who have been in Afghanistan never live. Afghanistan stay in but they not share Taliban or al Qaida. They been Russia time and they cannot go back to their home with their corrupted government. They stayed there and when America invaded Afghanistan parliament. They had been arrest. They never have been with Taliban or the others. So many people consider them as enemy but they are not. Because definitions are very wide definition so people they came after October of 2002, 2001. When America invaded Afghanistan, they just arrive in Afghanistan cause the[y] hear there enemy. They don't know what it means al Qaida or Usama bin Laden or Taliban. They don't care about these things. They heard they were enemy in Afghanistan they just arrived. As they heard first time Russia invade Afghanistan. They arrive they fought when back than they came. They don't know what's going on and Taliban they been head of government. You consider me even Taliban even the president of whole government. Many people they join Taliban because they are government. . . . So, many Taliban fight even the be fighters because they just because public. The government is Taliban then until now CIA don't have exactly definition well who is Taliban, who is al Qaida. Your Tribunal now are discussing he is enemy or not and this is one of your jobs. So this is why you find many Afghanis people, Pakistanis people even, they don't know what going on they just hear they are fighting and they help Muslim in Afghanistan. Then what. There are some infidels which they came here and they have to help them. But then there weren't any intend to do anything against America. Taliban themselves between Taliban they said Afghanistan which they never again against 9/11 operation. The rejection between senior Taliban of what al Qaida are doing. Many of Taliban rejected what they are doing. Even many Taliban, they not agree about why we are in Afghanistan. Some of them they have been with us. Taliban never in their life at all before America invade them the intend to do anything against America.

They never been with al Qaida. Does not mean we are here as American now. They gave political asylum for many countries. They gave for Chinese oppositions or a North Korean but that does not mean they are with them same thing many of Taliban. They harbor us as al Qaida does not mean we are together. So, this is why I'm asking you to be fair with Afghanis and Pakistanis and many Arabs which been in Afghanistan. Many of them been unjustly. The funny story they been Sunni government they sent some spies to assassinate UBL [Usama bin Laden] then we arrested them sent them to Afghanistan/Taliban. Taliban put them into prison. Americans they came and arrest them as enemy combatant. They brought them here. So, even if they are my enemy but not fair to be there with me. This is what I'm saying. The way of war, you know, very well, any country waging war against their enemy the language of the war are killing. . . . But if you and me, two nations, will be together in war the others are victims. This is the way of the language. You know 40 million people were killed in World War One. Ten million kill in World War. You know that two million four hundred thousand be killed in the Korean War. So this language of the war. Any people, who, when Usama bin Laden say I'm waging war because such such reason, now he declared it. But when you said I'm terrorist, I think it is deceiving peoples. Terrorists, enemy combatant. All these definitions as CIA you can make whatever you want. . . . So, finally it's your war but the problem is no definitions of many words. It would be widely definite that many people be oppressed. Because war, for sure, there will be victims. When I said I'm not happy that three thousand been killed in America. I feel sorry even. I don't like to kill children and the kids. Never Islam are, give me green light to kill peoples. Killing, as in the Christianity, Jews, and Islam, are prohibited. But there are exception of rule when you are killing people in Iraq. You said we have to do it. We don't like Saddam. But this is the way to deal with Saddam. Same thing you are saying. Same language you use, I use. When you are invading two-thirds of Mexican, you call your war manifest destiny. It up to you to call it what you want. But other side are calling you oppressors. If now George Washington. If now we were living in the Revolutionary War and George Washington he being arrested through Britain. For sure he, they would consider him enemy combatant. But American they consider him as hero. This right the any Revolutionary War they will be as George Washington or Britain. So we are considered American Army bases which we have from seventies in Iraq. Also, in the Saudi Arabian, Kuwait, Qatar, and Bahrain. This is kind of invasion, but I'm not here to convince you. Is not or not but mostly speech is ask you to be fair with people. I'm don't have anything to say that I'm not enemy. This is why the language of any war in the world is killing. I mean the language of the war is victims. I don't like to kill people. I feel very sorry they been killed kids in 9/11. What I will do? This is the language. Sometime I want to make great awakening between American to stop foreign policy in our land. I know American people are torturing us from seventies [REDACTED BY PENTAGON FOR SECURITY] I know they talking about human rights. And I know it is against American Constitution, against American laws. But they said every law, they have exceptions, this is your bad luck you been part of the exception of our laws. They got have something to convince me but we are doing same language. But we are saying we have Sharia law, but we have Koran. What is enemy combatant in my language?

[KSM speaks in Arabic; translator translates to English] Allah forbids you not with regards to those who fight you not for your faith nor drive you out of your homes from dealing kindly and justly with them. For Allah love those who are just. There is one more sentence. Allah only forbids you with regards to those who fight you for your faith and drive you out of your homes and support others in driving you out from turning to them for friendship and protection. It is such as turn to them in these circumstances that do wrong.

[KSM speaks in English] So we are driving from whatever deed we do we ask about Koran or Hadith. We are not making up for us laws. When we need Fatwa from the religious we have to go back to see what they said scholar. To see what they said yes or not. Killing is prohibited in all what you call the people of the book, Jews, Judaism, Christianity, and Islam. You know the Ten Commandments very well. The Ten Commandments are shared between all of us. We all are serving one God. Then now kill you know it very well. But war language also we have language for the war. You have to kill. But you have to care if unintentionally or intentionally target if I have if I'm not at the Pentagon. I consider it is okay. If I target now when we target in USA we choose them military target, economical, and political. So, war central victims mostly means economical target. So if now American they know UBL [Usama bin Laden]. He is in this house they don't care about his kids and his. They will just bombard it. They will kill all of them and they did it. They kill wife of Dr. Ayman Zawahiri[1] and his two daughters and his son in one bombardment. They receive a report that is his house be. He had not been there. They killed them. They arrested my kids intentionally. They are kids. They been arrested for four months they had been abused. So, for me I have patience. I know I'm not talk about what's come to me. The American have human right. So, enemy combatant itself, it flexible word. So I think God knows that many who been arrested, they been unjustly arrested. Otherwise, military throughout history know very well. They don't war will never stop. War start from Adam when Cain he killed Abel until now. It's never gonna stop killing of people. This is the way of the language. American start the Revolutionary War then they starts the Mexican then Spanish War then World War One, World War Two. You read the history. You now never stopping war. This is life.

QUESTIONS FOR READING AND DISCUSSION

1. What is Muhammad's central argument? Who is his audience? To what degree can his statement be considered truthful? Does it provide evidence you consider important or revealing?
2. What point was Muhammad trying to make by his statements about the "language of war"?
3. Why did he say "when you said I'm terrorist, I think it is deceiving peoples"? What is deceptive about his being labeled a terrorist?
4. Why did Muhammad refer to George Washington and events in American history? Was he in fact, as he claimed, not "making myself hero"?
5. What point did Muhammad attempt to make by discussing the connections between America, Russia, the Taliban, and Afghanistan?

---

[1]**Dr. Ayman Zawahiri:** A prominent member of Al Qaeda.

DOCUMENT 31–3

A Christian Leader Argues That Evangelical Christianity Has Been Hijacked

The political potency of evangelicals in the Republican Party and the administration of President George W. Bush raised questions about the proper role of Christianity in politics and vice versa. In his book Speaking My Mind, *evangelical Baptist minister Tony Campolo criticized evangelical Christians for violating central doctrines of Christianity. In a 2004 interview for an evangelical Christian audience, excerpted below, he outlined his claim that evangelical Christianity had been "hijacked." Campolo's comments challenge the political stances taken and the issues prioritized by the Religious Right.*

Tony Campolo
Interview, 2004

[Interviewer]: It's a common perception that evangelical Christians are conservative on issues like gay marriage, Islam, and women's roles. Is this the case?

[Campolo]: Well, there's a difference between evangelical and being a part of the Religious Right. A significant proportion of the evangelical community is part of the Religious Right. My purpose in writing the book [*Speaking My Mind*] was to communicate loud and clear that I felt that evangelical Christianity had been hijacked.

When did it become anti-feminist? When did evangelical Christianity become anti-gay? When did it become supportive of capital punishment? Pro-war? When did it become so negative towards other religious groups?

There are a group of evangelicals who would say, "Wait a minute. We're evangelicals but we want to respect Islam. We don't want to call its prophet evil. We don't want to call the religion evil. We believe that we have got to learn to live in the same world with our Islamic brothers and sisters and we want to be friends. We do not want to be in some kind of a holy war."

We also raise some very serious questions about the support of policies that have been detrimental to the poor. When I read the voter guide of a group like the Christian Coalition, I find that they are allied with the National Rifle Association and are very anxious to protect the rights of people to buy even assault weapons. But they don't seem to be very supportive of concerns for the poor, concerns for trade relations, for canceling Third World debts.

In short, there's a whole group of issues that are being ignored by the Religious Right and that warrant the attention of Bible-believing Christians. Another one would be the environment.

I don't think that John Kerry is the Messiah or the Democratic Party is the answer, but I don't like the evangelical community blessing the Republican Party as some kind of God-ordained instrument for solving the world's problems. The Republican Party needs to be called into accountability even as the Democratic Party needs to be called into accountability. So it's that double-edged sword that I'm trying to wield.

From Tony Campolo, interview by Laura Sheahen, July 30, 2004, www.beliefnet.com/story/150/story_15052_1.html.

[I]: Are the majority of evangelicals in America leaning conservative because they see their leaders on TV that way? Or is there a contingent out there that we don't hear about in the press that is more progressive on the issues you just talked about?

[C]: The latest statistics that I have seen on evangelicals indicate that something like 83 percent of them are going to vote for George Bush and are Republicans. And there's nothing wrong with that. It's just that Christians need to be considering other issues beside abortion and homosexuality.

These are important issues, but isn't poverty an issue? When you pass a bill of tax reform that not only gives the upper five percent most of the benefits, leaving very little behind for the rest of us, you have to ask some very serious questions. When that results in 300,000 slots for children's afterschool tutoring in poor neighborhoods being cut from the budget. When one and a half billion dollars is cut from the "No Child Left Behind" program.

In short, I think that evangelicals are so concerned with the unborn—as we should be—that we have failed to pay enough attention to the born—to those children who do live and who are being left behind by a system that has gone in favor of corporate interests and big money.

So as an evangelical, I find myself very torn, because I am a pro-life person. I understand evangelicals who say there comes a time when one issue is so overpowering that we have to vote for the candidate that espouses a pro-life position, even if we disagree with him on a lot of other issues.

My response to that is OK, the Republican party and George Bush know that they have the evangelical community in its pocket—[but] they can't win the election without us. Given this position, shouldn't we be using our incredible position of influence to get the president and his party to address a whole host of other issues which we think are being neglected?

[I]: Like what you just said—poverty, or our foreign policy?

[C]: Exactly. And we would also point out that the evangelical community has become so pro-Israel that it is forgotten that God loves Palestinians every bit as much. And that a significant proportion of the Palestinian community is Christian. We're turning our back on our own Christian brothers and sisters in an effort to maintain a pro-Zionist mindset that I don't think most Jewish people support. For instance, most Jewish people really support a two-state solution to the Palestinian crisis. Interestingly enough, George Bush supports a two-state solution.

He's the first president to actually say that the Palestinians should have a state of their own with their own government. However, he's received tremendous opposition from evangelicals on that very point.

Evangelicals need to take a good look at what their issues are. Are they really being faithful to Jesus? Are they being faithful to the Bible? Are they adhering to the kinds of teachings that Christ made clear?

In the book, I take issue, for instance, with the increasing tendency in the evangelical community to bar women from key leadership roles in the church. Over the last few years, the Southern Baptist Convention has taken away the right of women to be ordained to ministry. There were women that were ordained to ministry—their ordinations have been negated and women are told that this is not a place for them. They are not to be pastors. . . .

I'm saying, let's be faithful to the Bible. You can make your point, but there are those of us equally committed to Scripture who make a very strong case that women should be in key leaderships in the Church. We don't want to communicate the idea that to believe the Bible is to necessarily be opposed to women in key roles of leadership in the life of early Christendom.

[I]: What position do you wish American evangelicals would take on homosexuality?

[C]: As an evangelical who takes the Bible very seriously, I come to the first chapter of Romans and feel there is sufficient evidence there to say that same-gender eroticism is not a Christian lifestyle. That's my position.

[I]: So you mean homosexual activity?

[C]: That's right. What I think the evangelical community has to face up to, however, is what almost every social scientist knows, and I'm one of them, and that is that people do not choose to be gay. I don't know what causes homosexuality, I have no idea. Neither does anybody else. There isn't enough evidence to support those who would say it's an inborn theory. There isn't enough evidence to support those who say it's because of socialization.

I'm upset because the general theme in the evangelical community, propagated from one end of this country to the other—especially on religious radio—is that people become gay because the male does not have a strong father image with which to identify. That puts the burden of people becoming homosexual on parents.

Most parents who have homosexual children are upset because of the suffering their children have to go through living in a homophobic world. What they don't need is for the Church to come along and to lay a guilt trip on top of them and say "And your children are homosexual because of you. If you would have been the right kind of parent, this would have never happened." That kind of thinking is common in the evangelical Church. . . .

But the overwhelming proportion of the gay community that love Jesus, that go to church, that are deeply committed in spiritual things, try to change and can't change. And the Church acts as though they are just stubborn and unwilling, when in reality they can't change. To propose that every gay with proper counseling and proper prayer can change their orientation is to create a mentality where parents are angry with their children, saying, "You are a gay person because you don't want to change and you're hurting your mother and your father and your family and you're embarrassing us all."

These young people cannot change. What they are begging for, and what we as Church people have a responsibility to give them, is loving affirmation as they are. That does not mean that we support same-gender eroticism.

[I]: What do you wish evangelicals might accept in terms of salvation for non-Christians?

[C]: We ought to get out of the judging business. We should leave it up to God to determine who belongs in one arena or another when it comes to eternity. What we are obligated to do is to tell people about Jesus and that's what I do. I try to do it every day of my life.

I don't know of any other way of salvation, except through Jesus Christ. Now, if you were going to ask me, "Are only Christians going to get to heaven?" I can't answer that question, because I can only speak from the Christian perspective, from my own convictions and from my own experience. I do not claim to be able to read the mind of God and when evangelicals make these statements, I have some very serious concerns. . . .

I think that Christianity has two emphases. One is a social emphasis to impart the values of the kingdom of God in society—to relieve the sufferings of the poor, to stand up for the oppressed, to be a voice for those who have no voice. The other emphasis is to bring people into a personal, transforming relationship with Christ, where they feel the joy and the love of God in their lives. . . . We cannot neglect the one for the other. . . .

It's necessary to know Jesus in an intimate and personal way. That's what it means to be an evangelical. I don't think it means evangelicals are necessarily in favor of capital punishment. I'm one evangelical that is opposed to capital punishment. I do not believe being an evangelical means women should be debarred from pastoral ministry. I believe women do have a right to be in ministry. It doesn't mean evangelicals are supportive of the Republican party in all respects, because here's one evangelical who says "I think the Republican party has been the party of the rich, and has forgotten many ethnic groups and many poor people."

I am an evangelical who . . . is a strong environmentalist. I am an evangelical who raises very specific questions about war in general, but specifically the war in Iraq. The evangelical community has been far too supportive of militarism. . . .

To George Bush, I'd say "The God of scripture is a God who calls us to protect the environment. I don't think your administration has done that very well. The God of scripture calls us to be peacemakers. We follow a Jesus who said those who live by the sword will die by the sword, who called us to be agents of reconciliation."

I would point out to George Bush that the Christ that he follows says "blessed are the merciful, for they shall obtain mercy" — which doesn't go along with capital punishment.

QUESTIONS FOR READING AND DISCUSSION

1. Why does Campolo believe "that evangelical Christianity had been hijacked"? Who hijacked it and why, according to Campolo?

2. What does Campolo mean by declaring, "The Republican Party needs to be called into accountability even as the Democratic Party needs to be called into accountability"? What does he see as the proper role of evangelical Christians in politics?

3. Why does Campolo believe that "Christians need to be considering other issues beside abortion and homosexuality"? What other issues does Campolo think are important for Christians to consider?

4. According to Campolo, how have evangelical Christians influenced American foreign policy? How should they influence it, according to him?

5. Why does Campolo think that evangelical Christians "ought to get out of the judging business"? How would that influence their role in politics and government?

DOCUMENT 31–4

President Barack Obama Declares a New Beginning in U.S. Relations with the Muslim World

Relations between the United States and the Muslim world deteriorated sharply after the September 11, 2001, attacks on the World Trade Center in New York City, the subsequent wars in Afghanistan and Iraq, the continuing conflict between Israelis and Palestinians, and the intensification of terrorist violence across the globe. In June 2009, President Barack Obama traveled to Cairo, Egypt, and announced his support for a "new beginning" in relations between the United States and the Muslim world. In the following excerpt from his speech, Obama outlined the major sources of tensions between Muslims and the United States and argued that, despite differences, both parties shared common goals and interests.

On a New Beginning, June 4, 2009

I am honored to be in the timeless city of Cairo, and . . . proud to carry with me the goodwill of the American people, and a greeting of peace from Muslim communities in my country: Assalaamu alaykum. (Applause.)

We meet at a time of great tension between the United States and Muslims around the world—tension rooted in historical forces that go beyond any current policy debate. The relationship between Islam and the West includes centuries of coexistence and cooperation, but also conflict and religious wars. More recently, tension has been fed by colonialism that denied rights and opportunities to many Muslims, and a Cold War in which Muslim-majority countries were too often treated as proxies without regard to their own aspirations. Moreover, the sweeping change brought by modernity and globalization led many Muslims to view the West as hostile to the traditions of Islam.

Violent extremists have exploited these tensions in a small but potent minority of Muslims. The attacks of September 11, 2001, and the continued efforts of these extremists to engage in violence against civilians has led some in my country to view Islam as inevitably hostile not only to America and Western countries, but also to human rights. All this has bred more fear and more mistrust.

So long as our relationship is defined by our differences, we will empower those who sow hatred rather than peace, those who promote conflict rather than the cooperation that can help all of our people achieve justice and prosperity. And this cycle of suspicion and discord must end.

I've come here to Cairo to seek a new beginning between the United States and Muslims around the world, one based on mutual interest and mutual respect, and one based upon the truth that America and Islam are not exclusive and need not be in competition. Instead, they overlap, and share common principles—principles of justice and progress; tolerance and the dignity of all human beings.

I do so recognizing that change cannot happen overnight. . . . I am convinced that in order to move forward, we must say openly to each other the things we hold in our hearts and that too often are said only behind closed doors. There must be a sustained effort to listen to each other; to learn from each other; to respect one another; and to seek common ground. As the Holy Koran tells us, "Be conscious of God and speak always the truth." (Applause.) That is what I will try to do today—to speak the truth as best I can, humbled by the task before us, and firm in my belief that the interests we share as human beings are far more powerful than the forces that drive us apart.

Now part of this conviction is rooted in my own experience. I'm a Christian, but my father came from a Kenyan family that includes generations of

From President Barack Obama, "On a New Beginning," Speech in Cairo, Egypt, June 4, 2009, https://obamawhitehouse.archives.gov/the-press-office/remarks-president-cairo-university-6-04-09.

Muslims. As a boy, I spent several years in Indonesia and heard the call of the azaan at the break of dawn and at the fall of dusk. As a young man, I worked in Chicago communities where many found dignity and peace in their Muslim faith.

As a student of history, I also know civilization's debt to Islam. It was Islam . . . that carried the light of learning through so many centuries, paving the way for Europe's Renaissance and Enlightenment. It was innovation in Muslim communities . . . that developed the order of algebra; our magnetic compass and tools of navigation; our mastery of pens and printing; our understanding of how disease spreads and how it can be healed. Islamic culture has given us majestic arches and soaring spires; timeless poetry and cherished music; elegant calligraphy and places of peaceful contemplation. And throughout history, Islam has demonstrated through words and deeds the possibilities of religious tolerance and racial equality. (Applause.)

I also know that Islam has always been a part of America's story. The first nation to recognize my country was Morocco. In signing the Treaty of Tripoli in 1796, our second President, John Adams, wrote, "The United States has in itself no character of enmity against the laws, religion or tranquility of Muslims." And since our founding, American Muslims have enriched the United States. They have fought in our wars, they have served in our government, they have stood for civil rights, they have started businesses, they have taught at our universities, they've excelled in our sports arenas, they've won Nobel Prizes, built our tallest building, and lit the Olympic Torch. And when the first Muslim American was recently elected to Congress, he took the oath to defend our Constitution using the same Holy Koran that one of our Founding Fathers — Thomas Jefferson — kept in his personal library. (Applause.)

So I have known Islam on three continents before coming to the region where it was first revealed. That experience guides my conviction that partnership between America and Islam must be based on what Islam is, not what it isn't. And I consider it part of my responsibility as President of the United States to fight against negative stereotypes of Islam wherever they appear. (Applause.)

But that same principle must apply to Muslim perceptions of America. (Applause.) Just as Muslims do not fit a crude stereotype, America is not the crude stereotype of a self-interested empire. The United States has been one of the greatest sources of progress that the world has ever known. We were born out of revolution against an empire. We were founded upon the ideal that all are created equal, and we have shed blood and struggled for centuries to give meaning to those words — within our borders, and around the world. We are shaped by every culture, drawn from every end of the Earth, and dedicated to a simple concept: E pluribus unum — "Out of many, one."

Now, much has been made of the fact that an African American with the name Barack Hussein Obama could be elected President. (Applause.) But my personal story is not so unique. The dream of opportunity for all people has not come true for everyone in America, but its promise exists for all who come to our shores — and that includes nearly 7 million American Muslims in our country today who, by the way, enjoy incomes and educational levels that are higher than the American average. (Applause.)

Moreover, freedom in America is indivisible from the freedom to practice one's religion. That is why there is a mosque in every state in our union, and over 1,200 mosques within our borders. . . .

So let there be no doubt: Islam is a part of America. And I believe that America holds within her the truth that regardless of race, religion, or station in life, all of us share common aspirations—to live in peace and security; to get an education and to work with dignity; to love our families, our communities, and our God. These things we share. This is the hope of all humanity. . . .

For we have learned from recent experience that when a financial system weakens in one country, prosperity is hurt everywhere. When a new flu infects one human being, all are at risk. When one nation pursues a nuclear weapon, the risk of nuclear attack rises for all nations. When violent extremists operate in one stretch of mountains, people are endangered across an ocean. . . . That is what it means to share this world in the 21st century. That is the responsibility we have to one another as human beings.

And this is a difficult responsibility to embrace. For human history has often been a record of nations and tribes—and, yes, religions—subjugating one another in pursuit of their own interests. Yet in this new age, such attitudes are self-defeating. Given our interdependence, any world order that elevates one nation or group of people over another will inevitably fail. So whatever we think of the past, we must not be prisoners to it. Our problems must be dealt with through partnership; our progress must be shared. (Applause.)

Now, that does not mean we should ignore sources of tension. Indeed, it suggests the opposite: We must face these tensions squarely. And so in that spirit, let me speak as clearly and as plainly as I can about some specific issues that I believe we must finally confront together.

The first issue that we have to confront is violent extremism in all of its forms. . . . America is not—and never will be—at war with Islam. (Applause.) We will, however, relentlessly confront violent extremists who pose a grave threat to our security—because we reject the same thing that people of all faiths reject: the killing of innocent men, women, and children. And it is my first duty as President to protect the American people.

The situation in Afghanistan demonstrates America's goals, and our need to work together. Over seven years ago, the United States pursued al Qaeda and the Taliban with broad international support. We did not go by choice; we went because of necessity. I'm aware that there's still some who would question or even justify the events of 9/11. But let us be clear: Al Qaeda killed nearly 3,000 people on that day. The victims were innocent men, women and children from America and many other nations who had done nothing to harm anybody. And yet al Qaeda chose to ruthlessly murder these people, claimed credit for the attack, and even now states their determination to kill on a massive scale. They have affiliates in many countries and are trying to expand their reach. These are not opinions to be debated; these are facts to be dealt with.

Now, make no mistake: We do not want to keep our troops in Afghanistan. We . . . seek no military bases there. It is agonizing for America to lose our young men and women. It is costly and politically difficult to continue this conflict. We would gladly bring every single one of our troops home if we could be confident that there were not violent extremists in Afghanistan and now Pakistan determined to kill as many Americans as they possibly can. But that is not yet the case. . . .

And despite the costs involved, America's commitment will not weaken. Indeed, none of us should tolerate these extremists. They have killed in many countries. They have killed people of different faiths—but more than any other, they have killed Muslims. Their actions are irreconcilable with the rights of human beings, the progress of nations, and with Islam. The Holy Koran teaches that whoever kills an innocent is as — it is as if he has killed all mankind. (Applause.) And the Holy Koran also says whoever saves a person, it is as if he has saved all mankind. (Applause.) The enduring faith of over a billion people is so much bigger than the narrow hatred of a few. Islam is not part of the problem in combating violent extremism — it is an important part of promoting peace. . . .

And finally, just as America can never tolerate violence by extremists, we must never alter or forget our principles. Nine-eleven was an enormous trauma to our country. The fear and anger that it provoked was understandable, but in some cases, it led us to act contrary to our traditions and our ideals. We are taking concrete actions to change course. I have unequivocally prohibited the use of torture by the United States. . . .

So America will defend itself, respectful of the sovereignty of nations and the rule of law. And we will do so in partnership with Muslim communities which are also threatened. The sooner the extremists are isolated and unwelcome in Muslim communities, the sooner we will all be safer.

QUESTIONS FOR READING AND DISCUSSION

1. What accounted for "tension between the United States and Muslims around the world," according to Barack Obama?

2. What did Obama argue were the building blocks for "a new beginning" between Muslims and the United States? Were his proposals realistic? Do you believe that relations between the United States and the Muslim world have improved since the president visited Egypt? Why or why not?

3. What did Obama ask Muslims to do? What did he promise the United States would do? How realistic were Obama's requests and promises?

4. Do you think most Americans would agree with Obama's speech, as excerpted here? If so, why? If not, why not?

DOCUMENT 31–5

President Trump Addresses the Conservative Political Action Conference

At the annual meeting of the Conservative Political Action Conference in March 2019, President Donald J. Trump walked onstage and hugged the American flag to the cheers of his audience of conservative activists. Trump delivered a two-hour speech on what he considered his achievements in delivering on his campaign promise to make America great again. Impartial fact-checkers found more than a hundred falsehoods in Trump's claims about bringing jobs back to America, boosting the economy, building a wall on the southern border, imposing tariffs on goods from China and other countries, resurrecting the coal industry, cutting taxes, and many other matters. Regardless — or perhaps because — of Trump's false claims, his conservative audience applauded and cheered enthusiastically. Though several high-level members of his administration had been found guilty of various crimes, including collaborating with Russia to influence the 2016 presidential election for which the president himself was under investigation, Trump's embrace of the flag was meant to suggest to his audience that he remained an all-American president who loved his country.

President Donald J. Trump Hugs the Flag, **2019**

Tasos Katopodis/Getty Images

QUESTIONS FOR READING AND DISCUSSION

1. What political messages are conveyed by President Trump's embrace of the American flag? What does the photo suggest to Trump's supporters? What does it suggest to his political opponents?

2. Why might Trump have capitalized on this photo opportunity by taking this pose? What does he stand to gain by posing for photos of himself hugging the flag?

3. What evidence suggests Trump's genuine affection and heartfelt devotion to the flag and what it stands for?

4. What does this photo suggest about patriotism? What does patriotism mean to Trump and his supporters? How might their views differ from views held by those with more liberal political beliefs?

COMPARATIVE QUESTIONS _____

1. In what ways did the terrorist attacks of 9/11 influence the views of George W. Bush and the national security strategy of his administration?

2. How did Barack Obama's views of the Muslim world differ, if at all, from those of George W. Bush? How would you account for the differences?

3. How did the world orders envisioned by Khalid Sheikh Muhammad and Tony Campolo compare to those envisioned by Presidents Bush and Obama? How did religion influence these views?

4. How did the message sent by President Trump's embrace of the American flag differ, if at all, from the messages expressed in the speeches of Presidents Bush and Obama? Were their views less patriotic or less American than his? Why or why not?

ACKNOWLEDGMENTS

Chapter 22 22–3. "Anonymous soldier to Elmer J. Sutters, 1918" (pp. 162–67), from *War Letters: Extraordinary Correspondence from American Wars* (New York: Washington Square Press, 2001), edited by Andrew Carroll. Reprinted by permission of Andrew Carroll.

22–5. Stanley B. Norvell, Letter to Victor F. Lawson, 1919. From Stanley B. Norvell to Victor F. Lawson, in William Tuttle, ed., "Views of a Negro during the Red Summer of 1919," *Journal of Negro History* 51 (July 1966), 211–18. Copyright © 1966 by University of Chicago. Used with permission of University of Chicago Press.

Chapter 23 23–2. Diary Entries, 1925–1928. From Reinhold Niebuhr, *Leaves from the Notebook of a Tamed Cynic* (Chicago: Willet, Clark & Colby, 1929). Reprinted by permission of Westminster John Knox Press.

23–3. From Hiram W. Evans, "The Klan's Fight for Americanism," *North American Review* 223 (March–April–May 1926). Reprinted by permission of North American Review.

23–4. From Margaret Sanger, *Motherhood in Bondage*, 1928. Used with permission of the Ohio State University.

Chapter 25 25–1. Grant Hirabayashi, Oral History, 1999. Transcribed by Claire Cage. Courtesy of Go For Broke National Education Center.

25–2a. "Memorandum Submitted to the President of the United States at the White House on Tuesday, December 8, 1942 at Noon by a Delegation of Representatives of Jewish Organizations..." The Yiddish Scientific Institute/YIVO, The Institution for Research and Training in the Jewish Social Studies, New York. Reprinted by permission.

25–4a. David Mark Olds, Letter, July 12, 1945. David Mark Olds World War II Collection (PR 287). Reprinted by permission of the New York Historical Society.

Chapter 26 26–5. Donald M. Griffith Interview, 2003. From 30 *Below on Christmas Eve: Interviews with Northwest Ohio Veterans of the Korean War* (Toledo: University of Toledo Press, 2011). Reprinted by permission of Pamela Parsons on behalf of the Estate of Donald M. Griffith.

Chapter 27 27–2. "The Status Seekers, 1959," from Vance Packard, *The Status Seekers: An Exploration of Class Behavior in America and the Hidden Barriers That Affect You, Your Community, and Your Future.* Copyright © 1959 by Vance Packard. Reprinted by permission of Curtis Brown, Ltd.

Chapter 28 28–1. Martin Luther King, Jr., "Letter from Birmingham Jail." Copyright © 1963 Dr. Martin Luther King, Jr., © renewed 1991 Coretta Scott King. Reprinted by arrangement with the Estate of Martin Luther King Jr., c/o Writers House as agent for the proprietor, New York, NY.

28–3. National Organization for Women Statement of Purpose (1966). Reprinted by permission.

Chapter 29 29–2. Colonel Robert D. Heinl, Jr., "The Collapse of the Armed Forces" from *Armed Forces Journal*, June 7, 1971. Copyright © 1971 Sightline Media Group - Military. All rights reserved. Used under license.

Chapter 30 30–3. Oral History, 1983. Excerpted from *Hearts of Sorrow: Vietnamese-American Lives*, by James M.Freeman. Copyright © 1989 by the Board of Trustees of the Leland Stanford Jr. University. All rights reserved. Used by permission of the publisher, Stanford University Press, sup.org.